Accumulation on a World Scale

Samir Amin

Accumulation on a World Scale

A Critique of the Theory of Underdevelopment

Translated by Brian Pearce

Volume 2

Monthly Review Press
New York and London

Library of Congress Cataloging in Publication Data
Amin, Samir.
Accumulation on a world scale.
Translation of L'accumulation à l'échelle mondiale.
Includes bibliographical references.
1. International finance. 2. Saving and investment.
3. Economic development. I. Title.
HG3881.A5613 332.4'5 72-92028
ISBN 0-85345-272-5

First Printing

Monthly Review Press
62 West 14th Street, New York, N.Y. 10011
21 Theobalds Road, London WC1X 8SL, England

Manufactured in the United States of America

Contents
Volume 2

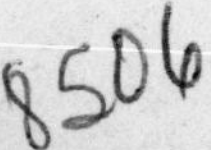

Chapter 2
The Formations of Peripheral Capitalism
Part 3: The Social Formations

The tendency of the capitalist mode of production to become exclusive when it is based on expansion and deepening of the internal market is accompanied by a tendency of the social structure at the center to approach the pure model of *Capital,* characterized by polarization of social classes into two fundamental classes, the bourgeoisie and the proletariat. The social classes formed on the basis of former modes of production (landowners, craftsmen, merchants, etc.) either disappear or are transformed (e.g., into an agrarian bourgeoisie). True, the social system gives rise to new stratifications at the same time as it becomes simpler: white collars and blue collars, cadres and unskilled workers, native and foreign workers, and so on. But these new stratifications are all situated within the framework of the essential division between bourgeoisie and proletariat, for all the new social strata in the course of development are made up of wage-earning employees of the capitalist enterprise. The relevance of the new stratification is therefore not economic (since from this standpoint the positions of the new strata are identical, being all sellers of their labor power), but political or ideological. In addition, the concentration of enterprises, the formation of monopolies, modifies the forms in which the bourgeoisie manifests itself. However, the alleged dichotomy established between ownership (dispersed) and control (said to have passed into the hands of the "technostructure," to employ Galbraith's neologism) is a delusion. The "technocrats" who take the decisions take them in accordance with the logic and interest of capital, exercising an increasingly concentrated control—which merely means that objectively the time is ripe for socialization. Nevertheless, the fact that in the capitalist mode of production the social structure is thus directly shaped by the movement of the economy itself leads to the *ideologization of economics,* or in other words to *economism as an ideology.* The illusion is created that the economy is a power above society, which the latter cannot control. This is the source of modern alienation, in contrast to alienation in precapitalist societies, which takes place in the sphere of ideology, with religion as its form of expression. This is also why economics claims to fill the entire field of social science.

If, however, as I have shown, the capitalist mode of production, introduced from outside—that is, based on the external market—tends to become not exclusive, but only dominant, it follows that the peripheral formations will not tend toward this essential polarization. Contrasting with the increasing homogeneity of the social formations of the center is the persisting heterogeneity of those of the periphery—by which I do not mean mere juxtaposition ("dualism"). Just as the precapitalist modes of production are here integrated into a system, subjected to the distinctive purposes of dominant capital (the peasant goes on producing within the setting of his old mode of production, but he is henceforth producing goods that are exported to the center), so the new social structures form a structured, hierarchical totality, dominated by the "great absent member" of colonial society: the dominant metropolitan bourgeoisie. It results from this, of course, that, just as the economic system of the periphery cannot be understood by itself, because its relations with the center are crucial, so the social structure of the periphery is a mutilated structure, which cannot be understood unless it is properly situated: as an element in a *world* social structure.

The form assumed by the peripheral formations may therefore be varied, depending, on the one hand, on the nature of the precapitalist formations subjected to aggression, and on the form taken by this external aggression, on the other. The precapitalist formations that were attacked seem to me to fall into two main types: the Eastern and African formations, and the American formations.

I have already said, regarding the first group, that they were structured combinations made up, on the one hand, of a variety of modes of production, the tributary mode being predominant (in a primitive form, based on a still-living village community, or in a developed form that was evolving toward a feudal mode of production), with the simple commodity mode and the slave-owning mode being in the service of this predominant mode; and, on the other hand, of long-distance trade relations with other formations. I have said that the simple primitive variety was the "African" type, while the developed one was "Asian and Arab."

The formations known as "American" are different. The New World was not uninhabited when the Europeans discovered it, but it was rapidly peopled with immigrants, most of whom arrived before the definitive victory of the capitalist mode of production at the center—in other words, before the Industrial Revolution. The native inhabitants were either driven back or exterminated (North America, West Indies, Argentina, Brazil) or else entirely subjected to the requirements of European merchant capital (the Andean areas of South America). Merchant capital, ancestor of fully developed capital, established annexes in the New World, in the form of enterprises for the exploitation of precious metals (mainly silver) and the production of exotic crops (sugar, later cotton, etc.). European merchant capitalists, who held the monopoly of this exploitation, thus accumulated the money capital needed for the subsequent complete development of capital. The forms assumed by the exploitation might be various: pseudo-feudal (the *encomienda* of Latin America), pseudo-slave-owning (mines), slave-owning (the plantations of Brazil, the West Indies, and the British colonies in the southern part of North America). They were nonetheless in the service of nascent European capitalism: they produced for the market, which forbids us to confuse them with the true feudal or slave-owning modes of production. Moreover, these annexes themselves developed annexes of their own—the enterprises needed to supply food for their labor force and materials for use in their exploitation. These enterprises sometimes had a feudal look about them, especially in Latin America, with its big ranches, but they never became really feudal, being destined to produce for the capitalist market. They belonged in most cases to the simple petty-commodity mode of production, being formed on free land and in free towns by European immigrants. Farmers and craftsmen also produced there for the market constituted by the plantations that were annexes of merchant capital.

The forms of aggression were also diverse. The Americas, Asia and the Arab world, and Black Africa were not transformed in the same way, because they were not integrated at the same stage of capitalist development at the center, and therefore did not fulfill the same functions in this development.

Peripheral Formations in America and in the East

The Americas played a vital role in the mercantile period. It was then that Latin America acquired the main structures that characterize it to this day. These are based on agrarian capitalism of the latifundia type, with labor power provided by peasants of degraded status (peons and former slaves). To this was added a local commercial bourgeoisie of the comprador type, when the metropolitan monopoly became overstretched. Along with it a petty urban community of craftsmen, small shopkeepers, officials, domestic servants, and so on came into being, in the image of that which existed in the Europe of those days.

Independence consecrated, at the beginning of the nineteenth century, the transfer of power to the landlords and the local comprador bourgeoisie. The structures described were to persist and become reinforced throughout the century, parallel with intensified exchanges with the new metropolitan center, Great Britain, which set up a network of import-export firms and banks all over the continent and drew extra profits from financing the public debt of the new states. The installation of (largely North American) oil and mining capital during the twentieth century, and then of industries producing goods to take the place of imports, gave rise to a limited proletariat, the higher categories of which were to appear all the more "privileged," comparatively speaking, because the agrarian crisis brought about a steady impoverishment of the poor peasantry and an increase in rural and urban unemployment. Sometimes, and from the start in association with foreign capital, the oligarchy of landlords and comprador merchants invested capital from agriculture and trade in the development of the new light industry or in the highly profitable activities connected with increasing urbanization (property, the tertiary sector, etc.). What is characteristic of this type of social formation is (1) its oligarchic character, the new (urban) bourgeoisie being the same class, made up of the same families, as the class of big landlords and comprador merchants, and (2) its development in the wake of the dominant foreign capital.[177]

In Asia and the Arab world the start came much later. It was only in the second half of the nineteenth century that the former feudal classes transformed themselves into big capitalist landowners producing for the world market. Developments of this kind, moreover, were highly uneven, affecting only a fringe, sometimes a very narrow one indeed, of the huge continent. Egypt, entirely transformed into a cotton farm for Lancashire by its few thousand big landlords, was the most extreme case. The power of survival of the village community resisted for a very long time, in a number of regions, the development of agrarian capitalism—less in India, where the British authorities granted the Zemindars ownership of the soil, forcibly breaking up the village communities; more in China and in many areas of the Persian and Ottoman empires, which avoided direct colonial subjection, Egypt being the extreme exception of a development along capitalist-latifundia lines. Only in the present period (sometimes only after the Second World War) did small-scale agrarian capitalism, with rich peasants of the *kulak* type, make its appearance on a serious scale, especially where agrarian reforms ended or restricted large-scale landownership. The belated and limited development of agrarian capitalism, and phenomena distinctive of the structures of urban life and of the ideology and culture of the new dominant classes that had emerged from the transformation of the old ones, or which were characteristic of the forms of colonial subjection, restricted to a greater or lesser degree the extension of the comprador commercial sector, either to the advantage of the European firms or to that of a partly Europeanized bourgeoisie of cosmopolitan background ("Levantines," for example). Subsequently, as in Latin America, sporadic industries set up by foreign capital enabled the local oligarchies to engage in new activities. The structure of these formations then tended to become markedly similar to that of Latin America, the late start made up for all the faster because of the powerful penetration of modern forms of foreign capital.[178]

Peripheral Formations in Africa

It is this lag that Black Africa, the last region to have been incorporated in the system, is now engaged in overcoming. For three centuries Black Africa was an annex to America, with the function of providing that continent's slave labor. The hunt for slaves, which extended all over Black Africa, had the effect of transforming the previously existing formations even before actual colonial conquest. It contributed substantially to the establishment of military monarchies superimposed on solid village communities. In certain coastal regions in direct contact with the slavers' bases it resulted in the introduction of a new slave-owning mode of production.[179] Subsequently, Black Africa, conquered at the end of the nineteenth century—but hardly opened up before the war of 1914–1918 and only to a limited extent between the wars, which was a period of relative stagnation of capitalism on the world scale—underwent a form of colonial subjection that was direct, crude, and simple, providing no opportunity for the appearance among the natives of any equivalent to the big agrarian capitalists and comprador merchants of the other two continents. Black Africa has, however, been closing this gap at a faster rate since the end of the Second World War.

The idea that Black Africa is the most backward and least-changing part of the underdeveloped world is certainly one of the most mistaken of prejudices—a survival of racism, perhaps. In fact, Black Africa is probably that part of the Third World which has undergone the most thoroughgoing transformations during the last half-century, and it is still changing with amazing speed. This process of change is certainly uneven between the different sectors of social life and different regions, and full of contradictions. This is because colonial subjection has been applied in Black Africa to societies that were among the most primitive, and apparently the least fit for adaptation to the new conditions of the dominant capitalist economy. Most of these societies had hardly grown beyond the level of primitive village communities, and state forms were still too recently arisen for the degradation of these village communities or their domination by the state machine to have reached an advanced stage. There was nothing comparable to the great states of the East or to the modern-type states of Latin America. Under these conditions, the ruling strata, the tribal chieftains, were less capable than elsewhere, economically, politically, and culturally, of transforming themselves into national bourgeoisies of the agrarian comprador type, well inserted in the totality of the new social and economic relations.

Elsewhere, in the Eastern and Latin American worlds, it was generally on the basis of large-scale landed property and the higher strata of state service, and sometimes also of the commercial community, that the new national bourgeoisie was formed. Large-scale landownership, which was often identified with political responsibility, became reinforced and transformed into landownership of the bourgeois type by adapting itself to agricultural production for export. This large-scale landed property was absent in Black Africa. Agricultural production for export was here often undertaken by big European plantations, as in the Belgian Congo and French Equatorial Africa. In other regions the *économie de traite* involved millions of small peasants organized in village communities. The survival of these community relations was bound to slow down the inevitable processes of differentiation that accompany the commercializing of agriculture. Nevertheless, under certain conditions, it was in this petty peasant economy that a rural bourgeoisie most easily took shape. On the other hand, in some cases the *économie de traite* stimulated the formation of social organizations which (for want of a better term and to be brief) I will call semi-feudal, notably in the Moslem savannah country, in Senegal, Nigeria, and the Sudan, where there came into being, not large estates of the bourgeois type, but hierarchical theocratic chiefdoms wielding political domination over village communities obliged to pay tribute.

In the great states of the East, with highly urbanized civilizations, there were often, before the colonial period, merchants similar to those of precapitalist Europe who were capable, by virtue of their technical knowledge, culture, and wealth, of adapting and transforming themselves into modern bourgeoisies. Black Africa had nothing like this. In the absence of great urban civilizations, the traders appeared here as an extension of large-scale Arab trade. Dyula, Sarakulle, and Hausa traders of the West African savannah appeared as a result of contact across the Sahara with the Arab-Berber world, which was seeking to obtain the products of the forest zone. In Eastern Sudan and on the coast of the Indian Ocean, Arab traders carried out these functions. The slave trade with the European trading centers on the Gulf of Guinea or the Arab bases on the East Coast was usually carried on by new elements, alien to traditional society, the *traitants,*[180] who were often half-breeds. In these circumstances, in the towns that were established from scratch after the colonial conquest, the new commercial tasks, even the most subordinate ones, were reserved either for the colonial companies or for foreign communities: Lebanese ("Syrians"), Greeks, and Indians.

Finally, the absence of solid political superstructures such as those of the East also had the effect of delaying the appearance of the bourgeoisie in Black Africa. It was often from the native members of the administrative organization that the modern national bourgeoisies of the Eastern and Latin American countries were formed. In Black Africa, however, the cadres of the administration, like those of the modern business enterprises, were recruited, down to quite a low level in the hierarchy, from among the foreign colonists. This situation was still further heightened where, as in Kenya or Rhodesia, a system of settlement in the colony enabled "poor whites" to fill *all* these functions, to the detriment of the formation of local elites of the modern type.

The very pattern of direct colonization, the *pacte colonial* that went with it, the lack of big towns, were also bound to delay the creation by colonial capital of light industries such as arose in the East or in Latin America. This delay itself held back the formation of technical cadres that would have served for the constitution of a national bourgeoisie. It is characteristic that the principal exceptions in this sphere are Kenya and Rhodesia (as well as South Africa, of course): colonies whose light industry was formed almost exclusively by and for the European minority. The Belgian Congo thus forms the only real exception, explained by the international statute governing the Congo basin, which deprived the Belgians of the privileges of the *pacte colonial.*[181]

The handicap constituted by the primitive rural structures of Black Africa—the absence of large landed property—was to become an advantage in the present epoch. Whereas in the East and in Latin America the solidity of semi-feudal structures very often presents a major obstacle to capitalist development, in several regions of Black Africa a rural bourgeoisie of modern planters has come into being very quickly. This progress has, of course, not affected the whole of Black Africa, for—even apart from the Moslem savannah zones, which, under the influence of the commercialization of agriculture, have evolved toward semi-feudal types of society—extensive regions are still stagnating quite outside the area of this transformation.

Comparative study of the zones in which a rural bourgeoisie has succeeded in developing leads to framing the hypothesis that four conditions need to be present in order that this occur.[182]

The first seems to be the existence of a traditional society organized in a sufficiently hierarchical way, so that certain strata of the traditional chieftainry possess enough social power to appropriate substantial tracts of tribal land. It was in this manner that the traditional chiefs of Ghana, Southern Nigeria, the Ivory Coast, and Uganda succeeded in creating a plantation economy rarely found among the nonhierarchical Bantu peoples. It should be noted, though, that excessively pronounced, more advanced hierarchies of the semi-feudal type, as in the Moslem savannah country, have *not* been favorable to the development of a rural bourgeoisie.

The second condition is that there be an average density of population of ten to thirty inhabitants per square kilometer. Densities lower than this make private appropriation of land ineffective and the potential supply of wage-labor inadequate. Excessive densities, as in Rwanda and on the Bamileke plateau in Cameroon, make it difficult for tribal chiefs to appropriate sufficient areas of land. The mechanism of proletarianization is considerably facilitated, moreover, when a labor force of ethnically alien origin can be drawn on, as with the workers from Upper Volta who work in the Ivory Coast. At a second stage of the process the younger members and dependents of the families of the original planters may in their turn be proletarianized.[183]

The third condition is the existence of rich crops, such as to enable a sufficient surplus to be obtained per hectare and per worker from the very first phase of the opening-up of the territory, when mechanization is at a low level of development and the productivity of agriculture, still largely extensive, is not high. Cotton in Uganda, or groundnuts in the Serere country,* and in general the production of foodstuffs, are forms of production too poor to make possible what coffee or cocoa beans have allowed to develop elsewhere.

The fourth and final condition is that the political authority be not unfavorable to this type of spontaneous development. The facilities offered for private appropriation of the soil, the freedom of labor, the availability of individual agricultural credit, have everywhere played a big role in the formation of this rural bourgeoisie. Characteristic in this connection was the abolition of forced labor in the French colonies in 1950. The bourgeois demand for freedom of labor enabled the planters of the Ivory Coast to turn to their own advantage a flow of immigrants incomparably greater in intensity than the supply of labor provided by the forced recruitment of workers—who, moreover, had until then been made available only to the French planters. It also made possible the organizing of a great political campaign in the countryside, with the peasantry who had been the victims of forced labor lined up behind the native planters. Contrariwise, the paternalism of the Belgian *paysannats* undoubtedly played a negative role, slowing down tendencies to bourgeois development in certain regions, such as the Lower Congo. Is it not significant that it has only been since the collapse of this policy, following independence, that a bourgeois development of this sort has succeeded in making progress?[184] True, it must also be mentioned that, in the Lower Congo, another condition—the possibility of calling on an ethnically alien labor force—has been present only since 1960 (the refugees from Angola). The policies of apartheid and of "defense of African traditions" practiced in South Africa, Rhodesia, and Malawi are also, of course, obstacles to the advance of a rural bourgeoisie.

Is the same true of policies of cooperative rural development? Carried on everywhere in accordance with the same rather naïve paternalistic principles, based, no doubt, on the Utopian desire to see the whole countryside progress without inequality, at one and the same steady pace, these policies have neither prevented the plantation system from developing where it was possible nor caused any noticeable qualitative changes.

It remains true that huge areas are immune to movement, because the

* A region in Senegal which has retained less hierarchical forms of social organization than the Wolof country.

conditions that make change possible have not been present there: the Africa that "has not started," that "cannot start."[185] This is the rural Africa which is "free from problems" in the sense that it can cope with population increase without modifying structures, by merely spreading wider the traditional subsistence economy. The insertion of this Africa into the colonial world has brought about a very limited development of export crops, often imposed by the administration as necessary for the payment of taxes. Sometimes, when the terms of trade between these exported products and the manufactured goods they make it possible to buy have grown worse, or simply when the administrative pressure that imposed them has weakened, we see these crops being given up in favor of subsistence agriculture. It would be superficial to describe this change as retrogressive, since rationality is here on the side of the peasants, not of the administration that strives to impose the cultivation of these noneconomic crops. The development of a parasitic urban economy, with the inflation it brings in its train, often lies behind this worsening in the terms of trade, the most spectacular example of which is the setback given to the cotton-producing economy of Congo-Kinshasa. Similar phenomena have occurred elsewhere (in Mali and Guinea, for example). There is much matter for reflection in a comparative study of these cases, especially regarding the role of different family structures and religious ideologies (animism, Islam, etc.), some of which seem to have adapted themselves more easily than others to the requirements of the new development.

In the regions affected by progress, the social upheavals have been radical and fast. Numerous strata of planters have broken with tradition; they engage in precise economic calculations and adopt European ways of life and consumption. Growth rates that are sometimes exceptionally high have been realized in agriculture: rates of 7 percent per year over ten or twenty years are not unknown.[186] Undoubtedly, the transformations undergone by these rural areas of Africa during the last three decades contrast with the relative immobility of the rural areas of the Eastern world as a whole, and are closer to certain parts of Latin America.

Under these conditions, the "average rate of growth" of agriculture in Black Africa is a meaningless concept. Whereas in the East such average rates do in fact reflect the slow progress of an agriculture that is broadly homogeneous, in Black Africa they conceal the exceptional progress of regions that are moving into the capitalist mode of production. The conclusions drawn by the international organizations which, accepting these meaningless averages, put Black Africa at the bottom of the list, are superficial and deceptive.[187]

The capitalist mode of production that is installing itself in some areas of Africa has its limits, however. Landed property, there as elsewhere, forms a protective monopoly. The possibility of geographical extension of the system reduces the need for an intensification that would in turn call for investment in land and the development of a local industry to provide machinery and fertilizers for it. Subsequent development based on commercialized production of food crops, when the possibilities of the external market start to level off, will also necessitate an intensification that will be more difficult.

In the Eastern world the urban bourgeoisie usually appeared earlier than its rural equivalent, the development of which was hindered by the semi-feudal relations dominating the countryside in the East. Moreover, the antiquity of urban civilization facilitated the rapid transformation of old-style merchants into a bourgeoisie of the modern type to which the Chinese Marxists have given the classical description of "comprador": intermediaries between the dominant capitalist world and the rural backwoods. As a rule, this commercial bourgeoisie, in association with the rich landowners and the upper circles of the administration, cooperated at a later stage with foreign capital in the creation of industries. It was on the basis of these higher strata of society and not of the rural bourgeoisie and the "third estate" made up mainly of craftsmen and clerks, numerous in the big cities of the East, that the essential nucleus of the national bourgeoisie was formed. As for the strata of the "third estate," in particular the craftsmen, the competition of foreign or local industry either proletarianized them or doomed them to hopeless decline. The mass underemployment found in the big cities of the East is due largely to this phenomenon.

This pattern of the formation of a national bourgeoisie differs both from the European pattern and from that of present-day Black Africa. In Europe the bourgeois strata of the *ancien régime* did not usually play the main role in the formation of the new industrial bourgeoisie. In many cases they were "feudalized" through purchase of land, leaving the new rural bourgeoisie and the craftsmen to provide the principal contingent of entrepreneurs in the nineteenth century. In the East the extreme weakness, or even nonexistence, of the rural bourgeoisie, together with the impossibility for craftsmen to rise in the world in the face of industrial competition, necessarily caused the national bourgeoisie to be highly concentrated numerically from the very start.[188]

The concentration of landed property, of which India and Egypt provide perhaps the best examples, with the continual movement of fortunes made in the towns into the countryside, to buy land, accentuated this centralization of wealth and the merging of large-scale landownership with the new urban bourgeoisie.

In Black Africa, where urban development has taken place only recently, in the colonial period, and where large-scale landownership is lacking, the formation of an urban bourgeoisie has been delayed for a longer period. The traditional traders, such as those of West Africa, were not capable, for lack of adequate financial resources (and probably also because of their rigid traditional culture), of modernizing themselves and entering the circuits of modern commerce. Their development has therefore remained limited, with their field of activity very often confined to traditional exchanges (cola,[189] dried fish, etc.). Some of their activities, moreover, have ceased to exist, such as the trade in salt and in metals. In certain sectors, however, a noticeable enrichment has taken place, the volume of exchanges having considerably increased. Examples of this trend are the cattle merchants of the Niger bend, of Nigeria, and of the Sudan, and the dried fish merchants of Mali, Chad, and the Bight of Benin. A few of these merchants have sometimes ventured into modern trade, in textiles and hardware, but they have, as a rule, failed to secure more than a very limited position in these branches. Yet the spirit of enterprise is not lacking among them, as we see from the emigration of Sarakulle and Hausa merchants to the distant Congo, attracted by the trade in diamonds. Nevertheless, the numbers involved remain very few, their financial means meager and their technical know-how slight.

As is well known, colonial conquest was preceded, over several centuries, by the operations of the coastal bases of the *économie de traite.* In these centers a trading bourgeoisie, European by origin on the West Coast, Arab on the East Coast, but in both cases rapidly becoming half-caste, might have served as the nucleus of a national trading bourgeoisie. These men did indeed follow the advance of colonial conquest, but they did not establish themselves as *traitants* in the new market towns of the interior, in the midst of areas where agriculture was becoming commercialized. Their development was cut short, owing to its late start, through the victorious competition presented by the big monopolies of colonial trade at the opening of the twentieth century. Here examples can be quoted of the bankruptcies suffered by merchants of Saint-Louis and Gorée at the end of the nineteenth century, as a result of competition by Bordeaux and Marseilles firms. Their children all went into state service.[190]

The development of commercial relations within the countryside should also have given rise to a bourgeoisie of small traders. Here too, however, the power of the big trading monopolies prevented them from growing above the level of very petty trade and moving into wholesale and import-export trade. One special field, however, seems to have been reserved for the local trading bourgeoisie: the trade in locally produced foodstuffs, which has so far remained a highly atomized business often carried on by women. Even here, tendencies toward concentration seem to have made themselves felt in some places.

All these groups with bourgeois inclinations have also suffered from the absence of a rich landed aristocracy by association with whom they might have speeded up their accumulation of capital. The narrowness of the African markets has also played a negative role. A very limited number of branch offices of the big concerns, in the *escales,** together with small traders of immigrant origin (Greeks, Lebanese, and Indians), sufficed to meet the needs of commerce. Only in quite exceptional circumstances, when, as a result of independence, European traders withdrew, or the state intervened actively on behalf of native traders, have the latter succeeded in breaking into the wholesale and import-export trades. The case of Congo-Kinshasa is particularly illuminating from this standpoint: here, the distribution of import licenses, together with inflation, have enabled a rich new trading bourgeoisie to develop, and to attain within only a few years an exceptional degree of maturity. Organized in a strong trade association (the Aprodeco), the Congolese merchants today account for perhaps 20 percent of the wholesale and import-export trade—something unparalleled in the rest of Black Africa. It is interesting that this bourgeoisie has originated from humble circles without great wealth or traditional social prestige with a modern education: clerks, teachers, nurses, etc.

The process of industrialization in Black Africa also offers some striking differences from the Eastern and Latin American patterns. This process is much more recent in Black Africa. The *pacte colonial* and the narrowness of the markets doubtless provide the explanation for this late development. Only since the Second World War has the process begun, sometimes becoming so rapid as to enable large areas of Black

* Market towns in the interior where the trading concerns had their agencies.

Africa to make up for their delay in starting, as compared with the East. This has happened in Senegal, Ghana, Southern Nigeria, the Ivory Coast, Congo-Kinshasa, Congo-Brazzaville, Kenya, Rhodesia, and Cameroon. Everywhere, however, even when it has taken place following independence, industrialization has been carried out almost entirely by foreign capital. Modern industry (even light industry) requires resources too great for an association of local national capital, deprived as it is of the source of accumulation represented in the East by large-scale landownership. Consequently, there are practically no small African-owned industries. Those that are usually classified as such in statistical tables are really examples of urban crafts (bakeries, carpenters' shops, and the like), in which the possibilities for accumulation are very limited. European enterprise reaches very far down in the scale of industrial activity.

For the same reasons the African rural bourgeoisie is unable on its own to create a modern industry, to follow the example of its European equivalent. It has neither the financial means nor the technical capacities for this. Its younger generation escapes into state service. Nevertheless, exchanges of capital do take place between town and country. Those who have become officials invest the money of their country kinsfolk in sectors which do not require excessive capital: road haulage, taxis, services, building. Conversely, officials buy plantations or tracts of land destined for market-gardening. The small scale of private fortunes in the towns restricts the scope of such transfers.

The African pattern of development of capitalism is thus different from the Eastern and Latin American patterns as regards the fundamental point of the respective places occupied by the rural and urban bourgeoisies and the relations between these two classes. Whereas in the East capitalism began in the towns, to spread later, and with difficulty, into the countryside, in Black Africa the reverse seems to be more typical. In Black Africa, rural capitalism has the good fortune to strike deeper roots, being scattered among tens of thousands of planters. On the other hand, Black Africa lacks a highly concentrated urban big bourgeoisie, allied to large landed property, such as is found in the East and in Latin America.

The new tendencies toward a development of state capitalism which are common to the Third World as a whole are doubtless due to the dominant position held by foreign capital and the weakness of the urban national bourgeoisie which results from this. Consequently, these tendencies are likely to be more pronounced in Black Africa than elsewhere.

The development of foreign capitalism in the towns has indeed created in the Third World national communities which are mutilated, insofar as the classes and social strata whose existence is (negatively) related to foreign capital are absent. In Black Africa this feature is all the more marked because urban development is recent and the dominance of foreign capital more complete.

The towns of Black Africa contain few social survivals from the past comparable to the craftsmen and petty traders of the East. The occupied native population is made up almost entirely of officials and office workers. The working class is weak in numbers in proportion to the up-to-dateness of industry. The mass of the people consist, apart from the lower strata of public employees and the employees of foreign private concerns, of a large number of unemployed, usually young men, who have come in from the country.

Under these conditions, the national movement has been led by the urban petty-bourgeoisie of officials and office workers, together with the bourgeoisie of small businessmen and planters, where this exists. The traditional rural elites have usually lined up with the colonial order, which they see as safeguarding tradition, threatened in the towns by cultural modernization. The urban bourgeoisies, with few exceptions, have been overwhelmed by the petty-bourgeois nationalist movement.

Independence has strongly reinforced the specific weight of the new state bureaucracy in the national community, especially because the rural bourgeoisie, where it exists, remains scattered and has a limited outlook, and because the bureaucracy inherits the prestige of the state, something that is traditional in non-European societies and that is reinforced in Africa by experience of the apparently absolute power that was wielded by the colonial administration and by the fact that the petty bourgeoisie from which this bureaucracy is recruited holds a monopoly of modern education and technical knowledge.

The new bureaucracy tends in these circumstances to become the principal driving force in society. The relations between this social group, on the one hand, and, on the other, the bourgeoisies arisen from the planters and from small-scale urban business, and foreign capital, constitute the essence of the problem of relations between political power and economic responsibility in these countries.

The question then arises: what will be the most probable form of development of African national capitalism under these conditions—private capitalism, or state capitalism? Comparative analysis of the recent evolution of African states suggests that these two forms are being combined in different ways depending on the stage of evolution at the end of the colonial period.

The development of capitalism within the colonial framework was based on the transformation of subsistence agriculture into agricultural production for export, and on mining. The growth rate of colonial capitalism was determined under these conditions by that of the demand of the advanced countries for the primary products originating in the colonies. At a later stage, the local market created by the commercialization of agriculture and the urban development that was bound up with this made possible the establishment of groups of light industries financed almost exclusively by colonial capital. It has already been shown that, on this narrow basis, the mechanisms of capitalist development become blocked at a certain level. Examples are plentiful to illustrate this analysis. A large number of African states—Senegal, Ghana, Southern Nigeria, Congo-Kinshasa, for example—reached this level ten or fifteen years ago. A new leap forward would require both an advance in the productivity of agriculture producing foodstuffs for the markets of the new towns and the establishment of groups of basic industries the outlet for which would be industrialization itself rather than direct consumption.

In certain cases where foreign capital had not exhausted the possibilities of this type of development at the moment when independence was achieved, the new local administration was obliged to leave unchanged the economic structures inherited from the colonial period. Often, however, when foreign capital had already exhausted these possibilities, the new administration has gradually come to desire to take over the foreign-owned sector, this being the only way open to it to secure rapid expansion by providing itself with an economic basis. It then tends to transform itself from a classical administrative bureaucracy into a state bourgeoisie.

In the first of these two cases, parallel with the development of the foreign-owned sector, a certain scope can be found for national development, in small and medium business activity. Efforts are sometimes made by the state to promote this type of development. It can be shown, however, that this scope is necessarily limited. The development of national capitalism at the expense of the foreign sector offers, in contrast to this, a greater range of possibilities, and it can assume a variety of forms, to the advantage either of private national capital or of the state. Transfers of ownership of foreign plantations to the well-to-do strata of urban society and the taking-up of shares in new foreign-owned industries furnish examples of the first type of process, with Congo-Kinshasa as probably the best example. Nationalization of large enterprises, like the Union Minière du Haut Katanga, provides examples of the second type.

In every instance, however, the state is the instrument needed to bring about this process, which cannot occur through the mere working of economic forces. The local bourgeoisie of planters and merchants does not possess the financial means to buy up the investments of foreign capital. To do this it needs the backing of public funds. It is this drift toward state capitalism that seems to me to constitute the essence of what is conventionally called "African socialism."

Certain circumstances have favored the radicalization of the current tendency, giving it a bias toward types of organization that are called socialist (in the sense that they are inspired by the Soviet statist pattern); other circumstances have favored development toward forms that are described as liberal (in the sense that they are inspired by the mode of economic organization characteristic of the West). The history of the national movement, and the role that has been played in it by the popular masses in the towns, or at least by the lower strata of the petty bourgeoisie, and sometimes by the rural masses (which have shown themselves capable of substantial revolts, in Kenya, the Congo, Cameroon, the Sudan, and Nigeria), are not without influence in this connection. When the blocking of advanced colonial-style development has already been effective for a long time, and the problems are therefore all the more acute, the pressure of these masses may have led to the adoption, after independence, of sharper attitudes toward the private bourgeoisie, as began to become apparent in Ghana. Similarly, though paradoxically, when this private bourgeoisie is nonexistent, owing to a delay caused by the form of colonial development, as in Mali or Guinea, the specific weight of the administration in the country's life may reinforce tendencies toward statism. Conversely, a process of colonial-style development under way as in the Ivory Coast, Biafra, or Cameroon may strengthen liberal tendencies and modify the relations between the private bourgeoisie and the administration. Generally speaking, however, the state bourgeoisie has in no case in Africa eliminated the private bourgeoisie, but has been content to absorb it or to merge with it. Indeed, the rural bourgeoisie of planters has always retained a leading economic role and an important political position.

The place occupied by the bourgeoisie—thus conceived in the widest sense of the term—in the political life of Black Africa today seems to be a decisive one. It is characteristic, in this connection, that the great ethnic movements that are in the process of upsetting the map of Africa by breaking through the artificial frontiers inherited from the colonial period are experiencing very different fates, depending on whether they affect ethnic groups that have been transformed by the development of capitalism or, on the contrary, groups that have remained unaffected by modernization. The national bourgeoisie gives an ethnic movement consistency, coherence of aims, and a definite program which peasant revolts have proved unable to combine under present circumstances. The contrast between the Biafran succession, organized around a local bourgeoisie, and the rebellion in Southern Sudan, a country without bourgeois elites, is illuminating in this respect. In the Congo, when independence came, the ethnic groups most affected by the development of capitalism, the Bakongo and the Baluba, immediately organized their provinces into a national state, and remained aloof from the great peasant revolts that involved the zones that were lacking in a bourgeois framework, namely, the provinces of the East and North, and Kwilu.[191] In Ethiopia, the Eritrean opposition, grouped around the bourgeoisie of that province, possesses a coherence that is lacking among the Galla peasants and the Somali nomads.[192]

The national bourgeoisie continues with greater or less success the work begun by foreign capital, namely, the development of plantation economy and light industry. During a certain period it may even perhaps enlarge its scope by gradually taking over the foreign-owned enterprises. Progress beyond that point demands the overcoming of serious handicaps standing in the way of rapid advance by food-producing agriculture and the creation of large economic spaces, which are the necessary conditions for further development.

True, there are examples to show that the transformations effected in export agriculture can also be effected in the production of foodstuffs for the market (the cases of the Senufo district in the Ivory Coast and of the Lower Congo are among the most illuminating), although, it seems, this is more difficult, for reasons that need to be analyzed. The spontaneous tendency runs in this direction, but at a rate that is inadequate to the needs of the present epoch, given the acceleration of urban development and the economic disequilibria this entails. In order to proceed much faster it may be necessary to bring in active participation by the rural masses. It is hard to say how this could be secured (though a systematic analysis of peasant revolts might provide valuable pointers), but it can be stated that a paternalistic egalitarian policy, whether in the traditional style, like the *paysannats*, or in the modern style (*animation rurale* and cooperation), has little prospect of producing any better results in the future than it has produced in the past.

As regards the need for large spaces, moreover, it is not to be forgotten that, having been created within the setting of the small artificial states of today, the national bourgeoisie will rise only with difficulty above the limited horizons of these states. Social forces that have no immediate interest in maintaining these micronational forms are nevertheless bound to appear on the scene.

International political hierarchy derives its structure from relations of economic inequality. The age is past in which bourgeoisies of different origins could coexist, each operating in a relatively independent sphere. The transformation of the relevant problems into *world* problems threatens young bourgeoisies with the prospect of being kept at the level of appendages to the most powerful forces on the world scale. This will continue to be the case at least as long as the underdeveloped countries remain what they are now—exporters of primary products, deprived of basic industries.

It is true that the development of capitalism in Black Africa remains embryonic, in the sense that vestiges of the past, especially the survival of structures that are still living realities (tribal ties, for example), often continue to hide the new structures (ties based on class, or on groups defined by their position in the capitalist system).

The numerical weakness which still frequently characterizes the bourgeois classes, and the modest income at their disposal, contribute to this impression of the indefiniteness of capitalist relations. The belated incorporation of these new bourgeoisies into a world unified, organized, and hierarchically ordered by capitalism makes the prospect even more uncertain. While they have not yet succeeded in building bourgeois national states, the bourgeoisies of Black Africa are already having to cope with problems of a new kind: destructuring of the rural community, development of towns accompanied by inadequate industrialization, a growing gap between the excessively slow pace of economic growth and that of the progress of education, cultural traumas—all of which reflect not the general difficulties characteristic of capitalist development, but those peculiar to the development of peripheral capitalism.

GENERAL FEATURES OF PERIPHERAL FORMATIONS

Despite their different origins, the peripheral formations tend to converge toward a pattern that is essentially the same. This is not surprising: it simply reflects the increasing power of capitalism to unify the world, relegating regional peculiarities to the museum of survivals from the past, and organizing the center, on the one hand, and the periphery, on the other, into a single hierarchical world structure. The development of agricultural production for export tends to give rise to an agrarian capitalism throughout the periphery and, furthermore, the latifundia form of this agrarian capitalism, both in Latin America and in the East, is continually threatened by the rising power of the rich peasantry, so that the *kulak* form of agrarian capitalism is tending to become general and to expand in scope. Integration into the world market tends everywhere to create comprador bourgeoisies. Even where, as in Black Africa, old-time mercantile colonial capital used to fulfill this function, its positions are being challenged by the first generations of national capitalists, who press their claim to take over. The shifting of the center of gravity of foreign capital from this old-time colonial capital to the great interterritorial mining and industrial concerns helps to make possible this nationalizing of trade, which has lost its former importance among the mechanisms of domination by the center.[193] By creating in the periphery, in the sectors that are of interest to it, organizations for mining and industrial processing on the scale required by modern technique, the center everywhere blocks the path for the development of a national industrial capitalism capable of competing with it. Hence the general tendency of local capitalism to assume statist forms.

The formation of colonies of settlement by Europeans has played its part in the gradual creation of a periphery. We have seen that, in Latin America, European settlement served to establish from the start that peripheral structure toward which national communities tended in the other regions of what was to become the Third World. The settlement of "poor whites" in North Africa or in Kenya fulfilled the same functions in relation to peripheral capitalism in the agrarian and commercial spheres. Only in the extreme (and exceptional) cases of North America, Australia, and New Zealand (and also, with special features of their own, South Africa, Rhodesia, and Israel), did the establishment of colonies of settlement result in the creation of new *central* formations.

The function fulfilled by New England was a special one from the outset. A model, such as history has rarely provided, of a society based on petty-commodity production, it took England's place as the new center (at first only partially) in relation to the periphery constituted by the slave-owning colonies of the South and the West Indies. Having thrown off control by the monopolies of metropolitan merchant capital, New England became a fully developed center, and later, as the United States of America, rose to its present status as the metropolis of the world. This offers the best available example that the simple commodity mode of production necessarily gives rise to full-blown (autocentric) capitalism, and that the less this mode of production is hindered by other modes the more striking will be the capitalist development it engenders. A partial analogy is to be seen in the original formation of the countries of White Oceania, also based on petty-commodity production. These countries, however, remained for a long time principally agricultural producers, exporting to Europe and not to the periphery, as with North America. For this reason Australia and New Zealand had more difficulty advancing to the industrial stage. Here too, however, the dynamism of the simple commodity mode of production, unhindered by precapitalist modes of production, showed its power to achieve this stage. The same can be said of South Africa, which was at first a mere agricultural appendage to the British center. At that stage, the white community remained isolated from the surrounding black world, and did not exploit it, merely driving it back. When it had reached the industrial stage, owing to its own dynamism as an unhindered simple commodity economy, white South African society found its own potential periphery ready to hand. This, it seems to me, is the explanation of the remarkable triumphant imperialism of South Africa, which has virtually annexed Rhodesia and does not hide its ambition to reduce the whole southern half of the continent to the status of its periphery. On a smaller scale, Israel exemplifies the same phenomenon in the Middle East.[194]

All the peripheral formations thus share three essential features: (1) the predominance of agrarian and commercial capitalism in the national sector of the economy; (2) the creation of a local bourgeoisie in the wake of dominant foreign capital; (3) the tendency to a peculiar bureaucratic form of development which is characteristic of the periphery in our own day.

Predominance of Agrarian and Commercial Capitalism

The predominance of agrarian capitalism forms the most striking and obvious of the classical features of the underdeveloped societies. The classical image of the dominant class in the underdeveloped world is the large landowner—not the feudalist but the planter (producing for export).

This predominance shows itself in one or another of the three forms of which I have analyzed the process of formation. The most complete of these is certainly the latifundia form that is found in Latin America, Cuba having provided the most thoroughgoing example, because this form was established there from the start to fulfill this very function, without any process of internal evolution or transformation of precapitalist formations. The fact that this latifundia form made use of servile labor (slaves or peons) for a long period before evolving toward general employment of wage labor offers a further confirmation that, whenever capital lacks a labor force, it does not hesitate to resort to political means in order to create this labor force.[195] The slavery and peonage of the Americas, like, closer to our time, forced labor on plantations (as in the Ivory Coast until 1950), or confinement of the African peasantry to inadequate "reservations" (South Africa, Rhodesia, Kenya before independence), constitute so many methods of implementing this policy.

When the formation of a capitalist latifundia proceeds by way of transformation of precapitalist formations, it comes up against the resistance of internal social forces that are all the livelier because the village community forms the basis of these precapitalist formations. When these forces are completely overcome, the finished pattern is realized, as in Egypt. Very often, however, development proves unable to reach this point. The consequence is the creation of agrarian capitalist formations that are integrated into the world market by their essential function but are nevertheless clothed in feudal forms. The systems of groundnut cultivation in the Murid country of Senegal and in the sultanates of Northern Nigeria, or the Sudanese economy, exemplify this incomplete transformation. The new ruling classes take for themselves only part of the land, often quite a small part. They continue to benefit from the tribute-paying system on which their position was originally based. Very often—as in the African countries mentioned—this tribute is levied in the name of new religious functions, the peasant community being integrated into a system of brotherhoods (Murid, Tidjane, Ansar, Ashiqqa, etc.).[196] This new religious force has been born not of a distinctive internal dynamic but of a need to collect a larger amount of tribute than in the past. Isolated from the world market, the local ruling class can only levy a tribute in subsistence goods, to provide for its own consumption and that of its hangers-on and its machinery of government. Once integrated into the world market, it can commercialize this tribute and adopt European patterns of consumption. Its appetite becomes limitless, and it can secure the increased tribute it needs only if a new force—here, religion—causes the peasantry to give its assent.

Paradoxically, where this path is closed because the original precapitalist formations are not sufficiently well developed, it is the most dynamic and modern form of agrarian capitalism that establishes itself. This has happened in the areas of native-owned plantations in Black Africa, where it is the rich peasant, the *kulak*, who has become the central figure in the new formations, whereas elsewhere the internal contradictions of a latifundia system integrated into the world market had to develop before agrarian reforms were imposed which favored "kulakization" (Egypt, India, Mexico, etc.). Here, too, it is absurd to try to ignore politics and reduce the significance of the process to strictly economic terms. It is interesting to observe that even where the conditions for transforming precapitalist formations integrated into the world market into formations of *kulak*-type agrarian capitalism are not at all favorable, it is nevertheless in this direction that the tendency runs. We then see meager forms of sporadic agrarian microcapitalism, as in the savannah country of Niger.[197] The concentration of modern means of production (tractor-drawn machinery), through the cooperatives, and the hiring out of these means, which is frequent in Africa, reflects the power of this tendency toward capitalism, even though in a setting that is very poor and confined.[198]

The predominance of agrarian capitalism brings in its train the agrarian crisis which is also a general feature of the Third World. Natural population increase being unable to find its normal outlet in industrialization, pressure on the land becomes intense. Moreover, capitalist forms in agriculture cause the excessive agricultural labor force to be thrown out of employment. In the precapitalist systems, the whole population, regardless of the theoretical surplus of labor, has the right of access to the land, but as capitalist forms develop, this right is lost. An increased proportion of landless peasants, and the driving of ever larger numbers of them right out of production, with the consequent appearance of unemployment, are the results of this process. At the same time the mechanisms of unequal exchange reduce the countryfolk to poverty despite the increased productivity of their labor. These are fundamental reasons for the flight from the countryside, and why it is accelerated despite the inadequacy of the urban outlet.

The Dependent Character of Local Capitalism

The control exercised by foreign capital over native-owned enterprises is more, or less, effective, depending on whether or not these enterprises are situated within the circuits exposed to external exchanges and therefore dominated by foreign capital. Analysis of some historical experiences of the development of national capitalism in the periphery shows clearly what these mechanisms of domination are: for example, in the case of Senegal, of the vicissitudes of whose national trade between 1820 and our own time I have made a study.[199]

This history makes sense only if one clearly distinguishes between the concepts that are essential for an analysis of accumulation: the concept of expanded reproduction and the concept of primitive accumulation. There is expanded reproduction when profit—the income from invested capital—is saved and reinvested in order to expand productive capacity. In contrast to this, in the prehistory of capital, the income that is originally turned into capital cannot itself be derived from the profit from a previous investment of capital, but must emerge from exploitation of noncapitalist sectors: this is primitive accumulation. In the relations between advanced and underdeveloped countries we observe mechanisms (up-to-date ones) belonging to the type of primitive accumulation, which operate to the advantage of the dominant foreign capital and therefore restrict the possibilities for development of the local capital, which remains peripheral. Politics thus plays a vital role. The case of Senegal between 1820 and our own day is a striking illustration of this truth.

This is why, in examining relations between the center and the periphery, we must never forget what is fundamental, namely, *the mechanisms of primitive accumulation for the benefit of metropolitan capital.* Integration into the world market determines the essential price structure, that which defines the ratio between prices of exported products and internal prices. This structure makes possible a systematic transfer of value from the periphery to the metropolitan center. This being a process of unequal exchange, it is a mechanism not of normal expanded reproduction but of primitive accumulation. The latter not only went on before the historical appearance of expanded reproduction: it continues to go on today, and is characteristic of all the relations between the center and the periphery of the world system.

National capitalist activities are nevertheless not absent from these relations. This is why we can also observe mechanisms of expanded reproduction for the benefit of the national bourgeoisie which has arisen in the circuits by which the periphery is integrated into the world market. This was the case in Senegal with the native *traitants* dealing in gum, and later in groundnuts, and with the import merchants of today. But this circuit is dominated by the capital of the center: the margin in which accumulation for the benefit of the national bourgeoisie can be carried on is wholly determined by the hierarchical relations between the bourgeoisie of the center and that of the periphery. Left to the unmodified working of spontaneous economic laws, this margin continually tends to be reduced to zero, because changes in relative prices transfer the benefit from the national bourgeoisie to the bourgeoisie of the center. These are the mechanisms that account for the ruin of the Senegalese bourgeoisie between 1900 and 1930, just as they explain the meager results obtained today in the sectors grafted on to the world market (forwarding agents, for example). Extraeconomic (political) relations between the bourgeoisie of the center and that of the periphery, which define the distinctive characteristics of the social formations of the center and of the periphery, either mitigate or aggravate this tendency for transfer of the capacity to accumulate from the periphery to the center. Other examples (of which there are many in Africa, such as that of the forest entrepreneurs) lead to the same conclusions.[200]

Only to a very minor degree do we observe mechanisms of primitive accumulation or normal expanded reproduction to the advantage of the national bourgeoisie operating in sectors that depend only indirectly on the external market, being mainly bound up with the expansion of the home market. Here the possibilities of rapid accumulation are greater, being much less subject to control by foreign capital. (This is the situation, for example, of the meat salesmen in Senegal.) These mechanisms belong to the sphere of primitive accumulation, when local capital is in relations with the noncapitalist sector of the local economy; otherwise they belong to the sphere of normal expanded reproduction.

G. Arrighi has used the expression "*lumpen* bourgeoisie" to describe this micro-bourgeoisie that comes into being in the wake of foreign capital and can develop only within the narrow limits allotted to it by the policy of the dominant capital.[201] This wretched form of national capitalism is frequent in Africa where the bourgeoisie is chiefly recruited from the ethnic group traditionally engaged in trade (Dyula,

Hausa, Bamileke, Baluba, Bakongo, etc.) or, in some countries, from women (the "market-mammies"). Though abject and narrowly restricted by the degree of tolerance shown by the dominant capital, this bourgeoisie may flourish and, amid the general poverty, constitute a local social force of decisive significance. This is the case in Southern Nigeria, where this type of African enterprise is often cited as an example of the success of promoting indigenous private enterprise.

It is quite clear that where the chief form of colonial economic dependence was through commercial relations and the chief form of foreign capital was old-style colonial merchant capital, even this limited and miserable type of national capitalism had no chance of developing. In the French colonies in particular, the mediocre dynamism of the metropolitan capitalism itself meant that excessive relative weight was given to this old-style merchant capital of Bordeaux and Marseilles, with its background in the monopoly companies of the *ancien régime* and the slave trade. In our time, of course, the center of gravity of the dominant foreign capital has, even in this case, shifted from the commercial houses to the big interterritorial mining or industrial concerns, so that the trading sector is rapidly losing its importance and being abandoned to local capital.[202] The change in political relations resulting from political independence also has a decisive influence here. The blossoming of this national bourgeoisie is all the more pronounced because the many ties that link it to the machinery of state—family, connections, corruption, etc.—favor its formation. In the most extreme cases of concentration of local power it is the upper strata of the bureaucracy, themselves merging with the landed oligarchy, which, either openly or through intermediaries, become a new bourgeoisie of the comprador type. They are then able not merely to take over their trading functions from the colonialists but even to secure an association with foreign capital in the modern sectors (mines, industries, banks).[203]

It remains true that, even in these most favorable situations, the very mechanisms of integration into the world market—both the economic ones (unequal exchange, lack of independence of the financing structures, vulnerability of the balance of payments, etc.) and those that belong to the domain of ideology and politics—forbid the national bourgeoisie to go beyond a "desire for autonomy."[204]

Contemporary Tendencies to the Development of National Bureaucracies

It is a commonplace that the world of today is witnessing the development, in all fields of social life (state and business administration, political and trade-union activity, etc.), of bureaucratic machinery that is unprecedented in its scope and effectiveness, at least in the capitalist formations of the center. Some explain this phenomenon as being necessitated by modern technique, adding, in the case of Burnham and Galbraith, that it reflects a transfer of political power from parliamentary democracy to state technocracy. Proof that it is a deep-rooted consequence of technical progress is said to be provided by the developments proceeding in Russia and Eastern Europe, the "convergence of the systems," despite the difference in ownership of the means of production—public in the East, private in the West.[205] Transposed to the periphery, this body of socioeconomic theory seeks to identify the bureaucratic phenomenon observable there with that which is characteristic of the center in our time. The demands of accelerated development in the Third World are said merely to reinforce a tendency that is general in the age we live in.

Although this theory fits the facts so far as their *appearance* is concerned (but *only* so far), it does not stand up to analysis. Here, too, we find the center and the periphery treated as though they were the same, so that it is not impossible to grasp the specific functions each fulfills within the same world system, and the real mechanisms by which each of them operates.

It seems to me that, at the center, the capitalist mode of production implies the polarization (which has in fact taken place) of society into two classes, bourgeoisie and proletariat (even if increasingly important sections of the latter—cadres of every variety—although they are employed for wages, deny that they belong to the proletariat). I think, too, that in the exercise of political power and management of the economy, the bourgeoisie cannot itself directly take on all the functions of direction and execution that its position demands. The farther society progresses the more complicated do its mechanisms become, and the more intensified this phenomenon. This is why social groups are formed that are entrusted with these functions: the higher administration, police and army, the technostructures of big firms, groups of professional politicians, and so on. Some of these groups have lost their traditional function: this has happened to the more professional politicians, who carry out, within the framework of parliamentary democracy, the function of negotiators on behalf of the different interests within a collective capital which at that stage is still scattered and intracompetitive, but who, with the coming of monopoly, have lost their function to the technocracies of the big firms and the state.[206] Only in periods of serious crisis, such as that from which Nazism arose, does the bourgeoisie lose control of these groups, which then seem to constitute an independent social force, for a time at least. In my view, the strengthening of the technocratic machinery in the countries of Eastern Europe, and their demand for "democracy" (restricted to this bureaucracy), reflect an evolution toward a new form of generalized state capitalism, which is essentially marked by the reestablishment of market mechanisms and the ideology (economism) that necessarily accompanies this. Investigation of the origins of this evolution, especially in Russian history, and discussion of whether or not this evolution is "inevitable"—in other words, the problem of the future of China after the Cultural Revolution—though matters of importance, are not our business here.

For nothing justifies us in transposing these analyses to the periphery. The bureaucratic developments in the periphery need to be interpreted, in my opinion, in relation to their own setting, which is that of the formations of peripheral capitalism.

In the East and in Latin America the domination of central capital has given rise, as we have seen, to social formations that include local ruling classes (big landowners and comprador bourgeoisie) who wield political power locally. This power has been exercised by these classes within the framework of a world system, that is, for the benefit of the center and of themselves, whose own development was determined from outside. Matters proceeded differently in other parts of the periphery, especially in Africa. In North Africa, direct colonial rule and the settlement of "poor whites" restricted within very narrow limits the formation of social classes similar to those in the East. In Black Africa, generalized direct colonial rule, in a particularly simple and crude form, reduced for a long period the local population of vast areas to what was in effect an undifferentiated mass, the traditional hierarchies having largely lost their meaning, while all the new economic functions were directly taken over by foreigners.

Within the setting of political independence and the formation of national states under these conditions, the connection between the new bureaucracies and the social structures has assumed a variety of forms, having different significances and opening up prospects of different types of development. Where the peripheral formations are advanced, the national bureaucracy has found itself in a relation to the social structure that is—in appearance—similar to that which obtains at the center. In appearance only, for the reason, at least, that the system does not constitute a truly *national* whole, that is to say, one that is coherent and self-sufficient. Just as the peripheral economy can be understood only as an appendage of the central economy, so is peripheral society a mutilated society: the important element absent from it is the metropolitan bourgeoisie whose capital dominates it. Owing to the weaker and one-sided development of the local bourgeoisie, the weight of the bureaucracy in this society seems much greater. Moreover, a specific contradiction may develop from this fact. Either the state fulfills its functions within the framework of the system, that is, at best, helps to promote the advancement of a local peripheral bourgeoisie, or it undertakes to free the nation from domination by the center, through promoting national industrial development—which can only be public in form—and then it risks coming into conflict with the social formation from which it has arisen. Where the peripheral formations are not very advanced, this conflict does not occur, since the local bureaucracy is practically alone on the scene.

Such important phenomena as those of the role played in the Third World by the classes and strata described as "privileged" cannot be interpreted without analyzing the structure as a whole. There is a popular attitude that the wage-earners (in general) are "privileged" in comparison with the rural masses. This is not true, however, in the more developed formations, where their "privileges" shrink beside those of the local property-owning classes. The contradictions characteristic of the periphery, resulting in increasing unemployment in town and country, give all skilled workers (even those at the lowest level who enjoy relatively stable employment) a scale of income that is beyond comparison with that (in theory, nil) of the unemployed. However, there are systems of redistribution—which are deplored but which at bottom represent society's necessary response to its own situation (and which are not so much "survivals from the past" as responses to problems caused by the development of capitalism at the periphery)—that are not allowed for in the national accounts. Moreover, the pressure of unemployment has its effect on the organization of the wage-earners themselves, and, as we have seen, explains unequal exchange—meaning that these wage-earners receive rewards that are lower than those paid at the center for the same productivity.

The "privileged" situation of the wage-earners is more pronounced in the less developed formations. In Black Africa especially, colonial rule tended, in the phase preceding independence, to foster certain differentials in wages. Direct colonial rule, simple and crude, became less and less bearable. The development of towns and the creation of industries necessitated an increase in the payment of urban wage-earners, living as they were in contact with European modes of consumption. The solidarity of traditional social relations in the countryside, which were as yet breaking up only slowly, restricted the influx of labor power into the towns. The social order imposed a revision of the reward of labor *in the towns*. The shifting of the center of gravity of foreign capital, from old-style merchant capital to the capital of big concerns with high productivity, made this revision possible and not very expensive.[207] The case of the Belgian Congo, the most highly industrialized country in Africa, is eloquent in this respect. Between 1950 and 1958, real wages in industry were doubled. This increase, incidentally, had no harmful effect on the newly established industries, but, on the contrary, stimulated them to modernize and expand.[208] Here, then, the wage-earning sections did become relatively privileged. The colonial power thought it was gaining something useful at a low price: instead of basing itself on a dependent peripheral bourgeoisie, it imagined it could restrict its concessions to social strata with a low level of skill, thus avoiding the formation of "elites" that might be more demanding. It was then that the present social structure took shape, to be inherited by the independent states.[209]

The amount and distribution of these petty privileges were modified, however, after independence. Here, too, the case of Congo-Kinshasa is significant. The Congolese inflation of 1960–1968 resulted in a considerable change in the distribution of income within the country, the share going to foreign capital not being affected: the formation of a local bureaucratic machine (and so of a bureaucracy which, to be sure, is made up of several grades, but the highest grades of which are today by far the most privileged sections of Congolese society) was financed (1) by a drastic cut in the real income of the peasants producing for export (an internal worsening of the terms of trade for them which was much greater than that of the external terms of trade) and (2) by a no less drastic cut in the real wages of wage-earners in industry and commerce, which were brought down to the level of 1950. The IRES group of economists have shown the retrogressive character of these changes: the higher proportion of expenditure on imports and on consumer goods in the new distribution of income; the two-fold structural crises, potentially permanent, in public finance and the balance of payments, which is inherent in this situation, and the increased dependence on the outside world which it implies.[210]

I have shown that, without the factor of inflation being present, phenomena similar to this are characteristic of the development of the countries of the franc area, and also, with only a moderate degree of inflation, of some other countries, such as Ghana. The mechanism is thus as follows: freezing of wages and of prices paid to agricultural producers, increasing indirect taxation to balance the budget, leading to an internal price increase and a decline in the incomes of peasants and wage-earners. The most dramatic examples are found in countries where there is no adequate basis of industry or agriculture producing for export and where a transformation of the same type, aimed at by the new bureaucracy, comes up against the practical impossibility of extracting revenue from the country, so that the latter is reduced to hand-to-mouth dependence on external factors, and chronic inflation with no prospect of any end (the case of Mali). Everywhere the peasants react to this worsening of their position by withdrawing from the market, by a return to subsistence economy, which constitutes their only economically rational way of defending themselves: the basis from which the state derives its revenue is thus made narrower.[211] The political and social significance of the analyses made by Arrighi and Saul, mentioned above, seems liable, therefore, to be overtaken by the current processes of change.

One must go further than this, however. There is a deep-rooted tendency throughout the Third World today toward political and social changes that move in the same direction, namely: overthrow of the local political power of the big landowners and the comprador bourgeoisie, where these exist; direct exercise of power by the bureaucracies (civil or military, with the army often appearing as the vehicle of the new regimes—being the best organized corporation, and sometimes the only one available); and the creation and subsequent development of a publicly owned sector of the economy. A similar evolution is observed even where there is no former power to be overthrown, taking place through a continuous development. Contradictions characteristic of peripheral formations account for this phenomenon. The inadequate level of industrialization and the absence of the foreign bourgeoisie enable groups of a petty-bourgeois character (officials, office-workers, in some cases old-style craftsmen, small traders, middle peasants, etc.) to assume major importance in local affairs. The spread of education and the increasing unemployment bring about a profound crisis of the system. The very need for hastened industrialization in order to overcome this crisis leads to the development of a publicly owned sector, since the rules of profitability (which determine the flow of foreign capital) and the insufficient capacity of local private capital would otherwise slow down the pace of industrialization.

The consequent strengthening of the state bureaucracy may result in a regime of state capitalism becoming general. This is more radical or less so, depending on whether it proceeds to nationalize foreign capital (as in Egypt and, to a less advanced degree, in Congo-Kinshasa and Zambia), and on the extent to which it tolerates a local private sector with which it associates itself (as in Tunisia). Even, however, in the most extreme cases (Egypt), state capitalism tolerates—or, rather encourages—the development of private capitalism in the countryside (the "kulakization" that results from agrarian reforms is part of this tendency), although it may endeavor to organize and control this development, by means of cooperatives, for example. If it does not challenge integration into the world market, but merely plays upon secondary contradictions which are in any case on their way out (Western market versus Eastern market), this state capitalism is bound to remain fundamentally peripheral, like its private predecessor, and merely expresses the new paths of development taken by capitalism in the periphery, and the transition from old forms to new in the international specialization between center and periphery.

These processes, too often hastily reduced to the alleged profound and ancient tendencies of non-European societies ("Asiatic despotism"), are in reality expressions of the integration of the Third World in the process characteristic of the world of today, under the specific conditions of the periphery.

Summary of Conclusions

1. Economic theory interests itself occasionally in the problems of "transition from a subsistence economy to a money economy." Owing, however, to its lack of a set of concepts making possible an exact analysis of the various precapitalist formations, the theory currently offered is painfully meager. The pattern of transition to peripheral capitalism is, in fact, fundamentally different from that of transition to central capitalism. The onslaught from without, by means of trade, carried out by the capitalist mode of production upon the precapitalist formations, causes certain crucial retrogressions, such as the ruin of the

crafts without their being replaced by local industrial production. The agrarian crisis of the Third World is largely the result of these setbacks, rather than of alleged "demographic determinism." The subsequent investment of foreign capital does not have the effect of correcting these retrogressive changes, because of the extraverted orientation of the industries that this capital establishes in the periphery. These distinctive problems of transition to peripheral capitalism largely escaped Marx's notice, and this accounts for his mistaken notion about the future development of the "colonial problem."

2. Unequal international specialization is shown in three kinds of distortion in the direction taken by the development of the periphery. The distortion toward export activities (extraversion), which is decisive, does not result from "inadequacy of the home market" (the "vicious cycles of poverty"), as the commonplace analysis suggests, but from the superior productivity of the center in all fields, which compels the periphery to confine itself to the role of complementary supplier of products to which natural advantage is relevant (exotic agricultural and mineral products). When, as a result of this distortion, the level of wages in the periphery has become lower, for the same productivity, than at the center, a limited development of autocentric industries will have become possible in the periphery, even though at the same time the terms of trade will have become unequal.

3. This initial and essential distortion brings another in its train—the hypertrophy of the tertiary sector in the periphery. Here, too, the attempts of current economics to reduce to a single model the distribution of activity between sectors at the center and in the periphery avoid the real problems. Neither the evolution of the structure of demand nor that of productivity can explain the hypertrophy of the tertiary sector in our time, both at the center and in the periphery. At the center it reflects the difficulties of realizing surplus value which are inherent in the advanced monopoly phase, whereas in the periphery it is from the beginning a result of the limitations and contradictions characteristic of peripheral development: inadequate industrialization and increasing unemployment, strengthening of the position of ground-rent, and so on. A fetter on accumulation, this hypertrophy of unproductive activities, expressed especially in the excessive growth of administrative expenditure, is manifested by the quasi-permanent crisis of government finance in the underdeveloped countries today.

4. Unequal international specialization also underlies the distortion in the periphery toward light *branches* of activity. The current marginalist doctrine, which accords a decisive role to the rate of interest in

the "choice of techniques," sets out in the economics taught at the universities a series of pseudo-problems resulting from the alleged preferential choice of light *techniques* in the developed (?) countries. The facts, as also the theoretical analysis of the mechanisms of investment, contradict this current doctrine. The contradiction really characteristic of the periphery (namely, a tendency toward light branches), which results from the complementary nature of development in the periphery, is the source of the special problems that dictate development policies in the periphery that are different from those on which the development of the West is based.

5. The theory of the multiplier effects of investment cannot be extended in a mechanical way to the periphery. The significance of the Keynesian multiplier is indeed restricted to the situation at the center in the phase of advanced monopoly, characterized by difficulties in realizing the surplus. Neither hoarding nor imports constitute, in the periphery, "leaks" that reduce the multiplier effect. What in reality annuls this effect is the export of the profits of foreign capital. Furthermore, unequal specialization and the marked propensity to import that follows from this, and which is typical of the periphery, have the effect of transferring the effects of the multiplier mechanisms connected with the phenomenon known as the accelerator from the periphery to the center.

6. The increasing volume of profits on foreign capital, destined to be exported, ought to attract serious attention to the question of the origin and dynamics of the superprofits of monopolies. Here too, however, marginalist theory, by locating the origin of monopoly not in the relations of production but in the form taken by demand curves, avoids the real problems. Analysis of the strategies of foreign monopolies in the underdeveloped countries is restricted merely to the field of the "concrete study," without any concern to develop theory. This analysis proves that, so long as the dogma of the periphery's integration into the world market is not challenged, the periphery is without economic means of action in relation to the monopolies.

7. Underdevelopment is manifested not in the level of production per capita, but in certain characteristic structural features which oblige us not to confuse the underdeveloped countries with the countries now advanced as they were at an earlier stage of their development. These features are (1) the extreme inequalities that are typical of the distribution of productivities in the periphery, and in the system of prices transmitted to it from the center, which result from the distinctive nature of the peripheral formations and largely dictate the structure of

the distribution of income in these formations; (2) the disarticulation due to the adjustment of the orientation of production in the periphery to the needs of the center, which prevents the transmission of the benefits of economic progress from the poles of development to the economy as a whole; and (3) economic domination by the center, which is expressed in the forms of international specialization (the structures of world trade in which the center shapes the periphery in accordance with its own needs) and in the dependence of the structures whereby growth in the periphery is financed (the dynamics of accumulation of foreign capital).

8. The accentuation of the features of underdevelopment in proportion as the economic growth of the periphery—in other words, the development of underdevelopment—necessarily results in the blocking of growth, in other words, the impossibility—whatever the level of production per capita that may be attained—of going over to autonomous and self-sustained growth, to development in the true sense.

9. While at the center the capitalist mode of production tends to become exclusive, the same is not true of the periphery. Consequently, the formations of the periphery are fundamentally different from those of the center. The forms assumed by these peripheral formations depend, on the one hand, on the nature of the precapitalist formations that were there previously, and, on the other, on the forms and epochs in which they were integrated into the world system. In this context we can distinguish between the American formations, the Asiatic-Oriental formations, and the African formations. Only this type of analysis enables us to grasp the essential difference that contrasts the peripheral formations with the young central formations, the latter, based on the dominance of the simple commodity mode of production, possessing for this reason a capacity for independent evolution toward a fully developed capitalist mode of production of a particularly dynamic kind.

Whatever their differences of origin, the peripheral formations all tend to converge upon a typical model, characterized by the dominance of agrarian capital and ancillary (comprador) commercial capital. The domination by central capital over the system as a whole, and the vital mechanisms of primitive accumulation for its benefit which expresses this domination, nevertheless subject the development of peripheral national capitalism to strict limitations, which ultimately depend on political relations. The "truncated" nature of the national community in the periphery (the foreign bourgeoisie being the "great absent member") confers an apparent relative weight and special functions upon the local bureaucracy which are not the same as those of the bureaucratic and technocratic social groups at the center. The contradictions typical of the development of underdevelopment, and the rise of petty-bourgeois strata reflecting these contradictions, explain the present tendency to state capitalism which is general in the Third World. This new path of development for capitalism in the periphery does not constitute a path of transition to socialism so long as integration into the world market is not challenged, but rather the future way of organizing new relations between center and periphery, based on a new state in unequal international specialization.

Chapter 3
The Monetary Mechanisms in the Periphery and the World Monetary System

The monetary field is a very weak section of current economic theory. Strictly speaking, the subjective theory of value can have nothing to say regarding the value of money, except tautologically ("the value of money is that of the goods it enables one to acquire") or by resorting to a subterfuge "liquidity"—which conceals another piece of tautological reasoning (to say that money derives its value from its "liquid" character, that is, from its nature as money, is like saying that a sleeping pill possesses "soporificity" . . .). This is why marginalism and neo-marginalism have to call in the quantity theory of money to help them.

It is not surprising that money has become the focus of the most widespread illusions, such as that of "management" of the conjuncture, of prices, of external equilibrium, and so on. At the same time, of course—this is what always accompanies such illusions—the true role of money in the mechanism of accumulation is evaded by means of a theory that runs off in the direction of Byzantine discussions and quantitative observations which are as confused as they are plentiful.

When carried over into the setting of the underdeveloped countries, monetary theory produces the oddest results. A violent attack is launched against what are called "perverse monetary mechanisms," said to be characteristic of the underdeveloped countries, while ignoring the real features distinctive of the system, which, moreover, merely reflect on the monetary plane the fundamental relations of dependence which prevail at a different level.

What I wish to analyze here are these monetary mechanisms that function in the underdeveloped countries (within the differing institutional frameworks that exist there: foreign-exchange standard or "autonomous" national currency), after first recalling the theory of the role of money in the mechanism of accumulation. We shall then see the theoretical error that the monetary illusion is based upon. Current theory, in contrast to this way of proceeding, completely ignores the essential fact—"the integration of banking"—the fact that, until recently, the functions of bank credit have been looked after in the underdeveloped countries almost entirely by branches of foreign banks. Monetary integration—a foreign-exchange standard, with unlimited and unrestricted transfers at a fixed rate—was accompanied by bank integration.

The forms of the institution of the foreign-exchange standard have been various, ranging from simple circulation of banknotes of the dominant economy (the dollar in Liberia, Cuba, and Central America) to the issuing of a local currency, entrusted to a bank of issue, transfers being uncontrolled and at a fixed rate (the system that existed in Egypt between 1916 and 1947, the French colonial system, and the current system in the franc area), and including the original system of the British Currency Boards (British colonies in Africa, Central America and Southeast Asia, with the Portuguese colonies having a similar system). In these countries, at these periods, monetary and banking integration by the commercial banks of the dominant country, themselves dependent on the central bank of that country, is accompanied by the circulation of notes that are issued, in the last analysis, by this central bank. Nowadays only the African countries of the franc area (former French West Africa and French Equatorial Africa, Togo, Cameroon, and Madagascar), the Portuguese colonies, the West Indies, and some Central American countries are still integrated in this way in a highly centralized currency area.

Elsewhere this integration either has become, or always was, imperfect. It was usually confined to the activity of expatriate commercial banks on an underdeveloped territory where the state, having stayed independent, had retained the sovereign right of creating currency. Nearly everywhere in Latin America paper money issued by the local state treasuries, and put into circulation through the budget, whether balanced or not, and sometimes through the discounting of bills that was also undertaken by the state treasuries, constituted the only legal tender. Here, the exchange fluctuated and transfers were unlimited and unrestricted, including, of course, those effected by the branches of foreign banks, which played the main role in banking.

With the coming of independence to the Third World there were born, all over Asia, the Middle East, North Africa, the English-speaking countries of Black Africa, and Latin America, central banks entrusted with the task of bringing order into the system of paper money where this existed, of "controlling" or "managing" credit, in accordance with the illusions of the monetary theory. To varying degrees, systems of national commercial banks, either public or private, took over from the branches of the big foreign banks, and, to varying degrees, transfers were subjected to control. Finally, the system of fluctuating exchanges which governed international relations (including those between the advanced countries in the first phase after abandonment of the gold standard) was replaced by a world system of rigid exchange rates (revised by devaluations when these occurred) which has been symbolized since 1945 by the organization of the International Monetary Fund. Has this withdrawal, to varying degrees, of the underdeveloped countries from the system of monetary and banking integration seriously modified the mechanisms by which the underdeveloped countries are really integrated into the capitalist world market? This is what the monetary illusion implies. But we shall see that, in fact, the means of action at the disposal of the central authorities of the underdeveloped countries remain very limited. Analysis of the monetary mechanisms and of the types of inflation in these countries shows that money remains, whatever the monetary system, fundamentally what it is—the form of exchange relations. Insofar as these continue to be based on international specialization, that is, on integration into the world market, money continues to be the effective instrument for organizing the transfer of value from the underdeveloped periphery of the world system to its advanced center: the transmission of the value of the dominant currency or currencies, and that of the price structures of the center, constitute the forms of this transfer. Past history—that of the integration of the countries that have become underdeveloped in the world market of precious metals, which preceded their banking integration—as also current history—that of the crises of international liquidities, with which I end this study—show that the mechanisms whereby the center exercises real domination over the periphery cannot be overcome by monetary illusions.

THE FUNCTIONS OF MONEY IN THE ACCUMULATION MECHANISMS

Money fulfills four essential functions: it is the instrument by which value is measured, it is the concrete instrument of circulation, it is the licensed instrument of legal tender, and it is the instrument by which value is stored. Marginalist theory emphasizes the role of money as a circulation medium from which all the other functions are derived. Keynesian theory emphasizes money's function as "means of hoarding" (from which we get "liquidity preference"), regarding *this* as the most specific function of money. Rist and Nogaro give pre-eminence to none of these functions rather than any other, seeking to maintain a positivist and empiricist attitude. Some contemporaries (Lindhal, Myrdal, Lundberg, Harrod) ascribe a complementary, though secondary, role to the two functions in the mechanisms of accumulation, while the Chicago school (Milton Friedman) goes back to the quantity theory. Marx occupies a special place here, shared to some extent by Schumpeter. He is the only economist to have opened the way to a real discussion on the role of money in accumulation (in the realization of the product).[1]

"Classical" Thought

Paradoxically, the economic thinking that Keynes calls "classical" attributes, like the Keynesian doctrine itself, a decisive role in the mechanisms of economic development to the rate of interest, and a quite negligible one to the banking system.

Saving and investment are, for the writers whom Keynes attacked, real factors in the economy. However, the monetary form in which these quantities are expressed adds a new cause of maladjustment to the real causes of possible disequilibrium. There is a "natural rate" of interest that ensures economic equilibrium. The amount of saving made available, allowing for "preference for the present," is, at this rate, equal to the amount of investment demanded, allowing for the productivity of capital. This is the real, fundamental reason why equilibrium between the supply of saving and the demand for investment can be achieved.

Now, not only is this analysis tautological, since neither Fisher nor Böhm-Bawerk established the existence of the productivity of capital on any foundation other than "preference for the present," so that the so-called natural rate of interest is nothing more than the rate of depreciation of the future, but the mechanism of determination of the "natural" rate of interest at the point where the curves of supply of saving and demand for saving intersect actually explains nothing at all. Keynes showed this very clearly: when the demand for capital changes (some innovation calls for larger investments), incomes change, and therefore likewise the supply of saving![2] By resorting to history in order to solve the problem—supply of capital available today is determined by the distribution and amount of income that existed yesterday—the logical difficulty is dodged.

In any case, the first marginalist paid no attention to monetary conditions. It "went without saying" that monetary conditions caused the rate of the money market to "tend" toward the "natural rate," but they could not say exactly how this happened. Wicksell opened a new era when he showed how cumulative processes in the banking mechanisms allowed the monetary rate to diverge from the natural rate. This analysis, taken up later by Myrdal, Keynes, and Cassel, served to explain economic cycles.[3]

This being so, when these processes are not operative, the state of "monetary equilibrium" (understood in this sense) is realized. When the rate of interest directly determined by monetary conditions is equal to the natural rate, the banking system then plays the modest but technically perfect role of "transforming desired saving into desired investment." This is the mechanism that Robertson analyzes at length: if the public wish to increase the amount of their saving, they slow down withdrawals from their bank accounts. If the bank raises the level of its advances, the desired saving is transformed into desired investment. If the bank fails to do this, then, the rapidity of circulation of money having diminished, the quantity MV in the quantitative equation becomes smaller: prices fall and bank accounts increase in real value—the desired saving has been squandered without investment having taken place. But in reality the bank will always transform saving into investment because, when it observes that depositors are drawing less rapidly on their accounts, it will realize that they have "too much money," in other words, that they want to save more.[4]

How does this mechanism of adjustment of saving to investment differ from the Keynesian mechanism? Two basically different problems are in fact involved here. Keynes analyzes the lack of adjustment between saving and investment due to liquidity preference that is too strong relative to the marginal efficiency of capital—in other words, the lack of adjustment due to the fact that capacity to produce is greater than capacity to consume, so that the profitability of investments (their "marginal efficiency") is too low. Robertson studies the technical mechanisms by which banks transform saving into investment. Needless to say, a bank may fail to do this, not for technical reasons but for more fundamental ones. Let us suppose that clients are withdrawing less from their accounts, but are also declining the credits offered to them, because investment would not be profitable. This means that the level of activity has fallen, since the money derived from previous sales has not been returned to production, in order to finance new production. This is why part of Robertson's argument seems unsound: although velocity (V) has fallen, and so the quantity MV has diminished, prices do not fall, because the volume of production has diminished too. It is even this decline in the volume of production that is reflected in the fall of V! This does not mean, of course, that the contraction due to inability to sell does not impel entrepreneurs to reduce prices later on. But this subsequent fall is secondary, and is not determined by the contraction in the amount of money available.

Can this subsequent reduction in prices restore activity to its previous level? The classical writers believed that only a fall in real wages could restore the profitability of investments. Keynes denies this, noting that although wages are a cost for the entrepreneur they are an income for the worker. Pigou maintains that the fall in prices and in nominal wages, taken together, must restore profitability, by giving greater value to the savings previously hoarded.[5] But if these sums were hoarded it was not done voluntarily, but because the gap between capacity to produce and capacity to consume made new investment unprofitable. So long as this gap persists (and if prices and nominal wages both fall, so that *real* wages do not increase, there is every reason to suppose that this gap will remain unaltered), then, whatever the real value of the amounts hoarded, investment will continue to be unprofitable, because the entrepreneur looks to the future, not to the past. But that is a different problem.

The banking system thus plays an important technical role, but not the fundamental economic role of adjusting savings to investment by varying the rate of interest—the role that the Swedish school assigns to it. For that to happen it would be necessary for the rate of interest to govern the volume of saving as well as that of investment. But it does not. Saving depends essentially on the absolute and relative amount of incomes from property. Investment responds only slightly to variations in "i"; essentially, it depends on the degree to which capacity to produce corresponds to capacity to consume.

Keynesian and Contemporary Thought

In Keynes the same paradox is found, between the excessive role attributed to the rate of interest and the passive role attributed to the banking system. The imbalance between saving and investment is ultimately ascribed to liquidity preference, which prevents the rate of interest from falling below a minimum level. Replying to classicist critics, Keynes formulated with clarity the way this mechanism functions.[6] The rate of interest is determined by the state of liquidity preference, allowing for the volume of money supplied by the banks (for interest is exclusively monetary, according to Keynes). Equilibrium forces then determine relative prices such that the marginal efficiency of different capitals is in every case equal to this rate. From that moment there is no longer any gap between "i" and the efficiency of capital, and consequently there is no further net investment. The equilibrium state of the Swedish school has been attained, in which, the monetary rate being equal to the natural rate, profits are nil (Joan Robinson's "zero net saving"). Clearly, however, this equilibrium may well be an equilibrium of underemployment, because whatever the volume of money, the rate of interest cannot, owing to liquidity preference, fall below a certain level. The banking system is then quite helpless, as Hicks has plainly demonstrated.[7]

This is why many Keynesians condemn the policy of monetary expansion, which, after passing a certain point (when the rate of interest has reached its minimum level), cannot but engender inflation, even without full employment.

The whole of this analysis is based on the idea of liquidity preference, that is, of propensity to hoard. But does such a propensity really exist in the capitalist mode of production? And what in fact is meant by "the need for liquidity"? On the one hand, it is the need to have ready cash with which to finance transactions. To what extent is an entrepreneur prepared to pay out the funds needed to keep his current production going? Clearly, he will do this until the point is reached at which these charges reduce his profit to zero. Here, too, Ricardo's analysis shows itself to be more realistic than that of the marginalists. On the other hand, it is the need to have cash for hoarding. But in a capitalist society, for fundamental reasons, there is no propensity to hoard. Once he has ensured the reserve savings he needs, the entrepreneur has no desire to hoard. He wants to save in order to invest; so long as investment brings a return he will use his funds to expand his enterprise. The question is thus not why the rate of interest cannot fall below a certain level, but why the level of the marginal efficiency of capital can fall so low. On this point, Keynes's explanations remain extremely vague.[8]

If an entrepreneur wished to hoard, would he be held back by the volume of active money? Not at all, for the banks would see that they can without risk increase the ratio of advances to reserves, which they had previously lowered, thanks to this increase in the volume of reserve savings. The harmful effect of hoarding on employment is automatically cured by an extra dose of credit (as Robertson, quoted above, has shown). Should the hoarder decide one day to invest the money he had been hoarding, the banks would correspondingly restrict the credits they accorded to industry.

What is disappointing in Keynes's theory is that the banking system appears helpless not merely beyond a certain point but *all the time.* One might think that money plays a passive role, in the sense that its supply is adapted to the need for liquidity. Keynes considers that this supply is rigid. It is this rigidity that, faced with a fluctuating demand, determines the current variations in the rate of interest. True, variations in this rate are sometimes due to the quantity of money becoming adapted to demand. But these difficulties are only temporary, and cannot explain the average level at which this rate remains over a long period;[9] "where Keynes speaks of adaptation of monetary demand to available supply there is in reality rather adaptation of the quantity of money to demand."[10] The "passive" conception of money (in this sense, and not Say's) is the very opposite of the quantity theory. Keynes's notion of the rigidity of the supply of money, however—its inability to adapt automatically to demand—causes him to slip back into the quantity theory.

The banking system thus plays no *fundamental* role in the mechanism of accumulation. But its role is nevertheless not a negligible one. It will be seen, moreover, that this role goes much further than a mere automatic adaptation of the quantity of money to the product "PT" of the quantitativist equation (general level of prices multiplied by level of economic activity, allowing for habits of payment).

The Passive Function of the Banking System

The first question to be answered is how the adaptation of "MV" to "PT" takes place. Total saving does not constitute a homogeneous mass: we must distinguish the *creative saving*—the money put aside by entrepreneurs with a view to subsequent expansion of production—from the *reserve saving*—the money put aside either by consumers with a view to future expenditure on ultimate consumer goods, or by entrepreneurs in order to finance all the productive expenditure needed to ensure the *present* level of production of the system and the normal disposal of this production. These last-mentioned sums (to which I shall confine the term "liquidities," although in current writing this term is applied to both types of saving in money form) are certainly hard to distinguish in practice from saving waiting for investment. It is from cash in hand that the entrepreneur pays the wage and buys the raw material and machinery needed to ensure current production and to expand his enterprise. However, the fact that the two kinds of saving are mixed together in the same till is not a reason for denying that current expenses are met from *gross* income, whereas creative saving is taken from *net* income, after ultimate consumption has claimed its share. The frequent overflows from the money market into the finance market, and vice versa, do not justify a denial of the logic and useful nature of this distinction. There is indeed a minimum amount of money needed for the mere functioning of the economic mechanism, in other words, needed just for the "staggering" over a period of time of expenditure and receipts. This amount of money constitutes a mass of liquidities of a particular type. If we merge with this, in "total saving," the liquidities that fulfill the *complementary* function of constituting reserves of money waiting for investment, the procedure leads us into a blind alley.[11]

It is this volume of liquidities that constitutes the primary social need for money. The banking system adjusts the amount of money in circulation to this need, by means of short-term credit. It is at the request of entrepreneurs that commercial banks grant short-term credits to them, in other words, introduce bank notes and representative money into the economic circuit. These credits serve merely to finance the current functioning of the economy, that is, to spread over a period of time the receipts and payments of enterpreneurs.

The whole question is whether or not this social need for money is predetermined—that is, if we assume habits of payment to be stable (which is true in the short run; in the long run, the improvement in banking techniques speeds up the circulation of money, in view of the increasing need for this to be done), whether or not the size of the national income is predetermined, or, in other words, whether or not the levels of economic activity and prices are predetermined. If the banks can modify these levels by injections or withdrawals of money, then to say that the banking system "adjusts the quantity of money available to the need for it" is meaningless.

Here, too, we need to know whether, fundamentally, the level of activity and the level of prices are determined by the quantity of money, or whether these levels ultimately depend on other economic factors. It is not a question of denying that credit facilities (lowering of the discount rate, for example) influence the level of future activity (by encouraging the formation of stocks of goods through making this more easily bearable financially, for example), and thereby influence the amount of money needed.

This is what Keynes, paradoxically, refuses to see: for him, the supply of money is rigid, an "independent factor." Warburton has shown that "i" affects the level of activity and thereby the demand for money.[12] In the course of the cycle the bankers, faced with this increased demand, often confine themselves to increasing the volume of short-term credit, without raising the rate of interest: the supply of money then adjusts itself quasi-automatically to demand.

But does that mean that it is the rate of interest that determines the level of activity (and consequently, in the last analysis, the amount of money, which is the decisive variable)? This is what Keynes thinks: the margin between interest and the marginal efficiency of capital determines the volume of investment and thereby of activity. But if we give some thought to the matter, this analysis appears inadequate, for what determines the marginal efficiency of capital? Keynes has nothing to say on this point. Actually, this efficiency, which is nothing but the profitability of investments, is directly bound up with the degree of correspondence between society's capacity to produce and its capacity to consume. If the capacity to produce ever became greater than the capacity to consume, the profitability of investments would soon shrink to zero, so that, whatever the rate of interest, economic activity would shrink.

A big step forward has been taken since modern theoreticians accepted this common-sense observation that variations in the rate of interest are too slight, as compared with variations in the profitability of investments, to be decisive.[13] Rist protested long ago against the lack of common sense shown by economists. Neither a fall in the discount rate nor open-market operations can do more than stimulate further an upward movement that has begun for other reasons. In a depression, sums of money artificially put into circulation will find their way back to the banks, and nothing more than a stock-exchange operation will have taken place.[14]

This is why, when, at the end of a boom, the capacity to consume starts to diverge dangerously from the capacity to produce, the lowering of "i" cannot avert a crisis. This fall enables entrepreneurs to maintain the burden of increasing stocks of unsold goods, but it does not enable these goods to be sold. It runs counter to the movement of real economic forces. It enables the crisis to be postponed, but not averted: indeed, the longer the period of artificial animation by means of credit, the deeper the depression when it comes. This is why it is recognized that variations in the rate of interest do not play a leading role in the cycle. This is why the "hawtrey solution" remains a fanciful notion based on an overestimation of the role of money in relation to the real forces in the economy. Moreover, modern theories of the cycle and the conjuncture, like those of "chronic depression" and "overdevelopment" in the 1940s, concern themselves solely with analyzing the "real" difficulties that arise from the possibility of disparities—whether cyclical, conjunctural, or lasting—between the capacity to consume and the capacity to produce.

Fundamentally, then, the level of activity depends on something other than the quantity of money. Is this also true of the price level?

Quantitativism associated the value of money in a mechanical way with the quantity of money. Although this mechanical connection, as shown in Fisher's equation, has now been abandoned, it does not follow that every trace of quantitativism has been eliminated from theory. There has even been an attempt to rescue quantitativism by showing its link with the subjective theory of value. Thus, Von Mises declared that when M increases, certain incomes have increased and, since the marginal utility of money declines for individuals when their incomes increase, prices therefore rise.[15] Is this reasoning well founded? When M increases, it is usually the case that production has increased, for the additional money has entered the economy through concrete channels. To an increased demand there corresponds an increased supply. Again, even if there be no increase in production, why should the additional money not go to swell the hoards? Why should it automatically and wholly find its way onto the market?

Economic theory seems to have taken a new path: that of studying the function fulfilled by money of "satisfying the need for liquidity." The discovery of "liquidity" was made by Hicks, who, in 1935, analyzing the *Treatise on Money,* set out explicitly the three theories of money contained in it: a theory of marginal choice between liquidity and profit (liquidity having a price due to the cost and risk of investment). Much earlier, however, an approach had been made to the theory of liquidity, in the course of investigation of the supply of and the demand for money. As early as 1921, Cannan, asking how "demand" for money was made up, rejected the demand for money for hoarding purposes, this being the *specific* service rendered by money. (Yet the other "service," that of facilitating circulation, is no less specific!) On this basis, Ellis tried to save Fisher from downfall, noting that to each level of the rate of interest there corresponds a particular allocation of money between the categories of hoarded and active money, an allocation that determines the level of prices, in accordance with the formula MV = PT, in which M stands for the amount of "active" money. All that Ellis did here was to show that Keynesianism is not fundamentally opposed to the quantity theory.[16]

Has liquidity analysis radically eliminated quantitativism? There is reason to doubt this. In the Keynesian model, the supply of money and the rate of interest being given, the level of liquidity preference determines the proportion of money that will be hoarded (and, consequently, the proportion that will be active). As the rate of interest determines the volume of investment (because the marginal efficiency of capital is an independent variable which does not depend on the quantity of money) and thereby the volume of national income, all the factors in the economic system are present except the general level of prices, which must be determined, according to the quantitative formula, by the ratio between the real national income and the quantity of active money. Keynes therefore remains, so to speak, a second-degree quantitativist. This is why, when the effect of liquidity preference ceases to be felt, quantitativism reasserts itself. This way of looking at the matter, in which the quantity of money is a factor to which the other factors adapt themselves (for Keynes, the quantity of money determines both the level of the national income and that of prices, instead of determining the latter alone, as the classicists hold), rather than being itself a variable dependent on the demand for money—in other words, on the level of income and prices—has made it easy to reintegrate the Keynesian system into the classical system. This reintegration, carried out by Modigliani in a general model, is liable to all the reproaches directed by Nogaro at the "mathematical" method and the quantity theory.[17] An anti-quantitativist position is, in fact, incompatible with any theory of general equilibrium, since there has to be an independent variable in the system! The Chicago school (Milton Friedman) has made this return to quantitativism. It is then led, once the quantitativist assumption has been accepted, to orient all its investigations in the only direction open to an empiricism that condemns itself to seeing only appearances—seeking for direct correlations between the quantity of money and sundry variables of the system ("permanent income"), "psychological" analysis of the "desire for cash," and all sorts of other problems that are false because badly conceived.[18]

If, then, all forms of quantitativism are rejected, the problem of how the value of money is determined remains to be solved. This being so, we can distinguish between two cases: that of a currency convertible into gold and that of an inconvertible one.

In the first case it is certain that the cost of production of gold plays a decisive role in the mechanism of determination of the general price level. Marjolin, in his study of price movements over the centuries, notes: "A rise in the price of goods is a necessary consequence of the opening up of gold mines in which the cost of production is lower than hitherto. It follows from the choice of gold as the measure of values." Wicksell made the same observation when he studied, at the end of the nineteenth century, the rise in prices that resulted from the opening up of new goldfields in Australia. If, indeed, a reduction in the cost of gold production is assumed, then the extra profits realized in this branch of economic activity will attract capital into it. This inflow of capital does not, however, bring about, as normally occurs, a fall in the price of the commodity produced, because gold is bought by the banks at a fixed price. Profits continuing therefore to be exceptionally high, they constitute a mass of additional income which, applying itself to the market for consumer goods and to that for capital goods, the supply of which has not increased, brings about a general rise in prices. This upward movement cannot ease until the general price level has rendered the cost of production of gold normal, that is, one that leaves the entrepreneur only a "normal" margin of profit. The production of gold will then be stabilized at this level. This analysis is not abstract construction: it corresponds to the account given by Paish of the general price increases experienced in South Africa following the opening up of richer mines. Robertson thinks that variations in the cost of gold can engender only very slight variations in its value, since gold production represents only 2 percent of the stock of precious metal, so that the value of gold is indeed equal to the marginal cost of production, but is not determined by it. It is because Robertson thinks the value of gold arises from its quantity (that of the existing stock plus new production, together making up the total supply of gold) that he is able to raise this objection.[19]

However, if the currency is *not* convertible, then the safety barrier constituted by the value of gold is no longer present. Up to this point, no expansion of credit could exceed the limit of needs because any excess credit that was offered would not be taken up by entrepreneurs. Only in the form of a distribution of purchasing power without any real backing (issue of paper money in wartime, for example) could the quantity of money be increased. An increase in prices, resulting from an imbalance between income and production, and not from the quantity of money, makes it necessary to abandon convertibility. When the banks no longer buy gold at a fixed price, the expansion of credit, or issue of purchasing power, can then (given certain structural conditions, to be examined later) take place without any limit, since they draw the price of gold into the general upward movement. The fundamental dependence of the supply of money on the demand for it therefore seems to have been eliminated.[20] It only seems so, however: while a general increase in prices *may* occur, this actually happens, as will be seen, only if certain conditions exist. It is still true that there is no longer any normal price level. This is why Hicks and Lange consider that under this regime a divergence between supply of and demand for money can bring about a general price movement.[21]

Analyzing the "monetary effect," Lange notes that if the price of a commodity that is being overproduced falls, if the elasticity of expectations is higher than unity (that is, if the public expects a further fall), and if the banks keep stable "the supply of money in real terms," then all goods will be in a state of overproduction, and the fall will be general. The banks' attitude certainly causes this development to happen all the sooner; but the problem remains, *why* is it that the public sometimes expects overproduction to become general, and sometimes does not? It may be that experience has taught them that there are situations in which, for real reasons, general overproduction does exist, and other situations in which such general production does not occur.

Finally, we see that the role of the banks is to adjust the quantity of money to this primary need, which is itself determined by the level of activity and that of prices. Needless to say, however, under a regime of inconvertibility a general price movement may itself be started by the banks, together with the entrepreneurs: the latter ask for credit greater than the need measured by the actual lever of activity and prices, and the banks grant this credit. (They run no risk if the Central Bank automatically rediscounts these advances, creating a quantity of bank notes corresponding to the volume of representative money issued by the banks.) I say "may" and not "must" because it is possible for a general price movement to originate elsewhere than in the attitude of the banks, which then merely adapt the quantity of money to the changing level of prices.

The Active Function of the Banking System

The last case shows that the banking system is in fact more powerful than it has seemed up to now in this analysis. It does not confine itself to adapting the quantity of money supplied to the product PT of the quantitative formula. It plays a more active role than this in the mechanism of accumulation.

Capitalist accumulation requires, in fact, an increased quantity of money not just because the gross national product is increasing but also because, in order that the transformation of saving into investment may take place, it is constantly necessary that new money be introduced into the circuit *before* the gross national product has increased. New investment has no outlet at the moment when it is made, since all the outlets existing at a given moment cannot exceed the volume of production at that moment. But new investment will soon create this new outlet by expanding production. In order to invest, however, the entrepreneur needs a certain amount of money. It therefore seems that some previously existing outlet must enable him to sell that part of his production the value of which is destined to expand production, so as to realize in money form the "saving" he has accomplished, his extra capital. The problem appears insoluble, for the entrepreneur can find no such outlet, since the outlets available when the entrepreneur wants to sell cannot exceed the volume of present production, and the entrepreneur has to find today an outlet equal to the volume of tomorrow's production. In reality, it is enough for an extra quantity of money equal to the value destined for accumulation (which will create its own outlet tomorrow) to be placed today in the entrepreneur's hands—from whatever source this money may come.

As we see, this is the problem raised by Rosa Luxemburg in *The Accumulation of Capital.* Contrary to her view, and in conformity with that of Marx himself, the only problem here is not the outlet (which investment itself will create) but the preliminary increase in the volume of money available. This quantity of new money comes to the entrepreneur either through gold production or through the banks. The channels whereby this gold penetrates the economy were analyzed a century ago by Marx, and I shall not go over that ground again.[22] Let me say merely that the production of new gold makes possible a special kind of sale: the producer of gold buys with his profits, which are in the form of gold, products from other entrepreneurs which he requires either for consumption or in order to expand his production. The gold producers can thus sell their surplus product (in which their real saving is crystallized) and realize in the form of money the value destined to effect expansion of their industry. With this money they can buy means of production and hire workers. The outlet existed potentially, but a special monetary mechanism was needed to enable the entreprener to obtain today in monetary form the benefit of the outlet that was to be created by the investment made possible by this monetary technique.

Today it is through the channel of credit that the quantity of extra money is created *ex nihilo* by the banks. Schumpeter has shown how this money put at the disposal of entrepreneurs enables production to be expanded.[23] Naturally, the bankers claim not to possess such great power. They claim that the banks keep an eye on the accounts of the enterprises they finance, so as to make sure that the latter do not tie up in long-term uses the short-term credits they are granted.[24] True; but this does not affect the matter, since expansion of production calls for long-term investments (purchase of machinery) and also for short-term investments (purchase of raw materials, payment of wages). The entrepreneur makes use of this latter need to borrow sums of money which, in economic reality (whatever may be the case in accounting), will serve to finance the expansion of production. Insofar as the new investment creates its own outlet, the entrepreneur is able to repay the bank loan with interest. The national product is then increased, and also the need for money, in the first sense defined here.

But even this service rendered by the banking system, which in this sense is not passive, is not fundamental in character. It is, indeed, only when the investment has created its own outlet that the advance can be repaid. Real reasons of a profound nature may cause this not to happen, and then the issue of money does not solve the problem of the absense of any outlet for the extra production.

Nevertheless, however secondary in relation to the general equilibrium this double role played by the banks may appear, it is decisive in making accumulation possible. Without a quantity of money constantly adapting itself to the necessary liquidities, no accumulation is possible. Without concentration of savings, without mobilizing reserve savings and making them available for investment, this development is greatly hindered. We must see whether the banks fulfill these two complementary tasks correctly in the underdeveloped economies.

THE MECHANISMS OF ISSUING MONEY AND CREDIT IN THE PERIPHERY

In current writing about the underdeveloped countries we find with increasing frequency the statement that their monetary and banking systems are defective. Issuing of money in these countries is said to be not in accordance with need, already defined as the second member of the quantitative equation (PT). It is said to be, on the contrary, automatically determined by the external balance (reduced, for greater clarity, in the rest of this outline, to the trade balance), and therefore both too plentiful in times of prosperity (when the balance shows a surplus), which gives rise to local inflation, and too slight in times of depression (when the balance shows a deficit), which delays recovery.

I reject this statement categorically, as resulting from a quantitativist view of the matter. I reject the alleged amplification of the economic oscillations by a "perverse" monetary mechanism. I will show that, while it is true that disturbances in the trade balance automatically give rise to changes in the issuing of money, the credit policy of the commercial banks can *and should* counterbalance these movements when they go beyond the limits fixed by the "need for money."

I will show that the monetary system of the underdeveloped countries fulfills its role just as well as in the advanced countries, adjusting circulation to local need: that it is "passive" (and also "active" in the sense defined above, namely, that it enables capital to be accumulated where this is possible). This fundamental function is fulfilled no less well by the system of foreign-exchange standard for a currency than by the system of a "managed" national currency.

The Foreign Exchange Standard: The Apparent Mechanisms of Issue

The British currency boards.[25] There are a number of foreign-exchange standard systems. The essence of the mechanism, however, is the same: a certain organ agrees to exchange the local currency for the dominant currency, and vice versa, at a fixed rate and in unlimited amounts. The local currency no longer constitutes a different currency from the dominant one: it is the latter that really circulates, though under a different name, in the underdeveloped economy.

For clarity of exposition I will take the British Currency Board. This is a public organization endowed with reserves of sterling and entrusted with the task of exchanging currencies in unlimited amounts and at a fixed rate. The Board invests its reserves in short-term sterling securities (British Treasury bonds).[26] The product of these investments is paid to the government of the given colony, together with the small commission of ½ to 1% which is paid for the exchange operation, a commission that does not in the least resemble a rate of exchange determined in the market. Whenever an individual (or a bank) wants some local currency, he pays out sterling in London and the Board gives him local currency on the spot. The Board's assets increase, as also do its liabilities, the local currency in circulation. Thus the two entries—assets and liabilities—evolve in parallel.[27] If they are not always absolutely equivalent, this happens because the value of the treasury bonds that constitute the Board's reserve may fluctuate on the market.

The first Currency Board certainly began to function when, at the end of the last century, the British government suspended the free minting of silver rupees, thenceforth supplying these rupees in exchange for sterling in London, and vice versa, in unlimited quantity and at a fixed rate. In the colonies of British West Africa silver coins circulated as legal tender from the beginning of the colonial period (1886), being minted in those countries in exchange for sterling deposited in London. The increased import of silver by the colonial governments (increasing from 550 pounds in 1885 to 1,259,450 pounds in 1910) reflects the penetration of money into the local economy.[28] When the Currency Board for this region was set up in 1912 it made no change in the situation apart from deciding that from that time onward it would print the sterling banknote no longer "on silver" but on paper. Subsequently this system was extended to other colonies.

The cost of the creation of this system was often a heavy one for the local economy, the Currency Boards having been endowed with gold found in those countries and transferred to London (as happened with Iraq, Palestine, and Transjordan). The same thing happened, *mutatis mutandis,* in the case of Egypt, where the National Bank, which from 1898 issued notes backed by gold to the extent of 50 percent and by British Treasury bonds for the rest, and which played the role of a currency board (exchange at a fixed rate and in unlimited quantity), adopted the practice of retaining in Egypt only the legal gold cover, and exporting whatever exceeded it, even momentarily. In 1916 the six millions in gold that represented this cover were transferred to London, and the issue of notes, thereafter inconvertible, was covered by British Treasury bonds. Here the cost of setting up the system was very heavy, for with this gold an autonomous system could have been created. When, after the Second World War, it was decided to establish such a system, Egypt was obliged to pay for the creation of a gold cover for its currency, as Great Britain declined to reverse the operation of 1916, that is, to reconvert into gold the treasury bonds which had then been exchanged for the precious metal. The same thing happened in the countries that had no gold stocks (the African colonies). The Currency Board was endowed at the outset with a sterling reserve paid for by the colony itself, a reserve that was, of course, less than the local circulation. It was regularly added to, the colony paying every year into the reserve fund a proportion of its revenue, so as to build up eventually a reserve equal to 100 percent of the circulation.[29] In this sense the circulation was actually equivalent to a 100 percent gold circulation; in other words, it was paid for in real values (exports) until the day when the entire circulation was covered by the reserve (the process can start all over again if the Board decides to make the reserve greater than the circulation). This does not apply when the Board remains content to carry out exchange without making any unilateral increase in its reserves.

The circulation of a foreign currency: the example of Cuba. I chose the system of the British Currency Boards for the foregoing explanation because it is clearer when, as in their case, the banking function and the function of exchange at a fixed rate and in unlimited quantity are attributed to two different organs. In reality there may, however, be no exchange organ at all, and the banknotes of the dominant currency may circulate as legal tender in the colony (Madagascar until 1925; Cuba, where the U.S. dollar circulated; Liberia; etc.). Again, a commercial bank, which may enjoy the privilege of local issue, may be entrusted with exchange operations (Egypt between 1916 and 1947; the French Union).[30]

The U.S. dollar was legal tender in Cuba, while alongside this fundamental currency there circulated pesos issued by the Cuban Treasury which were also legal tender, freely convertible into dollars in unlimited quantity, but without a rigidly fixed rate of exchange. The peso was introduced into the economy through the budget, even when this was balanced (the state paid its creditors in pesos). Thanks to restraint in the issuing of currency, the rate of exchange always stayed around unity. The peso, which circulated as "odd money" to make up amounts (the dollar remaining the fundamental currency of capitalist exchanges, both internal and external), tended to depreciate slightly in relation to the dollar, but was nevertheless sometimes worth more, when the internal need for make-up money was very high.[31]

The French colonial monetary system.[32] France very soon conceded the privilege of local issue in its colonies to private banks in these countries, which operated both as banks of issue and as commercial banks: in 1848 in the old colonies; in 1851 in Algeria (Bank of Algeria, which in 1885 became the Bank of Algeria and Tunisia); in 1875 in Indochina (the Bank of Indochina); in 1901 in French West Africa (the former Bank of Senegal, of 1848, became the Bank of French West Africa, Madagascar, where the notes of the Bank of France circulated as late as 1925, was the only exception.

Originally it was a matter of little systems copying that of the metropolitan country: the local banks of issue were endowed with gold reserves and authorized to rediscount the bills of the commercial banks. However, the difference of strength soon made itself felt between, on the one hand, the colonial branches of the great commercial banks with their practically limitless resources (able to draw on their metropolitan funds, in the absence of any control over transfer and despite the independence of the rates of exchange of the colonial currencies), and, on the other, the local banks of issue, with their limited gold cover. This imbalance would certainly not have led to the ruin of the banks of issue. During a boom the commercial banks could do without the rediscounting that the banks of issue would decline to undertake, owing to the inadequacy of their gold cover; they could import the funds they needed from the home country. These imports, by pressing on the demand for local currency, would have caused it to appreciate up to the gold point of entry. Gold would have flowed into the colony and the gold reserve of the banks of issue would have increased. But the abandonment of the gold standard prevented this mechanism from operating. Thenceforth the cash in hand of the banks of issue consisted of liquid assets in francs: "The old conception of cash in hand tends to be replaced by a new one, that of the amount of liquid assets in francs adequate to ensure transfers."[33] There is here, indeed, a risk for the banks of issue, which, being independent and not branches of a French organization, have only limited amounts available in francs. If obliged to change metropolitan francs into colonial francs at a fixed rate and in unlimited sums, the cash in hand of these banks may prove inadequate if the policy of the (quite independent) commercial banks is too expansionist. What we see here is, therefore, somewhat of a caricature of the French system.

True, the Treasury guarantees the transfer in exchange of this obligation, if the bank lacks the sufficient francs. This led the banks of issue to become semi-public organizations subordinate to the Treasury, until they were nationalized (Bank of Algeria, 1946; creation of the CCFOM for French Equatorial Africa and the colonies in 1944, replacing the old private banks; the Institution d'Emission of French West Africa taking the place in 1955 of the Bank of French West Africa). Released from their commercial function, these institutions become joint branches of the Bank of France and the Treasury. The replacement of these issue institutions, after independence, by central banks (of West Africa, Equatorial Africa, Cameroon, and Madagascar) has made no change in the economic mechanism I have described.

The functioning of this system is completely analogous to that of a Currency Board, except that a commercial bank that needs liquidities can either import them from its head office in Paris or rediscount them with the local bank of issue. The "control of credit" exercised by the latter is thus quite illusory, since, if rediscounting be refused, the commercial bank can always apply to its head office. It is therefore the Bank of France, and it alone, that ultimately controls advances of credit to commercial banks, not only in the home country but also in the colonies and the associated countries overseas.

The Egyptian monetary system.[34] Free minting of gold prevailed in Egypt at the time of the British conquest. Turkish, French, and British gold coins circulated simultaneously. The first crucial measure taken by Britain was the undervaluation in 1885 of the pound sterling, which was fixed at 97.5 Egyptian piastres, whereas in weight of pure gold it was worth 98.4. Thus the gold sovereign drove the other currencies out of circulation. The standard of the Egyptian currency was no longer gold, but *sterling* gold. The country, which every year imported gold in order to finance the cotton harvest, and then re-exported it, thenceforth gave preference to the British banks.

In 1898 the National Bank of Egypt was founded, with the privilege of making an issue covered by gold to the extent of 50 percent and for the rest by sterling securities. In 1914 banknotes were made obligatory legal tender, and the Bank was authorized to issue against increased gold cover (which had to be kept at 50 percent) in London and not, as before, in Cairo. The National Bank bought and sold gold in London in accordance with its issue needs. The Egyptian currency had ceased to be independent. The banknote that was inconvertible into gold in Egypt had become convertible into sterling: against Egyptian pounds the National Bank supplied British pounds in London at a fixed rate and in unlimited amount; this sterling was obtained by the National Bank by selling its gold in London. When, in 1916, the British government declined to sell gold to the National Bank, and the latter decided to buy sterling securities instead, Egypt bowed its head to the sterling standard. The National Bank thus fulfilled at one and the same time the functions of a bank of issue, a commercial bank, and a Currency Board.

The expatriate commercial banks in Egypt were in no way subject to any control by the National Bank. When they were short of banknotes in Egypt they had only to pay sterling into the National Bank in London to obtain what they needed.

The exchange control established in 1939 between Egypt and the countries outside the sterling area (with free exchange inside the area) reinforced the position of sterling. From then on, two new problems were faced by Egypt: unblocking the sterling assets that had been accumulated, and converting them into other currencies. When in 1945 Egypt joined the International Monetary Fund it remained a member of the sterling area. Nevertheless, it acquired the right to determine freely the parity of its exchange—the right not to devalue if Britain did so. But at the time Egypt was definitely setting its course toward monetary independence.

The thesis of "perverse monetary mechanisms." This can be summarized in the following three propositions:[35]

1. The amount of money in circulation in a country that is on the foreign-exchange standard is determined by the state of the external balance. Not a single bank note is issued in the given country unless its equivalent in the dominant foreign currency is deposited. It is thus strictly the state of the external balance that determines this issue. The question arises: what entries go to make up this balance? It will be seen that the answer totally refutes this pseudo-determination of issue by the external balance of payments. The supporters of this theory nevertheless stick to their vague claim. They add that, as the use of checks is not widespread in the underdeveloped countries, this issue constitutes the main element in liquid assets in money form. Consequently, in the short run at any rate, the ratio between the fiduciary circulation (notes) and the circulation of representative money (deposits) cannot but be constant (it depends on habits of payment which are slow to change);

therefore, no sudden increase in the use of checks, in order to remedy the shortage of notes, can take place, and ultimately the total volume of liquid assets depends on the state of the external balance.

2. Any excess or shortage of currency affects the general level of prices. Without adopting a mechanistic quantity-theory standpoint, it is alleged that pressure is exerted on prices in this way.

3. In a period of prosperity the external balance is favorable, and the influx of money makes prices rise, whereas in a depression the opposite mechanism takes effect.

The facts, as they crudely appear, seem fully to confirm this point of view. Chabert shows from the example of El Salvador, where 80 percent of total monetary resources are of external origin (as measured in net assets in gold and foreign exchange), that when exports increase the mass of money increases too (between 1940 and 1945), whereas it decreases when exports go down (between 1945 and 1947). The movement of the mass of money of internal origin does not make up for that of the external component. This phenomenon is a general one. It is true in the cases of Cuba, Egypt, and Iraq, countries on the foreign-exchange standard, where, consequently, the whole circulation of money (notes) can vary only under the influence of the balance of payments, and where the movement of money of local origin (deposits) has not made up for the movement of this circulation of external origin, since the volume of liquid assets in money (the sum of both components) has varied parallel with the volume of circulation, not only year by year but over the whole period 1937–1951. It is true also of other countries where the monetary circulation is of mixed origin (internal and external), as these countries do not form part of a foreign monetary system (their currency is "independent": Mexico, Brazil, Argentina, Turkey, etc.). Thus, during the war these countries accumulated assets in foreign exchange, while their total circulation increased.

The writer then makes a close study of the coefficient of correlation and dependence between the indices of monetary circulation per capita and those of wholesale prices, for fifteen Latin American countries, four Middle Eastern countries (Iran, Iraq, Turkey, Egypt) and two advanced countries (the United States and Great Britain), for the period 1937–53. The correlation he reveals is clearly better for the underdeveloped countries than for the two advanced countries, despite a certain number of exceptions (notably for the period 1937–41, for the countries of Latin America, and the period of 1946–52 in Turkey). It should be added that, for a number of underdeveloped countries, a month-by-month correlation is observed between issue of currency, which increases seasonally, and prices, which follow this movement, though at a much lower level (Salvador, Mexico, Brazil). Finally, the priority of the movement of circulation over that of prices seems to be proved by the improvement of the coefficient of correlation when there is a time-shift, circulation preceding prices. For the United States, however, the best coefficients are those of the series in which wholesale prices precede circulation. Furthermore, the movement of prices cannot be attributed to that of the exchange, since the percentages of increase were lower than those of monetary circulation or prices (Bolivia: increase in the rate of exchange, 200 percent; increase in prices and circulation: 1,000 percent). Sometimes even the influence of the rate of exchange has been a factor stabilizing internal prices, imported goods having increased in price less than domestically produced ones, as we see from the example of Venezuela. To conclude, it can be said that the cyclical variations in monetary circulation and prices, after elimination of the trend calculated for the period 1937-52, show a remarkable degree of correlation in the underdeveloped countries, whereas this is not apparent in the case of the United States.

This thesis of the "perverse mechanisms" of issue is basically wrong. It is not true that monetary circulation is determined in countries on a foreign-exchange standard, by the external balance.

Let us assume that the external balance (reduced for greater simplicity to the trade balance) is positive. A local importer obtains foreign exchange from abroad. He takes it to the Currency Board, which gives him local notes, which he then deposits in a (foreign-based) commercial bank. The cash in hand of this bank having increased, it may grant more credit to the local economy (the coefficient of liquidity—that is, the ratio between liquid and mobilizable assets, on the one hand, and, on the other, payments due, whether on demand or short-term—has increased). I say that it *may* do this because the bank may offer credit but no one may wish to take it. It is still true that if advances are asked for and the bank agrees to grant them, so as to bring the coefficient of liquidity back to its former level, the volume of liquid assets in money form will have increased more than the surplus of the external balance.

Thus, the volume of liquid assets appears to depend *both* on the surplus in the balance of payments and on the needs of the economy, the former constituting a ceiling that cannot be surpassed. There seems to be, at any given moment, a fixed ratio between the use of fiduciary money and that of representative money, determining a rigid coefficient of liquidity—even if the local producers should ask the bank to agree to let them have more credit than it is able to give. This is just where the mistake in this argument lies.

If a local producer asks the bank for credit and wants a certain amount in the form of an overdraft and the rest in banknotes, all the expatriate bank has to do is apply to its head office for sterling to be paid over to the Currency Board, and it can have the banknotes it needs there and then. A bank need never lack local currency if it has plenty of sterling in London.

There have already been cases where this mechanism has operated. In Southern Rhodesia between 1946 and 1951, the external balance was negative. Local currency was therefore being taken to the Board to be changed into sterling in order to meet the deficit. At the same time, however, the banks were changing their own sterling into Rhodesian banknotes in order to finance a big increase in their local credits.[36] It will be said that the deficit in the balance is here being compensated by an influx of short-term credit from abroad. This needs to be rejected as ambiguous, because it suggests that the influx of credit is induced by the gap in the balance and is necessarily equivalent in amount to this gap.

This is not so. It is better to distinguish clearly the balance of real payments, made up of exports and of the influx of capital intended for long-term investment, which make up the credit side, and imports and the outflow of profits from foreign investments, which make up the debit side, from the balance of the movement of bank capital (import and export of sterling by the banks on their own account, and not as representatives of a client).[37]

The balance of real payments is whatever it is. I think there is a tendency toward long-term equilibrium in this balance through the income-effect (a deficit constitutes a transfer of purchasing power), but that the deficit is not necessarily reabsorbed automatically—especially given that exchange is rigid and unlimited. In the case of independent currencies, there is added to this income-effect an exchange-effect (disequilibrium entails devaluation, which affects the balance in a favorable or perverse direction, depending on elasticities) which sometimes contributes to *short-term* equilibrium (not long-term, as devaluation brings about an increase in prices which cancels out this effect).

As for the balance of movements of bank capital, this is entirely independent and is not induced by the balance of real payments, so that, although the balance of real payments automatically affects circulation, this effect is without importance since it can be either counterbalanced or not by the movement of bank capital, which is always determined solely by the economy's need for money, and is limited by nothing else.

This is why it is possible for the volume of liquid assets in money and even the volume of circulation to increase although the balance of payments shows a deficit. There is no proof that imports and exports of money are induced by external payments, declares I. Greaves, after studying the experience of the British West Indies. A bank changes sterling into local currency because it needs this currency for the requirements of depositors; when it changes local currency into sterling, it does this not because it lacks foreign exchange but because its local cash-in-hand exceeds the requirements of the economy. This is why, between 1912 and 1950, the Currency Board of British West Africa issued £115.28 million against payment of sterling in London, whereas it transferred only £55.88 million of African currency into sterling.

As for the quantitativist explanation, this does not stand up to criticism. On the one hand, as we have seen, it is not the external balance but the economy's needs that determines the volume of money in circulation, and, on the other, it is not the volume of money in circulation that determines the price level but precisely the reverse, here as elsewhere.

The data for Egypt between 1920 and 1940 (trade balance, monetary circulation, price indices) show that, in conformity with the theoretical schema, the external balance tends to be better in a period of prosperity than in one of depression. In a period of prosperity, exports increase at first faster than imports (the surplus increases between 1922 and 1924), then more slowly—so that it was possible for the surplus to turn into a deficit in 1926. The movement runs the other way in a depression period. The other elements in the balance of real payments (entry of long-term capital, exit of profits, stable extra-economic factors—services, tourism, British Army), on which no data are available, probably intensify the movement (entry of capital during prosperity, cessation of this in time of depression).[38]

On the other hand, there is an obvious correlation between the movement of the balance of payments and that of issue (which increases when there is a surplus in the balance and decreases when there is a deficit). Although the coefficient of correlation, calculated crudely, is not high, it is possible to accept the assumption that there is a strong correlation owing to the intervention of factors in the balance of real payments other than the exchange of commodities. These elements, by accentuating the movement of the balance, bring the latter into line with the movement of circulation (whereas here the variations in the circulation are less than those in the trade balance alone).

Must we then conclude that the quantity theory is correct? Not at all. Prosperity is reflected in increased prices, in Egypt as elsewhere. True, prosperity improves the trade balance, but it is not this balance that causes the movement of prices. That is quite normal. It needs to be added that not only does the price of cotton improve on the external market and, correspondingly, the price of imports rise (as a result of the prosperous situation of Egypt's suppliers), which tends to raise the general level of prices in Egypt, but also the general solidarity of prices, on the one hand, and, on the other, the automatic transmission of the fluctuations in the value of the dominant currency, due to the psychological element (the Egyptian currency being sterling), intensify the general movement. Prices being higher, the need for money increases, and the circulation expands. There is indeed a correlation between the two movements, but the logical priority lies with prices.

It nevertheless remains true that price fluctuations are greater in Egypt than in Britain. Must we attribute this fact to the perverse quantitative effect of the external balance? Certainly not. The price of cotton, a raw material, fluctuates more than that of British manufactured goods—this is the reason for that feature of the situation. Also, throughout the period 1922–1938 the general trend was downward; but the decline was more marked in Egypt than in Britain. I attribute this to the general behavior of prices in highly monopolized economies (such as Britain) as compared with those in economies with a low degree of monopoly (such as Egypt). In any case, the fact that this trend was more marked cannot be attributed to the external balance, which was negative throughout the period in question.

Finally, there is the alleged priority of circulation in relation to prices which Chabert found to apply in the bulk of the underdeveloped countries between 1937 and 1953. This is only an illusion. The period was generally one of prosperity. The tendency for circulation to increase faster than prices is easily accounted for. On the one hand, the real national income increases, and with it the need for money, at constant prices. On the other, hoarding in the underdeveloped countries, in "modern" money (notes and deposits), subjects the system to an increased need for currency. Finally, and above all, the velocity of circulation of money slows down with development, as Chabert himself shows at some length.[39] Under these conditions it is normal for the volume of money to increase faster than the price level rises. By calculating the correlation that exists between the increase in prices and the increase in circulation, with a displacement of the latter toward the past, we find a greater proportionality between the phenomena, which gives the illusion that money is the cause and prices the effect. It should be added that, during the war, when the movement ran parallel to the accumulation of substantial amounts of foreign exchange in the underdeveloped countries, owing to the impossibility of importing goods, the illusion of a mechanical link between the state of the external balance, the circulation of money, and the level of prices was complete.

The fact remains that the parallelism between prices and circulation is much more obvious in the underdeveloped countries than in the advanced ones. I am inclined to ascribe this difference to the fact that in the underdeveloped countries the issuing mechanism is automatic, so that circulation adapts itself immediately to requirements, whereas in the advanced countries the management of credit by the Central Bank—that is, the numerous manipulations of the monetary situation that the state carries out—has the effect of concealing the connection between circulation and requirements. We shall see later on the significance and implications of this absence of management of credit in the underdeveloped countries.

In cases where a foreign currency circulates (as in Cuba in former times), the monetary phenomena are no different. There is an apparent correlation between the external balance, the volume of liquid assets in money form, and the volume of bank credit. The example quoted shows, however, that improvement in the external balance between 1931 and 1936 did not bring about any inflation of the circulation, which continued to be linked (like the volume of bank credit) with the general economic situation. This clearly indicates the independence of the balance of real payments and that of bank capital. Finally, in the case of Cuba, the positive balance of the external real payments as a whole and of bank accounts led Wallich to declare that the circulation of money was paid for in real terms.

The "cost" of the circulation of money. The mixing-up of the balance of real payments with the balance of bank capital in a single balance of payments has induced many economists to say that the foreign-exchange standard system is equivalent to a system of 100 percent gold circulation. It is alleged that if, in the long run, the use of checks does not spread quickly enough to make up for the increased demand for notes, then real exports will have to "pay for" the necessary influx of foreign notes.

As soon as one distinguishes between the two balances, and recognizes that it is only the balance of real payments that tends toward equilibrium (through the transfer of income), the theory of the excessive cost of the foreign-exchange standard collapses.

Nevertheless, insofar as the colony has "bought" its monetary circulation, at the outset, by transferring gold to London, or by forming a reserve to endow the Currency Board, by means of an allocation from the local budget (signifying a real levy upon the economy), it is true to say that the *initial* cost of the system in question *is* extremely high.

On the other hand, the balance of real payments tends toward equilibrium; and if this is attained, and the colony imports currency in order to meet its increased need for liquidities, then the balance of real payments and of bank payments taken together shows a surplus (equal in amount to the import of bank funds). The impression is thus given that it was the foreign-exchange standard system that gave rise to the need to export more than was imported, in order to "pay for" the import of monetary media.

"Managed" Currency and the Monetary Illusion

Criticisms of the foreign-exchange standard system, which are becoming more and more severe, can be grouped around three poles:

1. The foreign-exchange standard automatically transmits fluctuations in the values of the dominant currency. Acutally, there is no transmission here, since it is the currency of the dominant country itself that circulates. It will be seen what causes and consequences of this "transmission" are, and whether the system of managed currencies succeeds in preventing the harm done.

2. The foreign-exchange standard reinforces economic integration in the economic area dominated by the particular advanced country.[40] This is so, first and foremost, because the freedom of economic movements (absence of exchange control) favors the penetration of foreign capital, the export of profits, and commercial exchange. This is fundamental. Further, the dominated country enjoys no freedom to carry out an independent trade policy. It is deprived of resources in foreign exchange, since these go to feed a pool which is situated abroad and which is not under the dominated country's control. This is why Portugal possesses a strong currency, thanks to the surplus in the balance of its colonies' dealings with the United States: these resources in dollars benefit Portugal alone, and not the colonies. So long as the

dominant currency is freely convertible into foreign currency, the system is still tolerable. As soon, however, as this convertibility is suspended, the system becomes quite intolerable. This was how it happened that during the Second World War Egypt accumulated £415 million sterling which not only were convertible but are still blocked in London. India, Burma, and the Middle East accumulated £1.732 billion in similar "sterling balances," the Dominions £384 million, and the rest of the countries of the sterling area £607 million. There are thus territories at every stage of colonial history which "feed" the metropolitan country in this way. After the war, it was Ghana that, along with Nigeria and Malaya, supported the pound in withstanding the attacks of the dollar, thanks to the reserves held by the Marketing Boards.[41] It is true that there are cases, such as the French colonies since 1945, in which the balance is often negative where foreign exchange as a whole is concerned. In such cases the metropolitan country supplies the colony with the foreign exchange it needs. In return, however, the colony is obliged to give the metropolis preferential entry on imports—a preference which is, moreover, forced on the colony owing to the uniform regulation of exchange control and the ban on trade with other countries, a ban both legal and economic (owing to the lack of any reserve of foreign exchange controlled by the colony itself).

3. The foreign-exchange standard prevents any "management of credit" in accordance with local needs. This is the criticism most frequently levelled at the system, and yet the weakest.

The statement that issue is mechanically linked with the state of the external balance is quite false, as we have seen. On the contrary, indeed, it is acquisition of real monetary independence (autonomous exchange control) that brings a real danger, in an underdeveloped country, that this statement will come true, that is, that the external balance will become the factor ultimately determining the local issue!

In fact, under the foreign-exchange standard system, local issue is controlled to the same extent as issue in the metropolitan country, by the Central Bank of that country, through "credit control"—the importance of which economists have tended to exaggerate. Generally speaking, by showing that circulation adapts itself to requirements, the possibility of really *managing* the issue of money has been refuted. Nevertheless, we shall see later how, with inconvertibility on the one hand, and the development of monopolies on the other, the possibility of an inflationary issue, with the agreement of the Central Bank, has become a real one. In this sense, "management of credit" (restricting or approving this issue) has acquired a meaning, even if only a negative one (impossibility of issue if the economic system does not allow of this, possibility only of restricting an issue which is desired by the producers). Acquiring the possibility of doing this on the local scale, or, more precisely, getting free from the necessity of following the policy of the dominant country, has become the content of the new doctrine.

The doctrine—strongly inspired by the international organizations—has suggested three axes along which the chief reforms have been carried out during the last twenty years: (1) expansion of the embryonic money and finance market, (2) abandonment of the foreign-exchange standard in favor of a flexible system without a rigid exchange, and (3) creation of central issuing institutions endowed with their own reserves in gold and foreign exchange.

It will be seen that, in fact, all these efforts fail to secure the desired freedom to manage credit (in the sense of liberation from the power of the expatriate commercial banks) unless control is established over transfers, and *a fortiori*, the banks are nationalized. In the event these measures are taken, the country concerned really has "broken out of international monetary integration." Even in such an extreme case, though, we shall see that the new system does not safeguard the local economy against transmission of fluctuations in the value of the dominant currency. Moreover, the new system brings a number of disturbing elements into the local economy. Without control over transfers, issue remains independent of the state and of the external balance. But the rate of exchange, which is no longer rigid, becomes a factor of disturbance: in the event of disequilibrium of the external balance, due either to economic causes (disequilibrium in the balance of real payments) or to monetary ones (export of funds resulting from a crisis that has caused a surplus of liquidities), the rate of exchange depreciates. If control over the exchange is established, then determination of issue by the external balance becomes a reality!

All this has caused the countries that have taken the path of monetary independence to move further and still further along that road. Before the Second World War, the foreign-exchange standard system prevailed in two of the underdeveloped continents, Africa and Asia (China excepted), and in part of Latin America (the Caribbean). After the war, the movement to set up local monetary systems began in Asia. Today nearly the whole of Asia, the Arab world, and the English-speaking countries of Africa enjoy more or less real monetary independence. French-speaking Africa is almost alone in remaining subject to the classical foreign-exchange standard. In Asia and the Middle East, certain countries have gone all the way, setting up Central Banks with their own reserves in gold and foreign exchange, and establishing exchange control. Egypt is a typical example. Others have gone less far and adopted a more flexible regime. These countries sometimes continue to feed a pool of foreign exchange somewhere abroad. At the same time they have set up central systems and decided to fix freely their own rate of exchange, and, in order to make this freedom real, have kept at home at least part of their assets in foreign exchange and gold (India, Pakistan, Ceylon, etc.). As for South America, like China in former times it never knew the foreign-exchange standard. A system of local paper money operated there throughout the nineteenth century. Acquisition of monetary independence was reflected in the setting up of a central system of issue control (that is, by replacing paper money with an inconvertible fiduciary currency), and in some cases by the establishment of exchange control.

This brief outline of the old system will enable us to see that, even given the earlier hypothesis of paper money, the mere presence of expatriate banks enabled issue to be adjusted to requirements.

Paper-money systems in the periphery in the nineteenth century. The foreign-exchange-standard system, which is typical of the underdeveloped countries, was not introduced without prolonged tentative measures. True, often the system was introduced without its theory having been worked out: thus, for a long period, cash vouchers circulated in the West Indies which were not convertible into gold but *were* convertible into bills in the metropolitan country. The exchange fluctuated with the state of the external balance, because there was no organ that ensured exchange at a fixed rate and in unlimited amounts.[42]

In general, all through the nineteenth century, the colonies and the countries of the East and Latin America made use of gold, or more commonly silver, coins (China, Japan, Dutch East Indies, India, and Persia, and Latin American with the exception of Brazil). Only gradually was the foreign-exchange-standard system introduced: in 1899 in India, in 1903 in the Philippines, in 1904 in the Straits Settlements, Siam, Cuba, and Mexico. A direct gold exchange standard (without passing through the intermediary of a gold coin of a particular country's currency, as was the case in India from 1898 onward) was introduced in Argentina in 1899, when the Conversion Office undertook to exchange gold for local currency and vice versa. The same system was set up in Brazil a little later. China continued to use silver coins and silver ingots. Latin America was, all through the nineteenth century, the favorite region of paper money, which circulated alongside silver coins that were more or less at a premium, depending on the volume of issue. Mexico moved belatedly from this situation in which the rate of exchange fluctuated with the price of silver, to the foreign-exchange standard. The other states were unwilling to come to this decision, and only in the twentieth century did they at last stabilize their currencies by setting up central systems of the modern type (inconvertible credit money). The experience of Latin America, where paper money issued by the state treasury circulated, is worth some attention.

There is no point in detailing the internal flaws of the regime. Money, here introduced into the economy not by way of bank credit or commercial credit (bills) but through the budget, may prove to be excessive in quantity. In the case of a budget deficit, money incomes are created *ex nihilo,* without any real counterpart: prices rise, the external rate of exchange collapses. But let us assume a balanced budget—which was not the actual historical reality in Latin America or China.

A mere disequilibrium of the external balance results in a fall in the rate of exchange. This brings inflation through the increased price of imports. If the disequilibrium of the external balance is part of a permanent tendency, as is the case with the underdeveloped countries unless exchange control is applied, then what occurs is an endless series of devaluations, price increases, and fresh devaluations.

Let us now suppose that the balance of real external payments is, like the budget, in equilibrium. The money in circulation may prove to be insufficient even so. Money is introduced into the economy, as already mentioned, only by way of state expenditure. A trader who finds himself momentarily short of liquidities applies to the foreign commercial banks. In order to respond to his application, the latter need an extra quantity of the local paper money. They import funds that belong to them, and buy local currency on the exchange market. This transaction tends to raise the rate of exchange, which in turn causes prices to fall. In this case the amount of money does indeed adjust itself to requirements, but only at the cost of continual upsets in the level of the exchange rate and prices. The solution in these countries is replacement of paper money by fiduciary currency, that is, establishment of a Central Bank endowed with the privilege of issue and capable of coping with the country's increasing demand for money.

And as, here too, the bank encounters, in its foreign competitors, a force that is stronger than itself, it will be necessary to resort to control of transfers.

This outline is not fictional: the history of Latin America (Brazil, for example) has conformed closely to the line of development indicated.[43]

Modern systems of managed currency. Independent monetary systems are today being increasingly established, in Latin America, in place of the paper-money system previously in use, and in Asia, the Middle East, and the English-speaking countries of Africa, in place of the previous foreign-exchange standard system. Only French-speaking Africa remains outside this movement.

Freedom to fix the rate of exchange does not mean that the latter ceases to be determined by the cover and the state of the external balance. If the cover of the issue is still made up of foreign exchange, fluctuations in the value of the foreign currency will continue to be transmitted. To alter this situation the local issue will need to be covered by gold. We shall see once more that price movements in the advanced central countries always eventually spread to the periphery. As for the external balance, this operates via the rate of exchange to influence the market—whether free, official, or "black." Only exchange control is capable, by imposing equilibrium on the country's balance, of keeping its currency in good condition.

Although many illusions have been cherished regarding the creation of a local finance and money market, both to encourage the mobilization of national capitals and to enable the central bank to manage credit by a monetary policy, the results have so far proved highly disappointing.

The setting up of a central bank is undoubtedly the crucial element in the new system. Let us see how far the adaptation of issue to requirements—which, as we have seen, was perfect under the foreign-exchange standard system—is modified by the creation of a central bank. Technically, issue follows the same pattern as in the advanced countries, either in that the reserve held by the central bank has to constitute a certain minimum proportion of the issue (as in Egypt, India, Pakistan, Indonesia), or that the volume of banknotes issued over and above a certain maximum has to be fully covered (Burma). Sometimes the rules governing issue are extremely liberal (Ceylon, Thailand, Philippines).[44] The nature of the cover (gold or foreign exchange) is of great importance in whether the value of the currency of the dominant economy is automatically transmitted to the underdeveloped economy. For the moment I will deal only with the problem of whether or not the local central bank can manage credit. In order to do this I must examine (1) the assumption of freedom of transfers and (2) the assumption of control of transfers.

1. Under freedom of transfers, the central bank has no influence over the policy of the expatriate commercial banks.

Management of credit implies that in the relations between the central bank and the commercial banks the balance of strength is in favor of the former. This is not the case in any of the underdeveloped countries. Banks of issue with meager reserves of foreign exchange are confronted by branches of the great American or European banks with almost unlimited funds at their disposal. Although the laws establishing the central banks give them the right to fix the proportion between the reserves and the liabilities of other banks, freedom to practice open market operations, and so on, issue in fact eludes control by this central authority.[45]

What has to be realized is that the commercial banks in the underdeveloped countries do without rediscounting by the bank of issue. While this is also true in Britain, for historical and technical reasons (which in no way prevents these banks from depending on the Bank of England), the reason is quite different in the underdeveloped countries: here, the commercial banks do not have recourse to the services of the central bank simply because they are richer than this native institution which is legally their superior! In case of need, the expatriate banks draw advances from their head office to be repaid when they fall due. This disparity of financial strength, besides making impossible control of issue by the central bank, has for secondary effect a deplorable high liquidity preference. Insofar as the banks of local nationality do not possess open credits in the central countries, unlike their foreign competitors, they are obliged to keep an amount of cash in hand that would seem excessive in an advanced country. The history of Cuba has shown that when the local banks, lacking open credits in the advanced countries, allow themselves to grant credits to their clients in the same proportion to the reserves they hold as applied in the case of expatriate banks, they very soon find themselves, in the event of crisis, in a situation verging on bankruptcy.[46]

This high liquidity preference is reflected in a high level of cash and balances held in the central bank, relative to total liabilities. It is a situation thoroughly detrimental to mobilization of the local savings deposited in the native banks. It applies in the capitalist sector—in other words, in that sector of the economy where there should be no justification for it. The "feudal" hoarding that is characteristic of the underdeveloped economies is a feature of a sector where saving is not by nature destined for investment. Under those conditions it has no deflationary effects, and is akin to luxury consumption rather than to the baneful liquidity preference of which Keynes writes. In the case we are now considering, however, we find a true high liquidity preference of the Keynesian type.

For the same reasons, if the central bank alters the proportion between the reserves and the liabilities of the commercial banks, the latter are not at all obliged to restrict the volume of credit: they can import from the home country the funds they need to bring up the level of reserves. Finally, the open market system is itself impossible in countries where the market in treasury bonds is practically nonexistant.

Thus, under this assumption the central bank controls nothing, and the expatriate commercial banks remain masters of the country's monetary fate. It is to be observed, nevertheless, that the volume of liquid assets in money form remains adapted to the volume of local requirements, just as under the system of the foreign-exchange standard.

Monetary independence has contributed nothing new from this standpoint, while at the same time it has introduced serious disorders. Under the new system, indeed, the rate of exchange is of real importance. Disequilibrium in the external balance causes the rate to go down and prices to rise. As in the Latin American system in the nineteenth century, this disequilibrium may result from bank policy. If we assume that the central bank refuses rediscounting so as to restrict credit, and the expatriate commercial banks decide not to submit to this, and import liquidities from their head offices, what happens? Serious pressure is suddenly brought to bear on the rate of exchange, which rises, entailing an increase in prices. The upset is liable to become permanent.

Any violent conflict due to disagreement on general policy thus brings the danger of a clash between the central bank and the foreign-owned commercial banks. In this conflict the government possesses, to be sure, one effective means of coercion, namely, possible control of transfers. All the means by which the foreign banks can get around the regulation of credit by the central bank can in fact be neutralized by control over transfers. But this signifies real independence by the underdeveloped country from the international capital market. How, indeed, is it possible to distinguish between the capital that comes in "to be invested" and the capital that the banks import in order to feed the economic system with the liquidities "necessitated by development"? Wallich is perfectly aware of this dilemma. Despite the advantages of exchange control where the monetary domain is concerned, he rejects it because such control isolates the country from the international capital market.[47]

Let us assume, nevertheless, that an exchange control office is clever enough to detect these imports of liquidities by the foreign banks. In that case the central bank can certainly dictate to the commercial banks, forcing them to have recourse to its services. But at what price?

2. Under control of exchanges and transfers, the central bank can dictate to the expatriate banks, forbidding them to import liquidities. This advantage is nevertheless bought at a very high price: (a) because now the fluctuations in the external balance affect issue directly, (b) because now the backing of the currency in gold and foreign exchange is paid for in real exports, and (c) because now the foreign-owned commercial banks make the economy pay for a service they can no longer render—providing advances backed with the guarantee of a strong foreign currency.

a. Credit and fluctuations of the external balance: A deficit (or surplus) in the balance of payments results in an exit (or entry) of foreign exchange. These movements can determine fluctuations in the general level of prices in the underdeveloped countries, by way of the exchanges. These fluctuations in turn bring about variations in the quantity of money required. More harmful still, however, is the fact that these fluctuations in the volume of the reserves that make up the cover of the local issue oblige the banks to regulate the volume of credit in relation to the vicissitudes of a balance of payments the state of which does not depend on the underdeveloped countries but on the economic situation in the advanced countries.

We have already heard and rejected the allegation that cyclical fluctuations were intensified in the underdeveloped countries by perverse alterations in the quantity of money. Nevertheless, without accepting any of the schemas inspired by quantitativism, we must acknowledge that the response made by the local banking system to the state of the balance of payments does risk aggravating the difficult situation as regards external payments.

Thus, when a deficit in the external balance causes the local system's foreign exchange to be drained away, the banks may (not "must") be led, if the drain is too great, to restrict the volume of credit accorded to the economy in general, and to activities working for export in particular. These activities may find themselves compelled to restrict production, which will cause the external deficit to get still worse. On the other hand, a surplus in the external balance brings no benefit to the local economy. Not only may the banks be put in a situation where, further credits not being required by local producers (in particular because the volume of exports, already substantial, cannot be increased), the surplus of foreign exchange is sterilized, but also, when an injection of credit could actually be effected, it may be that the tendency to a rise in prices that this entails (together, moreover, with such other effects as the excessive demand experienced by the local market owing to the country's prosperity following a good export drive) will prevent the volume of exports from increasing, or will even reduce it, and this will rapidly deprive the country of its favorable situation in its relations with the outside world.

In any case, this monetary dependence involves permanent disequilibria in the mechanisms of local issue: accumulation proceeds less and less regularly, becoming increasingly a jerky phenomenon at the mercy of the chances of the external balance.

b. The cost of the backing for the currency: It must also be said that monetary independence implies for the underdeveloped systems a heavy cost in real terms. The foreign exchange that constitutes the backing for the local currency is obtained through a real surplus of exports over imports, since the exchange-control office maintains equilibrium in the balance of real payments and bank payments, so as to keep the local currency in good condition. The regime is thus equivalent to a system in which the money in circulation is backed by gold. This extra cost, these overheads of the economy, are undoubtedly reflected in a corresponding contraction in the volume of saving. True, the cost is not so heavy as it may seem: the foreign exchange is never anything but the backing for local issue, and that only to a partial extent.

But it is only in the case of an independent currency that this real cost exists. In the case of the foreign-exchange standard it was not so.

This situation is not peculiar to the underdeveloped countries. In the advanced countries also, circulation is backed in part by gold and in part by foreign exchange. There it is a matter of overheads of the system of production. In those countries too, the policy of the central bank may be hindered by the way the external balance evolves.

Nevertheless there is a difference in *quantity* between the underdeveloped countries and the advanced ones. The cyclical fluctuations in the external balance, the sensitivity of external exchanges to the conjuncture, is much greater in the underdeveloped countries than in the industrial ones, and therefore the cost of the system is heavier.

c. The price of bank services: This being so, does the service rendered to local economic activity by the foreign-owned banking system justify what it costs? This question raises a serious problem indeed, that of the real cost of the banking system to the banks for the service constituted by short-term loans destined to ensure the normal functioning of the economy constituting a transfer of income whose explanation is to be sought in history. If all the entrepreneurs of the nineteenth century had possessed an initial stock of gold equal to the volume of "necessary liquidities," and if the production of new gold had kept in step with the pace of economic growth, then perhaps short-term credit would not have developed in the way it has done. But in fact gold circulated in increasingly inadequate quantities, although it was the only currency acceptable in the society of those days. The banks used this situation in order to issue fiduciary money: the convertible note, or representative money, in return for the payment of interest. They then ran the risk, to be sure, that was implicit in convertibility, since at any moment the entrepreneur might demand metal coins. It may well be claimed that since convertibility has been abandoned this risk no longer exists. It is true that commercial banks still run a certain risk, since the receiver of credit may always ask for bank notes. Insofar as the central bank does not automatically supply these to commercial banks, the latter incur a risk. But, provided these banks adapt their policy to the wishes of the central authority, there is no real risk involved. Nevertheless, even in this case, the central bank obliges the economy to pay for these quantities of new money.

Interest no longer corresponds to risk. The central bank has become a public service providing the economy with means of payment. Interest is no longer the reward for this service, but a convenient means of restricting the demand for money (which may account for Keynes's attempt to explain theoretically the role of interest on these grounds). There are other ways of restricting the supply of money; the quantitative and qualitative control of credit has multiplied these techniques.[48] In a planned socialist economy, the banks strictly limit advances to enterprises to the amounts laid down in the plan. As the enterprises have no right to extend credit to each other, the banks control the issue of money even more thoroughly than in the West. Obviously, since the plan has decided the volume of production, and both prices and the distribution of payments into and out of the enterprises are well known, the volume of credit to be granted is known in advance. There is no need to resort to a rate of interest as a means of restricting the demand for money. This is not the place to discuss which of the two methods is better. In any case, the payment of interest by borrowers of bank credit does not impoverish the economy in the least, since it passes from the hands of those for whom it would have constituted an extra profit (the entrepreneurs) into the hands of those for whom it will constitute the same kind of income (bankers' profit), even though this does have an effect on the pace of development, and the direction taken by it.

It is not at all the same in the underdeveloped countries, where this payment represents a real loss for the local economy. Let us take the example of Egypt. Until the nationalization of foreign banks in 1957, the banks took every year a fraction of the value of the cotton harvest as payment for a service of short-term lending that an issue of local paper money could have rendered just as well. Before 1914, around £10 million was imported by the banks every year in order to finance the cotton campaign. The risk that the banks ran, however slight, was at least compensated by the placing of gold coins at the disposal of the economy. After 1914 a mere book transaction between the foreign banks in Egypt and their head office in London expressed this short-term movement of capital. Here too, the cost of the operation (in interest) for the Egyptian economy can be justified by the fact that a form of foreign exchange was made available to the economy which constituted a solid guarantee for borrowers. Today, however, with exchange control, it is the local deposits, and no longer foreign capital, that finance this annual campaign. The extra amount needed (since these deposits are inadequate) is obtained purely and simply by an issue of paper and of local representative money. Yet the interest paid by the cotton producers is exported, because it forms the profit of banks that are legally foreign, a fact which provides no additional guarantee. If the cotton producers were unable to pay back their loans, the Egyptians whose savings had been advanced in this way would have no greater guarantee than if the banks that now found themselves in a state of nonliquidity were Egyptian, since exchange control in Europe might prevent expatriate branches in Egypt from importing capital. Given that the harvest is in reality financed not by local saving but simply by local *issue*, no such danger actually exists so far as the indigenous savers are concerned. If a slump in cotton sales should occur, the central bank would refloat the producers through an additional issue. It is the whole of the economic system that meets the cost of this inflationary operation. The foreigner provides no extra guarantee in this instance. This situation sufficed to justify the nationalization of foreign banks. Some years later, the same argument justified the nationalization of banking in Tanzania.

Ought one to suppose, this being so, that the creation of an independent central banking system has been negative in its significance for the underdeveloped countries? The previous system, that of the foreign-exchange standard system, fulfilled its task perfectly well, providing the local economy with all the liquidities it needed, and doing this at reasonable cost. This system, moreover, guaranteed monetary stability, the use of a currency highly esteemed on the world market, and the feasibility of a negative external balance. The system that has replaced it brings in many factors of disturbance to the economic mechanism, instability in the rate of exchange and prices, and furthermore is very expensive, since it implies that the cover for the issue of money is to be paid for in real terms. Finally, it makes the guarantee provided by the expatriate banks illusory and therefore causes the service they render useless, and the loans they provide expensive. All this in order to secure an illusory control over credit!

And yet monetary independence *is* a necessity. It is a condition for that control over relations with foreign countries which is needed in order to protect local industry (customs dues are not always enough—the quota system is sometimes better), to supervise and control the inflow of foreign capital and restrict the export of profits, to supervise and control the policy pursued by foreign-owned commercial banks, and so on. As for the negative features of the system, they are due not to the system as such but to underdevelopment. Effective control over relations with foreign countries is necessary for real, not monetary, reasons. Monetary independence is thus, though a *necessary* condition, not a *sufficient* one, for a policy of development.

THE CONCRETE FUNCTIONING OF BANK CREDIT AND THE LIMITS TO THE FINANCIAL MARKET

The criticism addressed to the monetary system of the underdeveloped countries—that it supplies the economy alternately with too much money or not enough—is therefore without foundation. The monetary and banking system, even when foreign-controlled, supplies the economy with as much money as it requires. But to *whose* requirements does the activity of the expatriate commercial banks correspond?

It is well known that the banks in the underdeveloped countries do not finance all the sectors of economic activity. It is not here a question of why these banks do not finance development, because it is not the task of banks in general to finance new investment (except to the secondary degree examined above under the heading of the "active" role played by the banks in the mechanism of accumulation. It is a question of why the commercial banks in these countries do not even provide all the sectors of activity with the liquidities needed merely for their current functioning.

One must, of course, eliminate from the discussion a certain number of false (or badly formulated) problems. Thus, the hesitation shown by the big commercial banks as regards financing the modernization of craft production, small-scale business, or agriculture is easily accounted for. What these sectors really need is special credits, medium-term and subject to favorable conditions, not so much in order to ensure speedier turnover of their funds—which is the role par excellence of bank credit—as in order to enable them to modernize themselves, if such modernization is practicable—that is, provided that the conditions of competition from local large-scale modern industry, or from imports, do not condemn them to inevitable disappearance from the scene. Similarly, appeals to the banks for finance to launch new enterprises are wrongly conceived, since that is the responsibility of a promotion fund. It must further be realized that this division of responsibility, excluding the commercial banks from this field, is that of the orthodox French and British tradition. Elsewhere—in Germany, in Italy, in the United States, and in Japan—the banks *have* played this role in relation to national capitalism.

In reality, the banks correctly carry out their task in relation to what exists, namely, peripheral capitalism, based on expansion of the external market. This peripheral capitalism is sometimes foreign-owned and sometimes national. True, in some cases the banking system seems to function exclusively in the service of the foreign-owned sector; but that does not constitute an absolute rule of conduct for the banks in the underdeveloped countries. It is, rather, an exception, due to the overall strategy—economic and political—of the particular dominant foreign capital.[49] Characteristically, the sectors of *non*-peripheral national capitalism—the independent capitalism based on the *internal* market—have almost always found difficulties in developing, *inter alia* because of the banks' abstentionist attitude. In this case the sectors that have proved able to develop with relatively greater ease are those in which it was possible for primitive accumulation to be financed directly by the primary economy.[50]

We give the name "inertia" to this restriction of the granting of short-term credit in the underdeveloped countries to the sector currently engaged in production for export.[51] This particular restriction is due to the fact that the semi-capitalist sectors of economic activity do not really require financing by the banks.[52] Let us consider, for instance, native agriculture. This sector functions in the old way. It possesses a certain quantity of liquidities which is usually sufficient to spread expenditure and receipts conveniently over the year. When, therefore, a peasant experiences a shortage of liquidities, this occurs not because his activity is developing too fast but because he is on the road to ruin. The peasant then has recourse to the services of a usurer. The banks do not wish to take on this function; they do not exist to help peasants on the brink of bankruptcy. That task may be undertaken by agricultural credit cooperatives, helping small producers to resist the triumphant competition of more powerful producers. The role of the banks is not to lend to enterprises that are threatened with ruin but to lend to those that are developing.

The same is true of the native crafts. Formerly they had no need to call for outside aid in order to function: they possessed their own funds for financing current activity. When a craftsman needs money, this is a sign that his economic situation is bad, that he has not managed to sell his products as he usually does, that he is being ruined by modern industry. This being so, why should a bank, which avoids risks, and has the task of supplying liquidities in increasing quantity to producers whose continuously developing activity is proof of their good economic health, come to the aid of a craftsman who is heading for bankruptcy? The usurer who hastens this bankruptcy, and sells off the craftsman's possessions by auction, fulfills this social function better than the banker, who avoids incurring such troubles.

This is why, in order to come to the help of agriculture and the crafts by reducing the monopoly of the usurers, in view of the banks' unwillingness to intervene, governments have taken the initiative in setting up cooperative organizations. But a cooperative cannot bring lasting aid to craftsmen unless they modernize their production so as to withstand industrial compeitition. Credit cooperatives have very quickly been led to finance the modernization of such activities, by means of long-term or medium-term credits. In the end the effect is to facilitate the more rapid break-up of the old-style forms of activity, to the advantage of the most dynamic forms. There are a few exceptional cases in which foreign banks *have* specialized in these operations, such as Dawson's bank in Burma, which financed the development of native agriculture. It hastened the end of the old-style agriculture, giving place to a new type. But such cases are extremely rare, and foreign banks nearly always confine themselves to financing the capitalist spheres of the economy, leaving to other organizations the task of disintegrating the local subsistence economy.

The fact is that the banks in the underdeveloped countries have a history that is closely linked with that of the installation of peripheral capitalism in those countries. The European banks established branches in these countries when international trade had reached large-scale dimensions, and with the intention of facilitating this trade. Historically, moreover, most of the expatriate banks were set up in the ports, in order to carry out foreign-exchange operations. Parallel with these activities, which were closely connected with the export trade, certain financial institutions financed state loans. Thus, in Egypt, banks were set up in order to serve as intermediaries between the great European finance houses and the Khedive Ismail.

Broadly, however, foreign trade was the banks' main concern. On that basis, their field of operations was gradually expanded so that they took over the financing of the sectors bound up with international trade. Thus, in Egypt, besides financing the sale of cotton, they financed narrow-gauge railways for the transport of cotton. In addition to these activities connected with foreign trade, the banks never stopped financing certain public services, so maintaining a very old tradition. They thus helped the local governments to create essential public services and to modernize the infrastructure needed for the development of external exchange. These operations were, it is true, very profitable at that time, and closely connected with external relations: the entrepreneurs who obtained the concessions to develop these services were foreigners. Their monopoly enabled them to derive substantial profits from the work, which they exported through these same banks.

In the end, this "inertia" of the banking system constitutes a powerful means of guiding the development of peripheral capitalism in a way that conforms to the needs of the center. The example of Egypt again supports this analysis. Every year the volume of currency is greatly inflated at the time of the cotton harvest. Nothing like this happens at the time of the wheat or the maize harvest. The sale of cotton can be spread over as many months as necessary: the banks are there to lend the money that will make this wait possible. The exporters can thus endeavor to conquer new outlets: the growth of the cotton-producing economy is greatly favored. Wheat, on the other hand, has to be sold quickly, in accordance with tradition. Should a producer wish to try and expand the production of wheat, and should he then find himself in difficulties in selling as quickly as usual the extra amount produced, the banks would not rally to his support, and he would have to struggle with insurmountable difficulties to make ends meet. Wallich thinks that this would be the position in Cuba if the agricultural producers wanted to expand the production of rice or maize. We have seen a similar problem in Senegal, in relation to the commercialization of cola nuts.[53]

The banks' "inertia" results in wasting part, sometimes a considerable part, of the country's savings. The banks receive substantial sums in deposits, which arise in spite of everything from the foreign-owned capitalist sector and the country's other activities. It is not merely a matter of liquidities, but also of actual saving of money, and even of hoarding, by the country as a whole. Instead of mobilizing these resources for long-term development—which could be done, but which would not be profitable—the banks prefer either to export these savings or to use them locally to meet state expenditure.

The consequence is that we often see, especially in the colonial period, a high degree of liquidity in the banking system in the underdeveloped countries. I have given a number of examples of this familiar fact, which reflects the imbalance between the increasing sources of deposits and the limited local possibilities for profitable use of these deposits.[54] It is this imbalance, especially marked when the development of peripheral capitalism has come to reinforce an agrarian capitalism of latifundia owners whose hoarded savings assume modern forms and amount to considerable sums, that accounts for the abnormally low rates of interest charged in many underdeveloped countries.[55] The accumulation of saving in the form of bank deposits withdrawable on demand is thus due to a marked liquidity preference on the part of the banks and not on that of individuals. The relatively small amount of loans to the local economy (which is reflected in the high liquidity of the system) causes the banks' profits to be too low for them to attract deposits by offering high interest rates. The banks do not need these overabundant deposits. They always pay a very low rate of interest (from 0.5 to 1.5 percent in Egypt), whatever the period of the deposit. Accordingly, the savers often keep their savings in current accounts.

It is easy to imagine the loss an underdeveloped economy suffers through the absence of a system that would enable these sums to be used productively. If they had been invested as fast as they were accumulated, this process would have left behind it a real production potential that would not have been subject to the depreciation that has affected the value of money.

The constant withdrawal of fiduciary and representative money from circulation by hoarders in the underdeveloped countries constitutes, moreover, a powerful deflationary force. The hoarding that goes on in the underdeveloped countries in the traditional form of accumulation of gold is comparable in its effects to luxury consumption. The modern form of this hoarding of the precapitalist type appears, however, to have deflationary effects—not in the Keynesian sense, for this hoarding is not forced, in that it does not arise from the insufficient profitability of investments, but is truly voluntary, but because it constitutes a siphoning-off of purchasing power which is thus prevented from swelling demand, and *that* makes the profitability of investments more precarious.

It is obvious that hoarding of this sort can have no influence on prices if the banks introduce into the circuit additional credit that is equal in amount. This is what would normally occur, as Robertson has shown: when the rapidity of circulation of deposits diminishes, the banks reckon that they can raise the level of their advances. They create extra purchasing power which replaces on the demand market the loss caused by saving. Prices remain stable. In this way, saving by some can finance investment by others. The rigid attitude of the authorities in forbidding commercial banks to provide both short-term and long-term credit, which is understandable in Europe, where the deposits in these banks are usually not savings deposits, should have been overcome by the prospect of large profits and by the great security of the operation. It was not a question of long-term immobilization of short-term savings (which the Germans have dared to effect) but merely of using for productive investment savings that their owners intended to keep for a long time. The explanation of this attitude has to be sought in the real facts of the system. Industrialization of the country is not profitable, owing to foreign competition. In addition, the banks, which are closely connected with the big foreign-owned enterprises established in the country, do not wish to compete with them.

This being so, the deflationary effect of this form of saving is unquestionable. If we assume that this effect is balanced by an active policy on the part of the banks, what would be the social significance of this accumulation of money savings? A certain amount of potential purchasing power is accumulated in the hands of this social category—a potential that each member of this category can use as he wishes, and which gives him extra leverage. Nevertheless, the totality of these funds could not be used all at once by all the hoarders, for this would bring about illiquidity and the collapse of the banking system. If we assume that the central authorities cover the banks by a massive rediscounting, the ultimate result of the operation would be a general inflation of prices (as a result of the sharp increase in demand without real equivalent in supply), which would cancel out the effects mentioned.

Besides, the foreign-owned sector itself, as a whole, shows little interest in these funds of local origin. Most of the industrial enterprises operating in the underdeveloped countries are branches of extremely powerful monopolies, which themselves have commercial banks at their disposal in the home country. Their financial resources are inexhaustible: they float big loans in Europe and mobilize the deposits of European savers. Undoubtedly, the big monopolies commit to long-term investment in their overseas branches only the funds they can procure for themselves. They do not like to call upon banks that are outside their network, for these would bring into the business a new, and perhaps rival, power. Even, however, in cases where these foreign-owned enterprises need short-term funds, they do not turn to the locally established banks. The mother concern sends them what they need, drawing upon its own banking system—which, if necessary, simply creates the amount of money required to finance the temporary deficit of the overseas branch. Thus, the interest on these short-term credits does not move outside the complex of firms that forms the monopoly.

There is no shortage of examples of procedures such as this. We may take the example of the United Africa Co., which has never borrowed, even on a short-term basis, from the banks of British West Africa. The line followed by the copper producers in Zambia and the Anglo-Iranian Oil Co. in Iran has been the same.[56]

If the expatriate banks are so little interested in local investment of their money resources, this is because they can always—provided there is no exchange-control—export these liquidities to the finance markets of the advanced countries. Examples of this massive export of local savings, facilitated by the centralization of the banking system, are plentiful. The Royal Bank of Canada drains off to the finance markets of North America the deposits of savers in Haiti; Cuba provides another such instance. One cannot, of course, say that the savings exported would have been automatically put to use within the country where they originated. Wallich considers, on the basis of the study of this question made by Aliènes, that this export is not an autonomous movement of capital but, on the contrary, an induced movement, caused by the state of the external balance and the economic situation generally. I do not agree, but see in this export of capital one of the autonomous forces that *determine* the state of the external balance. During a period of prosperity, the accumulation of savings in an underdeveloped economy is so large that the banks dispose of considerable funds that they can export. When depression comes, dishoarding reduces these funds. The correlation observed between the general economic situation and the state of the trade balance gives the impression that what we have here is an induced movement. We see everywhere the same tendency to keep abroad not only local savings but even sums that become temporarily available.[57]

The expatriate banks have a twofold tradition in underdeveloped countries, depending on whether they are foreign-exchange banks or have served as intermediaries between foreign lenders and local governments.

For a long time the underdeveloped countries, having become colonies, ceased to make use of these intermediaries, and floated their loans directly on the metropolitan market. At the same time, the banks invested their liquidities in metropolitan government stock, that is, they became lenders to the state in the metropolitan country. Examples are provided by the French Union and by Egypt.[58] Nowadays, however, there is a marked tendency in most of the underdeveloped countries for these disposable assets to be used for financing current administrative expenses.[59]

Thus, whereas in the advanced countries the financial institutions have facilitated the transformation of the reserve-savings deposited with them into long-term investments, in the underdeveloped countries everything tends toward the utilization of savings (including sums that the saver would like to commit to long-term investment) either for short-term financing of the economy (insofar as these savings, deposited in the banks, are used to finance foreign trade transactions) or even for financing state expenditure, much of which, unproductive so far as the country's economy is concerned, is only productive of interest payments to the holders of state bonds. The "transformer" mechanism is here working the wrong way round.

The expatriate commercial banks have thus not always fulfilled either the traditional role of banks supplying liquidities to all sectors of the economy or, *a fortiori*, that of business banks financing the country's industrialization.

Attempts made by some local private banks to carry out these functions have nearly always failed. The experience of Cuba during the First World War is particularly striking, together with the more recent experience of Nigeria, and the achievement of the Bank Misr in Egypt is almost the only exception.[60]

The attempts made recently by several states to create a money and finance market, to promote public or semipublic financial institutions—stock exchanges, savings banks, mortgage and industrial credit organizations—have produced only very modest results.[61] Well-known are the unfortunate consequences of the attempts made in India, Mexico, and Chile, where the establishment of stock exchanges in a climate of feverish speculation brought ruin to savers, with discouraging effects. The prosperous stock exchanges found elsewhere (in Southern Rhodesia, for example) are only branches of stock exchanges in the metropolitan countries, where foreigners deal among themselves in the shares of foreign companies. The ultimate reason for these setbacks lies in the real situation of the underdeveloped economy. The creation of financial institutions may well favor the mobilization and centralization of capital, but these funds will remain unused if local industry fails to come into existence owing to foreign competition.

MONETARY DISORDERS AND INFLATION

Critics of the foreign-exchange standard not only charge this system with insusceptibility to "management" in accordance with local needs, but also declare that it favors the automatic transmission of fluctuations in the value of the dominant currency. I will examine how far "monetary independence" frees the underdeveloped countries from this tie-up with the dominant economy. The importance of the subject derives from the circumstance that the advanced world of today exists in a permanent atmosphere of inflation.[62] This "transmitted inflation" may, of course, be in addition to monetary disorders of internal origin.

Transmission of the Value of the Dominant Currency

Transmission in the foreign-exchange-standard system. It is certain that, "when products are freely exchanged and the different masses of money are in practice all one mass, the price-level necessarily tends to be the same everywhere; if this is not so, the disparities are to be ascribed to structural reasons (cost of transport, of labour or of power, for example) that are immune to monetary manipulation."[63]

A good example of this automatic transmission of fluctuations in the value of the dominant currency is the parallel evolution of prices in France and in the overseas countries of the franc area. Similarly, between 1914 and 1939, price fluctuations followed parallel courses in Britain, Egypt, and India—although their dimensions sometimes differed, which confirms the presence of autonomous local forces that influence prices in spite of everything.[64] By causing falls in prices to be greater, and rises to be smaller, in the underdeveloped trading partners, the deflationary effect of hoarding and of the absence of monopolies in production has been increased. It is these local conditions—the imbalance between supply and demand reflects them—that, together with the transmission explained above, explain the special forms of inflation during the Second World War in the Middle East.[65] Britain paid its creditors in that part of the world by making payments into their blocked accounts in London. In exchange, the central banks of the countries concerned not only obtained the right to issue money to an equivalent amount but also, in effect, paid the local creditors of the British. The rise in prices resulted from the purchasing power distributed locally in quantity greater than the supply, since, their accounts in London being blocked, the Middle Eastern states concerned could not import goods of equivalent value. It was because of this imbalance between supply and demand, and not because of some alleged quantitative mechanism due to the additional issue of money, that prices rose. The amount of imports ought to have risen, but in fact declined sharply. This is the ultimate reason why the price rise was higher where the local supply was less elastic (Iraq) and where local military expenditure was heavier (Egypt, as compared with the Sudan). It remains true that the intervention of a psychological factor, constituted by the evolution of prices in the dominant economy, is shown by the very great rise in prices that occurred in Syria and Lebanon, although the imbalance between supply and demand caused by military expenditure was not higher there than elsewhere.

This psychological factor played only a secondary role so far as the countries of the sterling area were concerned, as prices rose in Britain by only 30 percent during the war. Here it was the imbalance between supply and demand (the excessive volume of demand) that was decisive. In the French dependencies, however, the psychological factor played a much more important role. The examples of Syria and Lebanon testify to this, although the imbalance between supply and demand intensified the price rise (which was of the order of 600 percent, as against 490 percent in France between 1938 and 1945). In North Africa and Black Africa we can also observe the results of the combined workings of the two factors, psychological and real (local imbalance between supply and demand). After 1943 the evolution of prices proceeded parallel with that in the metropolitan country.[66]

Transmission in the "managed" currency system. The direct influence of the value of the dominant currency on the value of the dominated one did not have to be proved in the case of the foreign-exchange standard, since where that applies there is no indigenous currency—what exists is merely the foreign currency itself in a disguised form. In cases, however, where unlimited exchange at a fixed rate has been abolished, and where there is a managed currency backed by foreign exchange, this one-way influence nevertheless remains basically the same: if the value of all the foreign exchange is reduced, so that the cover possessed by the local currency declines in value, this currency itself very soon loses its initial value, because it owes this, to a large extent, to public confidence.

It is not only because imports become dearer that the local currency loses value. One might well suppose that the rise in internal prices would be localized in the international sector, while the domestic sector remained unaffected. This is what usually happens in relations between advanced countries when exchange rates are readjusted. Here we have an apparently paradoxical situation: in the advanced countries, in which all the sectors of activity hold together, a price rise can be restricted to a single sector, whereas in the underdeveloped countries, where two sectors coexist without interpenetrating, and the economy does not form an integral unity, a rise in prices in the capitalist sector linked with the international market is passed on in full to the native sector which seems to be independent of it.

Perhaps the explanation of this phenomenon should be sought through analysis of forms of behavior in relation to money. There are some social categories whose behavior is "neutral": these persons seek to adapt their nominal income to the level of prices. They follow the economic movement. Others—and these are the economically dominant category—are constantly engaged in studying the future in order to know what the value of money is going to be be. These persons, who have at their disposal reserves of money intended for future use (which is not the case with the poorer categories), not only think about the future value of money but also, because a large fiduciary element enters into the determination of this value, exert a serious influence on the way it evolves.

Let us take, for example, an underdeveloped country. Here the individual with a big income is often a landowner. He dreams of how he will spend his income; and he knows that he has to buy the luxury goods that he wants *from abroad.* The value of money means for him the value of the relevant foreign currency. In an advanced country, on the contrary, the individual with a big income is normally an entrepreneur. He dreams of investing his money, and he knows that most of his production expenses—purchase of machinery, payment of wages—will be paid out in the country where he is. The devaluation of a foreign currency does not devalue the local currency, to his way of thinking, except, and only except, insofar as foreign trade supplies his country's internal market.

An example that illustrates this view very well is given by Wallich. In Cuba all attempts to drive out the dollar by increasing the issue of pesos proved fruitless, because the peso circulated only in limited areas. An issue of pesos that exceeded the wants of these areas did not oust the dollar but merely resulted in devaluation of the peso. The dollar was still in demand in external relations. Wallich formulates very clearly the idea that the peso circulates wherever money is essentially a circulation medium, but wherever the use of money as a "store of value" has become established, there the dollar reigns. The existence of two parallel circulations determines variations in the internal exchange between the two currencies. If the peso has at some moments enjoyed a slight advantage, this was not because its future value was considered greater than that of the dollar, but for a secondary and practical reason, namely, a shortage of make-up money and small denominations in dollars.[67]

Condillac devoted a chapter of his *Essay on the Nature of Commerce in General* to studying the mechanisms by which the tastes of the ruling class determined all prices and the amounts in which different goods were produced. Since his time a similar role has been attributed, to an exaggerated degree, to the behavior of the working class ("wage inflation"). Flamant has revealed, however, that in France's postwar inflation we can discern vicious circles in which speculative profits are linked with prices.[68]

A very good example of this dependence is given by the devaluation of the Egyptian pound in 1949. In 1947 Egypt had left the sterling area. Nevertheless, Egyptian currency being still mainly backed by sterling, Egypt was obliged to follow Britain when the latter devalued. This had to be done to prevent relations between Egypt and Britain, the dominant country, from deteriorating (increase in the price of Egyptian exports in British money terms), although it involved increased difficulties in relations between Egypt and other countries. Another factor was the economic bond between Britain and Egypt created by the sterling balances, which, if there were no Egyptian devaluation, would lose still more of their value. The most important consideration was that the Egyptian currency was secured upon sterling assets. F. Moursi invented the useful expression "flexible sterling standard" to describe the situation in which Egypt found itself—legally free to fix the rate of exchange, but economically forced to follow sterling. The Maghreb is today in this position in relation to France, as are several Commonwealth countries in relation to Britain.

Monetary independence does not emancipate the underdeveloped countries from the vicissitudes of the dominant currencies. There is, indeed, a curious possibility of influence by the value of the dominant currency through the external balance. Let us assume that the currency issued in the (independent) underdeveloped country is backed 75 percent by gold (75 millions) and 25 percent by foreign exchange (25 millions), and 100 millions are circulating in the country. Let us further assume that the external balance is in equilibrium. A price inflation now occurs in the dominant economies. The exports of the underdeveloped country increase; the balance becomes favorable, the surplus being paid in foreign exchange. It might be thought that the local currency would tend to rise in value. Yet this does not happen: paradoxically, Indeed, the contrary happens. The increase in the national income resulting from the new situation calls for an additional issue of money. This extra issue is backed not by gold, the stock of which has not changed, but by foreign exchange, the stock of which has increased. There are now 200 millions circulating in the country—75 millions backed by gold, and 125 millions backed by foreign exchange. The surplus of the balance being paid in a currency that has fallen in value, a psychological reason for an internal price increase is introduced into the underdeveloped economy.

As it falls, the value of the foreign currency drags down the local currency. The favorable external balance, while being constantly canceled out by devaluation of the local currency, is constantly put back as it was at the outset because, in the meantime, a new price increase has taken place at the center of the system. What makes the situation still worse is that when this rise comes to a halt for the time being at the center (period of stabilization), the underdeveloped countries suddenly lose their "lead": exports fall, and a tendency for the local currency to lose value is observed (because, while foreign currency is always accepted in the underdeveloped countries when there is a surplus in the external balance, the local currency is not automatically accepted abroad when there is a deficit). Devaluation offers no prospect of restoring equilibrium in external relations. The price elasticities of exports are high, those of imports are low, and consequently a perverse effect is to be expected.

These cases are not imaginary. They correspond to the considerable difficulties experienced by the countries of Asia, Africa, and Latin America when, around 1925 and again around 1948, the European economies recovered comparative stability. After a euphoric period which, generally speaking, left the underdeveloped countries with an accumulation of debts due them that depreciated day by day, there followed a period of difficulties in selling and of pressure for lowering of the exchange rates in these countries.

Does this transmission cease to occur when the backing by foreign exchange and foreign securities is replaced by a backing of gold and national securities? When this happens, the separation between the two currencies, that of the dominant country and that of the dominated one, is absolute: "monetary independence" is complete.[69] It is a costly operation, for the high degree of sensitivity of the external balance of the underdeveloped countries to the international economic situation, their great dependence on foreign trade, means that they are obliged to maintain a gold cover proportionately much bigger than in the advanced countries. Gold alone is international money; the bonds issued by the local Treasury do not possess this virtue. If too large a proportion of the cover were composed of the latter, it would not enjoy the confidence of exporters in the poor country, who are its most dynamic economic elements.

Eventually the underdeveloped countries do indeed take the path of acquiring gold cover, when they are able. But they are not always in a position to do so. It often seems to them to be pointless; a composite backing of international reserves, made up partly of gold and partly of key foreign currency (dollars and sterling), or even of other hard currency of the advanced countries (marks, Swiss frances, etc.), seems equally effective.[70]

This reasoning by the underdeveloped countries is well founded. Experience shows that the mechanism of domination that makes the value of the currency of the dominant advanced center decisive in appreciating the value of the currency of the underdeveloped periphery does indeed persist, even where the latter's backing consists entirely of gold. Devaluation of the dominant currency—the one the local ruling classes will use to obtain the goods they want—makes it necessary to devalue the local currency. The devaluations that followed that of the pound sterling in 1967 have proved the truth of this yet again.

On this plane too, then, the monetary illusion must be dispersed. Monetary structures are not the main thing in underdevelopment. Whatever these structures may be, the value of the currency in the periphery can only be that of the dominant currencies at the center. Furthermore, it is not merely the movement of the general price level that is thus transmitted from the center to the periphery, but the fundamental structure of relative prices, as will be seen later.

"Permanent Inflation" and Its Transmission to the Periphery

The nature of inflation.[71] The quantity theory claims that only an increase in the volume of money can bring about a general increase in prices. The facts of history, when hastily considered, seem to justify this theory—though it is the fall in the real cost of the production of gold due to the discovery of richer mines that provides the true explanation of the great price movements of the nineteenth century. After 1914, Aftalion was to show that the rate of exchange can also determine general price movements. Subsequent studies all emphasized that a general rise could be due to rigidity in supply caused by some bottleneck in relation to expanding overall monetary demand.

A situation like this is frequent in time of war, war preparation, or reconstruction, when the production of consumer goods is limited (or operates in conditions of increasing costs), while incomes to which there is no real equivalent are distributed by the state on a large scale. Finally, after the experiences of 1944-1948, economists have come to maintain that the struggle waged between social groups on the market, over their share of the national income, can in certain conditions, when the mechanisms of competition are functioning unsatisfactorily, create a general increase in prices. In all cases, monetary expansion followed the price rise and did not precede it.

This being so, economists, perhaps out of concern about seeming to break with the quantity theory, have managed to forget the only case that in former times had interested them, namely, that in which an issue of money in excess of requirements choked the channels of circulation and brought about a price rise. Today economists give the name inflation to any fairly widespread rise in prices. It is hard to see what is gained by this terminology. The expression "rise in prices" is both clear and capable of rendering nuances like "uneven," "general," or "partial rise in prices," which the bare term "inflation" too often conceals. "Inflationary rise in prices" will be used here only to designate a general rise in prices due to "monetary causes." "Inflation" means the choking of the circulation channels through an issue of money out of proportion to the need for liquidities. Inflation can lead to a rise in prices, but it need not, if the additional money introduced into the economic circuit makes possible greater liveliness in economic activity, in which case the quantity of liquidities required by the working of the economic system soon increases. But the fact that money has made possible this greater liveliness does not mean that it is the cause of it. This is what normally happens in a period of prosperity, which is for this reason wrongly identified with inflation by economists who have adopted the terminology criticized above. The vital difference between genuine inflation, when economic liveliness is no greater than before, and prosperity, when the amount of money and the level of activity advance together, vanishes when this terminology is used. Inflation may not lead to an increase in prices if the surplus money does not appear on the market but is instead absorbed by hoarding.

Accordingly, it can be seen that true inflation is impossible within the framework of convertibility. There may well be a general increase in prices under this system, as the result of a fall in the relative cost of producing gold or a rise in the real cost of producing goods in general (in case of war or of shortage, for example), but it is impossible to conceive that the channels of circulation should ever be choked. Credits are granted by the banks in response to demand. These credits serve to finance either current production or new investment. In the latter case, either the investment creates its own outlet, and the borrower is able to pay back the banker (and when this is so there is no increase in prices, because production has grown in the same proportion as the income distributed), or else it does not, and there is a crisis. Insofar as the bank does not wish to suspend convertibility, it will avoid financing investment beyond a certain limit, because it knows that, for real reasons of imbalance between production and consumption, new investment beyond a certain point can no longer create its own outlet, even if the borrower were prepared to pay a high rate of interest. This is why

Hawtrey's doctrine of continuous inflation necessitates abandonment of the gold standard.

As for gold, this too is incapable of choking the channels of circulation. If the rate of production of new gold is high, this means either that the central bank, which buys this gold at a fixed price, sees its reserves increasing without any increase in the credit it makes available, or that hoarders buy this gold in order to meet their needs. In any case, gold is put into circuit by the producers who sell it and not by the state, which would regulate its issue like that of paper money.

There is thus in this case no problem of inflation, either in the advanced countries or in the underdeveloped ones. There are, however, general price movements (during the course of the economic cycle) the transmission of which deserves to be studied (but that is another problem). Things are not the same when convertibility is abolished.

The general climate of rising prices in the twentieth century.[72] If we are considering the transmission of inflation and the general increase in prices from the advanced to the underdeveloped countries, this is because history has shown the dominant role played by the former in determining the general economic climate on the world scale. There are indeed general movements of prices that are peculiar to particular countries, whether advanced or underdeveloped. These general movements brought about by special local causes certainly have an influence on the external relations of the country which is affected by these troubles. Besides these particular problems, there is a major problem of the twentieth century which is common to all the underdeveloped countries—the effects on accumulation in these countries produced by the atmosphere of continuous increase in prices that prevails throughout the world today.

This atmosphere in which "the economic system no longer functions otherwise than with rising prices" has its source, without any possible doubt, in the advanced countries as a whole.

Fundamentally, it is the substantial changes in the conditions of competition that have radically altered the course of the general movement. During the nineteenth century, insofar as competition constituted the rule and monopoly the very rare exception (confined in the main to public services, which were, moreover, controlled by the state), an entrepreneur was unable to increase his prices, because he would have lost all his customers. Under these conditions the banks could not issue "too much credit" because, on the one hand, since the entrepreneurs did not expect an increase in prices they had no need of extra liquidities and, on the other, the central bank, concerned to safeguard convertibility, prevented the commercial banks from granting credits in excess of the need for liquidities. Convertibility could thus be suspended only in the very rare exceptional situation of wartime, when the state issued purchasing power in paper money without any real equivalent.

In addition to this, competition, by generalizing new techniques, brought about a fall in real costs that was reflected in a century-long tendency for prices to fall. This was offset by bouts of general price increase (which usually did not last very long) caused by sharp reductions in the cost of producing gold.

If we study the gross curve of wholesale prices between 1800 and 1900 in the United States, or in Britain or France, we do not observe any of those "long waves" that Kondratieff caused to emerge by means of skillful manipulation of statistics. This does not in the least mean that, in periods more frequently interrupted by wars, a certain tendency to increased prices (due to the increase in real costs that such situations usually engender) had the effect of offsetting the downward tendency of prices that marked the whole century. At other periods a mighty wave of innovations might, on the contrary, have served to intensify the downward movement. It is by means of concrete historical explanation that we must account for each period of price increase in the nineteenth century, and not by means of a general quantitativist explanation.

In the twentieth century, conditions have changed: monopolies dominate the main branches of production. Monopolies are not obliged to lower their prices. Competition between them proceeds by other methods.[73] In some situations they can easily *increase* their prices. The climate of increasing prices that has prevailed in the capitalist economies since 1914 has often been blamed on the rigidity of nominal wages. In reality, if today the trade unions concentrate their efforts on maintaining this wage level, it is because experience has shown them that the general price-level no longer diminishes. During the nineteenth century, despite opposition from the trade unions, nominal wages were often lowered. Falling prices sometimes came to the aid of employers' pressure in making such reductions possible. The struggle between social groups over the sharing of total income—a struggle that went on in the nineteenth century as well as the twentieth—has now taken the form of a fight to increase money income because it is proceeding in a climate of general price-increase which facilitates this increase in money income. In the nineteenth century other methods were more effective, such as reductions in nominal wages or changes in relative prices through fiscal or tariff policy. This is why we must consider the change that occurred at the end of the nineteenth century in the conditions of competition as being fundamental in this connection.

Chamberlin criticizes the classical theory of the price mechanism and constructs a model of price determination which he considers more realistic, and which lies between competition and monopoly: each producer enjoys a certain monopoly, insofar as his product bears the maker's name, is aimed at a clientele used to buying from him, and so on, but at the same time he is subject to competition from products similar to his, so that the volume of his sales depends on his price (though to a lesser extent than in the case of the true monopolist). This analysis does not seem very realistic. What is true in it is situated at the level of retail trade; but while Lux soap may be replaced by Palmolive, it is a very different matter with steel, for example, which no substitute has come forward to compete with in the 1970s. No one can enter the production of steel without a substantial amount of capital, which cannot be obtained without the support of the banks. This, it seems, is the fundamental cause of monopoly. Competition has been relegated to spheres of activity where entry into production does not demand an amount of capital that forces one to resort to those all-powerful intermediaries, the banks.

It was thus the resistance of prices, in the new structural conditions, to any downward movement which made it impossible (or at least difficult) to get back to the gold standard after the First World War. The first wave of difficulties that occurred swept it clean away, and along with it went convertibility into gold.

Since then there has been no further barrier to the increase in prices. Does this mean that this increase will be continuous? No, for if entrepreneurs want to raise the price level they have to apply to the banks for increases in the credits that the latter allow to them. Since convertibility has been abolished, the central bank is free to agree or to refuse to follow such a policy. In this limited sense, management of money and credit has become a reality unknown to the previous century. It is remarkable that whereas this expression was not found in the theoretical thinking of the liberal century, the most liberal of modern economists (e.g., Hayek) consider that "neutral money" is the outcome of a monetary policy that it is difficult to carry out. This is why, although I upheld the basic theory that the quantity of money plays a passive role in the economy, in the sense that it adjusts itself to requirements, it has been possible for me to speak of the impossibility of the central banks of the underdeveloped countries managing credit—in other words, refusing to follow the policy desired by the concerns connected with the foreign monopolies when the foreign commercial banks to which these enterprises apply grant them credits, or when there is simply no rigorous control of transfers.

But when the central bank follows a policy that accords with the wishes of the entrepreneurs, will the increase in prices be continuous? Actually, what should be asked is why the monopolies do not wish to raise prices indefinitely; why the increase has not been continuous since 1914; why periods of price stabilization succeed periods of sharp increase (apart, of course, from periods when the price increase is due not to the behavior of entrepreneurs but to real causes: increases in costs of production, or disproportion between money incomes distributed and actual production, such as occurs in wartime).

Niebyl gives a very illuminating explanation of this phenomenon. "If real incomes show a tendency to rise above the level that ensures the highest profit for industry, price increases intervene in order to effect that contraction in production that is the traditional accompaniment of monopolistic practices."[74] These practices were not possible in the nineteenth century. There is, then, a level of real income for workers that ensures the sale of a certain amount of production at a certain price, yielding the maximum profit. In the last century no such level existed: wages constituted a *donnée*, like prices, against which the entrepreneur, isolated from his competitors, could do nothing. Today the situation is not the same: the monopolist tries to influence these two formerly independent factors. To the extent that the workers refuse to allow their real income to be reduced so as to be adjusted to this level, wage inflation is inevitable. But who is to be blamed for the rise in prices? The workers, who refuse to let their wages be adjusted to the level that suits the entrepreneurs? Or the entrepreneurs, who refuse to adjust their profits to the level of wages acceptable to the workers?

A secondary influence is the general climate of war in which our century lives, and the splitting of the world into isolated economic and monetary systems (made possible, *inter alia*, by the abandonment of the gold standard), which have added historical causes to this structural cause of the increase in prices. Needless to say, monopolies, monetary decisions regarding convertibility, and world wars are all the responsibility of the great powers, not of the underdeveloped countries. This is why responsibility for the general climate of price increase prevailing in the twentieth century has been attributed to the great powers alone.

It needs to be added, for the sake of clarity, that this continuous inflationary tendency is not offset by the permanent deflationary tendency of the twentieth century: the imbalance between saving and investment in favor of the former, in other words, between supply and demand, between the capacity to produce and the capacity to consume. This reality (which I do not contest), linked with the "overdevelopment" of the "mature" economies, is a matter of the *real* equilibrium, whereas inflation relates to monetary equilibrium. The generalized use of the term inflation leads here, as elsewhere, to confusions that ought to be avoided.

The consequences to accumulation in the periphery. The development of capitalism in Europe and in the United States thus proceeded in a climate of monetary stability and declining prices (the fall in prices being brought about by development, which was reflected in a steady reduction in real costs). In the underdeveloped countries, however, the current development of peripheral capitalism is proceeding in a climate of price increase, and with price structures that are not basically due to the internal conditions of these countries' development, but are transmitted from outside.

In the developed countries, this steady increase in prices favors accumulation. By systematically reducing the value of sums hoarded in money form it encourages investment, since this provides a means, if not of gaining, then at least of not losing anything. True, hoarding may also take the form of the purchase of securities in the form of real values, the production of which requires a real expenditure of productive forces: gold, jewelry, etc. When this happens, hoarding, which then becomes comparable to luxury consumption, has no harmful effect on employment, though it does hold back the pace of development.

In the underdeveloped countries, free as they are from "overdevelopment," what is called inflation (it would be better to say the continuous increase in prices, regardless of whether this is due to monetary causes, when this increase is not determined by the internal necessities of the economic mechanism but is transmitted from outside) has a harmful effect on the mechanism of accumulation.[75]

In the first place, the orientation of saving toward the hoarding of real values which it determines results in raising the level of consumption at the expense of investment. In addition, the continuous rise in prices makes possible the transfer of income to the economically stronger elements, in the forefront of whom stand the big foreign-owned concerns. The price increase thus enables the re-exported profits of the foreign monopolies to reduce the share taken by the profits of the (weaker) national sector of the economy, and so hinders the formation of local savings. Accordingly, to say that inflation, by making possible a reduction in the cost of borrowing foreign capital (interest being calculated on the nominal value of these loans), has a favorable effect on development is not true, for the rise in prices merely cuts down the share of interest paid on state loans and bonds, but not the much more considerable share represented by re-exported profits. This transfer is no mere theoretical mechanism. The Africanization of some sectors of activity (road transport, exploitation of forests, building, etc.), in the majority of the countries of Black Africa where it has taken place during the last twenty years, has been accompanied by marked lowering of the profitability of these activities, to the advantage of those, both upstream and downstream, which are controlled by foreign capital. This lowering of profitability has been considerably facilitated by the increase in prices, which has operated unevenly between the different sectors.[76]

The other powerful elements in an underdeveloped economy are often the landed proprietors. They spend their extra income—income they owe to inflation—on luxury imports. This fact, confirmed many times from the example of Latin America, causes Spiegel to declare that inflation has little influence on the rate of accumulation.

It has often been maintained that inflation favors forced saving at the expense of free saving. This is true only when the state, the promoter of inflation, uses the purchasing power it has created for productive investment. This case, however, remains exceptional, restricted to periods of reconstruction, for it is usually only in wartime that the state issues paper money without any real equivalent, and in this case the extra currency does not serve for productive investment but for the financing of war expenditure. Therefore, in the most common case, all that can be said is that the increase in prices is a form of redistribution of income. We need to know who gains and who loses in this redistribution if we are to know whether, ultimately, propensity to save has been increased. We have just seen that, in an underdeveloped economy, the categories that gain are probably the foreign enterprises and the landlords; and so, in the end, local saving is *reduced* by the increase in prices.

This is not, however, the main point. A general price increase has a very different effect on the relation between wages and profits in the advanced countries and in the underdeveloped ones. In the former, very broadly speaking, wages follow the increase in prices, and the gains in productivity due to technical progress are thus constantly being shared out between wages and profits. Over a long period, experience shows that the share taken by wages remains more or less the same.[77] In the underdeveloped countries, however, wages follow much more slowly, for profound structural reasons, and in the first place because of the pressure of the excessive supply of labor resulting from the break-up of the precapitalist rural communities. At best, real wages are kept constant, despite the improvement in productivity. What is true of wages is here equally true of the incomes resulting from the work of the peasants producing for the market, and especially for export. The experience of the last fifteen years proves this, with a wealth of detail. On the basis of equal productivity, the rewards of labor are becoming more and more unequal. A massive transfer of income from the periphery to the center, which is what is meant by this worsening in the terms of trade, constitutes the essence of the phenomenon.[78] This transfer accelerates accumulation at the center and restricts it in the periphery.

Transmission to the Periphery of the Price Structures of the Center

I will touch on this problem here only in order to recall what I have written earlier.[79] Strictly speaking, the question of price structure is not really one of monetary theory, although this structure is, of course, expressed in money terms.

In the capitalist mode of production, the equilibrium prices that ensure the adaptation of supply to demand are prices of production, in the Marxist sense. These prices assume an equal reward of labor as between branches (a single labor market) and an equivalent rate of profit on capital (equalization of the rate of profit). Consequently, if the same fraction of profits has to be saved in order to ensure expanded reproduction in all branches (or, let us say, for simplicity's sake, if all profit is reinvested, ignoring consumption by the capitalists), then the structure of growth—the allocation of investment between the different branches—is determined by the structure of prices. If there were no capital market ensuring the circulation of capital from one branch to another, there would be no guarantee of coherence between the structure of growth and that of demand, which is modified in its proportions by this very growth. The circulation of capital is thus a necessary law of the functioning of the capitalist mode of production.

But this circulation comes up against a permanent obstacle: the private ownership of capital. The enterprises and branches that are called upon to undergo more vigorous growth as a result of the evolution of demand are afraid—if, in order to finance their investments, they have to call in capital from abroad to an excessive extent—that they may lose control of their affairs. They therefore try to include in their prices a margin sufficient to allow an adequate amount of self-financing. The conditions of competition make this operation more or less possible. A price system that was rational from the standpoint of growth would imply—leaving out consumption by the capitalists—a price structure such that each branch could finance its own growth, in conformity with demand, without resorting to foreign capital: this would mean different rates of profit, or the same rate of profit with a free circulation of capital. The actual price system in the capitalist countries is in fact something in between; and the margins of self-financing are very variable, depending on many different elements (the degree of monopolization of the branch, etc.). This system has, then, nothing rational about it—the private ownership of capital constituting the real obstacle to all rationality. To this must be added the distortions that unequal indirect taxation contribute to the price system.

Productivity is measured within this price system: it is said that an enterprise or a branch has a productivity higher than others if it ensures (given equal rewards of labor) a higher rate of profit, and this is the actual tendency if the branch is to grow faster in order to cope with changes in demand.

Now, the price structure at the center is, broadly speaking, transmitted to the periphery for the same fundamental reasons that underlie the mechanisms of transmission of the value of the dominant currency: psychological mechanisms in connection with patterns of consumption, competition by imported products, and so on.

This transmission of the price structure of the center determines inequalities in productivity between different branches in the periphery that express the uneven degree of modernization—of penetration by the capitalist mode of production. These inequalities in productivity are often expressed in unequal rates of profit, but also very often in unequal rewards of labor, especially where what are involved are sectors that do not belong to the capitalist mode of production (as is often the case with rural production). This price structure has nothing rational about it from the standpoint of the requirements of growth organized to overcome the historical backwardness—uneven as between sectors—that is characteristic of the periphery. The needs of this growth—its distribution between sectors—are necessarily different from those at the center. From this angle, therefore, the transmitted price system is doubly irrational.

Monetary Disorders in Underdeveloped Countries

We owe to Eli Löbel a systematic analysis of monetary disorders in the underdeveloped world of today.[80] This writer has shown that the analysis of these monetary disorders must be essentially concerned with the short run (in the long run an equilibrium is always established) and must be situated in a definite structural setting (that of the underdeveloped countries) marked by relatively low elasticities of response on the part of local production to demand, by small external reserves and slight possibilities of external aid "without strings," and by a weak prospect of effectiveness for any possible measures of strict control, especially in Africa (frontiers easily crossed, administrations lacking in experience and politically "committed," etc.).

He distinguishes between three types of disorder: the first two—disproportionate increase in consumption, public or private, and tensions connected with industrialization—originate within the economy and may have effects on the external balance, while the third originates in the external balance itself.

Increase in consumption, public or private, at a rate that exceeds the growth rate of the productive economy, with its manifestations—either in a budget deficit or in disproportionate increase in credits for consumption purposes, or to cover the structural deficits of enterprises—constitutes the most familiar example of disequilibrium of internal origin. In this case it may be necessary to devalue the currency: this will have effects comparable to an increase in the amount taken by taxes and the subsequent reduction in demand, although these effects will be less selective.

Some tensions can set off a price spiral, without total supply and demand being thrown off balance. This assumes a balanced budget, a neutral credit policy (the liquidities created not exceeding the desired increases in cash at hand), an equally neutral wage policy (wages rising in step with productivity), and no difficulties as regards the balance of payments. Nevertheless, a policy of accelerated industrialization may result in "inflationary tension" if the production of consumer goods (especially foodstuffs) develops more slowly than industrial employment, which risks bringing about an increase in the prices of agricultural products, and so an increase in wages and consequently of *all* prices, a subsequent deficit in the public finances caused by increased rewards together with delay in receipts, and tensions in the external balance because the price increase restricts export possibilities, and eventually has repercussions in the monetary sphere. There is no way of avoiding tensions of this kind, which necessarily accompany accelerated development: they can only be contained by means of constant readjustments (of the state's financial structures, etc.). It is clear that in this case inflation makes the situation worse.

Similarly, a policy of industrialization based on import substitution, even if we assume that the quantity of agricultural produce available keeps pace with industrial employment, may have the same effects if the infant industries produce at higher cost than the prices of imported goods. In such a case, the currency may have to be devalued, for this has the same effect as a protective tariff for the infant industries. It would have to be selective (through multiple exchange rates) if the aim were to avoid a general increase in internal prices.

Analysis of the imbalances originating in the external balance of payments starts from the case that is simplest but also certainly the most fundamental: the flooding-in of an external inflation, by way of a pilot currency. This is what happens to countries integrated in a currency area, or countries which have a bilateral foreign trade structure. Here the rigidity of the system does not allow of much adjustment. On the world scale, something like this happens when inflation spreads from countries whose national currency serves as reserve currency for others in the rest of the world.

The fall in the price of exports causes—quite apart from any action that may be taken to alter the rate of exchange, if this entails a disturbance in the external balance—a necessary contraction in imports which is not always parallel to the fall in the income of exporters, and, consequently, sectoral imbalances between the supply of and the demand for different products, and spiral increases similar to the preceding ones. What is essential here is to combat possible speculative movements by trying to maintain key supplies at a satisfactory level, but this cannot always be done.

The increase in export prices does not always produce symmetrical inverse effects. On the contrary, we see here a tendency for internal prices to become aligned with external ones, and a spiral of continuous increase may occur if the excess income comes up against a feeble elasticity of supply. This is how this situation, which theoretically provides the possibility of accelerated accumulation, often prevents this potential extra accumulation from being realized.

Accordingly, the structural conditions of underdevelopment reduce considerably the possibility of mastering external relations and putting them in the service of a development policy. The analysis of contemporary experience made by Löbel confirms my conclusions.

It should be added that achievement of monetary independence entails the risk that in the event of disequilibrium of the external balance the rate of exchange may go down. A fall in the rate of exchange under conditions of underdevelopment, even if it leads, very provisionally, to equilibrium being restored in the external balance (which is not at all likely, in view of perverse price elasticities), cannot in the long run solve the problem, owing to the increase in prices which it causes, and which cancels out its temporary effects. Should there be some real reason for the chronic imbalance in the external balance, then, whereas, with a foreign-exchange standard, the time needed for the income effect to complete its work of re-equilibrating the balance is allowed to the underdeveloped economy, if there is monetary independence the country is involved in an endless series of devaluations and price increases.

The assumption is not an arbitrary one. It corresponds to the monetary history of Latin America in the nineteenth century, as we see in the case of Brazil from 1840-1895.[81] Here we may note in passing the parallel evolution (down to 1940) of the circulation of money and of the total value of exports—which proves that currency is closely bound up with export activity, and does not circulate much elsewhere in the economy.

The history of underdevelopment is thus a history of "missed theoretical opportunities for accumulation." If, during the Second World War, prices increased despite the accumulation of foreign exchange and gold, as generally happened in Latin America and the Middle East, this occurred because of the inadequacy of supply, through the material difficulty in importing goods. Before that time it was the permanent disequilibrium in the external balance (the trade balance was favorable, but the burden of profits to be re-exported, allowing for imports of new capital, was extremely heavy) that forced down the rate of exchange, which resulted in a price increase in accordance with my schema. This increase was intensified, to be sure, by the frequent budget deficit and the inflationary issue of paper money. The cause of the deficit lies in the fact that the necessary expenditure of a modern administration has grown more rapidly than its revenue (as we see from the historical example of Brazil). The case of Brazil is not unique. In Peru and China, the fall in prices between 1930 and 1938 was relatively greater than the increase between 1920 and 1930, so that over the period 1920-1938 as a whole a fall in prices took place.[82]

A general imbalance can thus exist between supply and demand with an independent monetary system for the same reasons as in the case of countries with a foreign-exchange standard. The case of Brazil during the Second World War is typical: the external balance is favorable, and yet prices rise. The rate of exchange remains stable, foreign countries paying for their deficit in accumulating foreign currency, but the imbalance between demand and supply, the latter being restricted owing to import difficulties, causes prices to rise. The rise is due to this real imbalance more than to the fact that the accumulating foreign exchange is depreciating—though this latter psychological factor has some responsibility for the rise. The stability of the rate of exchange in this situation reflects a reality that is important: the dominant economies can pay for their trade deficit by means of their own currency. This possibility, due to the fact the poor country always accepts this foreign currency which has an international purchasing power, prevents the exchange rates of the rich countries from depreciating. The poor countries, however, which have to pay in gold for any deficit they incur, since their currency is not acceptable, are more often subject to depreciation of their rate of exchange.

It remains true that in the case considered above (Latin America during the war) the increase in prices took place not merely without any fall in the rate of exchange, but *despite* the stability of this rate, which played a stabilizing role, the increase in prices in the dominant countries (and so in those of the goods they imported) having been less than the increase in the prices of goods of Latin American origin.

After the war, this fundamental mechanism, which continues to operate, has been sometimes supplemented by a mechanism which, though inverse (difficulties in the balance of payments creating internal disequilibrium between supply and demand) has a similar effect in increasing prices.[83] In addition, with monetary independence two traditional causes of increased prices make their appearance: inflation through the budget and through the credit policy of the central bank.

In the epoch of the foreign-exchange standard, a budget deficit was out of the question, as the central bank (or the currency board) gave no help to the local state. In the nineteenth century in Latin America, when a budget deficit occurred it was paid for by an issue of paper money by the treasury. This paper money was legal tender. But in the

French or British colonies this was not possible. Any deficit was met by a subsidy from the metropolitan treasury, which caused inflation throughout the whole currency area and not just in the colony. Given the small scale of the colonial budgets, this inflation could only be very slight. With the acquisition of monetary independence this possibility of resorting to the bank of issue becomes a serious cause of inflation.[84] Added to it is the new possibility of the central bank, which "manages credit," financing inflationary credit demands, following the example of the advanced countries of today.[85]

The effort now being made by some underdeveloped countries to escape from this dependence by developing bilateral agreements should not give rise to any illusions. Most of these agreements organize new relations between the underdeveloped world and part of the advanced world (the Eastern European countries), and merely reflect the appearance of these countries on the world market. Agreements made among underdeveloped countries themselves affect as yet only insignificant transactions. Here, too, dependence reflects the asymmetry and inequality that exist in reality. It cannot be avoided, or even reduced, by monetary means or the organizing of external exchanges so long as the real problems have not been solved. The currencies of the underdeveloped countries can in no case become international payment media.[86] This being so, we must not confuse development inflation, which has actually been practiced by some countries at certain periods, with the inflation without development that constitutes the experience of the underdeveloped countries.

Inflationary experiences in the Third World, which were practically confined to Latin America down to the Second World War, have become a common feature during the last twenty years. Some of these experiences, such as, in Africa, that of Congo-Kinshasa between 1960 and 1968, and, in Asia, that of Indonesia, have been thoroughly studied. The Congolese inflation, as Ryelandt has very clearly shown, results from the sudden coming to power of a new social class, the state bureaucracy, which sought to annex a part of the national income but was unable either to encroach seriously upon the share taken by foreign capital (owing to the outward orientation of some of the activities of this capital—the extraction industries of Katanga—or even, as regards the autocentric industrial groups of Kinshasa, because these foreign-owned enterprises were strong enough to be able to adapt to inflation) or to levy tribute directly from the peasant masses (who resisted by either open rebellion or passive resistance through ceasing production for export). With the aid of the United States and the International

Monetary Fund, an equilibrium was restored after eight years of inflation, marked by very considerable changes in relative prices and real incomes in Congo-Kinshasa as compared with the situation in 1960, reflecting a transfer of income from the peasants and lower-paid wage-earners (the real wages of the working class were cut by half) to the new ruling class. This "equilibrium" is rightly called retrogressive by Ryelandt, since its content is more biased toward consumption (by the new privileged strata), so that the equilibrium of the public finances and that of the balance of payments (on which the former is based) are extremely fragile.[87]

Most of the inflations in the Third World of today are of this type: in the Indonesia of Sukarno, in Mali, or in a number of countries of Latin America.[88] In some cases there is juxtaposed to this type of inflation a process of credit inflation associated with a disordered process of industrialization, mediocre in its effect, being carried out for the same social reasons of predominance by the new bureaucracy.[89]

These particular processes of adjustment lie behind the structuralist thesis of inflation.[90] But it is important to appreciate that the same results can be secured without inflation. Thus, in the former French colonies of Black Africa, where the monetary system forbids any budgetary inflation, a progressive increase in the tax burden, in the form of indirect taxes, has reduced the real income of the agricultural producers and the wage-earners in the towns for the benefit of the same social strata as in the previously mentioned cases. The new equilibria have the same retrogressive character as in Congo-Kinshasa and elsewhere. In the cases of Mali and Ghana, moreover, the regimes that have emerged after the fall of their predecessors have changed nothing from this point of view, expressing as they do an authority that is based on the same bureaucratic strata.

The experience of Japan.[91] In order to industrialize itself, Japan resorted to inflation on a number of occasions between 1868 and 1914. Between 1868 and 1873, inflation was caused by the budget deficit destined to finance the country's infant industry. Although the central banking system assumed its modern form only later (the Bank of Japan, which from its foundation was a real central bank, dates only from 1882), the Japan of 1860-1880 was not integrated by means of the banks. Nor was it subsequently integrated into the international finance market: very little appeal was made to foreign capital. The inflation of 1868–73 was thus purely national, in the sense that it was not transmitted from the outside world—which, in any case, was at that time in a phase of monetary stability. As for the inflations of 1894-1904 and 1914, they were even more national, Japanese capitalism having grown stronger. The state's aid to the old merchant families who around 1870 became transformed into industrialists was effected by way of loans without security. These advances weighed heavily on the market, causing prices to rise, and thus made possible a transfer of purchasing power from the peasant masses to the new bourgeoisie, who used this purchasing power to pay for the machinery they imported.

The choking of the channels of circulation by excessive amounts of currency between 1877 and 1894 had a favorable effect on Japan's development. This deliberate inflation of credit made investment possible before real saving had been obtained from production. The issue of currency, always ahead of requirements, certainly entailed a secondary price increase, but basically it made possible an increase in the level of activity. Part of the purchasing power created by the state for the benefit of the entrepreneurs found its way onto the external market, as it was necessary to import large quantities of machinery. These imports were paid for by liquidating the nation's stocks of gold and silver. In the Japanese case, the surplus of imports over exports was due to a sudden increase in imports of investment goods, and *not* to an increase in imports of luxury goods resulting from a transfer of income to the rich classes, as happened with the underdeveloped countries which were subjected to the transmission of a price increase that was external to the mechanism of their economy. It was thus not external demand in general that had risen, but only the level of demand for investment goods.

The difficulties of the external balance were thus the *result* of the acceleration of growth through internal inflation, and not the *cause* of the increase in prices.

The experiences of the underdeveloped world. Does this mean that all "national" inflation, meaning inflation that is not transmitted by way of the involuntary channel of external payments, is favorable to development?

Okyar criticizes, on the basis of the Turkish experience, the Keynesian policy of systematic budget deficits, which claims that this creation of new demand can foster "blocked" development. In the period 1933–40, Turkey's development was financed through the budget, without deficit and without inflation: investment amounted to 9 percent of the national income every year. From 1940 onward the budget deficit created inflation. Investment took only 4 percent of the annual national income, which fell between 1940 and 1948, whereas it had grown steadily between 1933 and 1940. The example is actually not very convincing, for the war period prevented the budget deficit from being used productively: current public expenditure, which amounted to 15 percent in the period 1933–40, rose to 22 percent in 1943–48. Okyar certainly shows that the Keynesian mechanism did not function, for it was not the absence of demand that blocked growth (otherwise the unproductive wartime expenditure by the state would have favored development, by creating multiplier effects), but he does not show that no deliberate inflation can be directed toward productive investment (the case of Japan) because it is *also* possible to carry out state investment without a budget deficit.[92]

Very different from these schemas are that of inflation and the increase in prices in the underdeveloped countries during the Second World War. Here the price increase, though internal in origin, was nevertheless closely bound up with the balance of payments. However, it occurred in a special war situation, so that some of its negative effects on accumulation were unable to take concrete form.

Indeed, since the demand of the European countries and the United States increased during the war, as in a period of prosperity, and since the need, as well as the possibility, for these countries to export manufactured goods declined during this period, these circumstances resulted in an improvement in the terms of trade for the overseas countries, which favored local accumulation. A large part of this surplus income realized through the improvement in the balance of payments would in normal times have been spent on luxury imports. This surplus income thus constituted in part a forced saving that soon found investment locally, all the more so because the lack of foreign competition and the acute reduction in imports favored the creation of local industries. It is true that some contrary forces worked against this development, such as the decline in the productivity of agriculture due to the impossibility of importing fertilizers, and the difficulty in getting machinery from Europe and America. Accordingly, part of this surplus income was directed onto the local market for luxury goods (building of villas, etc.), where it caused a price increase. This unrestrained consumption of luxury products resulted, moreover, in investment in milk bars, which served as a pole of development for local luxury expenditure. Part of the deficit in the balance of the Allied countries was paid for by liquidating gold reserves, and also—and especially—by transferring foreign investments of local ownership—starting, of course, with the least profitable of these investments. In this way the war contributed to the formation of local capital, if only by this transfer of ownership, the consequence of which was that the profits subsequently realized would no longer be re-exported. Later, the deficit in the European balance was paid for either in depreciating currency or in war debts (sterling credits, for example), which also depreciated as the European countries were inflated. This European inflation was thus transmitted overseas, and was made worse by the expenditure of the foreign armies.

The final outcome, despite the particularly favorable conditions for local development, was meager. Inflation was reflected in increased gross investment, but at the same time the war involved such a squandering of capital (nonreplacement of worn-out equipment in railways, roads, ports, etc.) that it is very hard to know whether, ultimately, net investment was positive. In the end, this type of inflation seems to have been negative in effect. What did play a positive role was not the inflation itself but the momentary disappearance of foreign competition.

These last examples show how unfavorable the general climate of rising prices in which the world has lived since 1914 has been to accumulation in the underdeveloped countries. Even under the favorable conditions of the Second World War, development was restricted to a greater extent than it was favored by the transmission of price increases from without. In contrast, the Japanese example shows that a managed internal inflation can favor development. The example of inflation thus demonstrates how harmful it is to confuse the mechanisms of development within a national framework with the mechanisms of development within the framework of international integration. The same phenomena that in one case contribute to accelerating the accumulation of capital serve in the other to check this accumulation.

THE DISTANT PAST: THE INTEGRATION OF THE PERIPHERY INTO THE WORLD MARKET FOR PRECIOUS METALS

Some precapitalist economies were innocent of the use of money (as in certain regions of Africa) or were still lagging at the stage of the first appearance of money (use of shell, animals' teeth, etc.). In these cases it was the European merchant—usually following in the wake of the Arab or Indian merchant—who introduced metallic money. When he bought export goods from the natives he injected Maria-Theresa dollars or Mexican piastres into the economic system. When he sold the native imported goods he withdrew these coins from local circulation. This is why, in North America and the West Indies, where the European settlers arrived as poor men, precious metals usually stayed only a very short time. It was necessary periodically to cope with the need for currency by issuing paper money. However, this is of secondary significance. These colonies remained in the main circulation area of precious metals, so that prices were determined by the relation between the cost of production of a commodity and that of the metal used for money.

The point is that this metal has an intrinsic value. The subjectivist conception of value has, of course, led to the statement that, since the utility of money arises from its use as money, gold already at that time owed its value to this particular use that was made of it, and that therefore the intrinsic value of the metal was a mere fancy. If one wants to go all the way with this idea, one has to deny that a system based on gold is basically different from a system based on paper money, which has no intrinsic value although it has value (since each note represents a certain amount of purchasing power). And yet it is clearly necessary to distinguish between these two systems. Metal coins are introduced into the economic circuit by the producers of gold. For these entrepreneurs the production of gold is a profitable activity, and, so long as a difference between the price of gold and its cost of production makes it possible to obtain a profit equivalent to that which other entrepreneurs derive from their production, new gold is introduced into the economy. But the extraction of gold involves a real cost in labor and in capital. The production of paper money, however, costs nothing. Paper money, moreover, is introduced into circulation through channels very different from those followed by gold—through the channel of state issues intended to cover governmental needs, or through the channel of short-term credit.

For Ricardo, who is wrongly charged with being the originator of the quantity theory of money, gold was a commodity the value of which was measured by the amount of labor congealed in its production. However, since the quantity of money needed was decided by the level of prices and economic activity and by habits of payment, the presence of a quantity of gold differing from this magnitude entailed a variation in the price of gold above or below its value, exactly in the same way as the overproduction or underproduction of any other commodity determined variations in its price. Marx criticized Ricardo by pointing out that he had forgotten the hoarding that absorbs the extra gold, and thereby, through confusing the total quantity of money available with the quantity *in circulation,* had opened the way to the quantity theory. At all events, crude quantitativism is later than Ricardo. It dates from Walras. It was in fact the new economic doctrine based on the subjective theory of value that was to lead to quantitativism. By supposing that the utility of gold is due precisely to its function as money, economists fell into a vicious circle from which they could emerge only by adopting the quantity theory in a crude form. Nevertheless, even in a moderate marginalist view such as that of Nogaro, a monetary system made up of gold coins appears very different from monetary systems that use paper. Indeed, while, in the short run, utility directly determines the price of a commodity, in the long run the volume of production of this commodity is fixed at a level at which the price determined by utility leaves the entrepreneur with no more than a margin of "normal profit" over and above the cost of production. The production of gold undeniably does include such a cost, whereas the production of paper money does not. The mechanisms whereby currency penetrates the economy are therefore quite unlike in the two cases.

This being so, it is easily understood that the fact that the same metal is used in two areas of the world does not necessarily imply that these two areas belong to one and the same monetary system. Between one place and another the real cost of producing gold may differ. One may describe as a "currency area" the geographical area over which there is approximate uniformity in the cost of production of gold. If, more generally, an economic space is defined as the geographical area within which general economic conditions are the same—the prices of commodities as well as the rates of reward of the factors of production[93]—one has to observe that, down to comparatively recent times, "currency areas" coincided fairly closely with "economic areas." Precapitalist societies constitute, as a rule, entities (which are not merely economic but also political and social) that are turned in upon themselves. The absence of migration (except, of course, through conquest, which constitutes a different problem) and the relative slightness of relations between each of these entities and the outside world result in the division of the globe into heterogeneous economic and currency areas. The development of capitalism, on its "native" foundation in Europe, also allowed the coexistence of economically heterogeneous areas during the nineteenth century, although a single European gold market (the reserves of which lay outside Europe—in America, and later in Africa and Australia) had been in existence for about two centuries already. We know that the general level of prices, for example, was never the same between any of the countries of Europe. Even at that time, however, the dependence of certain extra-European countries on certain European states had created economic areas of a new type, the metropolitan country and its colonies, in which some conditions, including monetary ones, had been rendered homogeneous, although others remained diverse.

The subsequent development of the export of capital conferred even greater importance on this new type of economic space—bringing out more clearly its nature and limits.

There then started to become apparent what might prove to be the significance under these conditions of the first forms of "monetary integration" of the underdeveloped countries. The precapitalist economies of the overseas countries possessed their own stock of metal. Their integration into the international market did not alter this (except, of course, through the plundering that occurred when these countries were conquered). But the contact established between two previously isolated societies brought about a modification in the value of precious metal—either through a fall in this value in the European countries as a result of the discovery in the Americas of mines where extraction was easier (which is what happened in the sixteenth century: there is no need to appeal to the quantity theory in order to explain the general increase in prices that occurred at that time), or through the opposite process, as when the relatively lower cost of silver in Europe caused changes in some general conditions in the countries of the Far East into which the Europeans introduced their silver.

In his analysis of international exchange, Ricardo started from the assumption of wages that were equal in terms of gold, and a scatter of prices in terms of gold similar to that of real costs, so as to produce equivalence in these prices. The assumption of equal gold-wages resulted from Ricardo's having previously assumed perfect integration of the two countries in a single gold market. This latter assumption was not merely dictated by logical necessity, it corresponded to reality when two independent monetary areas came into contact with each other: Europe and America in the sixteenth century, India and Britain in the eighteenth, and so on.

Here, then, is a specifically monetary phenomenon: a change in the value of money as a result of the integration of two economies is a wider sphere of exchange, which takes place alongside phenomena of a purely economic kind—changes in economic conditions as a result of the establishment of trade relations between the two systems.

India provides an excellent example of the phenomenon under consideration. That country's currency (the silver rupee) gradually declined in value during the nineteenth century. Its value in pence fell by 35 percent between 1850 and 1900. The result was an increase in prices in India (index 90 in 1861, 116 in 1900) which contrasted with the fall in prices in Britain in this period (from 135 to 105 between the same dates). The decline of the rupee was arrested, at the end of the century, by the introduction of the sterling exchange standard system: suspension of the free minting of rupees, exchange at a fixed rate and in unlimited quantities of rupees for sterling, and vice versa (so that the rupee became "a Bank of England note printed on silver").[94]

This fall in the price of silver resulted in serious losses for India; the government had to transfer to Britain annually, around 1880, about £16 million (interest on the public debt, maintenance of the army, etc.). It issued bills which it sold in London and which competed with the remittance of silver, so that the price of these bills varied with the market price of silver. Every year India lost about 25 percent of the amount of these bills and had to raise new taxes in order to compensate for this transfer of revenue to Britain. Another negative effect of the same kind, resulting from this, was the worsening of the terms of trade over a period of thirty years, from 1870 to 1898. Thus, 100 kilos of Indian wheat were sold for 19.22 francs in 1886 instead of 23.05 francs in 1870, owing to the fall in the price of silver. All the countries where silver circulated—that is, not merely India and the Far East but also Latin America, Persia, and others—suffered heavily from the devaluation of silver.

True, the advanced countries that were silver-monometallist or bimetallist also suffered from this process. These countries, however (such as Germany, Holland, Scandavia, Austria-Hungary, and Russia), were able to go over with ease at the end of the century to direct gold-monometallism (Germany, Holland, Scandinavia) or the gold-exchange standard (Russia in 1894, Austria-Hungary in 1891). Only the poorer countries of Europe, like Spain, had to go over to paper money. The underdeveloped countries, however, with the exception of Argentina, were unable to do this. They all eventually went over to the foreign-exchange standard, except in those cases, as in Latin America, where they retained the paper-money system that had been very widespread since the beginning of the nineteenth century.

It would be interesting to know the general effects of these changes in the value of metallic money in the peripheral capitalist economies in process of construction. Study of these effects cannot be undertaken in terms sufficiently general to constitute a theory. Each distinct historical case needs to be looked at closely—the nature of the economic regimes that confronted each other, and also the policy followed by the conqueror.[95] The historical interest of such studies relates to a fairly short period, as integration of the underdeveloped countries through the banking system was very soon superimposed on their commercial integration, and this integration by the banks than became the main form of monetary integration.

PRESENT TIMES: THE INTERNATIONAL LIQUIDITY CRISIS AND THE UNDERDEVELOPED COUNTRIES

I take from Eli Löbel the actual terms, which are extremely clear, in which he analyzes the current crisis of international liquidity:[96]

"1. During the last fifteen years," writes Löbel, "an increase in international liquidities—or world reserves—slower than in the volume of international exchanges has been observed. In this connection I will quote the Annual Report for 1966 of the International Monetary Fund (pp. 12-13): 'World reserves, here defined as the reserves of countries other than the Soviet countries and Mainland China, may be estimated at close to $49 billion at the end of 1951, and at about $70 billion at the end of 1965 (Table 1). They rose at an annual rate of 2.6 percent during this period, but since world trade increased at an annual rate of about 6 percent, reserves as a percent of annual imports fell from 67 percent in 1951 to 43 percent in 1965 (Table 2).'

"This movement has been intensified during recent years: the increase in world trade was around 10 percent and 5 percent respectively during the years 1966 and 1967, whereas world reserves increased by an average of only 1.5 percent per year during this period (according to the IMF Annual Report, 1968).

"2. Such a tendency may at first sight appear disturbing. It needs to be stressed, however, that there is no reason to declare that the present level of world reserves is inadequate. Indeed, it can be claimed that the structure of international trade was especially disturbed just after the Second World War, and has now become more stable, so that the balances to be settled have grown smaller, thus requiring smaller reserves. Professor Triffin calculated that monetary reserves, essentially composed of gold in 1913, then covered only 37 percent of world imports.[97] The ratio of reserves to imports, including in the numerator the reserve positions of the IMF, is even higher in 1965 than in 1913 (see Table 2).

"3. Furthermore, one ought to take into account not only the *stock* of international liquidities but also its *velocity of circulation.* This aspect of the matter has been overlooked up to now, though there have been some very thorough analyses of it so far as the internal monetary plane is concerned.[98]

"4. It is also established that adjustment mechanisms have made their appearance in recent years which may operate to bring about a reduction in the total level of reserves needed. On this point I will quote the IMF Annual Report mentioned above (1966, pp. 14 and 16): 'It is not impossible that improvements to be made in the international adjustment process may be such as to permit a reduction in the general level of reserves required in relation to trade and, therefore, to

Table 42

World Reserves: Growth, 1951–65

	Reserves at the end of 1951 (in billions of $ U.S.)	Reserves at the end of 1965 (in billions of $ U.S.)	Increase 1951–65	Increase in percentage per year
Gold	33.9	41.9	8.0	1.5
Reserve positions in IMF	1.7	5.4	3.7	8.6
Currencies *of which:*	13.7	22.9	9.2	3.7
Claims on U.S.*	4.2	14.8	10.6	9.4
Claims on U.K.†	8.2	6.7	−1.5	−1.5
Other	1.3	1.4	0.1	0.5
*Total***	49.3	70.2	20.9	2.6

Source: IMF Annual Report, 1966, table in Löbel, art. cit.

* Covers short-term liquid liabilities to central banks and governments; foreign official holdings of U.S. government marketable securities; and foreign official holdings of U.S. government nonmarketable securities for those countries that are believed to include such holdings in their reserves figures.

† Covers liabilities to foreign central monetary authorities, including inter-central-bank assistance.

** Countries of the Soviet bloc and the People's Republic of China excluded.

permit, for a time, a relatively low rate of growth in the need for reserves. Discussions to this end have been recently taking place within the framework of the Organization for Economic Cooperation and Development; and the Fund itself, in its relations with member countries, continues to promote such improvements wherever possible. Appropriate enlargements and extensions of bilateral swap arrangements can also reduce reserve requirements insofar as these arrangements add to confidence in currency stability and thus deter speculative movements.' This is true only provided that instruments of this kind are not multiplied to the point where they have the effect of unduly delaying the necessary adjustments. The financing of deficits by means of such arrangements can also reduce to some extent the need for reserves.

Table 43
Countries' Reserves as Percentage of Imports
(1951–65)

	1951	1960	1965
A. Developed countries			
(a) Group of ten (United States, U.K., W. Germany, Belgium, Canada, France, Italy, Japan, Holland, Sweden)	73	60	43
(b) Other developed countries	46	44	41
All developed countries	68	57	43
B. Less-developed countries			
(a) Major oil-exporters	60	49	64
(b) Countries with high initial reserves	118	41	22
(c) Other less-developed countries	41	44	42
All less-developed countries	64	44	42
Grand total	67	55	43
Grand total excluding U.S.	39	43	39

Source: IMF Annual Report, 1966, table in Löbel, art. cit.

"However, and this seems to me of vital importance, such mechanisms have functioned largely, if not exclusively, between the industrialized countries. I shall return to this point later.

"5. The crisis in the international payments system therefore does not lie in a world shortage of international liquidities, at least so far as the industrialized countries are concerned.

"It is much more a matter of their distribution, especially in the case of reserve currencies, first and foremost the dollar. The figures are known. In 1951 the gold reserves of the United States amounted to $24.3 billion, whereas in 1965 they came to not more than $14.7 billion. Corresponding to these diminished reserves we find an indebtedness of the United States to the rest of the world that grew steadily from $8.3 billion in 1951 to $25.2 billion in 1965. This last figure is made up of about $14.8 billion indebtedness to foreign public authorities, and about $10.4 billion indebtedness to foreign commercial banks, private persons, and various organizations. Nearly the whole of this external debt of the United States ($24.1 billion) is short-term indebtedness, as against $1.1 billion long-term. On the other hand, U.S. credits abroad amount to $12.2 billion, of which $7.7 billion are short-term and $4.5 billion long-term. The following table sums up the external situation of the United States, in billions of dollars:

Table 44

	1951	1965
Gold reserves	24.3	14.7
External debt,	8.3	25.2
of which, short-term	7.7	24.1
of which, long-term	0.6	1.1
External credit,	1.4	12.2
of which, short-term	1.0	7.7
of which, long-term	0.4	4.5

"6. The international crisis thus consists essentially of this situation in which U.S. gold reserves, amounting to $14. 7 billion, are too small to cover the country's external debts, whether we take the gross figure—$25.2 billion, or only $24.1 billion for the short-term debts—or the net figure—$13.0 billion for total net indebtedness, or $16.4 billion for short-term net indebtedness.

"By way of the world monetary system we have thus arrived at this paradoxical situation that the whole world is lending considerable sums to the United States, mainly on a short-term basis. This situation, which has resulted from the strong position of the American economy at the end of the Second World War, is now all the more open to criticism because that strong position, while it has remained intact on the economic plane, has been gravely shaken on the financial and monetary plane, owing to the weakness of U.S. gold reserves in relation to its liabilities: hence the crisis.

"7. It is of little significance that the worsening in U.S. external finances is not due to a deficit in the trade balance, or in the total balance of goods and services (they both show a surplus). The worsening has its actual source in capital movements, including movements of publicly-owned capital. What signifies is that part of this capital has been retransferred by the world monetary system. If, as is currently agreed, the private investments of the United States abroad bring in a profit estimated at between 10 and 15 percent per year, while the short-term debts contracted by the U.S. through the monetary system cost that country only about 3 to 4 percent per year, this illustrates one of the aspects of the world monetary paradox, to the advantage of the United States, and correlatively, to the detriment of the rest of the world.

"But while it can be stated that there appears to be no real problem of shortage of international liquidities for the world as a whole, the situation is different where the underdeveloped countries are concerned."

Discussing the situation as regards Africa, Löbel writes:

"Taking the statistics for the twenty-eight African countries* for which we have a comparable series from 1960 onward, we perceive that their external reserves fell from $2.9 billion in 1960 to $2.2 billion in 1965. These are gross external reserves, that is, before deduction of short-term debts, these gross reserves including gold, foreign exchange and automatic drawing rights on the IMF (called 'reserve position' at the IMF, which is equivalent to these countries' 'gold tranche' at the IMF, that is, their gold subscription to this organization).

"Now, the imports of these countries increased substantially during the last five years, from $4 billion in 1960 to $5.9 billion in 1965. The movement in opposite directions of international liquidities and

* Algeria, Tunisia, Morocco, Libya, Egypt, Sudan, the thirteen states members of the franc area, Mali, Ghana, Nigeria, Ethiopia, Somalia, Congo-Kinshasa, the three states of former British East Africa.

imports caused the ratio of the former to the latter to decline from 72 percent in 1960 to 37 percent in 1965."

As regards the Asian countries, the gross reserves, so defined, of twelve non-oil-producing states* for which we have comparable statistics beginning in 1948 declined from $5.4 billion in 1948 to 3.7 in 1951 and 3.6 in 1966, whereas their imports rose from 4.4 to 5.1 and then to 9.5 billion for each of these dates. Asia, which possessed substantial reserves after the war, especially the Indian sterling balances (more than £1.2 billion for India and Pakistan), saw these reserves melt away—quickly between 1948 and 1951 (the ratio of reserves to imports fell from 122 percent to 73 percent), more slowly, but still steadily thereafter (the ratio stood at 38 percent in 1966). The reserves held by big countries like India and Pakistan are hardly sufficient to cover more than a quarter's imports. The fate of the reserves of smaller countries has been better, notably that of Thailand, whose reserves rose by $0.7 billion between 1948 and 1966. The reserves of the oil-producing countries of the Middle East increased greatly: those of Iran and Iraq from $0.3 billion in 1951 to 0.7 in 1966, while those of Kuwait (reserves of the Currency Board and of the Government) rose to $1.1 billion in 1966 and those of Saudi Arabia (Saudi Arabia Monetary Agency) to $0.8 billion.

As regards Latin America, my calculations based on sixteen countries for which we possess comparable statistics† show that the ratio of reserves to imports, which was about 50 percent in 1948 (reserves being $2.5 billion and imports $5.0 billion), remained the same down to 1953. By that date imports stood at $5.9 billion and reserves at $2.8 billion, Mexico having been responsible almost single-handed for effecting this improvement in reserves. From 1953 on, however, the situation was to get steadily worse. By 1962 reserves no longer exceeded $2.3 billion, while imports had risen to $7.9 billion (a ratio of reserves to imports of less than 30 percent). True, between 1962 and 1967 the situation seems to have improved, for while imports rose to $9.5 billion, reserves also rose, to $3.1 billion. This improvement came almost entirely from two sources: increase in the reserves of Venezuela, a

* Burma, Ceylon, India, Jordan, South Korea, Malaysia, Pakistan, Philippines, Syria, Taiwan, Thailand, Turkey. I have made these calculations on the basis of the IMF figures.

† Argentina, Bolivia, Brazil, Chile, Colombia, Costa Rica, Dominican Republic, Ecuador, Guatemala, Honduras, Mexico, Nicaragua, Peru, Salvador, Uruguay, Venezuela.

large oil-producer (increase of $254 million in five years), and, above all, the sharp increase in the reserves of Argentina (which rose from $132 million in 1966 to $625 million in 1967) as a result of that country's policy of deflation. If these two countries are excluded, however, the ratio of reserves to imports continued to fall, sinking from 30 percent in 1962 to 23 percent in 1967 (reserves $1.6 billion, imports $5.1 billion).

If we consider net instead of gross reserves we get similar results. Regarding Africa, Löbel writes: "It is interesting also to trace the evolution of the net external reserves of the African countries. In order to obtain this figure, we deduct from their international liquidities which, apart from the gold element in them, consist of these countries' claims payable at sight on the rest of the world (when you hold currency of a foreign country you have a claim on the latter), these countries' external liabilities payable at sight. Let it be kept in mind that what is involved is not long-term debt but only short-term debts that can, in principle, be called in at any moment. These external liabilities payable at sight include the debit balances of bilateral agreements (clearing accounts), when these sums were available. They amounted to about $0.5 billion in 1960, and increased to $0.8 billion in 1965. Thus, net external holdings which came to $2.4 (2.9-0.5) billion in 1960 had declined to $1.4 (2.2-0.8) billion in 1965. And the ratio of net external reserves to imports fell from 60 percent in 1960 to 23 percent in 1965." The same applies to Asia and Latin America, net reserves representing about two-thirds of gross reserves.

Continuing his analysis, Löbel writes: "It is usual to take into consideration also the conditional reserves, which are, in a sense, international liquidities that are at the country's disposal provided it obeys the rules laid down by whoever grants the liquid assets in question. Typical of these conditional international liquidities are drawing rights on the IMF . . . the blocks of credit at the disposal of the African countries, which stood at $0.2 billion in 1960, rose to $0.6 billion in 1965. This increase was due to the mass entry of the African states into the IMF. The fluctuations recorded for a certain number of these states (Ghana, Mali, Somalia, Sudan, Tunisia, UAR) resulted from the use by these states of the conditional credits granted by the IMF. They are conditional in that the IMF allows credit only on condition that the state receiving it takes steps to restore equilibrium to its external finances. By adding these conditional liquidities to the others, and relating the total to the volume of imports, we get higher percentages than those shown above, namely, 78 percent in 1960 and 47 percent in 1965.

"There are other conditional liquidities besides those just mentioned. The French-speaking countries whose national currencies enjoy France's unlimited guarantee (West Africa–BCEAO; Equatorial Africa–BCEAEC; Madagascar) possess, thanks to this guarantee, conditional reserves equivalent to the whole wealth of France. This, of course, is a hypothetical notion and not reducible to figures. It remains the fact that for this group of African countries the concept of international liquidities has not the same significance as for the others, owing to their special links with France. It may even be said that their effective external reserves, which are held almost entirely in the form of French francs, are conditional. In return for her guarantee, France has been able to ensure that the receiving countries practice a credit policy such that their issuing institutions have no need to resort to the automatic credit facilities that France is obliged to accord them by virtue of this guarantee. In the issuing institutions of Equatorial Africa and Madagascar, the fifty-fifty composition of the boards of directors enables the representatives of France to prevent, if need be, a relative decline in external reserves that they may consider too acute. The board of the BCEAO, the issuing institution for West Africa, has a majority made up of representatives of the African member-states. France's safeguards in this case are a statutory and classical type: an increase in the discounting rate and a limitation in the credit ceiling in the event of a relative decline in external reserves. In any event, should the African states seek to depart from these statutory rules, they could not do so without the consent of the French administrators.

"While it is therefore not possible to include in the external reserves of the African countries this type of very special external facilities, one ought, on the other hand, to take into consideration the conditional external reserves resulting from bilateral agreements. These reserves are conditional in the sense that, in most cases, they cannot be used for purchasing goods or services except in the country with which the agreement has been signed. Furthermore, the list of goods that can be covered by these bilateral transactions is often subject to restrictions. Insofar as triangular or multilateral compensations are provided for, or simply practiced de facto, the external reserves in question become less 'conditional' in the sense I am here giving to this expression. It remains the fact that, just as the bilateral swap arrangements between central banks in the advanced countries can serve to 'finance deficit spending' and reduce to some extent the 'need for reserves,' so do these agreements for payment by reciprocal credit play a similar role.

"The figures relating to these agreements have unfortunately not been published in continuous, comparable, and exhaustive form."

Eli Löbel has nevertheless provided a recapitulation of the bilateral payment agreements in Africa. Most of them—involving especially the UAR, Mali, Guinea, Ghana, and Morocco—have been signed with the countries of Eastern Europe, but a few have been made between African countries. The same is true as regards the bilateral agreements made by Asian countries (India, the Arab countries, etc.), which are very numerous, and some of the Latin American countries (apart from Cuba, of course).

"The bilateral agreements with payment facilities have certainly contributed to reorienting the external trade of the signatory countries in the direction of greater diversification as regards partners. However, the increase in imports coming from the group of countries that have bilateral agreements with the African countries is certainly due in large measure to the aid rendered by the latter to the African countries. The figures (quoted here) cover only the reciprocal commercial credits, which is quite logical in a study of international liquidities. In addition, numerous bilateral agreements on trade and payments provide that some goods and services that have especially 'appreciated' on the world markets shall be excluded from these agreements. Finally, it is current practice that even if the transactions proceed, in principle, by way of a bilateral account with a credit margin, part of the payment has to be effected, at the end of the transaction, in convertible currency. These two last clauses usually work to the advantage of the African countries.

"In fact, the statistical data that are of most interest in connection with a study of the monetary impact of the net work of bilateral payments are:

"a. the amounts of the reciprocal credit margins that the partners allow each other, and which constitute, in a way, 'conditional' international liquidities;

"b. the real movement of the bilateral accounts, which shows in whose favor the system has worked and answers the question whether it is the African countries that have lent, through the bilateral mechanism, to the rest of the world (mainly to the advanced countries), or vice versa. Since we are here studying monetary questions, the essential problem is indeed to discover who is lending to whom, on what conditions, and by what mechanism."

These observations, which are valid for all the underdeveloped countries, lead to a series of conclusions that apply with equal force to the countries of Asia and Latin America.

"The mechanism of bilateral payment agreements tends to compel the non-African partners, and in the first place the advanced ones, to grant automatic commercial credits to the African countries.

"All this shows that it is extremely difficult to state a view on the question whether there is a problem of external reserves for the African countries, despite the decline in the ratio of international liquidities to imports from 72 percent in 1960 to 37 percent in 1965. The ways of settling international transactions have evolved a great deal in recent years, in and for the continent of Africa. The make-up of the international transactions of these countries has also evolved, especially as regards imports. Strictly speaking, in order to form a judgment on the inadequacy of international liquidities, even in the context of a country fully integrated into the world monetary system, it would be necessary to compare these liquidities only with the imports that the African country concerned has to pay for out of its own funds (principally, private and public consumer goods and intermediate goods). Now, the share of equipment imported and financed from external resources has certainly increased in recent years. A detailed study of the statistics of external trade and of sources of finance is necessary. We also need to know the extent to which the official statistics include these imports of equipment goods financed from abroad. Finally, there must be taken into account, as an aggravating factor, the charges of the long-term external debt, which is the counterpart of external aid.[99]

"Nevertheless, it is possible to offer the following conclusions to this part of my survey:*

"The international monetary system contains, by its very nature, this distinctive feature, namely, that the African countries constantly lend to the advanced countries, by virtue of the fact that they hold the greater part of their reserves in foreign exchange, principally pounds sterling, French francs and U.S. dollars. And, in relation to what interests us here, it is of little significance whether external aid has or has not contributed to these reserves. Just as, on the world plane, the world at large, forming part of the international monetary system, lends through this system to the most powerful countries—the United States first and foremost—so, on the plane of Africa, the continent as a whole

* I.e., the survey by Löbel, art. cit.

lends to the advanced countries, primarily to the former colonizing powers. We have already seen that the amount of this loan came to 2.9 billions in 1960 and 2.2 billions in 1965 (in dollar units of account).

"In the setting of the international monetary system, and to the extent that the African countries form part of this system, as is the case, Africa has a problem as regards international liquidities, given that the ratio of external reserves to imports has dangerously declined in recent years.

"In contrast to what is happening on the world plane, where what is rather to be observed is a crisis of confidence in the reserve currencies, or in more political terms, resistance to the imposition of an international reserve currency issued on a national plane—that of the United States—the problem for Africa arises not so much at the level of the *composition* of external reserves as at that of their *total* amount. Whereas on the world plane it is the country which borrows on a short-term basis through the international monetary system (the United States) that is suffering from a deficit in its external balance, on the plane of Africa the deficit in external balances is found on the African side, that is, on the side of the lending countries.

"To continue the analogy, and due allowance being made for all differences, where the relations between Africa and the advanced countries are concerned, the nature of the problem is comparable to that which existed immediately after the war, when the countries that were lending through the international monetary system—the advanced countries as a whole—were also those that had a deficit in transactions with the countries to which the loans were made (primarily, the United States).

"Despite the recent tendency for a very marked fall in external reserves, their overall level still remains sufficiently high, at 37 percent, for Africa as a whole. Nevertheless, owing to the very uneven distribution of these reserves among the African countries, some of the latter possess 'surplus reserves' which they lend exclusively to the advanced countries, through the international monetary system. This is the case with Libya, Ethiopia, and, to a lesser extent, the ex-French West Africa group (BCEAO). Others, such as the UAR, Ghana, Tunisia, and Mali, are experiencing serious difficulties—still within the setting of an international monetary system—without being able to call on the facilities that exist elsewhere in Africa, or being able to do this only to a small extent. The currency unions (West Africa and Equatorial Africa) and payments agreements formed between African countries have brought about a certain degree of African solidarity.

"The system of reciprocal commercial credits, through a network of bilateral payment agreements, is, however, favorable to the African countries, on the purely monetary plane, which is all that concerns us here, in that it tends to bring about a situation in which the advanced countries lend to Africa. The system, though essentially bilateral, can be made multilateral to a considerable extent by means of clearing houses."

Summary of Conclusions

1. Monetary theory is the favored sphere of an economic science which, because it is given over to the major vice of economism, applies itself only to pseudo-problems. Money conceals the essential relations—the relations of production, scientific analysis of which requires that economic science be transcended in a total social science—and brings to the forefront relations that are superficial—exchange relations. This is why all non-Marxist monetary theories, old and new, are in the last analysis based on the false assumption of the quantity theory: the "refinements" of the Keynesian liquidity analysis and that of the neo-marginalists of Chicago have not succeeded in extricating monetary theory from this false basic framework. In reality the banking system fulfills only a passive function of adjusting the quantity of money to need. If it also fulfills an active function in the mechanism of accumulation (in the process of realizing surplus value), this is not suspected by current monetary theory.

2. Having been extended to the underdeveloped economies, monetary theory is said to have discovered there perverse monetary mechanisms of a special kind, which cause the supply of money to depend on the external balance and introduce specific disturbances into these economies. In fact, we have seen that the monetary mechanisms in the periphery of the system do not differ, despite appearances, from those operative at the center: the foreign-exchange standard fulfills these functions no worse than does the "managed national currency." The creation of a national currency confers on the local authorities no power of effective control so long as a country's inclusion in the world market is not challenged: even control of the exchange and of transfers does not prevent transmission to the periphery of fluctuations in the value of the dominant currencies of the center, nor does it prevent transmission to the periphery of the center's price structure. Money here constitutes the outward form of an essential relation of dominance, but it is not *responsible* for this relation.

3. The monetary problem therefore lies elsewhere, in the concrete working of the banking system of the preiphery. This is wholly at the service of the development of peripheral capitalism, whether foreign-owned or national, private or public—in other words, it exists in order to facilitate the growth of a capitalism ultimately based on the external market, which is the essential element in underdevelopment. Current theory turns its back on this real problem.

4. The world monetary system is an instrument in the service of the law of accumulation on a world scale: its function is to facilitate the centralizing of means of accumulation for the benefit of the center of the system (the advanced countries) and to the detriment of the periphery (the underdeveloped countries). This was so from the beginning, in the distant epoch of mercantile capitalism and of the integration of the periphery in formation into the world market of precious metals, and is so in our time, as is shown by study of the crisis of international liquidities from the standpoint of the Third World.

Chapter 4
The Role of the Periphery in the World Conjuncture

The cyclical form assumed by accumulation became very early on the subject of economic studies. For a long time, however, because current economic theory had made the "law of markets" an article of faith, the cause of the cycle was sought in money, in the psychology of the entrepreneur, or in the technical conditions of production: in other words, in what have been called external or independent variables. Such a view of the matter was inevitably superficial. The actual mechanism of the economic dynamic of the process was not investigated. This approach gave rise to a remarkable efflorescence of theories about the cycle. To be sure, Malthus, Sismondi, and then (and above all) Marx, were three impressive exceptions. But the validity of the law of markets was so little questioned that Marx's analyses remained uncomprehended, wrongly interpreted, and rejected without real examination by marginalist critics.

At the end of the last century, Wicksell was obliged to challenge the dogmatic status of the law of markets, as a result of his study of the causes of general price movements and his attempt to discover both the reasons why total supply and total demand can be unequal and the mechanisms that operate to readjust the balance between these two quantities. Myrdal, from 1930 onward, and Keynes, already from 1928 onward but especially after 1936, carried further this critique of the law of markets. Thereafter, study of the cycle could rise above psychological and monetary commonplaces, to engage in a more thorough study of the mechanisms that adjust the saving derived from total income to the investment required for economic growth.

Today it is generally accepted that the cycle manifests itself through an imbalance between saving and investment—which is only the form of a more fundamental imbalance between society's capacities to produce and to consume. Ironically, the rehabilitated theory of the cycle, which was to include certain analyses of Marx's, was worked out during and after the Second World War, that is, just when the mechanism of accumulation was losing its cyclical form. The monopolization of the capitalist economies, and the intervention by the state made possible, and even necessary, by this monopolization, which are typical of present-day capitalism, have done away with the regular cyclical pattern that was characteristic of the century extending from 1825 to 1940. The fluctuations of the conjuncture have replaced the elemental cycle. At the same time, because state policies operate in the spheres of money and finance, the theory of the conjuncture constitutes a step backward in comparison with that of the cycle: "monetarist" illusions arise again, and the empirical pragmatism of "income policies" prevails.

The theses of the 1940s, inspired by Keynes, on "stagnation," "overdevelopment," and "maturity," tended the same way as the theory of the cycle or of the conjuncture, in that they concentrated on analyzing the possible imbalance between saving and investment.

The crisis of 1929 had been so violent that all purely monetary, psychological, or technological theories, both of the cycle and of the long-term tendency, were inevitably discredited. Subsequent theories of growth attempted a deeper analysis of the dynamic mechanisms by which production, saving, and investment balanced each other along a more or less upward-moving line that extended over a century. The progress achieved by Western capitalism after the Second World War caused these theories of maturity, which had again come too late, to be forgotten. Theoretical study of the problems of the dynamic equilibrium of growth in our epoch, which is not only that of monopoly and state intervention but also that of a profound technical and scientific revolution, and of the great changes in political relationships that have marked the last forty years, is only now beginning.

In all these cases, theoretical research took the capitalist mode of production as its frame of argument. Study of the specific forms of the cycle and the conjuncture in the peripheral economies integrated into the world market has come later. This study has therefore lagged behind, and so its formulations are still often very superficial. Analysis of the "cycle" and of the conjuncture in the underdeveloped countries is still often closer to the old monetary and psychological theories than to modern theories of the dynamics of growth.

As for the study of international monetary mechanisms, this advanced both as a result of the new theoretical efforts arising from criticism of the quantity theory and also because of observation of the special situations engendered, after abandonment of the universal gold standard, by the monetary disorders of the 1930s. As the question of economic relations with the rest of the world is especially important for the countries of the periphery, investigators were to some degree led to conceive of the cycle and the conjuncture in these countries as merely dependent on fluctuations in the balance of payments. The determining role played by the developed countries of the center in these fluctuations, and, correlatively with this, the passive role played by the underdeveloped economies, were sufficient, at least in appearance, for those who renounced a specific analysis of the inner mechanisms of the dynamics of accumulation in the countries of the periphery. Accordingly, the cycle in the underdeveloped countries was spoken of as a phenomenon that was transmitted from outside by the movement of the balance of payments. Is it correct to speak in this connection of a cycle or a conjuncture (even "transmitted" ones), or of simultaneous fluctuations in supply and demand?

Finally, the whole of this problematic ignores the essential aspect of the matter where the periphery is concerned. For there *is* an international cycle, that is, a cycle of capitalist economy as a whole. The countries of the periphery have their place in this general movement, just as they have their place in the mechanism of accumulation on a world scale.

I will consider first the theory of the cycle and of the conjuncture in the capitalist mode of production, then that of the cycle and the conjuncture transmitted from the center to the periphery, and, finally, that of the conjuncture on the world scale and the representative roles of the center and the periphery in this conjuncture.

THE THEORY OF THE CYCLE AND OF THE CONJUNCTURE IN THE CAPITALIST MODE OF PRODUCTION

Capitalist development has not proceeded along a continuous and regular upward path without fluctuation. Rather, growth has followed a series of cyclical fluctuations accompanying a general upward tendency. Investment's capacity to create its own market accounts for the upward trend, while the relative regularity of the imbalance between the total volume of production and consumption, or of saving and investment, accounts for the sinuosity of the movement.

The possibility of continuous growth in a capitalist economy without an external outlet (meaning external to the capitalist mode of production) was proved by Marx, and then again by Lenin, arguing against Luxemburg. The saving derived from the income of a previous period can quite well be invested and so create its own market during a second period, deepening the capitalist market without "extending" it. In this sense, the "law of markets" is valid. This validity is, of course, only relative, in that the capitalist form of development implies a dissociation in time between the act of saving and the act of investment. Credit, and the momentary advantage constituted by the conquest of new external markets, facilitate the fundamental operation: the real investment of money saving. Real saving derived from income during the previous period must, before being invested, assume the form of money. The production of gold in the nineteenth century and the banking system today make possible the carrying out of this preliminary operation.

The essential claim made by the law of markets, namely, that investment of saving that has succeeded in assuming the money form through which it has to pass is effected automatically thanks to the finance market, is profoundly mistaken. Investment can create its own outlet—but it can also fail to create it. The special function of the theory of the cycle is, precisely, to determine the conditions under which investment does *not* succeed in creating its own outlet.

Money certainly confers flexibility on the economic system; but it also makes it possible for the system to break down owing to an imbalance between total supply and total demand. By enabling the act of saving to be separated from the act of investment, money creates the possibility of crises. Does this mean that it is ultimately responsible for them? If this were so, it would have to be explained why this imbalance is a periodic and not a chronic phenomenon, why it is periodically overcome, and, especially, why the phenomenon of the cycle is characteristic of the capitalist mode of production alone, and not of simple commodity economy.

Insofar as accumulation is inherent in the capitalist mode of production, in contrast to precapitalist modes, the problem of the cycle appears as a problem distinctive of capitalism. This is why, in economies in which, though they are precapitalist, the use of money is widespread, and where "liquidity preference," or, more precisely, preference for hoarding, forms a strong motive for saving, there is nevertheless no economic cycle or "endogenous" growth. What we observe in these modes of production is a slow growth dependent on demographic development and technical progress; but this growth takes place in a setting in which the functioning of economic mechanisms is profoundly different from that which is characteristic of capitalism. In these economies there is no dichotomy between saving and investment: investment is carried out simultaneously with saving. The motive for saving and the motive for investment are the same. The categories "saving" and "investment" are, indeed, distinctive of the capitalist mode of production. This is why the cycle remains unknown to all precapitalist economies.

If, then, the cycle is a monetary phenomenon in the capitalist mode of production, it is so no more and no less than all the other economic phenomena. This is why all theories of the cycle based fundamentally on a study of credit mechanisms deal only superficially with the problem. Money does not play an active role in exchange; the outlet—the market—has to exist already: money on its own cannot create it. All money can do is facilitate a transition in time. This is why all modern theories have ultimately adopted the view that the cycle was the specific form of development by which the regular imbalance between saving and investment was regularly overcome—the conception set out in Marx's analysis.

As, however, the cycle is grafted on to a more general tendency of long duration, analysis of the regular imbalances between supply and demand must be complemented by analysis of the long-term tendencies to equilibrium or disequilibrium between saving and investment. In this analysis post-Keynesian theory has allotted a more active role to money.

The "Pure" Theory of the Cycle: The Monetary Illusion.[1]

Keynes's analysis was described by Lutfalla as "metastatic." In *The General Theory,* the volume of investment determines, through the multiplier, the level of national income. The volume of this investment itself depends on two independent variables: the rate of interest, on the one hand, and the marginal efficiency of capital, on the other. There is no reaction from income on to investment—or, more precisely, investment is proportional only to income, not to the growth of income. The result is that the equilibrium which is established at the level of the national income at which saving and investment are equal is a stable equilibrium.

Klein schematized Keynes's analysis in *The General Theory* in a series of equivalent diagrams the most characteristic of which is certainly the following:

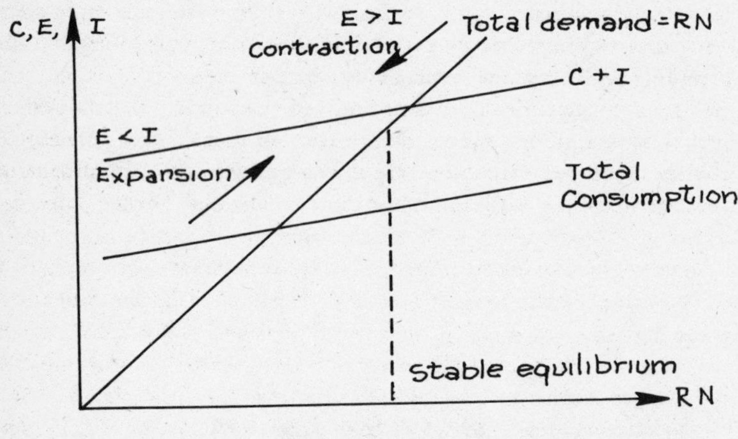

[FIGURE 6]

The General Theory does indeed contain a sketch for a theory of the cycle. A sudden fall in the marginal efficiency of capital is accompanied by a rise in the rate of interest, because it leads to an increase in liquidity preference. Investment suddenly slumps, and with it total demand: the national income shrinks to the point at which the amount of saving derived from this income no longer exceeds the diminished amount of investment. Basically, however, this analysis of Keynes's did not take the theory of the cycle any further than before, because the sudden fall in the efficiency of capital was left unexplained.

Keynes turns to human psychology, implying the impossibility of men entertaining indefinitely optimistic expectations of the future return on capital. It is clear, however, that if there were no objective reason why the level of this return should fall at a certain point in the development, such expectations would conform to a real state of affairs. At most, accidental historical causes might from time to time produce a psychological crisis, and so a contraction in total income. But the *regularity* of the cycle demands an explanation well rooted in the mechanism of the economic dynamic itself, not an explanation that is external to the phenomenon.

A bridge might then be thrown between this Keynesian conception and the theories of Lescure and Aftalion. The increase in production during a period of prosperity entails a general reduction in prices (because requirements are increasingly well satisfied), whereas costs of production increase, by virtue of the law of diminishing returns. One would, of course, still have to explain why it is possible for prices to fall while production is increasing, if incomes are increasing at the same time, and to reconcile the thesis of diminishing returns with the technical progress connected with the advance of industry. It appears that, on the contrary, the full utilization of production capacity during a period of prosperity makes it possible for costs to be reduced. Recourse to outside variables, whether psychological or technological, thus deprives the analysis found in *The General Theory* of a truly dynamic internal aspect.

It was by abandoning Keynes's assumption of stable values of the propensities to save and to invest that Kaldor gave the Keynesian analysis a real bearing on the cycle. Kaldor's schema assumes that propensity to invest is weak, both when the level of national income is low (owing to unused production capacity) and when it is high (owing to increasing building costs in a period of full employment). On the other hand, propensity to save will be high both when income is high and when it is low. The cycle is then clearly described by the schema outlined below:

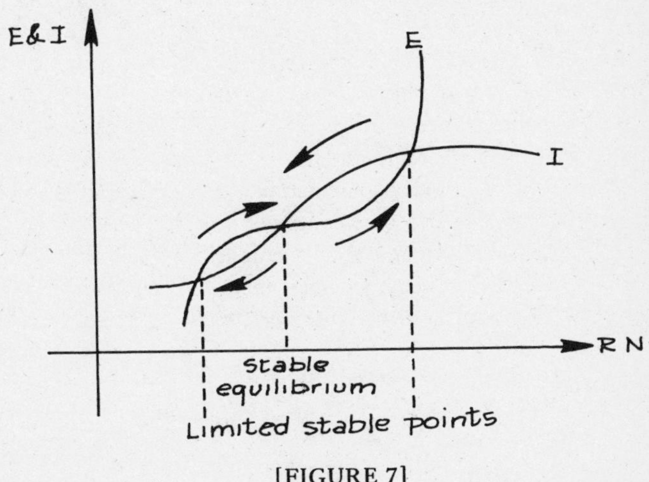

[FIGURE 7]

However, not only does Kaldor fail to explain why propensity to save is high when total income is low (logically, one would assume that this propensity rises regularly with income), but it still needs to be explained why the evolution of building costs can constitute a cause of downturn. So long as *any* labor remains unemployed, the possibility of additional construction is present. Let it not be argued that this work requires, in addition, to labor, raw material, machinery, power, etc., for it is precisely the utilizing of this labor that would make possible the production of all these goods necessitated by development. Recourse to this external factor—full employment—may well explain why the speed of development cannot be accelerated indefinitely, but it does not explain the downturn that has occurred historically when full employment was far from being realized when the crisis broke out.

Kalecki gives an equally rounded Keynesian description of the cycle: income determines investment, in the first place, and then, in its turn, investment determines income. But, in proportion as the level of total investment rises, the value of the propensity to invest diminishes. The cycle is then inevitable. Here, too, endogenous economic reasons are needed to explain the diminishing relation between propensity to invest and total investment. Unfortunately, it is to an exogenous psychological reason that Angell appeals: the gap between anticipations (form of the propensity to invest) and investment is due to the fact that the anticipations depend not on the investment itself but on its velocity. But why is this so?

Harrod has perhaps best analyzed the logical sequence linking all the factors that connect national income with investment, and vice versa. His description seems very complete. The imbalance in economic growth arises from the basic antinomy between actual saving, which essentially depends on the *level* of real incomes, and desirable saving, which essentially depends on the *rate of growth* of real income.

The balanced growth that is reflected in a stable value of G demands, in fact, stability in the ratio between investment ex post facto and the increase in the national income that it entails. The following equation shows that, if average propensity to save (s) is constant, growth (G) will not be regular unless the value of the coefficient (C) remains stable. In this equation:

$$GC = \frac{\Delta Y}{Y} \frac{I}{\Delta Y} = \frac{I}{Y} = \frac{S}{Y} = s$$

G represents rate of growth, C the capital-output ratio (the ratio between an investment and the income that this makes it possible to distribute), Y income, Δ Y increase in income, I investment, S saving, and s average propensity to save.

Now it is just the value of C, which measures the combined result of the phenomena of multiplication and acceleration, that cannot be constant, because acceleration (which Harrod calls "the Relation") calls for new investments that are *more than* proportionate to the increase in ultimate demand, and because, in its turn, the multiplier causes the increase in the volume of investment to bring about a more than proportionate increase in national income. In *The Trade Cycle* Harrod has constructed a model of the cycle by making the multiplier and the accelerator function in this way: an initial investment engenders an increase in national income, which itself determines a secondary investment (acceleration). The boom continues until the multiplier has lost magnitude sufficiently to annul the accelerating action of "the Relation." This is indeed what happens during prosperity, for propensity to consume diminishes in proportion as income increases, since the share of this income taken by profit increases faster than the share taken by wages.

Harrod is thus the writer who has come closest to Marx. There is no special chapter in *Capital* that brings together all the elements of a theory of the cycle, but nevertheless Marx revealed the essence of the process through his examination of the phenomenon known today as the multiplier and the accelerator. In the well-known chapter 21 of volume 2, which has caused so much ink to flow, Marx showed that it was possible for investment to create its own market, through the spreading and deepening of capitalism. In this same chapter, however, he analyzed the mechanisms by which what is today known as propensity to save was linked with total income. In proportion as income increases, so does the share taken by profit (the income essentially destined to saving and investment) relatively increase. This phenomenon corresponds perfectly to the diminution of the multiplier in Harrod's account. The multiplier is, indeed, merely the ratio between investment and that part of the income the distribution of which is connected with it which is spent (and so, the whole of this income less what is saved). When the volume of the national income increases, as the share taken by profits increases more rapidly than that taken by wages, the amount of expenditure engendered by a given investment diminishes. Accordingly, the ratio $\Delta Y / I$ falls.

If Marx considered that this diminution of the multiplier (in *Capital* this is expressed in the form of an imbalance between incomes spent, the source of ultimate demand, and production supplied, the source of this distribution of income) did not block development from the very outset, this was because he had previously analyzed what has subsequently become known as the accelerator.

When examining the replacement of fixed capital, he had suggested that an increase in ultimate demand might in some circumstances (those that are found together precisely at the end of a depression) engender a sudden investment which in turn, through the distribution of income it entailed, would create new possibilities for the investment of fixed capital. But Marx immediately denied that this phenomenon of replacement of fixed capital, analogous to the accelerator, owes its existence to the technical requirements of production: the need to build a machine that will last a long time, in order to respond to any increase, even a temporary one, in ultimate production. He ascribed this phenomenon to the most essential laws of the capitalist mode of production. An increase in demand, even a slight one, due to the opening up of a new market (internal, in the case of a demand connected with technical progress, or else external) at the end of the depression, causes a possible investment in fixed capital to seem a profitable prospect once again. All hoarded saving therefore suddenly moves into such investment. The new production engenders a distribution of income that makes this investment profitable indeed.

Marx thought that in a planned economy these constraints on technique would be reflected in fluctuations in the amount of reserve stocks, but that they would in no way determine the level of investment, which would be freed from its present dependence on immediate profitability.

Marx's analysis is in reality more complex in that, parallel with the analysis of the antinomy between multiplier and accelerator, it deals with the secondary problem of the cyclical fluctuations in wages, and is based on the theory of the tendency of the rate of profit to fall. During prosperity the amount of unemployment declines, real wages rise, and more intensive use is made of machinery. During depression an opposite movement takes place. These two mechanisms intensify the duration of both depression and prosperity. Dobb attaches an importance to this phenomenon, examined in volume I of *Capital,* which, in my opinion, is false to Marx's thinking.

The tendency of the rate of profit to fall shows itself by way of the cycle. At the beginning of the period of prosperity the countertendencies are stronger than the general tendency. At the end of this period the countertendencies are exhausted: the increase in the rate of surplus value which conceals the effect of the increase in the organic composition of capital comes to a stop. The rate of profit falls. But although this law manifests itself through the cycle, it is not the cause of the cycle. The cause lies in the combined working of the accelerator and the multiplier, that is, in the combined effect of the evolution of the capacity to consume, which does not increase as does the capacity to produce (owing to the increasing share taken by profit, and destined to saving) and of the immediate prospect of profitability which guides investment and which, thanks to the accelerator, delays the baneful effect of the diminution of the multiplier.

The Marxist formulations that come closest to this are those of Léon Sartre, Duret, and Paul Sweezy.

If Harrod arrives, in his study of the cycle, at a description that seems correct, this is because he breaks with the Keynesian analysis on an essential point. Harrod has linked propensity to invest directly to income, without going through the double intermediary of the marginal efficiency of capital and the rate of interest. He has thus taken as his starting point the antinomy between capacity to produce (linked with the saving derived from previous production) and capacity to consume (linked with the distribution of income that production engenders). He completely ignores interest, which he sensibly considers incapable of seriously affecting investment. He also ignores psychological phenomena, which he considers (again very sensibly) dependent, and not independent, variables.

Hicks—like Harrod a post-Keynesian, but much more attached to the traditional rate of interest—has sought to construct a bridge between Harrod's analysis based on the mechanism that links propensity to invest with total income, and the Keynesian analysis based on the antinomy between interest and the marginal efficiency of capital.

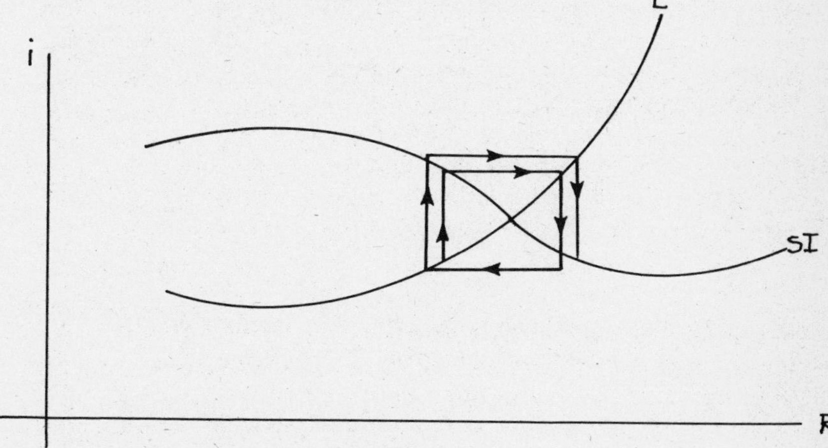

[FIGURE 8]

When he discusses the monetary aspect of the cycle, Hicks argues in Keynesian terms: a fall in the level of interest (if the marginal efficiency of capital remains stable) entails an increase in investment and thereby in income. But an increase in income increases the volume of money required for transactions. If the supply of money remains fixed, and if liquidity preference remains unchanged, the increase in the demand for money for transactions will in its turn bring about a rise in the level of interest. The development of these mechanisms, schematized by the two curves—liquidity (L) and saving-investment (SI)—is nothing other than the cycle.

Are we not here back in Hawtrey's utopia? An adequate injection of money, parallel to the increase in income, would make it possible, allowing for the stable level of liquidity preference, to satisfy the growing need for money for transactions without raising the rate of interest. Prosperity would be continuous, unless, of course, the efficiency of capital were to fall—something that would then have to be explained, as Harrod and Marx have explained it, by an imbalance between capacity to produce and capacity to consume.

Hicks clearly accepts the Keynesian hypothesis, namely that the point has been reached at which, whatever the amount of money injected, the rate of interest is already at such a low level that it cannot sink any further. No monetary measures can then avert the crisis. This analysis can be criticized for its inability to account for the cycle in the more general case, that of the nineteenth century, when the average rate of interest stood at a higher level than it does now. It can also be criticized for its static character: at best it might explain a permanent stagnation, but not the cycle. One could always go back to the marginal efficiency of capital: the cycle would then be seen as engendered by the independent movement of this variable, with the level of interest remaining at its lowest point throughout the whole process. Here, however, one would stumble over that very difficulty from which one had started out: what is the origin of the sinusoidal "psychological" movement?

The Theory of "Maturity"[2] and the Theory of the Surplus in Contemporary Monopoly Capitalism

For a century the cycle thus constituted the necessary form assumed by the development of capitalism. The cyclical imbalance between investment and saving was dictated by the very mechanism of growth, by the actual functioning of the accumulation of saving, which periodically becomes too plentiful in relation to possibilities for investment. The very outcome of cyclical development *is* growth. There is no superimposition of one phenomenon on another different in kind—the cycle on the one hand and the tendency over a century on the other. Construction of a pure model of the cycle in which the end point would be exactly the same as the starting point is a fantasy. The starting point of the movement—the sudden investment in fixed capital—is impossible to grasp apart from technical progress.

In the absence of the opening of an external market, only the introduction of new techniques enables the market to expand. The conquest of an external outlet does not resolve the imbalance between supply and demand on the world scale. It does, partly, resolve it for the economy that opens this outlet for itself; but only partly, for sooner or later it will have to import. This is why this solution is similar to that offered by credit. It is a temporary means only, and does not constitute the essential way of expanding the market.

In order to explain world recovery, all that remains is to analyze the effects of new techniques. This form of expansion of the market is absolutely necessary. In a period of depression the general stagnation furnishes a strong motive for technical improvements. The enterprise which succeeds in improving its technique recovers its lost profitability. The new method comes into general use and, since progress is usually expressed in more intense employment of machinery, a new demand appears inside the system. Production starts up again, thanks to the sudden investment called for by the construction of new machines. The subsequent development then takes cyclical form, but at the end of this movement the national income stands at a higher level. Something new has happened: a new technique has become general. Consequently, the volume of production has increased. The capitalist market is constantly expanding by this very means. *The cycle is thus inevitably a feature that runs all the way through an upward trend.* A stationary capitalism is pure fantasy. The long-term tendency, for its part, has no reality independent of the cycle: it is merely a useful abstraction derived by means of statistics and theoretical analysis.

Independent, however, of the mechanism of cyclical imbalance between saving and investment, there are real causes that tend to make these two overall quantities more or less easily "adjustable" in the long run. In this sense, the tendency over a century retains a reality of its own. But this reality manifests itself only through the cycle. If the imbalance between saving and investment becomes chronic, this is reflected, during the cycle, in a longer period of depression and a shorter period of prosperity. If, on the contrary, equilibrium becomes easier to achieve, for the real reasons mentioned, this is reflected, during the cycle, in a shorter period of depression and a longer one of prosperity.

What are these real reasons that cause equilibrium between saving and investment to be either easier or less easy?

Much was said in the years following the Great Crisis about "chronic stagnation," about the "maturity" of capitalism, and about "overdevelopment." Keynes discovered at that time the possibility of chronic underemployment. In fact, the analysis of maturity made from a Keynesian standpoint is ultimately monetary in character. I have already criticized the quantitativism that is the foundation of Keynes's thinking. It is therefore impossible to accept the thesis of the blocking of growth for purely monetary reasons. Even if one were to accept the thesis according to which, when the rate of interest has fallen to a certain level, no additional injection of money can cause this rate to fall any further, it would still be necessary to discover why the marginal efficiency of capital can be reduced to such a remarkable extent as to be comparable to the lowest rates of interest. If we say, with Keynes, that the low level of this marginal efficiency is due to the fact that past investments weigh heavily on expectations of profitability, which become chronically pessimistic, is this not an evasion of the difficulty?

This being so, must it be acknowledged that, since Ricardo and Marx, study of the development of capitalism has been given up for good? Ricardo thought he could prophesy a "stationary era" on the basis of diminishing returns operating on a historical scale.

Any conception of a stationary state is entirely alien to Marxism. The law of the tendency of the rate of profit to fall merely signifies that the contradiction between the capacity to produce and the capacity to consume must necessarily get worse and worse.

The ultimate reason for any overall imbalance remains the contradiction between the division of income between wages and profit, on the one hand (and thereby the division of income between consumption and saving), and, on the other, the division of production between equipment goods and consumer goods. A certain volume of ultimate production necessitates a certain volume of intermediate production. This latter quantity is merely a way of looking at the volume of investment required to produce the desired volume of ultimate goods. Harrod, by abandoning monetary analyses of the rate of interest and psychological analyses of the marginal efficiency of capital, in order to concentrate directly on the capital-output ratio, on the one hand—the ratio that measures the capital-intensity of production, that is, the ratio between the production of equipment goods and that of ultimate goods—and, on the other, on the division of total income between consumption and saving, comes remarkably close to Marx's analyses.

The relative strength of the century-long tendency to imbalance between total supply and total demand exerts a profound influence on the cycle. Superimposing the "pure" theory of the cycle (analysis of the multiplier and the accelerator) on the theory of the century-long tendency to imbalance between saving and investment reveals these effects clearly. Harrod's equation expressing the equivalence of actual saving, proportionate to income, and desired saving, proportionate to the growth of income, namely:

$$c(R_t - R_{t-1}) = sR_t$$

in which R_t represents income in time and R_{t-1} represents income in time $t - 1$—the first member the desired saving, the second the actual saving, s the propensity to save, and c a coefficient measuring the effects of the multiplier-accelerator tandem—can be expressed in the differential form:

$$c\frac{dR}{dt} = sR$$

Its integration gives:

$$R = R_o e^{\frac{s}{c}t}$$

This shows that income increases in geometric progression.

Insofar as the cyclical tendency to imbalance between the two quantities, actual saving and desired saving (investment), is aggravated by a tendency to imbalance over the century, the ratio of this geometrical progression is lower.

It appears that this is what actually happened. In the nineteenth century, the youth of capitalism, the huge possibilities offered by the break-up of the precapitalist economies were reflected in a tendency favorable to adjustment between saving and investment. Depressions were then less deep-going and less prolonged than the one that occurred in the 1930s.

But then, just at the very moment when the theory of "maturity" was forecasting the "end of capitalism" and "permanent stagnation"; at the very moment when a simplified version of Marxism was adopting, under the title the "general crisis of capitalism" (an apocalyptic vision alien to Marxism), the rate of growth of Western capitalism became faster and growth lost its cyclical character.

Marxist analysis brought up-to-date provides the only explanation of this development. We have already seen how Baran and Sweezy analyzed in new terms the "law of the increase of the surplus" and the forms of absorption of this surplus. At the same time, their theory of monopoly capitalism explains the disappearance of the cycle. The latter is due only to capitalism's inability to plan investment. Monopoly capitalism can do this, in a certain sense and within certain limits, given the active help of the state. As soon as capitalism escapes from the uncontrolled effects of acceleration, the cycle is no more, and all that remains is a conjuncture that is followed and observed, with the action taken by the state and the monopolies (the former in the service of the latter) to mitigate its fluctuations.

It may be asked why the cycle in its classical form should disappear, to give place to conjunctural oscillations that are close together, irregular, and of smaller amplitude, only after the Second World War, whereas the monopolies came into being at the end of the last century. It may also be asked why the crisis of the 1930s was the most violent in the history of capitalism, if the capitalism of the monopolies—which had already been formed—is capable of planning investment better than competitive capitalism.

The answer, I believe, must be sought in the way the international system functions. Monopolies are indeed able to plan investment up to a certain point: on condition, as we have seen, that the monetary system lends itself to this, which presumes that gold convertibility has been abandoned[3] and that the monetary authorities, together with the entire economic policy of the state, work in this direction. The "concerted economy"—planning, Western-style—means nothing more than awareness of this new possibility. Now, not only has this awareness, like all awareness, lagged behind reality, but also, and above all, the framework within which it can be translated into action is *national.* The international system has remained, long after the formation of the monopolies, regulated by automatic mechanisms. On the international plane, therefore, no "concertation" is possible. The attempt made by Great Britain (and France), after the war of 1914–1918, to re-establish the gold standard in external relations, although it had been finally abandoned internally, reflected this hiatus between the internal and the international orders. By making practically impossible any concerted internal policy, the international automatisms were, in my view, largely responsible for the exceptional gravity of the crisis of the 1930s. The monopolies, which make possible a conjunctural economic policy on the national plane, also cause the cycle to be aggravated if this policy is not followed. Keynes understood this. The maintenance of external controls after the Second World War was to make national economic policies effective for the first time; and it was at that time that there began, for example, France's "concerted planning."[4] The subsequent prosperity, with the Common Market and the liberalizing of external relations which has accompanied this prosperity, bring a serious threat to the effectiveness of these policies.

This is why the question of an international order is again on the agenda. The "order" that was established after the war, symbolized by the International Monetary Fund, is not order at all, for it remains based on confidence in automatic mechanisms. This confidence plays into the hands of the most powerful country, the United States. This is why, as I see it, a world economic policy is almost impossible. This flaw in the system expresses a new contradiction that has matured between the demands of the economic order, which can no longer be secured by national economic policy alone (because capitalism now has an essential *world* dimension) and the still national character of institutions and structures. If this contradiction is not overcome it is impossible to rule out the possibility of extremely grave "conjunctural accidents."

THE CONJUNCTURE OF THE SYSTEM IN THE PERIPHERY

Current economic theory is without the concept of social formation: it identifies the underdeveloped countries with the developed countries as they were at an earlier stage. To start with, then, current theory simply proceeds to apply to these young capitalist countries (in course of development) the schemas worked out for the capitalist mode of production, which are regarded as capable of explaining everything.

What results follow from the application of general considerations about the conjuncture and the century-long tendency to the underdeveloped economies? If the underdeveloped countries are regarded as countries where the capitalist economy is "young," where saving is always inadequate in comparison with possibilities, the conclusion should be that crises ought to be less serious in these countries than in the developed countries. The idea that the developed countries are marked by a chronic excess of saving, balanced by export of capital, whereas the underdeveloped ones are marked by a chronic inadequacy of saving, which makes possible continuous importing of capital, is a commonplace frequently encountered, though it is, strictly speaking, meaningless.

In identifying the underdeveloped countries with young capitalist economies similar to the European economies of the nineteenth century, one ought logically to conclude that the national income should grow at increasing rates in these countries, and that, consequently, consumption, as Harrod and Sweezy have shown, should progress at a pace that would ensure an increasing rate of investment.

In actual fact, fluctuations do seem to have been less pronounced in the underdeveloped countries *as a whole* than in the developed ones, at least in the twentieth century (meaning here fluctuations in total real income, not income in money terms). This does not exclude the possibility that they may have been more pronounced in *some* underdeveloped countries, as we shall see. But the growth of these countries' real income has not been fast but, on the contrary, slower than in the developed countries as a whole. Further, while the magnitude of conjunctural fluctuations is comparable in the different developed countries, there is a very wide scatter in the case of the underdeveloped ones. These fluctuations are the more violent the more closely the given country is integrated into the international market. In a well-integrated case they may be no less violent than in the most highly developed countries. This totally contradicts the theory which claims to apply mechanically to the underdeveloped countries a schema based on study of the capitalist economies.

The General Theory of the Cycle and of the Conjuncture Applied to the Underdeveloped Countries

The general theory of the cycle and of the conjuncture that has been outlined leads to the conclusion that fluctuations are more violent in proportion to the more pronounced character of the century-long tendency for saving to exceed investment. In the young capitalist economies in course of development, the oscillations of the cycle were therefore not very marked, but in economically mature countries they become increasingly so. The facts do seem to confirm the validity of this assumption.

When, however, we consider matters in the underdeveloped countries, it seems at first that the observations we are able to make refute the theoretical thesis worked out on the basis of the European model. What we find are cyclical oscillations that tend to become *bigger* than in the developed countries. Already in the nineteenth century the most advanced colonies—those that were best integrated into the international market—seemed to suffer worse during the depression periods than the European countries. In the 1930s, some countries of Asia, Africa, and Latin American again experienced difficulties at least as serious as those that shook the capitalist countries. Yet the degree of disturbance suffered in their cases cannot be attributed, as in those of the advanced economies, to "overdevelopment."

Nevertheless, an attempt has been made to account for the gravity of the fluctuations in the underdeveloped economies on the basis of theoretical generalities that are alleged to be universally valid.[5] Keynes noted that when propensity to consume is high, the multiplier mechanism is such that slight variations in investment give rise to very marked fluctuations in income and employment. In the underdeveloped economies, in which saving is relatively slight, the sinusoidal curve ought therefore to show greater width than in the developed economies, which enjoy greater stability (although the average level of employment may be lower).

This thesis, which is very popular in post-Keynesian writing because it seems to explain a fact, lies open to criticism. The Keynesian mechanism of the multiplier is not universally applicable. It is valid only in the mature economies, where saving is chronically greater than investment, and where, consequently, forced hoarding (which cannot be sterilized by an adequate monetary policy) results in a certain stagnation relative to possibilites of development. In this case, and in this alone, calculation of the value of the multiplier has meaning. It enables us to compare the overdeveloped countries one with another. Those that have attained a relatively more advanced degree of maturity (and where, therefore, propensity to consume is weakest) enjoy greater stability (because the value of the multiplier is lower) at a lower average level of activity: stagnation is quasi-chronic in these countries. But when the volume of saving does *not* tend to be chronically greater than that of investment, the Keynesian analysis ceases to be valid. In these conditions it is pointless to calculate the value of the multiplier because, whatever the level of saving, over the average duration of a cycle, investment is equal to it. The law of markets recovers its validity, over this average duration: here it is supply that limits demand, and not the other way round. The level of average propensity to consume is therefore incapable of accounting for the comparative degree of stability of these economies.

Closer attention to the facts leads one to reject this mechanistic application of the Keynesian schema to the underdeveloped countries. Actually, in nineteenth-century Europe propensity to consume was greater than it is today, and yet depression was less pronounced than it was to be in the 1930s. The fact is that the seriousness of the fluctuations depends not on the value of saving (in other words, the "size" of propensity to consume) but on its size in relation to profitable investment, which itself depends on the level of profits.

Subsequent rejection of the application of the same schema to developed and underdeveloped countries alike has led economic theory to take a different attitude. It is said that an independent cycle does not exist in the underdeveloped economies. These "dualistic" economies are said to be marked by juxtaposition of two sectors that differ in their economic nature. The native sector makes little use of money. It consists of a "wants" economy which is quite free from capitalist development through the investment of previously accumulated saving. The capitalist sector consists of a series of enterprises, usually foreign-owned, which are not integrated with one another, each of them being directly linked with the dominant capitalist economy. In this profit economy of a very special type, fluctuations are not engendered by mechanisms of the internal dynamic of development, but are transmitted by the fluctuations of external demand. The rate of development of the capitalist enterprises in these countries is itself dictated by the pace of the cycle in the dominant countries, to a much greater extent than by the internal requirements of accumulation in the economy in which the foreign firm is located.

In fact, the so-called dualism of the underdeveloped countries does not consist of simple juxtaposition of two sectors that turn their backs on each other: it is not a matter of a geographical extension of a capitalist country which possesses a few enterprises on foreign soil. In most cases an original local economy exists: an agriculture producing for export derives its income from external demand. In turn, this income impinges on the market for imports and on the local market. Through this channel an internal movement may occur. The cycle of external demand should thus engender in the underdeveloped economy a cycle of its own, even though this will be transmitted rather than autonomous.

The Theories of Transmitted Conjuncture

Haberler and the monetary transmission of the cycle through the balance of payments. Haberler argues in favor of three propositions, basing the distinctions he makes on the monetary systems of the partners brought into relationship.[6]

First of all, in the case in which two countries which are brought into contact with each other are subject to the gold-standard system, the transmission of fluctuations from one country to the other is perfectly symmetrical. This transmission reduces the intensity of the fluctuations in the originating countries by spreading wider the area over which the cycle exerts its effects. In a period of prosperity in country A, its imports develop more rapidly than its exports. This country has to face a drain of gold that reduces inflationary tendencies within it, while reinforcing them in country B.

Second, if country B has adopted the foreign-exchange standard, the cycle will not be propagated from the dominated country to the dominant one, but in the opposite direction this effect is reinforced. In a period of prosperity in the country that is dominated monetarily, this country pays for the deficit in its balance of payments in the currency of country A. The volume of credit exerts no stimulating influence in the dominant country because no transfer of gold, the ultimate form of money, has taken place. On the other hand, the natural development of prosperity in the dominant economy is not checked by a drain of gold, whereas the influx of foreign currency into the dominated country is reflected in a real increase in advances of credit.

Third, when each of the two countries has an independent managed currency, cyclical fluctuations are no longer transmitted at all. A boom in one of the two economies in contact entails a disturbance in the balance of payments which, since it cannot be adjusted by an export of gold or foreign currency, has to be adjusted by an alteration in the rate of exchange. This adjustment reduces excessive imports to the level of possible exports.

This is certainly a narrowly monetarist analysis.

In the nineteenth century, colonies and metropolitan countries used the same metallic currency. Yet the direction in which the cyclical movement was transmitted seems always to have been from metropolis to colony. On the other hand, the intensity of the fluctuations was not always greater in the originating country than in the dominated one. However, the adoption, during the twentieth century, of the foreign-exchange standard by the majority of the underdeveloped countries would certainly explain, from Haberler's point of view, the recent worsening of economic oscillations in the dominated country.

In fact, the *rapporteur* of the League of Nations used a mechanistic quantity-theory method without any scientific value. In his analysis, fluctuations in the volume of credit are mechanically linked with the volume of ultimate reserves of the monetary system, in gold or foreign exchange. Everything happens as though the ratio of money in circulation to reserves in ultimate money were rigid. In reality this is not so, for the ratio itself undergoes cyclical oscillation.

The post-Keynesians and the foreign-trade multiplier. Although this mechanistic outlook has generally been abandoned, the tendency to see in the economic cycle of the underdeveloped countries an original phenomenon, intrinsically cyclical although having its source outside the given country, an external phenomenon transmitted by the balance of payments, is still a tenacious one.[7] Haberler's thesis is now expressed not indirectly, through monetary quantitativism, but directly. It is said that the fluctuations are trasmitted *not* through the channel of the flow of gold and foreign exchange that they engender, but directly, through the channel of commodity movements. The cyclical oscillations in the dominant countries are reflected, in fact, in a real movement of exports and imports. Prosperity in some, by resulting in imports that are greater than exports, directly fosters the development in others of the inflationary tendencies characteristic of economic euphoria. The deficit in the balance is settled by way of foreign credits alone. No movement of gold or foreign exchange is necessary. No alteration in the rate of exchange takes place. Under these conditions, the quantity-theory mechanism does not function.

This new way of looking at the matter has enjoyed a great vogue, thanks to the elaborated form given to it by the theory of the foreign-trade multiplier. C. Clark's study of the Australian cycle is typical. The theory of the foreign-trade multiplier declares that a favorable trade balance (a surplus of exports) plays the same role as an investment: it sets going a process of induced growth. Thus, the deficit in the balance of the developed countries during a period of prosperity—that is, the surplus in the balance of the underdeveloped countries—is said to induce in these latter countries phenomena of "secondary" growth. Conversely, in a period of depression, the unfavorable trade balance of the underdeveloped countries brings about depression. There is indeed a cycle of the underdeveloped countries—a transmitted one, in the sense that its source is the cycle in other countries, but a true cycle nevertheless, with the trade balance playing exactly the same role as is played by investment elsewhere.

However, the theory of the foreign-trade multiplier is not valid for the underdeveloped countries—for the same reasons that cause the Keynesian theory of the multiplier, from which it is derived, to be false in the context of underdevelopment. A favorable trade balance has beneficial effects only if saving tends to be superabundant, in a context of overdevelopment. The surplus of exports then engenders a secondary demand, which creates its own supply. Apart from this, the theory lacks validity, and neither a favorable nor an unfavorable trade balance entails secondary effects.

Moreover, the state of the conjuncture has no absolutely definite effect on the trade balance. Prosperity brings about a parallel growth of exports and imports. Its effect on the balance varies: sometimes it causes improvement, at other times deterioration. While it is true that the balance of payments (not that of goods) tends to be favorable for the developed countries in a depression period, this is due to the cessation of the export of capital far more than to improvement in the trade balance. Similarly, for the underdeveloped countries, it is this cessation of the flow of capital, not the worsening of the trade balance, that causes the balance of external payments to show a deficit. It is for this reason that the alteration in the twentieth century, between a deficit balance and a surplus balance, depending on the state of the conjuncture, did not exist in the nineteenth century—that is, before the movement of capital had assumed the dimensions to which it later grew. Even at that time, however, it was never observed that a period of prosperity in Europe produced, through the appearance of a favorable balance for Europe (a "perverse" effect, but a frequent one), a depression elsewhere—or vice versa.

The nonexistence of a distinct cycle in the underdeveloped countries. The most general criticism to be made of all the theories of the transmitted cycle is that they have overlooked the fundamentally different character of the structures that are typical of the developed and the underdeveloped countries. When this essential reality is taken account of, a schema emerges that is profoundly different from those of Haberler and Clark.

The economic oscillations experienced by the underdeveloped countries are then seen to bear very little resemblance to a true cycle. When the conjuncture in the developed countries is favorable, the level of exports from the underdeveloped countries goes up. The incomes that benefit first and foremost in these countries consist mainly of ground-rent. Most of the profits of capitalist enterprises, which we will assume to be foreign-owned, are exported, and wages remain fairly stable. The elasticity of the rents drawn by the landowners, however, enables *this* income to absorb the supplement engendered by the increased price and volume of exports of agricultural produce. The small peasants also benefit to some extent from this prosperity (though less than the landowners, because they have to deal through intermediaries, merchants who absorb part of the extra income). This prosperity of ground-rents is reflected in a marked increase in imports of luxury goods, and a noticeable increase in imports of cheap manufactured goods that the small peasants buy.

Conversely, if the conjuncture is unfavorable in the developed countries, primary products are sold in smaller quantities and at lower prices. The whole economy of the underdeveloped countries suffers from this, but wages, being relatively rigid, are less affected than rents. As for profits, the volume of which also diminishes, they are still, by definition, exported, and therefore do not affect the situation in the underdeveloped countries. If, however, exports have declined, and with them ground-rents, then imports of luxury goods and goods for consumption by the peasantry will soon suffer the same fate.

The cycle therefore does not seem in the least to have been transmitted by way of the balance of payments. The latter continues to be kept even, in periods of prosperity and depression alike, since exports, rents, and imports all vary together in the same direction. Haberler's analysis, which might have some validity in relations among countries with a central capitalist structure (without prejudice to fundamental criticism of this theory on the grounds of its dependence on the formalism of quantitativist monetary relations), has none in the case of relations between countries with such profoundly different structures as those of the center and the periphery.

Can we at least say that the cycle is transmitted directly through the channel of fluctuations in the volume of exchanges? We cannot. The special role of the analysis of the foreign-trade multiplier is to show that the "primary" fluctuations of the volume of external exchanges (fluctuations due to the state of the conjuncture abroad, constituting an independent factor about which nothing can be done) give rise to "secondary" internal fluctuations. This theory serves to analyze the effects of the cycle of external exchanges on the internal mechanism of accumulation. Here, however, we have nothing of that kind. It is in this sense that there is no true cycle in the underdeveloped economies.

The fact that rent constitutes the elastic income in the underdeveloped economies means, quite simply, that the multiplier does not function there. The increased purchasing-power available in the underdeveloped country as a result of the increase in the value of exports is not mainly spent and partly saved—it is spent *in its entirety*. The increased demand does not give rise to induced investments. The accelerator is transferred abroad, as I have shown; the investments take place abroad and not in the underdeveloped economy. There is thus no true cycle, not even a "transmitted" one, but only a sinusoidal oscillation of total income.

Economic writing has emphasized heavily (and in my opinion wrongly) the negative effects of this "conjunctural instability" of the underdeveloped economies. This thesis of the negative effects of instability is based on the following three arguments:

1. In itself, the cyclical dependence of total local income on the conjuncture abroad means that, with every depression in the dominant economy, the capacity of the underdeveloped countries to save goes down, without this being necessitated by any internal mechanism of the economy.[8]

The instability of the export markets of the underdeveloped countries, it is said, has very harmful effects on local saving. The variations in the volume of exports from these countries are not compensated by the inverse variations in their prices. While foodstuffs like tea, coffee, cocoa, sugar, etc.—consumption of which is relatively stable in the developed countries—enjoy relatively rigid prices, this is not so in the case of industrial raw materials—minerals, textile fibres, rubber, etc.—variations in the prices of which tend rather to aggravate the fluctuations in the volume of exports. Depression in the developed world is therefore reflected in a serious loss for the underdeveloped economies.

This problem has been studied in detail by a commission of the United Nations. The published summary of their conclusions shows that fluctuations in the annual unit values of prices for primary products exported have varied from 5 to 21 percent, depending on the products. The magnitude of these fluctuations has grown in successive stages during three periods of peace: 11 percent per year in 1901–13, 13–15 percent in 1920–39, and 18 percent in 1946–50. Cyclical fluctuations of prices have averaged 27 percent. Annual fluctuations in the volume of exports averaged 19 percent. Since 1945 they have been 24 percent. Cyclical fluctuations in the volume of exports have been, on average, of the same magnitude as those of prices. Finally, fluctuations in receipts from exports (cumulative effects of fluctuations in prices and in volume) have amounted to 22 percent, both annually and cyclically. This magnitude gets bigger as time goes by: 19 percent in 1901–13, 21 percent in 1920–39, and 30 percent in 1946–50. The variations in real values (obtained by dividing these variations in nominal values by the index of prices in British manufactured exports) show that the variations in real value (13.5 percent for the period 1901–50) have been the same as the variations in nominal values (13.7 percent).

2. These flucutations in the value of exports are not compensated by equal and inverse fluctuations in the movement of capital. On the contrary, these oscillations reinforce the first-mentioned ones. It is during periods of depression that the least foreign capital flows in. While, therefore, the fluctuations in the total value of exports are compensated by equal fluctuations in imports (connected with the movement of ground rent), the oscillations in the movement of capital, which reinforce the terms of the trade balance, periodically upset the balance of external payments, in one direction or the other. True, the outward movement of the exported profits of foreign capital reduces this disturbance. In fact, it is in a period of prosperity, when foreign capital is flowing in, that the volume of profits exported is also greatest. However, the magnitude of the fluctuation in capital movements often proves greater than that in the movement of profits. Normally, moreover, fluctuations in imports are less great than those in exports, because the "flywheel" of hoarding mitigates the intensity of oscillations in consumption by the rich, just as that of reserve saving does in relation to consumption by the peasantry.

Does this cyclical disequilibrium in the external balance of the underdeveloped countries, first one way and then another, bring us back to Haberler's thesis? Not at all, since this movement of the external balance is not here the cause of the transmission of the cycle, but, on the contrary, a *consequence* of it.

Nevertheless, it is said, this imbalance—induced, not inducing—favors, under the conditions of the underdeveloped countries, a permanent tendency for prices to rise. This increase in prices has, under these conditions, a harmful effect on the formation of local saving. During periods of prosperity, the surplus in the external balance, paid for by foreigners with their own currency, facilitates excessive issue of credit. This credit, being unable to affect production, the volume of which is determined more by the inflow of foreign capital destined for long-term real investment than by that of short-term capital, will go to feed speculative circuits that will bring about artificial price increases. The banks, to be sure, cannot feed speculation unless this continues to be profitable to those who engage in it. This is why all the foreign short-term capital that enters the country via the surplus in the balance of payments is not poured back into the economic circuit. A considerable part of it is "sterilized." This sterilization is expressed in an increase of the ratio of ultimate monetary reserves to credits allowed. During depression periods, however, the external deficit presses heavily on the rate of exchange. Clearly, when the underdeveloped country is completely integrated as regards money, there is no alteration in a rate of exchange that does not in fact exist. The balance of payments can go on being negative for an indefinite time without any mechanism operating to affect the price level. When, however, the underdeveloped country possesses an independent currency, devaluation eventually has to be introduced. This devaluation will generally bring about a general increase in prices, not only because imported goods cost the economy more but also because foreign currency constitutes the backing for local currency. But this devaluation does not, in general, restore external equilibrium, because the price elasticities of the exports and imports of the underdeveloped countries are such that "perverse" effects are more to be feared from devaluation than "normal" corrective effects are to be hoped for.

3. The consequences that the transmission of fluctuations has for accumulation in the underdeveloped countries are all the more serious because no anti-cyclical policy can be pursued in these conditions.[9] The heart of an anti-cyclical policy (leaving aside here the question of the effectiveness of such a policy) is the exertion of influence on investment, the "dynamic" factor par excellence. In the underdeveloped countries, it is said, the dynamic factor is external trade. Now, exports cannot be regulated, because they depend not on the situation in the underdeveloped countries but on that in the developed ones. Further, it is not possible to make up for the oscillations in exports by a policy of major public works—first, because the depression does not release many productive forces in the underdeveloped countries, and it is not easy to transfer agricultural labor, engaged in producing primary products for export, to industrial tasks, and second, because such works necessitate large-scale imports of equipment, and the balance of payments would therefore be subject to too serious a deficit. These two reasons, it is said, render any anti-cyclical policy difficult and even ineffective under conditions of underdevelopment. Prebisch attributes the frustration of such a policy to the fact that large-scale public works, by distributing

income, would (owing to the high propensity to import) cause too serious a deficit in the external balance, since exports would remain held down at a very low level.

In reality, if the transfer of labor power from export agriculture to the public works sector were possible, no difficulty need be feared from that quarter. It would not be ground-rent, the connection between which and luxury imports is obvious (and which is reflected in the high propensity to import), that would annex the increased income. Wages and profits would gain from it, in the first place. It is true that an increased need to import equipment would then be felt. But part of the labor released from export agriculture could be devoted to producing this equipment locally. The country would then be launched, on the pretext of combating the cycle, on a real policy of conscious and planned independent development.

In the case where, to some extent, recourse was had to the external market, the cycle could then be transmitted in the opposite direction, from the underdeveloped country in course of development to the dominant country. The new activity in the underdeveloped country would be reflected in an increased demand for equipment produced in the developed countries, and prosperity would thus be spread to these countries. However, development taking place within the framework of international integration cannot lead to reversing the direction of the transmission of fluctuations. The point is that, so long as this framework is retained, industrialization of the underdeveloped countries remains bound up with the export of capital from the developed countries. It therefore takes place only during periods of prosperity in the latter. The underdeveloped countries import equipment only during those periods—at the very time when these countries can find markets for their exports. Demand for equipment cannot constitute a cause of transmission of prosperity from the underdeveloped countries to the developed ones.

THE CONJUNCTURE AS A WORLD PHENOMENON: THE ROLES OF THE CENTER AND THE PERIPHERY

Although a mechanistic application of the theory of the cycle and of the conjuncture to the underdeveloped countries turns out to be unhelpful, because the conjuncture is not, in these countries, an independent phenomenon, it nevertheless remains true that the view according to which the conjuncture appears a transmitted phenomenon, in which the underdeveloped countries play a purely passive role, is superficial. In reality, the conjuncture is not a phenomenon distinctive of the developed countries taken separately, and transmitted by them to the underdeveloped ones, but a phenomenon that is bound up with the actual functioning of capitalism on the world scale. The underdeveloped countries form an integral part of this world capitalist market. There is therefore only one true cycle, the world cycle in which the underdeveloped countries play an active role but one that is different from that played by the capitalist economies of the developed center.

A Short History of the World Conjuncture

Analysis of the respective roles played by center and periphery in the unfolding of the cycle, or, more generally, of the oscillations of the conjuncture, has to begin with observation of how external trade and the other elements in the balance of payments react to fluctuations in the level of activity. Although facts concerning this aspect of the underdeveloped economies are difficult to amass and to interpret, I have tried to trace the history of the international conjuncture, with special emphasis on relations between the center and the periphery in the course of this history.[10]

As regards the cyclical behavior of external trade, this seems to have been different during the nineteenth century from what it was during the crisis of the 1930s and during the "minor" fluctuations since the Second World War.

During the crisis of the 1930s, fluctuations in the trade of the periphery were more extensive than those in the center. The same applies to the post-1945 period. The "minor recessions" of 1949–50, 1954, 1958, and 1961 were more pronounced in the trade of the underdeveloped countries than in that of the developed centers.[11] For the world as a whole, the value of exports of manufactured goods fell from $12.4 billion in 1921–29 to $5.13 billion in 1931–35, a fall of 58 percent. In constant prices of 1913 the fall was less: from 7.688 to 5.591, which means that the volume of these exports fell by 27 percent. As for imports of these products, they were likewise reduced in value by 58 percent and in quantity by 26 percent. Total exports of primary products, however, fell in value by 58 percent (from $19.12

billion to $7.93 billion) and in volume by only 5 percent (from 13.447 to 12.767, in 1913 prices).

If we identify the developed countries with the exporters of manufactures and the underdeveloped countries with the exporters of primary products, we observe a substantial worsening in the terms of trade for the latter during the period of depression, with a fall in their import capacity, while the trade balance of the developed countries is comparatively stable, because most of their trade is done with other industrial countries, and consequently the total volume and value of their imports and exports vary in the same direction and in similar proportions. If, therefore, the terms of trade improve for the developed countries, this can occur only because exchanges take place between these countries and the underdeveloped ones, not because of relations among the developed countries themselves. Similarly, if the trade balance of these countries tends to improve, this is due to a worsening of the trade balance of the underdeveloped countries, resulting from a fall in their exports greater than the fall in their imports, and not to exchanges among developed countries.

The fact that the decline in the exports of the underdeveloped countries is greater than the decline in their imports is easily explained, through the effect of dishoarding in periods of difficult conjuncture. It remains secondary, however, in relation to the general movement, which is marked by a parallel fall in exports and imports, in not very different proportions.

Thus, when prosperity gives way to depression (the converse happens when depression gives way to prosperity), the trade balance of the developed countries, taken as a whole, improves, and that of the underdeveloped countries worsens. Further, the magnitude of the variation in the trade balance of the underdeveloped countries is usually greater than in the developed ones.

The experience of the nineteenth century shows rather different results, at least as regards the comparative experiences of the United States, Great Britain, France, and Egypt in connection with the four cycles covering the period 1880–1914 (recessions of 1886, 1894, 1901, and 1908).[12]

For Great Britain, during these cycles the decline in the value of exports was 15 percent, 17 percent, 2 percent and 12 percent, respectively, giving an average of 11 percent. The decline in the value of imports was 18 percent, 5 percent, 0 and 8 percent, thus appearing smaller (an average of 8 percent). Only twice did the volume of exports decline (once by 6 percent and once by 8 percent), and on the other two occasions it increased. Similarly, on only two occasions did the volume of imports decline (once by 4 percent and once by 3 percent). As for the terms of trade, not only did they improve continuously throughout the period, they seem to have improved in each depression. It is impossible to say, however, whether this improvement resulted from the general trend or from the conjuncture.

The experience of France leads to similar conclusions. Total value of exports declined successively by 11 percent, 19 percent, 2 percent and 9 percent (average, 10 percent), while that of imports declined by 17 percent, 14.6 percent, and 9 percent, in other words, in very much the same way, though slightly less (average, 9 percent). On three occasions the volume of exports fell: once by 3 percent, the second time by 13 percent, the third time by 3 percent (average, 5 percent). The volume of imports fell only once, by 8 percent. Here, too, the terms of trade improve in every crisis. The result is all the more convincing because over the whole period the terms of trade very slightly worsened.

The experience of the United States in 1907–08 was no different. The value of exports declined slightly (1 percent), that of imports to a greater extent (16 percent). The volume of exports rose, that of imports fell by 5 percent, and the terms of trade improved.

One would thus be tempted to draw the following conclusions: (1) the fluctuations in the value of foreign trade were fairly slight, and not to be compared to those of the period 1929–1932; (2) the slightness of these fluctuations was due both to the relative stability of prices and to the slightness of the fluctuations in the quantities exchanged. Very often, indeed, the volume of exports increased during the depression, which suggests that the crisis was to some extent overcome by conquest of new outlets abroad.

If we now consider the progress of the cycle in the underdeveloped countries—for example, Egypt between 1880 and 1914—we see that the phenomena to be observed here are typical: the fluctuations in the price of exports, while less violent than in the twentieth century, are nevertheless much greater than those affecting the exports of the industrial countries: 33 percent, 10 percent, and 20 percent (an average of 20 percent), as against, respectively, 13 percent, 12.5 percent, and 4 percent (an average of 9 percent), for the price of British exports. As for the total value of exports, it falls only once (by 30 percent) and increases three times (by 6 percent, 1 percent, and 1 percent). This is due to the obvious upward trend in the quantities exported. Despite the crisis and the worsening of the terms of trade, the upward trend in the volume of exports is so strong that the volume of imports increases too.

From these comparative experiences one would be tempted to conclude that the pattern is quite different from that of the twentieth century. Here we have the impression that each crisis at the center is overcome, in part, by the conquest of fresh outlets abroad, in the colonies. The parallel decline in the imports of the developed countries gives us reason to think that the outlets are not to be found in *those* countries. On the other hand, the increase in the imports of the underdeveloped countries during crises shows that the precapitalist markets are broken into all the faster during a depression period. As the expansion of exports follows that of imports, we rediscover the upward trend of the external trade of the underdeveloped countries, which proceeds faster than that of the developed countries.

Data for the earlier part of the century, between 1830 and 1880, are harder to come by, and are practically nonexistent for the underdeveloped countries.[13]

For Great Britain, during the crises of 1857, 1866, and 1875, the total value of exports declined successively by 5 percent, 5 percent, and 9 percent, that of imports by 12 percent, 6 percent, and 0. These figures, lower than those of the period 1880–1914, are accounted for by the competition that began to manifest itself after 1880 (France, Germany, the United States), depriving Britain of her privileged position on the world market. However, the fact that, from that period onward, trade with, and especially exports to, the colonies suffered less from crises than did trade with foreign countries shows the role played by the colonies in the mechanism of recovery. Imports from foreign countries fell by 11 percent, those from the colonies by 16 percent; exports to foreign countries fell by 8 percent, those to the colonies increased by 6 percent.

In the case of France, examination of the crises of 1825, 1836, 1847, 1857, 1866, and 1875 gives revealing results. The value of exports fell successively by 11 percent, 16 percent, 19 percent, 16 percent, 12 percent, and 18 percent (average 15 percent) between 1828 and 1830, 1836 and 1837, 1846 and 1848, 1860 and 1861, 1866 and 1868, and 1875 and 1878. The cycle of the balance seems therefore to have been more serious for France at this period than at the end of the century. It will be recalled that at this period France had no colonies. Perhaps this provides additional proof of the role played by the underdeveloped countries in the mechanism of recovery in the economies dominating them.

While the movement of the trade balance seems to have altered in the course of time, and to be different in the twentieth century from what it was in the nineteenth, the movement of capital and of the backflow of profits further complicate the matter. As regards the experience of the 1930s, the picture of a cycle in which the balance of the underdeveloped countries is positive and negative by turns, whereas that of the developed countries is, correspondingly, by turns negative and positive, fails to match up with reality.[14]

For Britain, for example, if we compare the periods 1925–29 and 1930–34, the balance of the main real flows (trade balance, long-term exports of capital, repatriation of profits) improved during the depression period, owing to the reduction in the surplus of imports over exports and the cessation of export of capital, these two factors being greater than the fall in income from investments abroad. This being so, we should not be surprised to find that a period when less gold was imported than was exported (the prosperity period of 1926–29: net exports of 21 million) was followed by one of net imports of gold (313 million between 1930 and 1934). The difference was also paid for through short-term movement of capital (increasing from 4 millions to over 21 millions), which did not have a disturbing effect, as had often been the case, but rather a stabilizing one.

For the United States in the same periods, this same real balance was improved during the depression due to the cessation of long-term capital export and despite the slight worsening of the trade balance, which remained favorable. This being so, the United States received gold during the depression and exported it during prosperity. It should be added that in this case the short-term capital movements do seem to have had a disturbing effect.

In France, however, in these same two periods, the balance worsened during the depression (almost in equilibrium during the first period, with the first four entries showing a deficit of 0.6 billions, and with a pronounced deficit—19 billions—in the second period). Thus, export of gold apparently made up for the deficit. The considerable size of the influx of floating capital both in the first period (movements of repatriation of French capital which had previously gone out of the country) and in the second (influx of short-term capital from abroad) made possible the steady and increasing import of gold that is a well-established feature of both periods.

For the developed countries generally, if the trade balance improves in a period of depression and, further, in accordance with the traditional schemas, the long-term export of capital ceases, then the total balance should improve, with gold and foreign exchange flowing in (the case of Britain). If, however, the trade balance worsens and the export of capital ceases, the total balance either improves or worsens, depending on the comparative strength of these two movements. In fact, it has almost always improved (as is shown by the examples we have already looked at, those of the United States and France, and by those of Holland, Switzerland, and Canada). By way of exception, persisting export of capital during a period of depression causes the balance to worsen, as we see from the example of Sweden. In any case the movement of capital prevails over that of goods. If, therefore, the balance of the developed countries improves in a period of depression, this is because of the cessation of exports of capital (the general phenomenon), and not because of the (exceptional) improvement in the balance of trade.

For the underdeveloped countries, the general worsening of the balance of payments in a period of depression is likewise more attributable to the cessation of imports of capital than to the worsening of the balance of goods. The latter often improves, but even so the cessation of the inflow of capital prevails heavily over this movement, as is shown by the examples of China and Chile between the two world wars. The situation is aggravated, of course, when to the stoppage of capital inflow is added a worsening of the current balance (as in the cases of India or Cuba). Sometimes, however, the sharp fall in interest to be paid has more than made up for the worsening of the balance (the case of Cuba).

When foreign capital has continued to flow in, it has generally not done so in proportions sufficient to make up for the worsening in the current balance (see, e.g., the experiences of the Dutch East Indies and Argentina during the 1930s). The reason is that the inflow of capital often entails an outflow of profits, which is extremely rapid—almost simultaneous when this inflow goes to finance large-scale infrastructural works.

Thus, it is the movement of capital that is mainly responsible for the worsening of the balance of the underdeveloped countries. This movement is subject to marked cyclical fluctuations. Nor is this situation peculiar to underdeveloped countries. A similar phenomenon is found in the developed countries that are debtors, i.e., that receive foreign capital. Not only do the examples of Denmark and Australia between the wars confirm this analysis, but also the examples of Germany and Japan, two big capitalist countries (and which do not specialize in export agriculture, as Denmark and Australia do). Having temporarily become debtors, these two countries, despite the marked improvement in their trade balance, found themselves in the position of countries whose balance was moving unfavorably.

Thus, it is *debtor* countries that are badly placed during cyclical depressions, not underdeveloped countries as such. True, all the latter countries are debtors. But it is to this feature—to the movement of foreign capital, and not because of a disparity between the movement of exports and that of imports—that the evolution of their situation is due. Everywhere, exports and imports evolve parallel, as explained by the theory of the transfer of purchasing power. It should finally be added that the short-term movement of capital, which was very often perverse, intensified the situation, as in the United States, France, and Canada (in the positive direction) or in Sweden, India, the Dutch East Indies, Germany, and Japan (in the negative direction). The movement was "normal" in three cases only: Britain (positive), and Denmark and Australia (negative).

The consequence is that the balance improves for the developed countries, taken as a whole, and worsens for the underdeveloped countries, in a period of depression. Thus, between 1929 and 1932 the reserves in gold and foreign currency held by six large creditor countries increased, and those held by eighteen debtor countries decreased. Similarly, in the sterling area, the sterling holdings of the central banks of fifteen countries were subject to an obvious cyclical movement. As for the holdings of the commercial banks, they showed the same movement, as was apparent from the evolution of the funds held in London by these banks. Now, this cyclical movement of the balance cannot be ascribed to the movement of goods, which improved for these fifteen countries between 1929 and 1931. The responsibility lies exclusively with the stoppage of capital exports from the developed countries, as is shown by the statistics of the balance of payments of ten countries of this area.

Regarding the nineteenth century, no details of balances of payments are available, but only the net results (surplus or deficit). The movement of these net results has been studied for each of the alternating periods of prosperity and depression (four cycle) that occupy the period 1880-1914.[15]

For France, in general, during depressions gold flows at a higher rate than in the previous or subsequent period of prosperity: it seems that the balance is therefore better in each depression, as it was after 1930. As for the trade balance for these different periods, it shows the following deficits (in billions): 1.5, 0.8, 0.6, 0.5, 0.3, 0.3, 0.6, 1.5. No definite conclusion can be drawn from these figures: on moving from depression into prosperity the balance twice improves and once worsens. Here, then, we again see the pattern of the twentieth century: whatever the evolution of the trade balance during the cycle, the movement of capital is strong enough to cause it always to be better in a depression period, through the slowing-down in the export of capital. Except for the crisis of 1901–03 and the prosperity of 1910–13, exports are greater during prosperity than during depression. It should be noted, however, that the fact that export of capital, though during a depression it usually goes on at a slower rate, nevertheless does go on, suggests that the crisis is partly overcome by the export of saving—sometimes at an increased rate (1901–03). In any case, this maintenance of the flow of capital during depression renders the total fluctuations in the balance rather slight.

For Britain, on the contrary, the external balance appears to have worsened in each depression period in the nineteenth century. The trade balance, which shows an increasing deficit—which reflects the fact that the country is becoming a more and more "mature" lender country—conceals the cyclical phenomenon. Here, too, however, the movement of capital largely depends on the level of activity. There are two exceptions: when depression gives way to prosperity in 1897, the flow of capital diminishes, whereas when prosperity gives way to depression in 1908, it increases. In this case also the conquest of external outlets for local saving may have helped to overcome the crisis. In Britain, then, in general, the worsening of the balance in each depression takes place despite the slowing down in the export of capital. The trade balance worsens rather severely, as I have already had occasion to mention (on the average, exports fell by 11 percent, as against a 7 percent fall in imports, whereas for France these two percentages are 10 percent for exports and 9 percent for imports). This may have been due to the special difficulties encountered by Britain at the end of the century as a result of the appearance of new competitors.

The schema of the nineteenth century is thus rather different from that of the twentieth. One cannot speak with certainty of an improvement in the balance of the developed countries during depressions. It must be added that the gold movements do not in themselves constitute very reliable barometers of the evolution of the balance, the net result of which was largely decided by the short-term capital movements for which we unfortunately possess no statistics.

There are virtually no statistics for the movement of the balances of the underdeveloped countries. Nevertheless, the case of Argentina has been studied for this period. In each depression the balance worsens. But the movement seems attributable to the cessation of the flow of foreign investment in 1891, rather than to the movement of the trade balance, which, adapting itself to the capital balance, seems not very regular: the flow of capital, slight during the years 1883-86 (depression), becomes greater between 1887 and 1891, stops completely from 1891 to 1896, and then picks up again, weakly (this balance of capital does not altogether reflect the phenomenon, owing to the backflow of profits which it includes).

There are no other studies available on the balance of the underdeveloped countries in the nineteenth century. One could, however, refer to those devoted to the debtor countries (Canada, Australia, the United States), whose behavior was similar from this standpoint—all the more so in that they were exporters of primary products—and one would arrive at the same conclusions.

Is it possible to carry the historical analysis further and to measure directly the magnitude of the fluctuations in income? There is an index of manufacturing activity, year by year from 1875 to 1939, for the principal countries.[16]

In the nineteenth century the oscillations on the world scale were, successively, 3,4, 3, 0, and 8 percent (crises of 1874, 1883, 1892, 1900, 1907), giving an average of 4 percent. They averaged 5 percent for Britain (3, 9, 5, 2, 6 percent). There is no comparison between these figures and those for the twentieth century, which have been, for the world as a whole, 13, 30, and 7 percent (crises of 1920, 1929, and 1937), giving an average of 17 percent, and for Britain 40, 12, and 8 percent (average 20 percent). Generally speaking, during the nineteenth century the average of the indices of the depression years was higher than that of the years of prosperity immediately preceding them. The development of capitalism was proceeding rapidly.

For India the cyclical oscillations were less marked. Between 1896 and 1914 production did not stop increasing, except during the minor recession of 1910 (3 percent). In 1920 the recession did not exceed 5 percent, and in 1930, 8 percent. What is noticeable here is the effect of craft production, less subject than industrial production to the rhythm of the cycle. For Chile the crisis of 1929 seems to have been very grave (index moving from 156.7 to 116.3, a fall of 26 percent): this was a mineral-producing country heavily dependent on world demand.

Comparison between these series suggests the following schema: in the developed countries the cycle of industrial production oscillated about 5 percent during the nineteenth century, but between the wars the oscillation was considerably greater (30 percent for the world as a whole in 1930). In the underdeveloped countries, insofar as their industrial production is intended for export (mining), the cycle is at least as pronounced as in the developed ones. When this production is destined for the local market, the magnitude of its oscillations depends on the relative importance of foreign trade as an element in the country's income. If this importance is high as in Egypt, the fluctuations in purchasing power resulting from exports affect internal demand. If, however, it is not very high, as in India, the fluctuations in exports have very little effect on the demand of the millions of peasants—who, moreover, buy from craftsmen rather than from manufacturing production.

The lack of statistical information prevents me from undertaking a systematic inquiry into this matter. Nevertheless, a few facts are available which support my analysis.

In the first place, there is the evolution of unemployment among the nonagricultural population, the fluctuations in which seem to be of the same order of magnitude for the developed countries and for the countries that export primary products (for lack of examples from the underdeveloped countries one may refer to those countries whose behavior is fairly similar from this standpoint). And the evolution of total profits is fairly typical.

In France, between 1929 and 1935, total profit (income from stocks and shares and income of industrial and commercial enterprises) decreased from 57 billions (23 percent of the national income) to 36 billions (21 percent), a reduction of 36 percent. In Germany between 1929 and 1932 the total income from industrial and commercial enterprises and from dividends and interest (total profits) decreased from 14.9 billions (20 percent of the national income) to 8.2 billions (18 percent), a reduction of 44 percent. In Britain the national income fell from £4,384 billion to £3,844 billion between 1929 and 1932, that is, by 12 percent, the share taken by wages increasing slightly (from 76.9 to 80.4 percent) and that of profit therefore falling a little more than 12 percent. In the United States the contraction in total income was 51 percent (from 81.92 billions to 39.49 billions between 1929 and 1930), the share taken by wages rising from 68.3 to 85.4 percent. The reduction in profit was thus about 75 percent. The profits index of sixty-five Egyptian companies (total capital, £E 31 million) shows a violent fluctuation, from 130 in 1929 ("100" being the period 1929-38) to 89 in 1933, thus falling by 31 percent. The profits index in India similarly shows a big fluctuation, from 100 in 1928 to 27.8 in 1931, a decrease of 72 percent. The size of this fluctuation, in contrast to the slightness of that for manufacturing activity, tends to show that in the foreign-owned industrial sector (the profits index is calculated on the basis of large enterprises which are frequently engaged in export), the oscillations are very wide, whereas in the sector of petty production destined for the local market (crafts and small-scale industry) this is not so.

Furthermore, the fluctuations in agricultural income in the underdeveloped countries depend on the nature of agricultural production. When what is involved is production for export, the oscillations are great, as we see from the example of Egypt, where the gross value of the harvests fell from an average of 145 in the years 1924-28 ("100" being 1939) to 75 in 1931, a reduction of 48 percent. If we assume that agriculture constituted 50 percent of the country's income, and that other activities did not suffer from the crisis, the national income must have suffered a contraction of 24 percent from this cause alone, that is, a contraction greater than that suffered by Great Britain, and close to what happened in the other big industrial countries (Germany, etc.).

This being so, one would be tempted to say that fluctuations in income are more violent in the underdeveloped than in the developed countries, at least as regards the countries that are integrated internationally, that is, those the volume of whose exports constitutes a high percentage of the gross national product. One would be tempted to measure these fluctuations by those of the country's exports.

We possess direct evaluations of the fluctuations of national income in some underdeveloped countries (India, Chile) and some countries which, though not underdeveloped, are producers of primary products (Australia, etc.). These direct evaluations do indeed tend to show that the magnitude of the cyclical oscillation of the national income of the underdeveloped countries depends on the degree to which they are integrated internationally (as measured by the importance of exports in their gross production). For Chile, a country closely integrated into the international market (as for Australia, a country which, though not underdeveloped, specializes in the export of primary products, and from this standpoint behaves like an underdeveloped country), the contraction was at least as great as in the developed countries where it was greatest. For India, a less integrated country, the contraction was only slight.

This result, which could be foreseen, leaves us to conclude that the cycle of the developed countries and that of the underdeveloped ones are profoundly different. The magnitude of the oscillation of the real income of the industrial countries was in 1930 about 25 percent. In the nineteenth century the corresponding figure seems to have been about

5 percent, as is shown by the cyclical evolution of the index of industrial production in Britain, France, Germany, and the United States. This oscillation could in no case be attributed to a shrinkage in exports. In a country where about a quarter of the national income is derived from exports, a reduction in the volume of the latter by 10 percent produces a reduction of only 2 percent in total real income. Yet, in 1929, the volume of the world's exports of manufactured goods (broadly equivalent to the volume of the total exports of the developed countries) fell by only 27 percent, which could have brought a reduction of only around 7 percent of real income—not 25 percent. In the nineteenth century the volume of exports seems to have remained stable all through the cycles, with only total value varying—and that not very much—as a result of price fluctuations. The crisis was thus caused essentially by the contraction of *internal* demand, and not by that of external demand, even though the latter might, in a given instance, aggravate the collapse of total demand.

Responsibility for the cycle lies with internal investment. The primary contraction of demand constituted by the reduction in the volume of investment and that of exports entails a secondary contraction, and so on.

Let me try to give figures for this movement in the case of the United States. Net investment represents about 10 percent of income in that country during prosperity periods. Its collapse there means a primary contraction in demand by 10 percent. A reduction of 50 percent of the volume of exports means another primary contraction of demand, of about 2.5 percent of the national income (since the share of exports in the national income comes to about 5 percent in the case of the United States). The primary contraction is thus, in all, of the order of 12.5 percent of income. As the ultimate contraction is 25 percent, the value of the real demand multiplier can be estimated at 2.

Toward a Theory of the Cycle and of the World Conjuncture

The experience of history leads us to the following seven conclusions:

1. There are no very precise rules for the way the trade balance behaves, in either the developed or the underdeveloped countries, because exports and imports vary in the same direction and in similar proportions. Even so, there is a certain tendency for the imports of the

underdeveloped countries to shrink less violently than their exports.

2. The shrinkage in the trade of the developed countries is due above all to that in the *volume* of their exports and imports. The shrinkage in the trade of the underdeveloped countries is due mainly to the fall in the *prices* of their exports, the worsening of the terms of trade that this reflects, and the decline in real import capacity that follows from it.

3. The undoubted cyclical movement of the balance of payments is due to that of *capital* far more than to that of the trade balance.

4. Fluctuations in national income became suddenly greater after 1914, both in the developed and in the underdeveloped countries, as did fluctuations in exports and imports, and in prices. After the Second World War these fluctuations lost their cyclical character, giving place to a shifting conjuncture, with movements of limited magnitude.

5. Fluctuations in industrial production in the underdeveloped countries depend on the destination of this production, and on the degree of the country's dependence on external trade.

6. Fluctuations in agricultural income in the underdeveloped countries depend on the same factors.

7. Fluctuations in the total real income of the underdeveloped countries are often smaller than those characteristic of the developed ones. Fluctuations in income *in current prices* are, however, notably greater, owing to the great volatility of prices in these countries.

From these conclusions I derive the following four theses:

1. The cycle does not seem to be transmitted through the channel of fluctuations in the quantity of money. Although it is true that, the balance of payments being favorable for the underdeveloped countries in a prosperity period and unfavorable in one of depression, these countries see their resources in international liquidities increase and decrease by turns, internal circulation remains "neutral," that is, proportional to monetary income (real income x level of prices).[17]

2. The cycle does not seem to be transmitted via the trade balance, either, through the working of the multiplier. The behavior of the trade balance is indeed extremely variable, as we have seen, both in different periods and in different countries. It is to be added that even when the balance is favorable in an underdeveloped country we do not observe a wave of "induced," "secondary" investments engendered by this net surplus.

3. The cycle seems then to be quite simply the cyclical aspect of the movement of the income of agriculturists living by exports, which takes the form of a cyclical worsening of the terms of trade for their

exported produce. This oscillation has secondary effects on industrial production destined for the local market, on services as a whole, and so on, but these effects are much reduced. The cycle of the underdeveloped countries is merely the cycle of their capacity to import.

4. In the international cycle, the underdeveloped countries play an important role at the moment of recovery by providing additional outlets for the exports of the developed countries, through the possible break-up of precapitalist societies. During recession, trade between developed and underdeveloped countries often declines less than that among the developed countries themselves, and very often, in fact, the volume of imports of the developed countries increases during depression (a very general case in the nineteenth century).

It is on the basis of these theses that it is possible to work out a theory of the international conjuncture that assigns a specific role to the periphery in the mechanism of accumulation. This specific role is especially visible when recovery takes place, but it is also apparent during the other phases of the movement of the conjuncture at the center.

The Role of the Periphery in the Mechanism of Recovery

The periphery plays a role that is far from negligible in the mechanism of international recovery.[18] The point is, however deep a depression may be, it can come to an end sooner in the underdeveloped countries than in the central capitalist economies, because it is more superficial in the former. During a depression in the developed countries a considerable mass of labor is thrown out of employment. All incomes contract—profits first and foremost, but also wages as a whole. During the preceding period of prosperity new enterprises were set up which are now reduced to idleness. The burden of unutilized productive capacity weighs heavily, making recovery all the more difficult.

In the underdeveloped countries, on the other hand, while oscillations in the predominant form of income, ground-rent, are considerable, this is not true of the mixed incomes of the bulk of the population. True, the craftsmen and peasants suffer from the unfavorable world conjuncture. A certain number of them are ruined, lose their economic footing, and are cast into unemployment. But the great mass of these social classes do not suffer from this misfortune to the same degree as the mass of the workers in the developed countries. The entire sector producing foodstuffs for consumption by the producers remains outside the sweep of the depression's effect, just as it was outside the influence of prosperity.

Moreover, in these countries, while during prosperity foreign capital flowed in and made possible the equipment of new enterprises, such development is less permanent than it is in the developed countries. In the countries of the periphery, capital shows a marked preference for investment in the tertiary sector, and for light investment.[19] Tertiary investment is often purely financial—purchase of buildings for resale, purchase of goods for export, securities, etc. This huge mass of capital which is not materially productive is destroyed by the depression without leaving behind it any productive capacity to weigh heavily and thus delay recovery. This destruction of fictitious capital impoverishes the country for the benefit of foreigners, leaving it with a financial burden that corresponds to nothing concrete. At the same time, all other things being equal, light investment leaves behind it unutilized productive capacity which is relatively less bulky and therefore less of a burden on the market than heavy investment.

If, then, the crisis is reflected in the collapse of the level of the external exchanges of the underdeveloped countries, this happens only insofar as, exports having dragged ground-rent down in their decline, luxury imports then cease. However, once these export activities have become dormant, the level of exchanges with the outside world is stabilized, because the income of the indigenous sector has been only slightly affected by the fluctuations caused by the capitalist mode of production. But in the developed countries the depression may get even worse. After making inroads on profits, it attacks wages. This is why, during depression, the volume of exchanges among the developed countries themselves generally declines proportionately more than the volume of exchanges between the developed and the underdeveloped countries.

After a certain moment, the relative rigidity of the underdeveloped markets may thus constitute a factor of recovery. The existence of exchange relations between the periphery and the center enables the latter to find new external markets in the disintegration of the indigenous craft sector. The foreign capital which, during the prosperity phase, found more lucrative investment in other activities, is now content with this outlet. Capital has better opportunities at the center during the prosperity phase than to establish enterprises in the periphery to compete with craft production there. In fact, during the course of development of the cycle, the rate of reward of capital shows more violent fluctuations in the developed countries than in the underdeveloped ones. Stock-exchange activity, and the very wide fluctuations in stocks and shares, by turns devalued and overvalued, which this speculative activity inevitably engenders, have the effect, in the advanced capitalist countries, of amplifying both the fall and the rise in the marginal efficiency of capital. The violence of these fluctuations in the profitability of capital in the developed countries thus enables certain activities to become lucrative enough in a period of depression.

The further disintegration of primitive indigenous production at the end of the depression is reflected in a new wave of exports from the developed countries. The mechanisms of monetarization start to work. The increase in money incomes in the underdeveloped countries resulting from this further disintegration of the wants economy is reflected in the formation of local saving which finds its way at once into the speculation circuits, revival of which is all the easier because they have left behind them no unutilized production capacity that would weigh heavily on the recovery of accumulation.

These multiplier phenomena in the underdeveloped economy are profoundly different from those characteristic of the way the mechanisms of prosperity operate in the developed countries. All that is involved is a development of money incomes in the underdeveloped countries. Generally speaking, this development is effected merely by reducing income in kind. This accelerated disintegration of primitive economies as a result of external trade worsens the situation in these countries, where an additional mass of ruined craftsmen become victims of permanent unemployment.[20] However, this disintegration, which is reflected in a fresh development of capitalism in these countries, makes possible the quicker formation of incomes of the capitalist type, and so the formation of a new element contributing to saving in money form. It is this saving that goes to feed the speculation circuits I have mentioned. Furthermore, this deeper disintegration of the native economy is reflected in reinforcement of the position of ground-rent. It therefore harbors in germ a future increase in imports. This is why the opening of new external outlets does not constitute a *final* solution of the problem. In theory, it is not needed in order that recovery may take place in the developed countries.[21] This recovery is indeed due very largely to a deepening of the *internal* market due to the generalizing of a new, more capital-intensive technique. Nevertheless, we observe, after each depression at the center, the opening of new outlets in the periphery. The countries of the Third World thus play an active role in the mechanism of international recovery.

Structural Adjustments of the Periphery to the Requirements of the Center

But it is not only in relation to the mechanism of international recovery that the underdeveloped countries play an active role in the international cycle. Throughout the cumulative process that characterizes prosperity they also play an active role that is far from negligible.

The development of prosperity, marked by the growth of total income, is reflected in an increase in the share of profits and consequently in an increase in the relative volume of saving accumulated. The relative share taken by wages decreases. Accordingly, capacity to consume falls further and further behind capacity to produce. Before long, the new equipment created by investment of the additional saving puts on the market a mass of consumer goods that cannot be absorbed. The working of the accelerator for a time maintains the illusion of the profitability of the new equipment made necessary by the increase in the *absolute* volume of consumption. There is thus overproduction of consumer goods, since the purchasing power distributed and destined for purchase of these goods (mainly wages) is less than the total value of this production. This overproduction, reflected, in Harrod's account, in the diminution of the multiplier (growth in propensity to save), is for a long time concealed by the working of the accelerator, with its inverse effects.

It must be pointed out that this overproduction is not due to a propensity to save that is too great, on the average. Whatever the level of this propensity, it is possible to imagine a division of total production between a production of equipment goods and a production of consumer goods corresponding to it, given which all saving could therefore be invested. This possibility constitutes, indeed, the very meaning of economic growth (if we ignore the cycle): when total income increases, the level of saving rises, and this makes possible a development of production of equipment goods which is faster than that of consumer goods. This more rapid development of the production of equipment goods, reflecting the rise in the level of productivity, in turn makes possible the subsequent growth of total income.

If this development has to take the form of a sine curve around an upward trend, this is because the propensity to save, whatever its average amount over an entire cycle, rises *too quickly.* The mechanism "bolts." It is this bolting, due essentially to the great elasticity of profits, that gives rise to the cycle. This does not in the least mean that the propensity to save ought to remain stable. On the contrary, development demands that this propensity rise, and at the same time makes it possible for it to rise. All that is needed is that this propensity should rise more slowly (or less quickly).

The point is that the overproduction of consumer goods is confronted with a real *under*production of equipment goods: a relatively increasing purchasing power (saved profits) is applied to the purchase of equipment goods the production of which seems constantly to be inadequate. In other words, prosperity is marked by an increasing imbalance between production of equipment goods and production of consumer goods. This increasing imbalance is concealed for a time, as has been said, by the antagonistic working of the accelerator and the multiplier.

Trade between the developed and underdeveloped countries also continues to conceal this imbalance—in other words, to prolong the periods of prosperity. Exchange between developed and underdeveloped countries in no way constitutes the solution to overproduction by the capitalist countries. Development of the capitalist countries is perfectly possible even when there are no precapitalist societies to be disintegrated. If external trade expands parallel with the development of capitalism, it is not, therefore, for this reason, but simply because the tendency to expand markets is inherent in capitalism.

Nevertheless, trade between developed and underdeveloped countries does play an active role in capitalist development.

The developed countries, which are always ahead of their backward partners in exchange, take the offensive, so to speak, by exporting to them.[22] Only later does the structure of the underdeveloped countries become modified, adapting itself to the evolution of production in the advanced countries so as to make possible the export of primary products to them. Imbalance is therefore a permanent feature of trade relations between the center and the periphery of the system. This permanent imbalance is, however, always being corrected, and so it plays, in the development of the most advanced countries, only the modest role of a catalyst, comparable to credit.

Here we need to go further, to grasp the mechanism by which the structure of the underdeveloped countries is adjusted to the requirements of the evolution of production in the developed countries. The latter have the advantage in all branches of production. It is therefore the products that tend to be overproduced during the prosperity phase that are the first to seek (and so to find) an outlet in the economies of the periphery. Manufactured consumer goods, which become more and more plentiful during this period, are those that are exported on the largest scale. Conversely, the growing demand of the developed countries, during the prosperity phase, for those products that are relatively least plentiful leads to adjustment of the structure of the underdeveloped countries to the needs of the more advanced countries. The underdeveloped countries specialize in producing goods the supply of which tends to be less than the demand for them in the developed countries during the prosperity phase: they specialize in producing primary products that contribute to the equipment of the developed countries—in the main, agricultural raw materials and mineral products.

Exchange of consumer goods—in respect of which supply is greater than demand—for intermediate goods—in respect of which, on the contrary, demand is greater than supply—facilitates that upward trend in the developed countries. To the same degree this exchange intensifies, where the capitalist sector of production in the underdeveloped countries is concerned, the inbalance between production of consumer goods and production of intermediate goods. This is why these countries, where the production of raw materials develops faster than the production of the manufacturing industries that use these raw materials, find themselves increasingly tied to external trade as the cycle develops. Once again, international specialization is seen to have nothing rational from the standpoint of society.

We can now appreciate better the real place occupied by the periphery in the world conjuncture. Although the extension of the capitalist mode of production to the periphery is not essential to the working of the mechanism of accumulation, this extension plays the role of a catalyst and an accelerator of growth at the center. It may therefore be important. But it is not the only force that works in this direction of accelerating growth at the center. It may even be only a secondary factor in this regard.

This is so, for example, in the present period, since 1945.[23] Since the end of the Second World War capitalism has been experiencing an extremely brilliant period of growth. In this phenomenon the extension of the capitalist mode of production to the Third World has played only a very secondary, almost negligible, part. It is the modernization of Western Europe—its Americanization—that has been the essential factor in this "miracle." Modernization means deepening (not spreading) the capitalist market, a solution that, always possible (as Marx and Lenin always said), has become real through the conjunction of elements situated on different planes (including the political plane: fear of communism, etc.), which rules out any mechanistic "economist" interpretation. The European Common Market and the influx of American capital into Europe constitute the most obvious expressions of this phenomenon.

Nevertheless, although during this period the extension of capitalism to the periphery has not played an important role, this does not mean that it has always been so, or that it will always be so in the future. In the past, the extraordinary wave of extension of the capitalist market to the colonies during the nineteenth century certainly played an important part in the relatively peaceful course taken by accumulation at the center. This first wave determined a first series of forms of specialization between center and periphery—the periphery, of course, adapting itself to the requirements of the center. These forms of adaptation implied, after a certain level had been reached, a relative blocking of the mechanism of the extension of capitalism: the extension of capitalism to the periphery in these forms therefore began to exhaust its possibilities—whence the special violence of the crisis of 1930.

It seems that the type of growth that the capitalist world has known since 1945, based on the Americanization of Western Europe, is tending in its turn to exhaust its possibilities. The world monetary crisis and the reappearance of chronic "deflationary tendencies" are perhaps symptoms of this. What may take over the role of ensuring the growth of capitalism?

I see three possibilities. First, progressive integration of the countries of Eastern Europe (Russia and its satellites) in the world market, and *their* modernization. Second, the contemporary scientific and technical revolution, which, along with automation, the conquest of the atom, and the conquest of space, may open up substantial possibilities for deepening the market. Third, and last, a new wave of extension of capitalism to the Third World, based on a new type of international specialization made possible by the technical revolution of our time. In this context, the countries of the center would "specialize" in ultramodern activities, while forms of classical industry hitherto reserved for them would be transferred to the periphery.

Once again, by "adapting" themselves to the requirements of the center, the countries of the periphery will have played an important role in the mechanism of accumulation on a world scale.

Summary of Conclusions

1. The fluctuations of the conjuncture—whether they assume a regular cyclical form (as was the case down to the Second World War) or not (as has been the case since then)—are manifestations of the internal contradiction between the capacity to produce and the capacity to consume which is distinctive of the capitalist mode of production, a contradiction that is constantly overcome by the deepening and spreading of the capitalist market. Current economic theory, by way of exception, explains this dynamic of the contradiction (though in economistic terms of the combined working of the multiplier and the accelerator which conceal the origin of the contradiction of the system), when this theory is able to raise itself above the monetary appearances of phenomena. It thus reformulates, though in mechanistic and oversimplified form, the analysis already made by Marx.

2. The historical law of this inherent contradiction of the capitalist mode of production is that it tends to *intensify* (as shown in the exceptional dimensions of the crisis of 1930). But this tendency/law does not lead to a "spontaneous catastrophic collapse," because the system can always respond by organizing monopolies and bringing about state intervention so as to absorb the increasing surplus. The historical conditions in the context of which accumulation on a world scale is proceeding are of vital significance in this connection. The scientific and technical revolution of our time, together with the progressive integration of Eastern Europe into the world capitalist system, will probably alter to a considerable extent, in the foreseeable future, the conditions of accumulation on a world scale. The spread of capitalism to the periphery, the adjustment of the structure of the periphery to the requirements of accumulation at the center (in other words, the forms of international specialization between the center and the periphery), must also occupy an important place in analysis of the conjuncture.

3. Current economic theory, which compares the underdeveloped countries to the developed ones as they were at an earlier stage of their development, does not succeed in accounting for the conjunctural phenomena distinctive of the periphery. It takes refuge in a mechanistic theory of the conjuncture being "transmitted" from the developed countries to the underdeveloped ones, either through monetary mechanisms or through the foreign-trade multiplier. In reality the economies of the periphery of the system do not experience true conjunctural phenomena distinctive to themselves, even "transmitted" from without, for they have no internal dynamism of their own.

4. The periphery nevertheless occupies a place that may be important in the course taken by the cycle—or by the fluctuations of the conjuncture—on the world scale. It provides a sphere of possible extension of the capitalist mode of production, at the expense of "precapitalist *milieux.*" Although such an extension of the capitalist mode of production is not *essential* to the working of the mechanism of accumulation, it plays the role of a catalyst and an accelerator of growth at the center. It certainly fulfilled an important function of that order in the first phases of colonial expansion. It seems to have lost this importance during the present period. But it may recover it in the future, in the context of a new structure of "international specialization."

Chapter 5
The Adjustment of the Periphery's Balance of External Payments

From a glance at the manuals of "international economics" that are widely used in the universities we learn that what is taught is that any disequilibrium that may occur in a country's balance of external payments should be automatically reabsorbed—just as the courses on "development policies" or "projects analysis" advise the underdeveloped countries to adopt, when calculating the "social profitability" of projects, an "equilibrium rate of exchange."

I propose to show in this chapter that the theory of the mechanisms of readjustment of the external balance, in its successive variants—the classical theory of price effects, the post-Keynesian theory of income effects, the theory of exchange—is always based either on unsound foundations, which nevertheless survive tenaciously in current theory (just as the quantity theory of money does), because it is not known what to put in their place without giving up the sacrosanct subjective theory of value, or else on cursory and superficial analyses derived from an empirical method. Present-day theory gets bogged down more and more hopelessly in a series of pseudo-problems or in a search for impossible answers to problems that are wrongly presented (because of an unwillingness to go beyond empiricism), and closes its eyes to what is essential. What is essential is that the equilibrium in the balance of payments, which at best is only a tendency, depends on a permanent adjustment of the international structures. The latter are, so far as relations between the developed and underdeveloped worlds are concerned, structures of asymmetrical domination by the center of the world system over its periphery. External equilibrium, international order, is possible only because the structures of the periphery have been shaped to conform to the requirements of accumulation at the center. In other words, equilibrium is possible only if development at the center causes and maintains underdevelopment in the periphery. This refusal to see what is vital exposes the ideological character of current economic theory, which is entirely based on the religiously held postulate of a universal harmony that must not be questioned and which therefore cannot be the subject of scientific criticism. Only in this way can theory perceive the appearances of things without perceiving what is essential. The result is that theory dooms itself to failure to understand either the nature of underdevelopment, or the dynamics of accumulation on a world scale, or the dynamics of the balance of payments, especially as regards relations between the developed and underdeveloped worlds.

This chapter will undertake, first, an external criticism of the theories in question that deal with the "spontaneous" adjustment of the external balance—after briefly reviewing what the constituent elements of this balance consist of—and then an attempt to make progress toward a theory of the structural adjustment of the periphery of the world capitalist system to the requirements of accumulation at the center (which is the direction in which the answer to the real question is to be sought), and to bring these elements of an answer to that question into confrontation with the history of the external relations of the underdeveloped world.

THE CONSTITUENT ELEMENTS OF THE EXTERNAL BALANCE

When we speak of the balance of payments, a certain ambiguity hovers over the expression we use. What, in fact, ought to be included in the balance of payments?

There are some elements that must obviously be included. These are the monetary equivalents of current transactions of a strictly commercial kind: export and import of goods, payment for commercial services (freight and insurance). Also to be included are the expenditures of visiting tourists, the remittances sent home by emigrants, and other such movements of funds. But should *all* capital movements be included in the balance of payments?

The objection to the inclusion of all these elements is that the totality of the balance of current transactions and that of the balance of capital transactions are always, by definition, in equilibrium with each other. All transactions must indeed be paid for. The debt that may appear to arise from consideration of the balance of voluntary transactions is offset by an equivalent amount of credit. This credit from abroad may itself, moreover, be either voluntary or forced. Must we then *exclude* all capital movements from the balance of payments?

The interest and profits on foreign capital invested in the country make up a mass that is fundamentally distinct from the other elements in the movement of capital. These payments arise from previous foreign investments. This is why there can be no argument about this matter. The inclusion of these sums in the balance of accounts is so little disputed that the movement of interest is classified among current transactions. Among the other elements that make up the balance of capital transactions, a special place must be given to long-term investment. Here, the exchange operation is merely a necessary means and not the essential content of the operation of capital transfer.

Short-term capital movements and short-term "forced" loans are of a profoundly different character. Under the one heading of "short-term capital movements" many operations which are different in their economic significance are all grouped together. We find here, side by side, purchases and sales of foreign currency motivated by the intention of making a profit from variations in the rate of exchange itself; momentary transfers that are basically due to movements of the discounting rate (the capitalists who have momentary liquidities at their disposal try to find short-term investment outlets for them in countries where the rate of money is highest); and, finally, those notorious erratic movements ("hot money") which are dictated by extra-economic considerations, usually political in character. All these movements have the distinctive feature of being *voluntary.* In contrast to this, the institutions that centralize holdings of foreign currency are sometimes obliged, in the absence of a "natural" equilibrium between voluntary movements inward and outward, to grant short-term credit to foreigners. Such credit is clearly "forced." When complete freedom prevailed in international relations this obligation did not exist, because it was always possible to find foreign currency, if one was prepared to pay the price. Today, the exchange control has to balance entries and exits of funds within a short period. If it is short of funds all it can do is refuse to hand over foreign currency to the trader who needs it. The foreign correspondent will then apply, in his own country, to an organ providing guarantees for foreign trade, such as has now been set up almost everywhere. This organ will settle the debt in its own currency. It thus acquires a claim on the trader in the country which is short of foreign currency, and so grants, perforce, short-term credit abroad.

Where there is no control over the exchange, abandonment of flexible exchange rates in favor of a system characterized, since the creation of the International Monetary Fund in 1945, by rigid rates, makes the purchase of foreign currency (purchase inevitably at a relatively fixed rate) not always possible, since at this rate there may not be a supply of foreign currency sufficient to meet the deficit.

Transfers of gold do not constitute, either, a homogeneous category within the balance of capital operations. Gold is accepted as a means of settling a debt, and it is also bought in order to speculate on fluctuations in its value, or to satisfy a need for long-term hoarding. This last requirement is sometimes what lies behind a substantial import of gold in the underdeveloped countries, as well as in the developed ones.

The elements that need to be taken into consideration in order to form an idea of the balance of payments are, therefore: commercial transactions and comparable transfers of income, repatriation of profits, long-term capital movements, and, finally, transfers of gold destined to satisfy the needs of local hoarding.[1] It is these items that in fact exhaust the list of elements corresponding to real economic forces. Short-term movements, even if "willed," reflect the working of momentary forces only. Although these movements have a certain influence on the rate of exchange, and thereby on general economic conditions, their evolution over a long period does not show any tendency that is sufficiently general for it to be taken into consideration.

It should be added that we need to distinguish between the balance of real payments, thus defined, and the balance of movements of bank capital. This distinction is necessitated by the fact that branches of foreign commercial banks often function in underdeveloped countries to which they supply monetary liquidities. Imports and exports of funds by these banks must be carefully distinguished from imports and exports of capital destined for investment, although their effect on the rate of exchange, if there is one, may be similar. This distinction is vital in the case of the underdeveloped countries which are integrated in highly centralized currency areas (such as, today, the franc area and the escudo area). Here the entire banking system consists of agencies or branches of big banks centered in the metropolitan countries, and the absolute freedom of transfer, guaranteed at a fixed rate, enables the banks to import or export liquidities in accordance with the local economy's requirement of monetrary instruments.[2]

Aftalion declines to include long-term international investments in the balance of payments because, "if new investments are to be brought into the picture it is hard to say how distinctions could be made among them, and all would have to be included. From the balance of payments one would go over to the balance of *settlements,* which is, by definition, always in equilibrium."[3] However, the reason he gives does not seem convincing. What has to be done here is to engage not in a *statistical* but in a *theoretical* investigation, which requires that we distinguish clearly between international investment and "erratic" transfers of funds. It should be added, moreover, that the figures of the entries in the balance of commercial operations are, from the statistical standpoint, sometimes just as inexact as those for capital operations. Aftalion points to the inaccuracy of customs documents which, ignoring the fluctuations in the rate of exchange in the course of the year, show only an average figure that distorts reality.[4] It is true that the balance of international indebtedness has only financial, and not real, significance.[5] It is impossible to know statistically to what extent the equivalent of claims on foreign countries is made up of real investment and to what extent it consists of what is called "liquid capital," that is, a sum of money kept abroad. Besides, the value of the investment abroad, as it emerges from this balance, is itself largely fictitious, since the portfolio of foreign securities is subject to fluctuations connected with the conjuncture. Furthermore, the external financial accounts themselves do not reveal all capital movements: they ignore profits reinvested on the spot, and undistributed reserves. It would therefore be naive to seek to draw valid conclusions regarding international investment on the basis of a mere examination of the external balance.

The fact remains that the balance of payments is an economic reality. This balance is usually regarded as being even when the net difference between the entries corresponding to real economic forces is nil.

The questions to be asked are these: (1) Is there a mechanism that causes the "real" balance (that is, excluding movements of monetary gold, foreign currency and "compensatory" credits, and also, where the given country's banking system consists of agencies of metropolitan banks, including movements that correspond to the flows of liquidities necessitated by the functioning of the monetary system) to tend toward spontaneous equilibrium? (2) If such a mechanism exists, and consequently a rate of exchange called an "equilibrium" rate (one could also call it a "natural" rate) likewise exists, what is the nature of the structural equilibrium corresponding to this? (3) Specifically in relations between the developed centers and the underdeveloped periphery, what is the nature of this "structural adjustment"?

THE THEORY OF MECHANISMS OF "SPONTANEOUS READJUSTMENT" OF THE EXTERNAL BALANCE

Is a momentary deficit in a country's balance of payments, whatever its cause, whether transient or structural, capable of becoming reabsorbed on its own, by influencing the level of the rate of exchange, if this is appropriate, or else by influencing prices and economic activity? Economic theory still answers this question in the affirmative, although analysis of the readjustment mechanism has been revolutionized by recent work.

Adam Smith allowed only the price mechanism to enter into the construction of international equilibrium. In this he was following the very old, mercantilist tradition of Bodin, Petty, Locke, and Cantillon, who had observed that disequilibrium in the trade balance was compensated by movements of gold. He was also following the quantitativist tradition, according to which the movement of gold in turn determined the general price level. The disequilibrium should therefore become reabsorbed on its own. It was only one step from there to declaring that the only possible cause of external imbalance was "internal inflation"—a step that the bullionists were to take, under Ricardo's leadership, at the beginning of the nineteenth century. The arguments of Bosanquet, who attributed the disequilibrium of the balance to nonmonetary causes (export difficulties due to war, together with the payment of subsidies to foreign countries), failed to convince contemporaries despite their high degree of logicality. It happened in this case as in the controversy about the quantity theory which was, a little later, to set Tooke against Ricardo: Ricardo's theory was demolished without anything positive being put in its place.

It was Wicksell who brought out, at the end of the nineteenth century, the role played by changes in demand in the mechanism of international equilibrium. A deficit in the balance was analyzed as a transfer of purchasing power. This extra purchasing power would enable the foreign country sooner or later to increase its imports, while the deficitary country would sooner or later be obliged to reduce its imports. International equilibrium would be achieved without any alteration in prices. This profoundly revolutionary contribution was taken up by Ohlin, who claimed, on this basis, that it was possible for German reparations to be paid. The extent to which the classical theory of price effects (connected with the quantity theory) continued to be influential, however, can be appreciated from the fact that so eminent a thinker as Keynes refused to give up the old outlook. If he alleged that it was impossible for Germany to pay reparations, this was exclusively because he believed that the working of the price elasticities of German exports and imports would bring about a "perverse" rather than a "normal" effect. It was a long time before the "income" view of the matter was accepted. It was not Keynes himself but only the post-Keynesians who incorporated in the theory of international equilibrium the essence of the method inaugurated by Bosanquet and taken up by Wicksell and Ohlin.

These two views—the "price" view and the "income" view—are often presented as being mutually exclusive. Chang's study, for example, leaves the reader to conclude that analysis of the responses of foreign trade to variations in incomes is enough to describe and explain the state of international exchanges.[6] The critical reply made by Viner, declaring that, the longer the period of observation, the greater seems the price elasticity, so that Chang's pessimistic calculations are ill-founded, is still too firmly attached to the tradition that declines to see demand as dependent on anything but price.[7]

Yet these are unquestionably two aspects of the same phenomenon, namely, demand. Does demand depend on price, or on income? A long controversy has produced a number of econometrical calculations.[8] The entire construction of Walras's general equilibrium remains based on the law of supply and demand. It was with the intention of replacing the labor theory of value by the utility theory that the first analysts of the market, Say, in particular, put forward the law of demand. The responses of demand and supply to variations in prices are then explained by the diminishing marginal utility of goods. Equilibrium is obtained without any elements other than these responses playing a part. In reality, however, this construction remains very fragile, incapable of replacing the whole content of the Ricardian and Marxist analyses. This weakness is due to the fact that Say and Walras overlook the fundamental element in demand that is constituted by *income.* They make the law of supply and demand contribute more than it is capable of contributing. The law of the diminishing utility of goods may well explain that demand falls when prices rise, but only provided that the level of incomes remains unaltered. Now, the distribution of incomes is, in the theory of general equilibrium, dependent on the relative prices of goods. Any change in prices alters incomes. Recourse has then been had to periodic analysis, in order to escape from the marginalist vicious circle. Today's prices depend on yesterday's incomes, and yesterday's incomes depend on the prices of the day before yesterday. This resort to history constitutes a real theoretical act of surrender, an admission of the fundamental impotence of marginalism. Analyses of the price elasticities of external trade are of the same order. They assume that the natural incomes of the partners in exchange are stable, and they thus lose all power to explain the real movements of international trade.

The introduction of the responses of supply and demand to variations in income in general, and of the responses of external trade to variations in the national income in particular, was a veritable revolution.[9] But the *descriptive* nature of these studies must be emphasized. It is noted that the level of incomes being so much at a certain period, the level of exchanges of a certain product was so much; at a later period the incomes, prices, and quantities exchanged were different. The assumption is then made that demand depends on price and on income. This assumption is expressed by a linear equation with three variables: two of these, price and income, are independent, and the third, demand, is bound. Partial correlation analysis enables us to determine the respective role played by the two independent variables in the determination of the dependent variable. This is Chang's method. It is based on analysis of variability. In economics one can always express a quantity in a linear relation with two others, and coefficients will always be found that render this relation statistically significant. What can be concluded from this is that the three magnitudes are indeed bound together, but not that the supposed connection is the only possible one, or even the most interesting. This method provides a more or less adequate description, but nothing more.

This is the weakness of a method that enables one to check the plausibility of an assumption but not to choose between assumptions that are equally plausible. To make that choice, the only valid method remains abstract economic analysis. And *that* requires that the fundamental problems of economics—the nature of value, the nature of money, and so on—be tackled directly: problems that no inductive statistical method can enable one to dodge.

The Classical Theory of Price Effects[10]

This theory was worked out at the beginning of the nineteenth century within its context of assumptions that corresponded to the reality of that time (the gold standard) and on the basis of the quantity theory of money. Since any importer has a choice between buying foreign currency (foreign gold coins) and sending gold abroad (in the form of ingots), a deficit in the balance of payments cannot bring down the national rate of exchange to a sufficient extent to influence the terms of trade and to favor exports. Therefore, disequilibrium can ultimately find reflection only in a drain of gold. The general decline in internal prices resulting from this drain, and consequently the decline in the prices of exports, as compared with the stability of foreign prices, and consequently the stability of the prices of imports, discourages the latter, favors the former, and enables equilibrium to be restored. It is the worsening of the terms of trade that reestablishes equilibrium.

The quantity-theory analysis of international relations was refined during the nineteenth century, notably by Goschen, who claimed that the natural reaction of the central bank when faced with a threat of diminution of its gold cash-in-hand was sufficient to restore equilibrium to the external balance.[11] By raising the discounting rate, this organ attracts short-term capital from abroad, and thereby covers the deficit in foreign exchange. Here we are in the realm of that ideology of universal harmonies that blinds the analyst to the point of making him commit elementary faults of reasoning. For Goschen is here going too far. Any rise in the discounting rate can attract short-term foreign capital only so long as it lasts. At the end of a certain time, when the gold cash-in-hand has been reconstituted, the central bank will lower this rate, and consequently the disequilibrium in the balance of payments is certain to reappear.

Though constructed on the assumption of the gold standard, this theory can easily be extended to the underdeveloped countries with a stable exchange, that is, the countries on a foreign-exchange standard. This is precisely what recent writers have done. In this case, disequilibrium in the balance of payments entails an outflow of foreign exchange. The deflation of internal credit that follows affects prices in a way that enables equilibrium to be restored. Where these countries are integrated through the banking system as well as through the currency, it is the totality of the balance of real payments and of bank transactions that tends to re-equilibrate from this standpoint. An outflow of foreign exchange, whether due to a disequilibrium in real payments (cessation of the flow of investments, bigger deficit in the trade balance, etc.) or to export of surplus liquidities by the expatriate banks, affects credit and prices in the same way. In the end it is this equilibrium of the overall balance that prompts the conclusion that the internal circulation is paid for by exports,[12] just as in a country on the gold standard, where the importing of gold for the needs of circulation has to be paid for in exports.

The logical link between this classical theory of price effects and the quantity theory of money is fundamental. The theory makes sense only if the quantity of money determines the level of prices. In the case of a country integrated through the banking system, it obliges one to suppose that the flows of banking liquidities must also be included in the balance that is in "spontaneous" equilibrium. This affirmation being necessary in order to save the theory, no further attempt is made to examine *why* it should be so: it is merely said that, since it *is* so, the real balance determines the volume of internal circulation of money. Here once again we are in the realm of the ideology of necessary universal harmonies.[13]

Only if the underdeveloped country is in a state of monetary independence (paper-money standard) is the theory held to be no longer valid, as in relations among developed countries—for then the disequilibrium of the balance affects the rate of exchange to an extent sufficient to alter the conditions of international exchange.

Price elasticities.[14] Only recently has it been perceived that the alteration in the terms of trade—attributed, rightly or wrongly, either to the internal movement of prices due to the flow of gold or of foreign currency, or to the rise and fall of the rate of exchange, effects that are similar from this standpoint—which on the one hand favored (or disfavored) exports, also lowered (or raised) their unit prices. An internal increase in prices, or an improvement in the rate of exchange—like a fall in these prices, or a decline in the rate of exchange—may affect the state of the balance for better or for worse, depending on the level of elasticities. The same is true, but the other way round, where imports are concerned.

Analysis of the effects of different combinations of price elasticities has become commonplace nowadays. The best formulation is given by Joan Robinson, who takes account of these four elasticities: that of the national export supply, that of the foreign import supply, that of the national import demand, and that of the foreign export demand. To be fair, it should be recalled that, long before the Keynesians, Nogaro had seriously criticized Augustin Cournot's theory of the exchange. This theory assumed what had to be proved, namely, that price elasticities are such that devaluation makes it possible to reabsorb the deficit.

Influence of prices of imports on prices of home-produced products. If the economy is perfectly integrated, a change in the price of imports must entail a proportional change in all internal prices, and, consequently, in the price of exports. Here, too, criticism has been made on the basis of the effects of alterations in the rate of exchange (and thereby in the price of imports) on internal prices. But it is the same when a change occurs in internal prices with a stable rate of exchange assured (when there is a fall in internal prices, for instance). Is not the relatively higher price of imports bound to influence all prices in an upward direction?

Aftalion showed that the level of the exchange itself had an effect, in some cases, on the internal price level. It ought not to be assumed that the rate of exchange affects only the prices of imported goods, through variations in cost, and that devaluation ultimately affects the price of goods only insofar as imported goods enter into their manufacture. Aftalion demonstrates, by means of historical examples, that the rate of exchange does sometimes influence all prices, through an increase in money incomes.[15] Will the influence of an alteration in the rate of exchange on the income of importers (through stocks of goods that have been acquired and paid for previously), on the income of holders of foreign shares, and on the income of exporters and producers for export, always be capable of determining a general increase or decrease in prices proportional to this alteration in the rate of exchange? If the influence goes far enough, if the fluctuations in money income are not compensated by fluctuations in hoarding, and if, finally, the whole of money income comes on to the demand market, then this will probably happen. In that case, the situation of the balance of payments, after devaluation has exhausted its effects, will be exactly the same as the situation of the external balance previous to this devaluation. The chronic disequilibrium, which had been temporarily reabsorbed, now reappears: there is no tendency to long-term equilibrium.

Numerous mechanisms of this type are to be found, especially in the monetary history of Latin America. In the nineteenth century successive devaluations took place there, particularly in Argentina. These devaluations were inoperative in the long run because they were followed by a general and proportionate increase in prices. I have shown how the mechanism of this general increase was closely linked with the behavior of the predominant income, namely, ground-rent.[16] These experiences prove that it is not possible to resolve a real disequilibrium of the external balance, due to profound structural maladjustment, by currency manipulations. They also show that the internal and external values of money cannot long remain different from each other. Despite the existence of home-produced goods which do not figure in international exchange, the domestic sector does eventually become subject to the influence of foreign prices. This influence is exerted through the channel of incomes. More recent experiences broadly confirm these views. For example, the devaluation of the Malian franc in 1967, which, according to the French experts, would restore equilibrium to Mali's external balance, in fact resulted in a proportionate and almost immediate increase in all prices, despite the freezing of wages. This is but an extreme example of how the structure of the dominant country's prices imposes itself on a dominated economy—an example that deserves to be thought about.

True, one might point out that, during the nineteenth century in Europe, the gold standard and the compensatory monetary policy of manipulating discount rates, a policy based on Goschen's theory, proved to be effective. But was this not merely because in the long run the balance of payments was in equilibrium, with disequilibria never more than momentary, conjunctural incidents? If disequilibrium had been structural and persistent, would not this method have failed sooner than it did?[17]

The Theory of Exchange Effects[18]

Direct price effect is based on the quantity theory, and this is the root of the error here.

Given the assumption of inconvertible currencies, the existence of a rate of exchange can vary widely at the whim of the balance of payments (that is, of the balance of real payments together with the balance of bank transactions, if we assume an underdeveloped country where expatriate commercial banks are functioning), does this not bring us back to the price effect without the quantity theory coming into the argument? In this case, indeed, the alteration in the rate of exchange entails an alteration in the price of imports, but there is no reason why the price of home-produced goods and the price of exports, which must relate to internal prices, should alter. Because the quantity of money continues to be stationary, say the quantitativists. Because the rate of exchange does not always necessarily influence internal prices, say others. Here, too, the analysis must be completed in the same way as before. On the one hand, depending on price elasticities, the alteration in the rate of exchange may have "normal" effects or "perverse" ones. On the other hand, the price of imports may, here too, influence the level of internal prices, and thereby that of exports, and in the same way: via costs, via the behavior of the dominant income, and via the transmission of price structures.

Here, too, short-term capital movement may prevent alteration in the rate of exchange (and in prices) just as formerly it prevented the movement of gold (and of prices). If the central bank raises the interest rate, it attracts foreign short-term capital, just as under a gold system, and for the same reason. In the event of a temporary deficit in the balance it can thus prevent devaluation (and the resultant increase in prices), just as under a gold system it could prevent a drain of gold (and the resultant decrease in prices). But this effect comes up against the same limit as before. If the deficit is structural, chronic, and profound, the inflow of foreign capital will not succeed in neutralizing it—all the less because the prospect of losing on the exchange in the event of devaluation is unattractive to speculators in search of a profit that is in any case rather slight, owing to an increase in the interest rate. At all events, once the rate of interest has been raised, the inflow of short-term capital will eventually come to an end.

Finally, what are we to conclude from the analysis of price effects? First, that there are no price effects, but only an exchange effect. Disequilibrium in the external balance does not influence prices directly, through the quantity of money. It affects the rate of exchange, and this in turn affects all prices. It follows from this that alterations in the rate of exchange can never, whatever the price elasticities may be, resolve the difficulties of a structural disequilibrium, since at the end of a certain period things go back as they were at the start. Second, even in the transition period, fluctuations in the exchange do not necessarily improve the situation of the external balance, owing to the existence of critical price elasticities.

If we consider that, in the countries of the periphery, the elasticity of demand for imports is particularly slight, owing to the lack of possible substitution of local production for foreign production; that in these countries the incomes of exporters are all the more important in proportion as the country's degree of international integration is high; that the influence of these incomes on demand is supplemented by decisive psychological considerations which link the internal value of the currency to its external value; and that there is a mechanism whereby the price structure of the dominant economy is transmitted to the dominated one—then we may conclude that, in nine cases out of ten, devaluation will in no way resolve the chronic disequilibrium of the balance of payments, either in the short run or, *a fortiori,* in the long; on the contrary, this devaluation will worsen the external situation in the short run.

The Theory of Income Effects

The new theory as presented by Ohlin. Wicksell and Ohlin presented the mechanism of the income effect in a very simple form. The deficit in the external balance is, as we know, settled by a transfer abroad of purchasing power. This new purchasing power must enable the economy that benefits from it to import more. On the other hand, the transfer obliges the deficit economy to reduce its demand for imports. Ohlin thus starts from a fundamentally correct position, whereas the price-effects analysis started from a quantity-theory position—in other words, it constructed its schema on a fundamentally mistaken basis.

As for the transfer of gold that takes place under the gold-standard system, this provides support for the transfer of purchasing power, and nothing more. Obviously, if we assume that convertibility and flexible exchange have been abandoned, then disequilibrium, which is on the one hand a transfer of purchasing power, and on the other has an effect on the rate of exchange (when disequilibrium has not been compensated by a transfer of some international money, either gold or foreign exchange—that is to say, after stocks of this money have been exhausted). These secondary effects of disequilibrium on the rate of exchange may obstruct the working of the re-equilibration mechanism, e.g., canceling out the transfer of purchasing power through a price increase. But the mechanism remains essentially of the same nature as before.

The superiority of Ohlin's theory in comparison with the former theory is that it enables us to explain the re-equilibration that takes place in the balance, however, the terms of trade may evolve. In the classical theory it is the alteration of these terms in a certain direction that reestablishes equilibrium. Now, experience has proved that re-equilibration takes place despite a perverse evolution of the terms of trade. This is easily explained from an income standpoint—the deficit is a transfer of income to foreign countries, which results in an increase in "their" imports ("our" exports), regardless of the terms of trade, whether better (the normal effect) or worse (the perverse effect).

The theory of transfer of purchasing power also has the merit of bringing out the point that there is only a *tendency* to restoration of equilibrium. Nothing is less certain than that the increase in purchasing power resulting from a surplus in the external balance should be wholly concentrated on demand for imports. Taking a Keynesian standpoint, Federici claims that an income paid to a foreign country not only transfers purchasing power to it but also automatically creates additional income and production in the paying country, through the mechanism of the multiplier.[19] When Britain buys from Argentina, it supplies pounds sterling to the latter. These pounds sterling can only serve, after a more or less lengthy circuit, to buy goods in Britain. This criticism assumes the problem solved. But what is not certain is that those who possess pounds sterling *want,* given the relevant prices, to buy goods in Britain.

This tendency to equilibrium is valid in all cases, whether the currency be stable (gold standard, gold-exchange standard, foreign-exchange standard) or not (paper-money standard), although in the latter case there is the further addition of an exchange effect. Besides, what tends to equilibrium is the balance of real payments, not the sum of the balances of real payments and of the flow of bank capital.

An import of capital destined for investment increases the country's income, whereas an import of liquidities by an expatriate bank in order to meet an increased need for currency does not increase any income. This being so, it is understandable why the underdeveloped countries have not paid in real exports for the increase in their circulation of money.[20]

The new theory as presented by the post-Keynesians.[21] Keynesian thinking, by putting in the forefront the multiplier effects of a primary increase in incomes, was to make possible the final perfecting of the theory, which was achieved by Metzler and Machlup.

Reduced to its simplest terms, the mechanism is as follows. A positive net result of the external balance operates like an independent investment; it determines, through the working of the multiplier mechanism, a greater increase in the national income, which, given the propensity to import, makes possible a readjustment of the external balance. Conversely, a negative net result of the external balance determines a shrinkage of total income which facilitates a reduction in imports that contributes to bringing the external balance back to equilibrium.

The simplest example of how the mechanism functions is given by Haberler. The factors that can cause disturbance (independent investment I, and net result of the external balance X - M) constitute the multiplicand. The multiplier is merely the converse of the propensity to save (c measures the propensity to consume). We thus have:

$$Y = (I + X - M) \frac{1}{1 - c}$$

Subsequently, attempts have been made to improve the formula by making more precise the independent factors and the induced factors distinctive of external exchange. This later work has not, however, altered the essence of the reasoning.

Colin Clark's initial formula:

$$Y = (I + X) \frac{1}{1 - c + m}$$

increases the multiplicand by deleting (- M) but decreases the multiplier by the propensity to import (m). It makes it possible to distinguish to some extent between the induced effects and the independent ones. Harrod's formula brings in a real element by distinguishing between imports on the basis of their real destination: imports destined for internal investment, or for production of goods for subsequent export. Clark's other formulae make possible a more exact distinction between induced effects and independent ones (his second formula appeared in the *Economic Journal* in 1938) and bring the time element into the scheme (Clark's dynamicized multiplier).

The model put forward by Machlup (a model with successive injections) enables one to take account simultaneously of the effects of variations in country A's balance on country B and of the reciprocal effects of B's balance on that of A. The same is true of Metzler's horizontal multiplier model. It must be said that Metzler draws attention to a very interesting case, namely, that in which the fall in the national income in the paying country and in the receiving country is such that the debtor country is unable to settle its debt. The possibility of internal equilibrium thus depends on the values of the propensities to consume and to invest in the two countries. This case is particularly interesting, for it ought to enable us to put our finger on the problem: it shows, indeed, that the equilibrium of the external balance reflects only a structural adjustment of the economies involved, the requirements for which it makes clear.

These post-Keynesian theories have been subjected to much criticism. The symmetrical character they attribute to increase and reduction in income has been questioned. Kindleberger has noted that, in an underdeveloped country, Duesenberry's "demonstration effect" is reflected in the fact that the extra imports that result from prosperity become permanent requirements that cannot be reduced when exports collapse during a period of depression.[22] These theories have also been criticized for assuming stable marginal propensities and rigorously stable prices, rate of exchange, and rate of interest.

These are, in fact, only secondary criticisms. The crucial criticism to be leveled at all the formulas of the foreign-trade multiplier is similar to that which multiplier analyses in general are subject.[23] If demand creates its own supply, this takes place, here as before, through the intermediary of production, the development of which calls for the investment of saving. What has to be taken into consideration is thus not the propensity to save but the propensity to hoard (Keynes's "forced" hoarding, not the precapitalist hoarding of real values). What then becomes of Haberler's formula of the foreign-trade multiplier?

In the developed countries, where the Keynesian propensity to hoard is *not* nil, this formula has some meaning, as has, along with it, that of the foreign-trade multiplier. Here, a surplus in the balance does indeed behave like an investment. A "gift," even a temporary one, to foreign countries contributes a certain animation to economic activity. This Keynesian propensity to hoard is merely a recognition of the contradiction between producing and consuming capacity that is characteristic of developed capitalist society.[24]

In the underdeveloped countries, however, where this propensity *is* nil, the value of the second member of the formula becomes infinite. The multiplier loses its distinctive significance. While in the underdeveloped countries a really productive investment does increase total income and so make possible subsequent additional imports, a mere surplus is not productive; as production in the underdeveloped countries is limited not by capacity to consume but by capacity to produce, a "gift" does nothing to enable society to become richer. On the contrary, this gift constitutes a loss, diminishing the national income by the corresponding amount.

Furthermore, the question of what the various "propensities" are—the answer to the question about the stability of propensities to import or what the alterations are that affect it—is not one of empirical fact but a basic theoretical question. For what is meant by the structural adjustment that is a condition of equilibrium in external payments? This adjustment is expressed precisely by alterations in propensities, including the propensity to import. We are therefore not entitled to imagine a variety of models, each characterized by different variations in these propensities. This empiricist attitude gets us no further. For propensities do change; furthermore, we need to know how and why they change. Models constructed on these income effects of the external disequilibrium are therefore incapable of throwing light on the problem of the external balances of the countries of the periphery.

From observation of the volatility of prices in the underdeveloped countries, which is incompatible with the foreign-trade multiplier analysis, the income effect has been rejected as a means of restoring equilibrium in these countries. Ohlin was overtaken by the post-Keynesians, and the modern theory has become that of the multiplier, and no longer that of *International and Inter-Regional Trade*. This was going too far, however. I reject the multiplier analysis for basic reasons which I have already explained; but I consider that Ohlin's analysis remains valid.

In rejecting the multiplier analysis, some contemporary authors have mostly gone back to the traditional price effect. They rejected the income effect because of the "low propensity to save" of the underdeveloped countries and the weakness of the multiplier that follows from this, owing to the volatility of prices in these countries. And as price fluctuations are observed in these countries that are independent of the rate of exchange, they revert to the crude price-effect.[25] During depression, the prices of exports fall, even though the local currency stands firm (monetary integration). In a period of prosperity these prices rise, with the local currency still stable. Should it not be concluded from this that the analysis made previously, in which direct effects by the external balance upon prices were rejected, retaining only the immediate effects of this balance upon prices through the rate of exchange, is incorrect? Should one not be convinced that the underdeveloped countries prove the possibility of a direct price effect? That in these countries the fluctuations in the balance of payments entail fluctuations in prices through the intermediary of international currency movements?

Not at all. Prices fluctuate at the mercy of demand in the underdeveloped countries just as in the developed ones. If the export prices of the underdeveloped countries fall in a depression period, this is due not to the deficit in the external balance but to a decline in the demand for these goods, a demand mainly from abroad. The volume and the price of exports fall together and for the same reason. The deficit in the balance has nothing to do with *causing* this fall: on the contrary, it results from it. Moreover, the quantity-theory schema is here caught red-handed, so to speak. The deficit in the external balance ought, according to the classical theory, to entail a drain of payment media that would itself bring about a fall in prices (a cumulative process). In a case where the local currency is independent, the exhaustion of local stocks of foreign exchange and gold is not the cause of the fall in prices but the consequence of this fall, which has contributed, along with the fall in the volume of exports, to make the external balance unfavorable. This exhaustion leads not to a subsequent fall in internal prices but to devaluation, and thereby to an increase in the price level. This general and proportional increase cancels out the effects of devaluation. These temporary effects have, in the circumstances, no positive significance. Devaluation under depression conditions does not in fact make possible an increase in the volume of exports. The external deficit is therefore temporarily worsened, since unit price in foreign currency has fallen.

The conclusions at which we arrive, where the theory of the readjustment of the balance of payments is concerned, are thus wholly negative. In the first place, despite appearances, the so-called price effect no more functions in the underdeveloped countries than it does in the developed ones. Second, the "exchange" effect does not tend to restore equilibrium. Alterations in the rate of exchange are often, especially in the underdeveloped countries, effective only for a limited period (until the internal increase in prices has become general and proportional to the fall in the rate of exchange), and are often effective in a perverse direction (owing to the price elasticities). Third, the "income" effect is only a tendency, and implies the pressure of structural adjustment that constitutes the very essence of the problem.

There is, then, no mechanism that automatically re-equilibrates the external balance. All that can be said for certain is that imports, in general, transfer purchasing power abroad in a precise monetary form, and that this transfer naturally tends to make possible subsequent exports. This tendency is a very general one. It is similar to that by which, in a market economy, any purchase makes possible a subsequent sale, provided some other conditions are fulfilled. But just as the existence of this profound tendency does not justify the "law of markets," so it does not justify the construction of a theory of automatic international equilibrium.

Yet the external balance was, broadly speaking, kept in equilibrium for a whole century. It must be concluded from this that the structure of the underdeveloped countries was at that time perfectly in conformity with the requirements of the dominant countries. The whole problem results from the fact that this "structural harmony" is not exempt from internal contradictions. On the contrary, these contradictions become more acute, because "equilibrium" corresponds, for the dominated periphery of the system, to a "blocked transition." Its true nature then becomes apparent, and the international specialization on which it is based is found unbearable. External disequilibrium becomes manifest and forces its victims to react. This reaction, if it does not go so far as to challenge the foundations of the system of international specialization, shows itself on secondary, nonessential levels—leading, for example, to changes in the monetary system. This is how the underdeveloped countries have often broken through the rigid monetary dependence which, by preventing the momentary fluctuations in the external balance from altering the internal conditions of the underdeveloped economy, facilitated the structural adjustment that was capable, broadly speaking, of establishing equilibrium in this balance. Today, when these temporary fluctuations in the external balance cause changes in the internal conditions of the underdeveloped economy, structural adjustment has become more difficult.

The new policy of capital export reflects awareness of this situation in the developed countries. The World Bank and the financial consortiums are not ignorant of the fact that "natural" structural readjustment no longer functions as it did in the nineteenth century. They rightly deduce from this that capital can be invested only where its utilization will immediately give rise to a surplus of foreign currency that can provide the means of exporting the profits. Chronic disequilibrium is thus resolved by reducing the degree of international integration, reducing the flow of foreign capital. But the underdeveloped economy remains basically what it was before: a peripheral capitalist economy, that is, one where the process of capitalist accumulation has been based from the start not on expansion of the internal market but on external demand. Since external demand and the flow of foreign capital continue to be the essential source of the development of capitalism in the underdeveloped economies, this development is itself held back by the external disequilibrium. This is the phenomenon of blocked transition.

Conditions and Significance of the "Natural Equilibrium Rate of Exchange"

Par as equilibrium exchange rate between convertible currencies. We have just seen that the real features of the two economic systems in contact with each other may be such that the balance of payments cannot be equilibrated in the context of free exchange. Since the automatic mechanisms do not function, it seems that in this situation there is no equilibrium rate of exchange. The structural disequilibrium goes so deep that, whatever the rate of exchange may be, the external balance remains unfavorable to one partner and favorable to the other.

What is called the equilibrium exchange rate is in fact a rate that ensures equilibrium in the balance of payments without restrictions affecting imports and the "natural" movement of long-term capital. If it be said that the mechanisms that readjust incomes have only a *tendency* to operate, this amounts merely to saying that such a rate does not always exist. To put it more precisely, as the mechanisms of the exchanges belong to the short term, whereas structural readjustment is a long-term matter, there is not always an equilibrium rate of exchange, and still less a "natural" or "spontaneous" one.

Yet it appears that an equilibrium rate did exist throughout the nineteenth century. Par was certainly at that time, from one point of view, the "normal" rate of exchange between two currencies that were both convertible into gold. Purchase and sale of gold by the banks of issue, at a fixed price and in unlimited amounts, confined the fluctuations of the exchange rate between the narrow limits of the gold points. Does this mean that par was a rate toward which the market rate actually tended? Aftalion showed that the mechanisms of the exchange do not differ in kind whether currencies are convertible or not. In both cases, variations in the exchange are determined by the same forces: the state of the balance of payments, how the future value of a currency is estimated within the given economy, and the speculative movements of capital. The only difference—which is here a substantial one, to be sure—is that the system of convertibility kept exchange fluctuations within narrow limits.

If there were international structural disequilibrium, the balance of payments of one of the partners would be constantly unfavorable and that of the other constantly favorable. The rate of exchange would be kept stable at the level of the outgoing gold point. This rate would entail a steady drain of gold from the country with the unfavorable balance toward the country with the favorable one. Such a state of affairs certainly could not last. The central bank would combat the gold drain by raising the discount rate. If the structural disequilibrium went too deep, this policy would soon be found ineffective.

Nevertheless, par would, in this case, have constituted an equilibrium rate. Chronic disequilibrium of the balance means that there is a tendency to import too much; in other words, that total demand is focused excessively on imports and not enough on home-produced goods. A price distortion is bound to appear eventually, with a decline in the prices of home-produced goods. Does this bring us back, then, to the price effect? Not at all. What we have here is not an influence by the quantity of money upon the general level of prices, but an influence by income upon relative prices. The decline in internal prices, and so in the prices of exports, means a worsening of the terms of trade and a decline in the income of local exporters, that is, in the country's income, which will bring about a decline in imports. The mechanism will continue to function so long as equilibrium has not been reestablished. Convertibility gives the system sufficient solidity for the income mechanism to be able to exhaust its effects, that is, eventually to re-equilibrate the balance.

What happens, though, if convertibility is suspended? What then happens to the theory of the exchange?

Disappearance of the "normal" rate of exchange when inconvertibility prevails. As the purpose of the theory of the exchange is to explain the ratio that obtains between the values of two currencies, it is plain that one's general conception regarding the value of money is what ultimately determines one's conception of the fundamental nature of the exchange. This is why marginalism, which defined the value of money as its purchasing power, arrived at the theory, on the question of the exchange, of the parity of purchasing powers. And just as it landed up with the quantity theory in the internal domain, so also was it to land up with an international quantity theory, determining an international distribution of gold that would ensure equilibrium of the exchanges at the level of purchasing powers.[26]

According to my analysis in which I reject the quantity theory, it is necessary, when determining the internal value of money, to distinguish the case of convertibility from that of inconvertibility.[27] In the former, the real cost of gold production is what ultimately sets limits to variations in the value of money. In *this* sense, par did indeed constitute the normal rate of exchange. When convertibility is abandoned, so that the central bank is no longer buying and selling gold in unlimited amounts and at a fixed price, this price may itself be drawn into the general upward movement, so that sight is lost of the concatenation of mechanisms that now seem to be perfectly reversible. Just as there is no longer a normal price level, so there is no longer a normal rate of exchange.

Aftalion studied exchange variations in situations of this kind (in the Europe of 1914–1925) and defined the way this mechanism works. Closely examining events in France and other countries, Aftalion showed that while, on the one hand, the purchasing power of a currency did indeed form an element in the demand for it, on the other, fluctuations in the rate of exchange could themselves, in a world where inconvertibility prevailed, draw prices along with them (through the two channels of costs and incomes), so that the theory of parity of purchasing power lost its reality. In his book, Aftalion undertook a minute study of the psychological mechanisms of speculation. Since the "safety-rail" of convertibility has gone, speculation drags the rate of exchange along with it, and this rate determines the level of internal prices and of the price of gold. In the end, the very expression "normal rate of exchange" loses all meaning. The existence of too great a gap, over a long period, between the official exchange rate and the purchasing capacity of a currency, whittled away by inflation, makes export difficult and increases the debit side of the balance. Economies finding themselves in this situation are then obliged to take the step of devaluing their currency in order to adapt its external value to its internal purchasing power. This devaluation may in turn give rise to a new wave of inflation that cancels out all its effects. There is no need to bring in the factor of speculation. Speculation is, indeed, in these circumstances based on reality. People speculate on a fall because experience has proved that such a situation contains the germ of a future devaluation. It is this actual situation that is the cause of devaluation, and not the speculation that precipitates these events.

All the conditions needed for a situation like this to develop are present in international structural disequilibrium. The chronic deficit in the balance of payments that reflects this profound structural disequilibrium compels states to devalue their currency. The devaluation of inconvertible money gives rise in its turn to a wave of inflation that brings the situation back to where it was before. Once again it becomes clear that chronic disequilibrium cannot be avoided except by way of control over external trade and capital movements, by direct influence on real movements. When the currency has become inconvertible the system no longer possesses the solidity it needs in order to wait for the income effect to exhaust its consequences and for equilibrium to be restored. The tendency to disequilibrium entails permanent instability.

The equilibrium exchange rate and full employment. Modern economists—in particular, Nurkse—lay down an additional condition when defining the equilibrium exchange rate, namely, that it must ensure full employment.[28]

It was Robinson who established a connection between the level of employment and the rate of exchange.[29] This connection is, at bottom, extremely artificial. It follows from an almost caricatural simplification of the Keynesian analysis. Robinson links the level of the national income to the rate of interest in a mechanical way, so that there is always a level of interest that ensures full employment—whereas Keynes rightly insisted on showing that it was possible for unemployment to become an insoluble problem. Robinson then links, in an equally artificial way, the international movements of capital with the rate of interest—whereas these movements are dictated by the absolute and relative volume of incomes from property in the developed countries and prospects of profitability of investment both in these countries and in the periphery (prospects that are largely independent of fluctuations in the rate of interest). Equipped with these mechanistic and artificial relations, she shows how to each level of interest (and therefore of employment) there corresponds a level of the exchange which equilibrates the balance of payments. This way of considering that one of a group of variables can always be fixed arbitrarily because the others then adjust themselves to this arbitrary value is typical of the method employed by the analysts of "general equilibrium." It is liable to all the criticisms that can be made of the empiricist method in economics. It is thoroughly formalist. It denies the existence of fundamentally irreversible causal relations. This is why the equilibrium rate of exchange cannot be connected with the problem of the volume of employment other than in an artificial and unrealistic way.

The equilibrium exchange rate as the rate of domination of the periphery by the center. In reality, this exchange rate may very well be—and even certainly is, in relations between developed and underdeveloped countries—an exchange rate of domination. To each level of the exchange there corresponds a certain distribution of relative profitability of investments in the different sectors. But it is not the exchange that determines the volume of absorption of foreign capital by the underdeveloped country. Precisely the contrary is true. Capital flows in to the extent that the developed countries have free capital to dispose of and that conditions make these external investments profitable; and by weighing upon the balance of payments, they determine an equilibrium level of the exchange—in other words, a level that makes possible payment of interest on imported capital and payment for the volume of imports determined by the degree to which the underdeveloped countries are integrated into the international market: that is, determined by the demand for foreign goods that the volume of exports (bound up with this degree of integration) makes possible. In other words, the mechanism of the exchange enables the structure of the underdeveloped country to be adjusted to that of the dominant country. In this sense, a "better" equilibrium, meaning one that makes possible an alteration of this structure, necessitates restrictions on imports. Clearly, in this case too, when the protection constituted by the gold standard has been removed, a passing change in conditions of trade or movement of capital entails an alteration in the rate of exchange which, by bringing about a different distribution of relative profitability between different sectors of the underdeveloped economy, influences the orientation of foreign investments and, consequently, the conditions of domination. But what always happens is an adjustment by the underdeveloped structure to the developed one.

STRUCTURAL ADJUSTMENT OF THE PERIPHERY OF THE WORLD CAPITALIST SYSTEM TO THE REQUIREMENTS OF ACCUMULATION AT THE CENTER

The Theory of International Structural Adjustment

The underdeveloped economies are not precapitalist economies or even dualistic economies characterized by the juxtaposition of two independent systems, one capitalist and the other not.[30] They are *peripheral capitalist* economies. That is, they are dominated by the talist mode of production, but this mode of production, which in their case is based on the external market, does not tend to become exclusive, as it does where it is based from the outset on the internal market, in countries where the break-up of precapitalist modes of production has preceded its victory.

It is therefore not surprising that when we deal with any large economic problem relating to these countries we always find ourselves considering the external balance. All the important economic changes that may occur during the development of these countries influence the different elements in the balance of payments. Can the same be said of the developed countries? Here, too, it is not possible to conceive of any big change that would not affect the conditions governing relations between the national economy and foreign countries. In fact, however, the two problems are different in kind. It is possible to construct a valid model of development of a capitalist economy without bringing international relations into it. This theoretical model is perfectly correct because capitalist economy forms a coherent whole which is logically self-sufficient. A model like this is out of the question for an underdeveloped country, which, by definition, cannot be isolated from the international market. The forms of its international integration condition the pace and direction of its development. The underdeveloped economy does not constitute a coherent whole in itself. It does not make sense apart from the world capitalist market which shapes it.

The problem is therefore not whether there are mechanisms that ensure "spontaneous" equilibrium of the external balance in general, and in particular in relations between the dominant developed center and the dominated underdeveloped periphery. It is clear that no such mechanisms exist, at least in a form that would ensure "automatic" equilibrium. It is only the ideological character of current economic science, its will to discover at any price the mechanisms of "universal harmony," that enables it to state the contrary, making use of anything and everything: a fundamentally mistaken theory (the quantity theory of money); an inadequate analysis of elasticities, full of errors; and recourse to empiricism and refusal to analyze—notably as regards the significance of "propensities."

The problem is, why, despite the absence of such mechanisms, the system does function, ensuring relative equilibrium in relations among developed capitalist countries and between them and the countries of the periphery. While, as regards relations among developed countries, the system certainly functions, this happens by way of repeated crises, which make up the history of the development of capitalism: the classical cyclical crises of the nineteenth century and the first third of the twentieth century, the crisis in states' monetary affairs and foreign relations, and, most recently, the "dollar-famine" crisis of the postwar period, followed by the present crisis of the international monetary system. Permanent structural adjustment constitutes the background to this story—an adjustment always marked by inequality, asymmetry, and domination, yesterday by Great Britain and today by the United States.

In respect to relations between the center and the periphery, which is what most concerns us here, the (fundamentally unequal) adjustment takes place through a permanent tendency to external deficit on the part of the underdeveloped countries, a tendency marked by increasingly chronic "difficulties" in their external payments.

This profound tendency is nothing other than an expression of the forces that make the exports of the capitalist countries more "necessary" (inherent tendency to export) than for the underdeveloped economies and that at the same time facilitate their sale. The dynamism of the capitalist economies and the growing absolute advantage that is the reflection of this in industrial production enables the exports of these countries to be always ahead of those of the underdeveloped countries. This constant tendency, reinforced when the capitalist economies become overdeveloped, is still further strengthened when, during the cycle, the moment of recovery arrives. In contrast to this, the development of peripheral capitalism, based on expansion of external exchange and investment of foreign capital, continues to be impelled from the outside. It therefore lacks an aggressive dynamism of its own that would oblige it to open new markets for itself. It merely adapts itself to the market that is opened to it by the dynamism of the capitalist center.

True, this chronic disequilibrium is continually overcome through adaptation of the underdeveloped structure to the requirements of the developed countries. This structural readjustment is effected thanks to readjustment of the structure of relative prices, which is such that the export products that interest the center are at every stage the most profitable ones. The generalizing of money circuits within the wants economy enables local production to be given a new direction dependent on capitalist profitability. This reorientation enables export activity to be developed further. Foreign capital itself, when it comes on the scene, moves, in accordance with immediate profitability, into activities that are bound up with the external market.

But this international specialization establishes itself only through a permanent struggle against increasing obstacles. Peripheral capitalism does not radically destroy precapitalist modes of production. On the contrary, it reinforces the precapitalist structures. This happens with the strengthening of the agrarian capitalism that is characteristic of underdevelopment.

In nearly all the underdeveloped countries, agrarian capitalism has constituted the principal form of capitalist development. On this basis, social classes of landed proprietors have come into being—latifundia-owners in some countries, rich peasants elsewhere—which have played a determining role in history.[31] This type of development has reinforced the dominant position of ground-rents—a reinforcement that is reflected in a high propensity to import luxury goods made in the most advanced countries.[32] These imports are larger in proportion as the conjuncture is favorable. This reinforcement of rent is also reflected in intensified hoarding, which calls for increased imports of gold (bought abroad). The specific character of this development, putting ground-rent in a dominant position, causes the investment of capital, both foreign and national, to be in part directed toward tertiary production, which is by definition unexportable. This exceptional profitability of unproductive activities attracts foreign capital into sectors that cannot give rise to the surplus of exports needed to pay the profits on investments.

The very mechanism of international specialization bears within itself its own contradiction. It means for the underdeveloped country a narrowing of the range of goods it produces (that it can supply) at the very moment when its demand is increasing (as a result of the growth of income that colonial opening-up implies), in other words, when it is demanding a more varied range of goods. The equilibrium of supply and demand is then possible only on condition that imports are able to grow very fast, faster than production. This is what is meant by "increased propensity to import." Such a mechanism can function only if exports are also able to grow very fast, that is, when the system of international specialization is being installed. For the periphery as a whole, and over a large period, the center's demand for products of the periphery can only grow at the pace of the center's own growth. Thus, the history of the periphery necessarily appears as an endless series of "miracles"—brief periods of very rapid growth when the system is being installed—followed by blockage, stagnations, even retrogressions: "miracles without a morrow," "failures to take off."

Specialization itself must constantly assume new forms. During its long history—three centuries in the case of Latin America, over a century for Asia and North Africa, eighty years for Black Africa—the periphery has successively fulfilled a variety of functions in this specialization in the service of capitalist accumulation at the center. In the period of mercantilist capitalism it provided superprofits for large-scale maritime trade: Africa supplied the labor (slave trade), America the product (sugar, etc.), the "feudal" consumer in Europe the means of realizing this superprofit. In the period of industrial capitalism international specialization at first took the form, principally, of commercial exchanges—the *économie de traite,* characterized by the exchange of agricultural products (the development of which gave rise to peripheral agrarian capitalism) for manufactured consumer goods. Then, with the investment of foreign capital, from the end of the nineteenth century onward, came mining activity and, after that, the establishment by this capital of light industry. The international specialization that obliges the underdeveloped countries to specialize in light production also necessitates that they import heavy goods. Through this channel the level of the propensity to import is raised.

At the present time the outlines of a new kind of international specialization are emerging: the developed center will specialize in automated forms of production requiring very highly skilled labor, the periphery will specialize in the classical (including heavy) forms of production of the industrial epoch, requiring only unskilled labor.

Upon this permanent and growing basic contradiction of specialization is superimposed that of the dynamic of foreign investment. The integration of the underdeveloped countries into the capital market weighs directly upon the balance of payments, owing to the outflow of funds to which it leads. The payment to foreigners of profits on previously invested capital increases very rapidly. The backflow of profits tends to become greater than the inflow of new capital. A very simple reckoning of compound interest shows that—whatever the rate of growth of the inflow of new foreign investment—the backflow of profits must very soon surpass it. Thus, the periphery moves from the stage of being a young borrower to that of being an old one. The monopoly character of the foreign capital invested in the periphery causes this "tribute" to be still greater. At the same time, the export of the profits of foreign capital annuls the multiplier effects of acceleration. Transfer abroad of the field of operation of the accelerator is itself reflected in a rise in the level of the propensity to import.[33]

The monetary and banking integration that has accompanied this hierarchical organization of international specialization facilitates the flight of local saving and its investment at the center. The mechanism functions as a powerful centralizer of capital at the center. The underdeveloped countries are not, as the false image of current theory presents them, countries that receive capital because they are lacking it, but, on the contrary, countries that *supply* capital to the center.

In the present period the increasing difficulties of international specialization cause a crisis of public finance to be general throughout the periphery. The state has to bear the social costs of this specialization—in particular the costs of infrastructures, which require very heavy recurrent expenditure. In its turn, public expenditure, growing both absolutely and relatively, entails an increase in propensity to import, for this expenditure has, directly and indirectly, a very high import content.[34]

The chronic deficit was continually overcome during the nineteenth century by a structural adjustment of this type which was greatly helped by the solidity of the metallic standard. For the countries with independent currencies (especially in Latin America), the cycles of repeated devaluation did not hinder their structural readaptation. Today this devaluation is done without. A rigid exchange rate, officially fixed, tends to become the rule. This rigidity has the result that the entry of foreign currency is inadequate to meet requirements. The foreign capitalists are thus always in danger of seeing their profits blocked. The risk element in foreign investment becomes greater. The intensity of the flow of new foreign capital declines or becomes irregular. This decline in the import of foreign capital worsens the situation, since it reduces one of the two main sources of foreign currency. Sooner or later the authorities have to adopt the only possible solution, a cut in imports.

For their part, the institutions of the center concern themselves with directing investment into the sectors that are immediately profitable, that is to say, those which produce a surplus of currency in the course of their activity—for example, raw materials. Foreign investors have no fear, in this connection, of any measure that may be taken by the public authority, since the product itself is wholly destined for export. Even if the local government were to decide that the profits of foreign investment should remain frozen, the foreign capitalists would still be able to repatriate their gains. All that would be needed would be to sell the raw materials to a daughter-concern at a slightly lower price. Whatever local legislation might be regarding exchange and the export of profits, the enterprise would continue to be profitable. This does not apply where capital is invested in other types of activity, such as those which dispose of their products inside the country itself. Activities of this order are in jeopardy from the measures that the local authorities may be led to adopt in order to deal with their external deficit.

The equilibrium secured in this way by the state authorities of the periphery—through measures of control which leave fundamental orientation of the economy (international specialization) unchallenged—amounts in fact to an adjustment *downward*, by checking the process of integration into the world market.

Thus, structural adjustment of the periphery to the requirements of accumulation at the center means above all an increasing transfer of capital from the periphery to the center. Unequal exchange, that is, the worsening of the terms of trade over a whole century, involving the exchange of increasingly unequal quantities of total labor (direct and indirect), has assumed extraordinary proportions.[35] Following Emmanuel, I have shown how unequal reward of labor (the different proportions of the value of labor power ranging from 1 to 20, whereas the relevant differences in productivity range only from 1 to 5), together with the law of the international equilization of profit, could signify a transfer of value of the order to $22 billion. If the trade of the periphery represents 20 percent of its total product, that means that 15 percent of this product is transferred in this way.

It is absurd, in these circumstances, to ascribe any natural value to the equilibrium exchange rate that facilitates the working of these mechanisms which centralize wealth on the world scale. Only the ideology of universal harmony prevents one from seeing the true nature of this structural adjustment. Development policies that recommend the adoption of a "realistic rate of exchange" that would ensure this equilibrium of the external balance, at least as a rate for calculating the social profitability of projects (a reference exchange rate), are, in fact, policies for the development of underdevelopment.[36]

This mechanism of structural adjustment has never been studied systematically by current economic theory. The crisis, manifesting itself through the crisis of external payments experienced by an increasing number of underdeveloped countries, is nevertheless impossible to ignore. Current economic theory therefore seeks to account for it, not as the outcome of a fundamental mechanism of the world market, but as a phenomenon peculiar to our time.

Prebisch and Kindleberger analyze the matter in this way. The former considers that it is a new phenomenon of the twentieth century, due to continuous decline in the propensity to import of the new center (the United States). The latter attributes the phenomenon to the "maturity" of the industrial countries. Both writers remain at the level of description, without analyzing the phenomenon as a symptom of blocked transition.

The Thesis of R. Prebisch[37]

The thesis maintained by Raul Prebisch as an explanation of the chronic deficit of the underdeveloped countries (the tendency for gold to leave these countries) is bound up with the decreasing propensity to import of the center of the twentieth-century world, the United States.

Fluctuations in income are assumed to have been greater in the nineteenth century in the developed countries (mainly Britain) than in the underdeveloped ones. During depression periods the fall in the national income, which was relatively more serious in Britain than in the countries of the periphery, entailed a fall in the imports of the dominant center which was relatively greater than the fall in the imports of the peripheral countries. Britain then attracted the gold of these countries to itself, since the balance (assumed to be in equilibrium throughout the cycle as a whole) was unfavorable to the underdeveloped countries. Conversely, during periods of prosperity, gold flowed back to the underdeveloped countries: the relatively greater expansion of the national income of Great Britain entailed an increase in the level of British imports that was relatively greater than that of imports into the underdeveloped countries.

In the twentieth century, Prebisch maintains, the phenomenon has lost its symmetry because the propensity to import of the United States is continually falling, while that of Great Britain remains stable. For the phenomenon to continue to be symmetrical it would have been necessary for the ratio of fluctuation at the center to fluctuation in the periphery to increase regularly in proportion to the decline in the center's propensity to import. But this is not the case. The result is that the volume of gold that leaves the underdeveloped countries for the developed ones during depression exceeds the volume that moves in the opposite direction during prosperity.

It is to be noted that Prebisch's proposition, namely, that the balance of the underdeveloped countries was in equilibrium over a long period in the nineteenth century and is now chronically unfavorable, is based not on the relative *size* of the fluctuations at the center and in the periphery, or on the absolute size of the propensities to import, but exclusively on the *movement* of the center's propensity to import.

To clarify this matter, let us assume that the world is divided into two countries: the developed center and the underdeveloped periphery. Let us then assume that fluctuations are greater at the center. In a period of depression the center's imports fall by 50 percent, say, and those of the periphery (which are the center's exports) by 10 percent.

The balance worsens for the periphery and improves for the center. The opposite occurs during a period of prosperity. Over a complete cycle, the external balance is in equilibrium. One might have assumed the opposite—that is, bigger fluctuations, or equally big ones, in the periphery—and the result would have been the same. The relative size of the fluctuations explains who gains in prosperity—the center or the periphery—and who suffers in depression. It does *not* explain any asymmetry that may show itself in the balance, with a chronic deficit for one of the partners.

Propensities to import explain the relative size of the fluctuations. Let us assume that propensity to import is low at the center and high in the periphery. A certain fluctuation, one way or another, in the income of the center causes a more or less pronounced fluctuation in the periphery, depending on the relative size of the two incomes. Here, a slight fluctuation at the center causes a more pronounced fluctuation in the periphery. Conversely, a pronounced fluctuation in the periphery has only a slight effect at the center. The fluctuations at the center are slighter than those in the periphery. Normally, it must be so because, the world being divided into two countries, their propensities to import are inverse to their incomes (the imports of the two countries being equal), and the income of the center must be the greater.

Let us now bring in a movement in the center's propensity to import. During a depression period the center's imports, the fluctuations in which we are assuming to be greater, fall by 50 percent, those of the periphery by 10 percent. The center has a surplus in its balance, the periphery a deficit. Prosperity arrives. Meanwhile, the center's propensity to import having decreased, its imports increase by only 20 percent instead of 50 percent. Those of the periphery increase by 10 percent. The balance of the periphery is favorable, but to a lesser extent than it was unfavorable during depression. There is a chronic deficit. It would be the same if the fluctuations were greater in the periphery. During depression the center's imports fall by 10 percent, those of the periphery by 50 percent. There is a surplus in the periphery's balance. During the prosperity period that follows, the center's imports increase by 20 percent, those of the periphery by 50 percent. There is a deficit bigger than the periphery's surplus had been.

Therefore, whether one accepts or rejects Prebisch's assumption (greater fluctuations at the center in the nineteenth century), his reasoning remains sound either way: if the center's propensity to import declines regularly, it is necessary, in order that the phenomenon may remain symmetrical, that, parallel with this, the quotient of fluctuation at the center by fluctuation in the periphery shall increase in the same proportion as propensity to import declines.

I think that, in the nineteenth century, fluctuations were approximately the same in size at the center and in the periphery—indeed, my calculations show that they were possibly even a little larger at the center. In the twentieth century, at least down to the Second World War, they seem to have been larger both at the center and in the periphery, but especially in the periphery. The quotient in question has therefore probably declined, which has aggravated the effect of the decline in propensity to import.

This is the essential point. What Prebisch can be criticized for is having chosen, as proof of the decline in the propensity of the developed countries to import from the underdeveloped ones, the figure for the general propensity of the United States to import (declining from 5.9 percent in 1919 to 3.0 percent in 1948). What in reality accounts for the phenomenon is not the evolution undergone by the propensity to import in general, but the evolution of the propensity of the developed countries, taken together, to import from the underdeveloped ones, also taken together. The general propensity of the developed countries to import increases regularly owing to the increasing trade of these countries among themselves. The propensity to import of the underdeveloped countries—and as these countries do not trade with each other, this propensity is equivalent to their propensity to import from the developed countries—has also increased. Altogether, the propensity of the underdeveloped countries to import from the developed ones has increased more than that of the developed countries to import from the underdeveloped ones, which simply reflects the fact that the ratio of the center's income to the periphery's has increased.

It is therefore not because the center's propensity to import has fallen that these difficulties have occurred, but because it has increased less rapidly than that of the periphery. This propensity seems to have diminished for the United States, since that country's general propensity to import has fallen, although it may be that its propensity to import from the underdeveloped countries has increased. But for the developed world as a whole this is not true.

It is true that, alongside this process, the size of the relative fluctuations in the periphery has increased, at least down to the Second World War—but by very little. On the other hand, the propensity of the underdeveloped countries to import from the developed ones has advanced from zero to about 30 percent (a little less than their general propensity to import). The propensity of the developed countries to import from the underdeveloped ones has advanced from zero to about 7.5 percent (three-tenths of their general propensity to import). The ratio of the center's propensity to import from the periphery to the periphery's propensity to import from the center, which was about unity at start, is today 7.5:30, or 25 percent (the inverse proportion is about 4).

Thus, the propensity to import of the developed countries as a whole has indeed increased less than that of the underdeveloped countries as a whole.

What does Prebisch's thesis mean, then? Quite simply, that the center's development is based on the home market (the market of all the developed countries taken together), whereas that off the periphery is based on the external market (the market of the developed countries). It is this fundamental asymmetry that accounts for the evolution of the ratio of propensities to import. But this movement is not new, not something special to the twentieth century. It has been permanent ever since the periphery was integrated into the world market. How, then, are we to explain the fact that the chronic deficitary tendency in the external balance of the periphery seems to have appeared only late in the day? By bringing in the factor that Prebisch neglects in his analysis: the movement of capital.

Prebisch takes into account only the trade balance, ignoring the other items in the balance of payments. The chronic tendency of the trade balance of the underdeveloped countries to be unfavorable can be offset by the influx of foreign capital. This influx, at certain periods of the cycle (prosperity), may indeed cause the fluctuations in the balance of these countries to be greater, but it nevertheless contributes to equalizing the surpluses and deficits over the cycle as a whole. It is true that this inflow carries the implication of an eventual backflow of profits that must exceed it in volume. It will be this backflow of profits, growing bigger and bigger, that in the end will become responsible, together with the movement of the trade balance already analyzed, for the chronic deficit in the balance of the underdeveloped countries in our time. During the nineteenth century the increasing flow of foreign capital, greater than the backflow of profits, made up for the progressive worsening in the trade balance. In the twentieth century the increasing backflow of profits, greater than the inflow of new capital, is added to the progressive worsening of the trade balance, and so makes the overall balance of payments even less favorable. These and other factors were brought by Kindleberger into *his* schema.

Kindleberger's Analysis [38]

It was not on the basis of the problem of relations between the underdeveloped countries and the developed ones that Charles Kindleberger made his analysis, but in connection with the problem of the "dollar famine" and the relations between Europe and the United States in the years following the Second World War. This problem gave rise to an economic discussion in which the chief participants were Harrod and Kindleberger.

Harrod, defending British interests, blamed the dollar famine on the policy of the United States, and in particular on the overvaluation of the dollar in relation to gold, together with the American customs tariff, which he considered too high. Kindleberger answered the British economist in the terms of a general theory. He began with the observation that the mechanism that causes the underdeveloped countries to be victims of the conjuncture in all its phases is similar to the mechanism that now operates in relations between Europe and the United States. In 1949 a minor recession in the United States resulted in European exports to that country falling by about 50 percent. Kindleberger considers that, for the effects of a variation in the national income in the United States and in Europe on international economic relations to be symmetrical, five conditions need to be fulfilled: (1) the degree of dependence by one region upon another (measured by the ratio of exports to national income in each of the two countries) must be of the same order of magnitude; (2) inflationary and deflationary pressures must work in the same direction in both countries; (3) price elasticities must be the same for the exports of both countries; (4) innovations must not always originate in the same country; and (5) in both countries the response of supply to demand must be identical.

Now, in the relations between the United States and Europe, just as in the relations between the developed countries in general and the underdeveloped countries, these five conditions are not present. There is therefore asymmetry in the balance of payments.

On the first point the same comment must be made as for Prebisch's analysis: the degree of dependence as regards external trade determines the direction in which fluctuations are transmitted, but cannot explain a chronic deficit. Thus, the heavy dependence of the underdeveloped countries upon their exports to the developed countries, and, conversely, the slight dependence of the developed countries on *their* exports to the underdeveloped ones, simply means that a slight fluctuation at the center produces a pronounced fluctuation in the periphery, whereas a pronounced fluctuation in the periphery is incapable of producing any great effect at the center. What counts is not the level of the propensities but the way they move. Let it be noted in passing that this does not mean that fluctuations are less pronounced at the center than in the periphery. The size of fluctuations depends not only on the size of exports and the share of the latter in the national income: it also depends on fluctuations in internal demand (on investment). The importance of this last factor is so decisive that, in fact, fluctuations at the center have often been greater than those in the periphery.[39]

The second point in Kindleberger's analysis deserves more attention, for it is new and opens up an interesting line of thought. By a deflationary tendency, Kindleberger means a tendency for saving to be overabundant. The deflationary tendency that prevails at the center in our time thus reflects a situation of "maturity." Kindleberger counterposes to this the inflationary tendency of the periphery, where saving is inadequate. There is a regrettable confusion here between investment that is desirable from the point of view of society and investment required by the system. True, saving is inadequate in the underdeveloped countries if our standpoint is the desirable development of these countries. But saving cannot be inadequate from the standpoint of the functioning of the present system. The fact remains that it is not overabundant. I do not agree with the use of the terms inflationary and deflationary, since the tendency called deflationary in the highly developed countries is in fact accompanied by a genuinely inflationary tendency (that is, by a tendency for the issue of currency to be excessive and consequently, by a tendency for prices to keep on rising). The road opened by Kindleberger is nevertheless a useful one. This tendency which he calls deflationary signifies that depression is more pronounced at the highly developed center than elsewhere, and prosperity less so.[40]

Thus, in a depression period the center's imports decline by, say, 50 percent, whereas those of the periphery decline by only 10 percent. The periphery's external balance is unfavorable. But when prosperity arrives, the center's imports do not increase by 50 percent above the average, but by only, say, 20 percent, whereas those of the periphery increase by 50 percent. The periphery's external balance continues to be unfavorable, and this situation becomes chronic.

As for price elasticities, these reinforce the tendency to chronic deficit. The prices of the developed countries are inelastic, those of the underdeveloped ones are hyperelastic. In a depression period, when the center's volume of imports falls by 50 percent, the prices of these exports from the periphery also fall (by, say, 50 percent). The value of the center's imports declines by 125 percent altogether. The periphery's imports, however, which diminish in volume by 10 percent, do not change in price. The surplus of the center's balance is greater in value than in volume. Conversely, in a prosperity period the price and the volume of the center's imports increase, the former by 50 percent, the latter by 20 percent, so that the value of these imports increases by 80 percent. The surplus in volume terms of the center's balance has become a deficit in value terms. However, the compensation is only partial. The great elasticity of the exports of the underdeveloped countries intensifies the chronic deficit. In volume terms the deficit of the periphery's balance was 70 percent of the average total trade of this part of the world (during the depression the periphery's deficit was 40 percent—fall in exports by 50 percent, and in imports by 10 percent, and during prosperity it was 30 percent—increase in exports by 20 percent, and in imports by 50 percent: a total of 70 percent). In value terms, however, the deficit becomes in a depression period 125 - 10 = 115 percent, the surplus in a prosperity period 80 - 50 = 30 percent, the total deficit being 85 percent.

Kindleberger's analysis, though interesting, nevertheless remains restricted to the sphere of the trade balance, and therefore needs to be completed in the same way as Prebisch's. Furthermore, this analysis remains, like Prebisch's, purely descriptive. *Why* is the propensity to import of the developed countries what it is, and that of the underdeveloped countries what it is; *why* are the price elasticities and the responses of supply to the pressure of demand, etc., what they are?

The answer is forced upon us: the place of the external market in the development of peripheral capitalism explains the way these propensities move. It is thus that the degree of dependence on external trade is the product of a historical movement the stages of which we have traced: what are called "deflationary" pressures are accounted for by the state of "maturity," the price elasticities by the degree of monopolization of the economy—monopolized industrial production resists a fall in prices more firmly than agricultural production which has remained competitive. As for innovations, obviously they must come from the developed countries, not the underdeveloped ones. These innovations and the "demonstration effects" they engender in the underdeveloped countries reinforce the propensity to import by diverting demand from local goods toward imports. Finally, supply is markedly elastic in a capitalist structure in which the dynamic entrepreneur runs ahead of demand, but not very elastic in a structure in which the enterprise follows demand (itself external). This situation intensifies the effect of the difference in the degree of monopolization of production on the relative elasticity of prices.

Neither Prebisch's analysis nor Kindleberger's can therefore take the place of the theory of the structural adjustment of the periphery to the requirements of accumulation at the center.

BALANCE OF PAYMENTS OF THE CAPITALIST COUNTRIES OF THE PERIPHERY

The balance of payments may thus be in chronic disequilibrium when there is profound international structural maladjustment. This chronic disequilibrium is always eventually overcome by the income effect, but over a period of time that may be quite long. It would therefore be more precise to describe the phenomenon as a *tendency* to disequilibrium.

Assuming a stable exchange (gold standard or foreign-exchange standard), the tendency to deficit is continually overcome by a slowing-down in potential growth. It is very difficult to trace statistically this phenomenon, which operates as a deep tendency and is not revealed by overt symptoms. When, however, the exchange is allowed to fluctuate freely, the tendency to disequilibrium is constantly reflected in devaluation of the currency. It is therefore easier to trace the phenomenon, although devaluation may have been caused by internal inflation rather than by the disequilibrium in the external balance. Knowledge of the history of the issue of currency enables us, however, to determine more surely where the responsibility lies. It is also possible to try and trace the phenomenon through the movement of the international reserves (gold and foreign currency) held by the underdeveloped countries.

Hoarding and the Balance of Payments

It remains true that it is dangerous to imagine that one can reveal a profound tendency in a system, such as the tendency to deficit in the balance of payments of the periphery, merely through observation of the movement of its international reserves. Once again, though empiricism enables one to discover the superficial appearance of things, it cannot do away with the need for analysis.

The point is that the movement of international money is not automatically determined by the balance of payments, which is in its turn determined by real forces. This movement is not merely "induced," it is also sometimes "inducing." International money is not only international money, it is also a means of hoarding (in gold and foreign currency), the backing for local currency, and a commodity (industrial gold). Now, hoarding and internal monetary requirements are determined by real forces, not by the state of the balance.[41] Hoarded international money passes in its turn from private persons into the banks and back again, which means that the movement of the reserves of the central bank is determined by forces other than those that have been analyzed up to now as determining the balance of payments.

What are the forces that ultimately determine the international movement of gold? On the one hand, the balance of real payments, and, on the other, the need for gold for internal monetary circulation and hoarding. In order to prove this I will argue in two stages: first, the balances, thus defined, of the two countries between which we assume the world to be divided (the developed center and the underdeveloped periphery) are assumed to be in equilibrium; second, disequilibrium in these balances is assumed.

It is easy to show in the first stage of my argument that gold is distributed between the center and the periphery in accordance with the need for money and the real need for hoarding. Let us ignore industrial gold, which is a true commodity like any other. Let us first consider the internal need for money. To begin with, imagine that gold constitutes the only form of internal money. There is a mechanism by which gold makes its way from the producing to the non-producing countries. In A the production of gold is expensive in real terms (gold prices are low). In B, however, gold is cheap (gold prices are high). A exports goods and B imports them. Gold moves from B to A. Nevertheless, B, the producer of gold (South Africa, for instance), does not import goods from every country in the world. Among the non-producers of gold, it applies to the most highly developed countries that are capable of supplying what it wants. Will there be a bad distribution of gold between Britain and India, for instance? Britain exports to South Africa, but India does not, although it needs gold for its monetary circulation. Is the balance between Britain and India equilibrated, then, without any movement of gold? Not at all, for the banks come into the process. They issue convertible notes in India in order to satisfy that country's need for currency. To obtain an adequate backing of gold it is enough for the central bank of India to buy gold from

South Africa, that is, to provide the gold producers with (convertible) Indian notes. Equipped with this purchasing power transferred from India to South Africa, the latter will eventually be able to import more goods. The income effect will re-equilibrate the Indian balance of payments, in which the entry of gold is not induced but inducing. Abolition of convertibility does not alter the schema, except that, under the influence of the initial disequilibrium of the balance following the importation of gold, the rate of exchange will fluctuate.

Let us now bring in the need for gold for hoarding. The Indian hoarder sells without buying, steadily withdrawing gold from circulation. This causes the need for money to be felt ever more strongly. The bank imports gold in order to make up for this constant hemorrhage. For its part, finally, the balance of payments brings about an induced movement of gold. The deficit in this balance means that the Indians are buying from other countries more than they are selling to them. They pay with their gold, which is being drained away from India. The bank serves as intermediary in this, but the departing gold is not the bank's, it belongs to private persons. Inconvertibility makes no change in this process except that the country's need for gold is now essentially determined by that of the hoarders, who buy from the bank the gold they desire. The bank, which has to ensure payment in gold of the country's debts abroad, imports gold in order to make up for the hoarders' withdrawals.

In all the foregoing arguments it would be possible to replace the word "gold" with "gold and foreign exchange." Besides, the foreign banks can always freely import their currency, or export it, by varying the state of their account with their head office.

International movements of gold and currency are thus not necessarily regular as the movements of the balance of payments are. Let us take an underdeveloped country whose balance worsens in a period of depression. A parallel dishoarding process intensifies the outward movement of gold (a mere cessation of hoarding itself, accompanied by cessation of imports of gold for this purpose, plays the same relative role). If, however, the balance improves during depression, the two movements in opposite directions may cancel each other out, partly or wholly. It should be added that the internal monetary need for gold and currency, which is less in a period of depression (contraction of income and prices), intensifies the outward movement of gold, or at least checks its inward movement. The opposite happens during a period of prosperity.

It is not helpful, when attempting to estimate hoarding, to examine the evolution of the world distribution of gold. India may have absorbed less gold, relatively, than Britain, and yet, the need for monetary gold being greater in Britain, this may be compatible with a high degree of hoarding in India and a low degree in Britain.

Finally, it is better to measure the evolution of the balance of payments on the basis of statistics of real flows (goods, long-term capital, repatriated profits, commercial services), rather than on the movement of international monetary reserves. Unfortunately, however, this is not always possible in practice.

Nevertheless, hoarding and the need for money intensify the tendency of the balance of payments of the underdeveloped countries to be unfavorable. The argument that follows is devoted to the question of measuring these two new real forces which have not been considered up to now.

The hoarding of gold and currency, insofar as hoarding in prosperity periods is greater than dishoarding in depression periods, constitutes a real disequilibrating force.

The growing need for money is itself the second force making for disequilibrium. This need, which increases in a period of prosperity and decreases in a period of depression, also increases over a long period of time. It is usual to distinguish between the internal need for money and the need for international money. The latter itself increases over a long period, so far as the underdeveloped countries are concerned, owing to the ever greater fluctuations in their external balance.

The internal need for money is satisfied by importing gold (the gold standard) or by local issue, without cover (independent currency) or wholly covered by gold and foreign currency (foreign-exchange standard). Only to the extent that internal circulation is covered by international currency does the need for money affect the balance. Again it must be emphasized that it affects the balance only if the *local* banks have to import this cover, that is, to pay for it (in local currency, which becomes additional purchasing power in the hands of foreign countries). If it is the expatriate banks that import these funds—in other words, transfer them from their head office—then there is in reality no purchase, no transfer of income, but a mere transfer of liquidities.[42] The same applied to the need for international currency.

I have tried to evaluate this independent movement of gold (and currency) for hoarding and monetary need (internal and external, since the two needs cannot be dissociated in practice, although conceptually they have to be) over a long period, for some of the underdeveloped countries: India, Egypt, and China.

Between 1835 and 1913, India absorbed an annual net average of £4.1 million of gold. This figure measures both the independent need for gold and the movement induced by the balance of payments after 1898. The independent movement was determined solely by the need for hoarding, since there was no internal circulation of gold in India. It was silver alone (between 1835 and 1884, £257 million was imported, and £270 million minted, the reminting of old coins accounting for the differing) that circulated in the country (silver monometallism). As for international money, there was no need for any down to the end of the nineteenth century. Until 1898 silver was exchanged for gold as a means of paying for the deficit (so that it is the fluctuations in the import of *silver* that reveal the state of the balance). After that date, the Indian importer paid silver rupees into the central bank, which paid out gold in London. In the event of a chronic deficit, this bank had to buy gold: there was therefore a monetary need for gold for external use. In passing, let it be noted that this system was unfavorable to India. When suffering from a deficit, that country had to buy gold on the international market with its own currency, that is, with depreciated silver coins. It is easy to see why the British commercial banks declined to finance so costly as operation, and why it was the Indian government that had to bear the cost of keeping its rate of exchange stable. Statistics show that dependence of the movement upon the cycle was not clear-cut. Before 1898 the movement represented merely the fluctuation in the independent need for hoarding. There was a certain tendency for fluctuations to follow the course of the cycle but nevertheless the upward trend often concealed this tendency for hoarding in depression periods to be less than in prosperity periods. After 1898 the upward trend became notably faster: to the independent need for hoarding there was now added the need for a gold reserve for external exchange purposes. The trend completely concealed any dependence on the cycle there may have been.[43]

For Egypt and China, which absorbed an annual average of £2.7 million of gold between 1890 and 1913, the rising trend concealed the cycle, which nevertheless was there: imports in a depression year were less than in the prosperity year that followed, not less in that which preceded it. For China, the movement reflected only the movement of hoarding (internal circulation being silver); in the case of Egypt, there was both the independent movement of hoarding and of the internal need for money and also the movement induced by the balance of payments.[44]

As regards Egypt, the rising trend shown by the movement of total gold imports (for the internal monetary need was covered by the gold imported and then re-exported) is quite clear. The cycle of net imports is equally clear. Here too we see the independent movement of hoarding and the movement induced by the balance. After 1914 the trend slackened, owing to the cessation of the internal need for gold. Nevertheless, hoarding continued to be very substantial, and eventually became greater than the former need of gold for internal circulation (after 1945). Also notable was the great dishoarding that occurred in the 1930s. Eventually a correlation becomes apparent between net imports of gold and the level of ground-rent as a whole. The latter constitutes a relatively stable percentage of the country's export. The fact is that rent and total exports vary with the quantity and price of cotton exported. My calculations show that this relation is a relatively stable one. This assumption enables us to calculate the proportion of ground-rent that was hoarded in gold between 1887 and 1950. The evolution of this proportion is typical. Before 1914 its steady rise reflects the enrichment of the landowners. After the First World War, modern practices largely replace hoarding in gold with hoarding in notes and bank deposits. Nevertheless, the cyclical dependence of hoarding remains clear. The increase in the percentage after the Second World War reflects both the continued enrichment of the landowners and the partial resumption of hoarding of gold, persistent inflation having to some degree deprived hoarding in the form of notes and bank deposits of the vogue it had enjoyed between 1920 and 1940.[45]

The hoarding of gold in the underdeveloped countries thus constitutes a considerable force, pressing hard upon the balance of payments. The general conclusion is well established. Kitchin estimates that 25 percent of the gold newly mined between 1920 and 1929 was absorbed by Indian hoarding, 50 percent having been devoted to monetary use and 21 percent to industrial purposes.[46] It is true that all through the nineteenth century it was above all the developed countries that absorbed gold. Between 1835 and 1889 hoarding in India absorbed no more than 13 percent of gold production, as compared with 16 percent between 1890 and 1929. It is also true that the absorption of gold by the developed central countries was substantial between 1870 and 1913. In the case of Britain, which absorbed £3.2 million a year at this time, the fact that dependence on the cycle does not emerge very sharply may be due to the strong upward trend of the internal need for money. France, between 1880 and 1913, absorbed 5.564 billion gold francs, or 163 million per year—more than India, in absolute terms. Britain took about half of the amount that India imported, and so a great deal more in relative terms (per capita, for example). But this was not gold for hoarding: it was the need for money that was increasing at this pace. This need was considerably greater than that of the underdeveloped economies. It is noteworthy that France, where the use of checks was less widespread, had to import more gold than Britain.[47]

Hoarding actually made its appearance in the West as something endemic only after 1929 (it had occurred episodically between 1914 and 1929). Gold began to be accumulated when the gold value of the currency was abandoned. Along with this, the depth of the depression of 1929 brought about dishoarding in the periphery—for the first time: during the nineteenth century, though hoarding diminished during depressions, it rarely became negative. In the course of the 1930s the landowners and the peasants of India, Egypt, etc., liquidated their hoarded resources. They sold their gold to the banks, which exchanged it in London against (devalued) pounds sterling, and it was this that enabled Britain to maintain the rate of exchange of her currency. This movement was a very extensive one, as can be seen from the table showing the sources of gold and the uses to which it was put between December 1930 and September 1937.[48] After the Second World War the practice of hoarding gold was reinforced in the developed countries, especially in France, owing to miscellaneous causes, mainly political in character.

Reduction of the External Assets of the Periphery and Devaluation Cycles[49]

At what date, approximately, did the balance of payments of the periphery become chronically unfavorable? This question is very difficult to answer, for the situation seems to have taken this turn at different periods in different countries. It appears that the balance of real payments of Cuba and of the French and British colonies in Africa, for example, was chronically unfavorable from an early date, so that some observers said, wrongly, that their imports of monetary liquidities must be paid for with real exports. Already in the nineteenth century, however, the rate of exchange in nearly all the states of Latin America was regularly falling. In Brazil the deficit in the external balance was as much responsible for this as the inflationary issue of paper money. It was the same in Argentina between 1880 and 1900. In other words, the external balance of these countries—the major suppliers of primary products in that period, which were already more closely integrated into the international market than the countries of Africa and Asia which had only recently been reduced to colonial status—was already chronically unfavorable in the nineteenth century.

For the twentieth century there can be no doubt about it. The gold value of the different currencies had fallen everywhere between 1929 and 1937 (on the eve of the crisis). Nevertheless, it declined to a noticeably greater extent in the underdeveloped countries than in the developed ones. If some of the former kept unaltered their rate of exchange with the metropolitan country (French, Belgian, Portuguese, Spanish, and British colonies, and colonial members of the sterling area), this was not because they experienced no difficulties in equilibrating their external balance. It was rather in spite of these difficulties that the metropolitan countries acted in this way, so as to allow the income mechanism to exhaust its effects, just as previously. Their reserves in foreign currency (which took the place of gold as international currency for these countries) were less in 1937 than they had been in 1929, which shows that there was a chronic tendency toward deficit in their balance of payments. (Latin America also reflects this chronic deficit.) Even at the depreciated rates which those countries adopted, the deficit persisted, as is proved by the fall in central reserves of monetary gold between 1927 and 1937 (an entire cycle), as in all their monetary reserves. In the developed countries all these reserves *increased* during the same period.

After the Second World War a system of relatively rigid rates replaced the fluctuating exchange rates of former times. Devaluations nevertheless occurred very frequently in the underdeveloped countries, with the consent and on the recommendation of the International Monetary Fund. These devaluations were sometimes made necessary by previous internal inflation; often, however, they were "necessitated" by the chronic external deficit, which had merely been reinforced by inflation.[50] Along with this, the international reserves of the periphery diminished.[51] It is true that the immediate postwar period was also marked by external deficits in several of the developed countries (Western Europe): the system was functioning at that time, the reconstruction period, almost exclusively for the benefit of the United States. The center (the United States, Europe, Japan) was to resume as a whole its traditional place in the world economy only after this first stage had been left behind (the stage of the "world dollar shortage"), though not without creating serious problems of readjustment among the advanced countries themselves (the present crisis of international liquidity).

The Lesson of History: From the Foreign-Exchange Standard to the Illusion of Monetary Independence

The historical functioning of the foreign-exchange standard. At the outset the precapitalist economies possessed a stock of money adapted to their needs. Their integration into the world market was reflected in the growing development of external exchange relations—first commercial, later financial. The external balance of payments, a new reality, had a constant tendency toward deficit, for the profound reasons already analyzed.

If these economies had possessed a well-developed financial organization, their central bank would first of all have tried to combat the draining away of gold by raising the discount rate and by a policy of gold-buying. Finding these measures ineffective, the central authorities would eventually have been led to establish a system of quantitative control over the real movements of goods and capital . . . unless, of course, they bowed to the "natural" evolution of things. They would then have allowed the gold reserves of the banking system to become exhausted, after which the gold standard would have been abandoned in favor of a system of inconvertibility and an unstable rate of exchange: or else growth would have been allowed to slow down until equilibrium was reestablished.

But is it not utopian to talk of underdeveloped countries possessing a well-developed financial organization? The precapitalist economies, which managed without credit and banks, were ignorant of modern financial organization. To the extent that the external balance, that new reality, showed itself constantly unfavorable, with the development of international relations, gold migrated from these countries to the developed countries, simply in order to pay for the deficit.

When the local economy, which at the outset had possessed adequate stocks of precious metal, had been stripped of its monetary reserves, how were internal commercial operations financed? Through the importing of gold coins by the foreign-owned banking system. The banks made a profit on the transaction, of course: this imported gold currency was lent to individuals, in return for interest. Thus, the foreign banks in Egypt imported from Europe each year sovereigns and gold francs which they lent at interest to Egyptian traders. In this sense the disequilibrium of the external balance imposed extra costs upon the local economy. The latter was no longer able to use local monetary reserves, which had been wholly liquidated, in order to obtain means of payment, but had to rely on credit from abroad.

This situation did not last. It was generally followed by complete monetary integration of the underdeveloped countries. This new system deprived the balance of payments of some of its reality. The rigid and unlimited exchange enabled the underdeveloped economy to obtain the foreign currency it needed to pay for any external deficit.

The complete monetary integration of certain underdeveloped countries eliminates the difficulties that can arise from disequilibrium in the balance of payments, even if this disequilibrium is persistent.[52] In the long run, however, this disequilibrium has to be absorbed through the functioning of the income mechanism. The balance of real payments tends to become even. In this sense the underdeveloped countries do not have to pay for their imported monetary circulation with a surplus of exports, though they do have to pay in real terms for the use of this money.

Adoption of the foreign-exchange standard thus allows the system to regain equilibrium by slowing down the growth of the underdeveloped country, thanks to a dominated exchange rate that facilitates structural readjustment. There is no need to stress the extent to which this mode of readjustment of the external balance is negative in its consequences for local capital formation—directly, since the restoration of equilibrium is effected by reducing local income (worsening of the terms of trade), and indirectly, since this mechanism facilitates structural readjustment in a way that conforms to increasing specialization, to the detriment of autocentric growth.

The alternative solution: monetary independence. The original draining away of stocks of money from an underdeveloped country is very awkward in its consequences if this country is politically independent. Only with increasing difficulty can the state meet its needs. This was why the states of Latin America had recourse to inconvertible paper money. At that time the very possibility of exchange control was not appreciated. This is undoubtedly why the system that was established more or less everywhere was that of freedom of the exchanges, which meant permanent devaluation of the local currencies.

Thus, already in the nineteenth century, certain independent states decline to adopt the technique of complete monetary integration offered by the Currency Boards system, with exchange at a fixed rate and in unlimited amount. They would certainly have liked to establish a convertible system, but they were unable to do this. Is this not a further proof of the correctness of the theory of international disequilibrium set out above? If Argentina had from the outset regulated its relations with other countries, would it not have succeeded in establishing a stable monetary system? Did it not prefer to sacrifice the advantages of this system to those of the absolute freedom of international trade and capital movements? Argentina paid for this freedom, first by the exhaustion of its initial stocks of international means of payment, and then by the institution of a local currency that was always unstable and continually depreciating. The instability of the inconvertible local currency simply reflects the permanent disequilibrium of the country's external balance.

There are thus in the end only two solutions open to these countries with independent currencies. They can either prefer to retain the "advantages" of freedom of international exchanges—which means sacrificing monetary equilibrium—or they can give up freedom in relations with the outside world—which ensures monetary equilibrium, but only at the price of a reduction in the growth of external exchanges.

The "liberal" choice facilitates the mechanisms of increasing international specialization with perhaps the investment of foreign capital and the development of peripheral capitalism, both foreign and national. But it provides no guarantee of stability of the rate of exchange, for in this case, as has already been mentioned, the value of the dominant foreign currency determines the value of the local currency backed by this foreign currency. This direct influence operates through the appreciation that the dominant economic categories confer upon the future of the value of the currency concerned. The wished-for rise in prices is made possible precisely by the absence of convertibility and the accommodating attitude of the banks. This mechanism is independent of the state of the external balance. Juxtaposed with it is that by which fluctuations in the balance of payments—by determining, independently of the rate of exchange, the volume of monetary reserves—influence production, prices, and accumulation. Furthermore, the deficit in the external balance affects the rate of exchange and this in turn affects prices and accumulation. We have already seen that the underdeveloped economies were especially susceptible to this mechanism, described by Aftalion.

There is thus an additional reason for the permanent increase in prices and continuous inflation in the underdeveloped countries. This continuous price rise, which is determined not by the functioning of the economy's internal mechanisms but by the state of external relations, may well favor accumulation in the mature developed countries.

It offers only disadvantages, however, in economies that suffer not from chronic inadequacy of demand in relation to production but from inadequacy of production itself.

Indeed, the accumulation of local capital is considerably hindered by monetary disorders of this kind. Absolute freedom of relations with the outside world thus checks the development of indigenous capitalism, even in peripheral form.

The fact remains that this freedom may facilitate the importing of foreign capital. The latter is not affected by the risk of devaluation. Foreign capital in search of a temporary refuge, speculators' capital, does certainly run the risk of grave losses on the exchange, and so this sort of capital avoids such countries. But capital destined for long-term investment has nothing to fear on that score. It does not come with the intention of leaving again: it comes to stay. What *will* leave the country are the profits on this capital, and there are no grounds for misgiving on their account: profits are proportional to the real value of the investment, not to its subsequent financial value, and so they evolve along with the rate of exchange.[53]

This imported foreign capital constitutes, nevertheless, an essential source of the development of peripheral capitalism within the underdeveloped economy, and around this development a local capital may also come into being. Although the multiplier mechanisms, under conditions of underdevelopment, operate only to a slight extent, it is clear that the rapidity of local capitalist accumulation depends, given conditions of structural stability, on the amount of foreign capital that flows in, on the degree of international integration.

However, capitalist development under these conditions remains peripheral. It occurs within the setting of intensified international specialization. It does not radically destroy the indigenous precapitalist structure. On the contrary, it reinforces the underdeveloped structure, its position as a dominated economy. The variable rate of exchange, constantly falling, continues here to be just as fundamentally a dominated exchange-rate, even though its position is unstable and permanently in jeopardy.

It is therefore proper to distinguish between two possibilities here. Either the surplus of the balance, during a period of prosperity, is equivalent to the deficit of the difficult years (a tendency for the balance to be equilibrated), or it is not (a state of chronic disequilibrium).

In the first case the exchange remains stable—or, more precisely, it is alternately devalued and revalued.[54] This was what happened with the exchange in Argentina, Bolivia, Colombia, and Peru, which went down in 1920 with the fall in prices of raw materials and the consequent deficit in the balance, only to rise again between 1922 and 1925. This phenomenon is fairly widespread. There is a close correlation between the price of oil, coffee, and tin and the state of exchange in Venezuela, in Brazil and Colombia, and in Bolivia. In this case it is possible that the underdeveloped country may possess a reserve supply of international money sufficient to avoid these fluctuations in the exchange. State intervention to avert them is a possibility. The system is in any case a costly one, since this stock of money has to be proportionate in amount to the size of the fluctuations in the balance.

If, however, there is a definite tendency toward deficit—in other words, for the deficit during depression to be bigger than the surplus during prosperity—then devaluation is inevitable. This is what happened in 1920, as in 1929: the revaluation of the years 1922–25 was at a lower level than the devaluation of 1920, and that of 1929 was not followed by any revaluation between 1935 and 1937. An exchange stablization fund, which is incapable in a developed country (its reserves having been exhausted) of combating the basic tendency, is even less capable of doing this is an underdeveloped one, as is shown by the example of Bolivia in 1941.

This is why the underdeveloped countries are moving more and more toward the other solution. Increasingly they are being led to consider exchange control as the only solution to the difficulties of the external exchange.[55]

If this control is seen, as is very commonly the case, as a makeshift, a "regrettable necessity," if the basic orientation of the type of development contemplated is not called in question, if this development is still conceived in terms of increasing international specialization, that is, of priority development of production for export on the world market, then it is quite clear that external equilibrium is being obtained only at the price of putting a brake on development, even in the peripheral form. This braking can provide no final solution, even to the problem of external equilibrium taken by itself. The profound tendencies to disequilibrium continue to operate, and the control eventually proves ineffective, so that the currency has to be devalued. The recent history of the underdeveloped countries is full of experiences of this kind. They show that "monetary independence," even when accompanied by the most effective controls over external relations, is illusory unless the strategy of integration in the world market be challenged and withdrawal from this market—the condition for development that shall be no longer peripheral but autocentric—seriously undertaken.

Summary of Conclusions

1. The mechanisms that are alleged to ensure automatic external equilibrium are of the same order as the Law of Markets—either an empty tautology or a false theory. The claim that such mechanisms exist (price effect, exchange effect, foreign-trade multiplier) is based, moreover, on a false theory of money (the quantity theory) and on a short-sighted analysis of "elasticities" and "propensities" which implicitly presupposes that which it endeavors to prove. Current economic theory thus evades the real problem, namely, why "elasticities" and "propensities" are what they are—different at the center and in the periphery of the system—and how they evolve. It is impossible not to see in this orientation of current economic theory a preoccupation with apologetics which, as in the case of the Law of Markets, is bound up with the ideology of universal harmony. As in relation to the Law of Markets, it is not possible here to speak of a general tendency to equilibrium.

2. But this tendency to equilibrium reflects a mechanism of structural adjustment. This is the heart of the problem, which current economic theory evades. In the relations between the center and the periphery of the system this structural adjustment is asymmetrical: it is the periphery that is shaped in conformity with the center's requirements for accumulation, the price structures and the distribution of relative profitabilities being shaped so as to ensure that the development of capitalism in the periphery remains peripheral—that is, based essentially on the external market. Adjustment is therefore inevitably accompanied by a chronic tendency to deficit in the external balance of the periphery. Attempts to account for these phenomena of asymmetry of the balance of payments without referring to structural adjustment (in other words, to the mechanism of international speculation) can at best be only partial and descriptive. This is the case with explanations such as those offered by Prebisch and Kindleberger, which describe the state and the movement of "elasticities" and "propensities"—states and movements which are as they are precisely because they express the most fundamental mechanisms of structural adjustment.

3. The history of the periphery's balance payments shows two phases in rapid succession: a first phase which is characterized by surplus in this balance (corresponding to the opening up of the colonies, the installation of the underdeveloped economy, the "development of underdevelopment"), followed by a second phase in which there is a chronic tendency to deficit (corresponding to the crisis of this system, the blocking of growth based on external demand). The foreign-exchange standard conceals for a certain time this tendency to external deficit; sooner or later, however, this deficit constrains the underdeveloped countries to opt for monetary independence. This, however, is an independence that cannot provide a real solution of the problem—a problem which is rooted elsewhere, in the most basic mechanisms of integration into the world market—and so cannot but give rise to further monetary disorders.

Afterword to the Second Edition

The first edition of this book was sold out in less than a year, and my desire that the book provoke discussion and criticism has been amply fulfilled. I have learned a lot from this discussion, and if I were to rewrite the book I would certainly not do it in exactly the same way. On the one hand, some of the shortcomings are now more clearly apparent to me; on the other, some attitudes that I continue to reject have been reformulated since I wrote, and this invites me, in my turn, to push my argument further.

Two questions have provided the principal themes for discussion: unequal exchange, and the future of the formations of peripheral capitalism. Although the former is the one that has caused most ink to flow in France, it seems to me the less important, and subordinate to the latter question. Elsewhere, particularly in Latin America, where analysis has gone much deeper, attention has been focused on the major question: Why has accumulation in the periphery not yet led to the development of completely autocentric capitalism? What are the prospects before the world system: is it moving toward an increasing dichotomy between center and periphery—or is this only a stage in evolution, with the system now tending toward a kind of homogeneous capitalist formation on the world scale?

This is clearly the context in which *all* the problems of the world today need to be placed, those of the class struggle as well as "national" problems—all of which, for this reason, are so closely intertwined that they form only a single question, the different aspects of which cannot be dissociated from each other.

I intend to present my opinion on these questions in this Afterword. First, however, I must clear up some aspects of the problem of method.

1. History did not stop in 1880, or in 1917, or in 1945. In each decade new facts appear which express new developments that had not been suspected in the previous phases. History is no more linear today than it was five centuries ago. Just as the pseudo-Marxist schema of the "five stages" (primitive communism, slave-owning society, feudalism, capitalism, socialism) results from a mechanistic outlook (similar, in its way, to that of Rostow), so is every attempt to reduce present-day developments to so-called "forecasts" made by Marx, Lenin, Trotsky, a result of religious dogmatism.

Uneven development continues to be the only rule, which always baffles the soothsayers. Besides, the outcome of political struggles determines at every moment new alternatives that were previously unforeseen and unforeseeable.

It is therefore necessary, at each stage, to integrate the new facts into one's analysis. This seems obvious, and yet there are always some in search of absolute certainties who refuse to do this, and are consequently forced either to ignore the new facts or else try and fit them at all costs into a schema that had not allowed for them.

A clear instance of the fundamental divergence between *that* way of analyzing reality and my own is furnished by the discussion that has gone on around the book by Baran and Sweezy.[1] It is still my view that this work is an important contribution which integrates vital new facts relative to the way in which, in our own time, the system overcomes at its center the fundamental, permanent, and growing contradiction between capacity to produce and capacity to consume. I have shown that the law of the tendency for the surplus to increase, which results from the policy of the state and the monopolies in the present epoch of monopoly capitalism, does not in the least contradict the law of the tendency for the rate of profit to fall; on the contrary, it is the way in which the latter law is expressed in the system in our time. And yet some commentators have reacted vigorously against this contribution by Baran and Sweezy. Why? Because it is awkward for them, since it shows that the system *can* function (and yet what is more obvious than that?). They prefer the religious and reassuring vision of an apocalyptic catastrophe, of a golden age realized miraculously at one blow, to the disturbing vision of perpetually changing conditions which oblige one to constantly bring oneself up to date.

Moreover, the method used by Ernest Mandel to refute Baran and Sweezy is typical. Instead of undertaking an internal analysis of the system being criticized, so as to expose any incoherences it may contain, Mandel is content to describe Baran and Sweezy as "Keynesians"![2]

And this he does because they take the criticism of Keynes seriously, because they see that Keynes's emergence reflected the necessity for current theory to find an explanation of some important facts. It is precisely by undertaking a thorough critique of Keynes (which, following the example of Baran and Sweezy, I have done in numerous pages of this book) that we reveal both the problem (that of the absorption of surplus in the age of monopoly) and the answer to it: we discover that the Keynesian liquidity theory conceals the real problem, that of the contradiction between capacity to produce and capacity to consume, which can be grasped only on the basis of the theory of the capitalist mode of production; and that it is therefore necessary to look in a different direction from the one taken by Keynes if we are to find out how the system overcomes this contradiction. This is what Baran and Sweezy have done and what has led them to analyze the methods whereby the surplus is absorbed. By declining to undertake this type of critique, Mandel condemns himself to become quite uninteresting: he is reduced, having dodged the *new* problems that arise, to merely popularizing Marx. This is undoubtedly why his *Marxist Economic Theory* resembles so closely the textbook of political economy published by the U.S.S.R. Academy of Sciences: the only difference between them is that Mandel places alongside a popularization of *Capital* a diatribe against the Soviet bureaucracy, whereas the Russian textbook-writers place alongside a similar populatization an apologia for the Soviet system. Trotskyism is rich in attitudes of this kind, which make it a real twin of Soviet official ideology, both being equally dogmatic.

2. There is therefore still a great deal to learn through criticism of current theory. This is indeed the only scientific method that enables one to make real progress. Economism as an ideology constitutes a permanent threat, because the evolution of the economic system recreates at each stage the conditions for new economistic illusions which penetrate the mode of thinking in a new and subtle way. It is therefore not enough just to proclaim one's rejection of economism. Slackness in criticism in this domain nearly always leads to a pendulum movement that oscillates continually between an insipid economism and a voluntaristic idealism that proclaims, absurdly, that "economics does not matter"—thus preparing a reversion to economism. We have, alas, all too many examples of this kind of thing—notably in one of the important fields dealt with in this book, that of the choice of branches and techniques of industry.

Ten years ago, progressives lined up unhesitantly with supporters of the systematic choice of modern-based industries, whereas liberals and conservative paternalists advocated choice by the underdeveloped countries of light techniques and industries. Today it is clear that both groups stood on the same basis of economism: either search for maximum acceleration of growth, or search for immediate individual profitability.

The search for maximum growth at any price finds expression in the slogan of the Stalin period: "overtake and surpass the United States in all fields of production." Formulated like that, both on the theoretical and on the practical plane this aim deliberately ignores the *content* of this measurable economic growth. Critique of the concepts of national accounting teaches us that the aggregates measured grasp only the commodity magnitudes, those that interest the capitalist mode of production. With one's mind focused on the gross internal product one forgets that the growth of this magnitude may in the last resort be achieved by the destruction of productive forces, namely, human and natural resources. These latter are merely *means* in the capitalist mode of production, whose only aim is maximization of profit. In economic jargon, "calculation of the profitability of the firm internalizes the external economies"—those external economies that arise precisely from the destruction of human forces and natural resources. It is for this reason that the capitalist mode of production possesses a capacity for growth—growth in the economistic sense that defines it, that is, in a relative and limited sense—greater not merely than that of all previous modes of production, but also, no doubt, than that of socialism as well, insofar as the latter makes man its objective instead of profit.

The discovery of the "problems of the environment"—even though the expression is a wretched one, compelling us to distinguish between the human environment and the physical environment—which is so fashionable at the moment, reflects this awareness of the *relative* character of economic magnitudes. It leads to fundamental criticism of calculations of profitability; it reminds us of the very short time-horizon of commercial calculation—twenty years at most[3]—a horizon that is very much lower than that of any society that controls its own fate; and it brings out the artificiality of attempts to broaden the calculation of profitability which do not go beyond the sphere of economism (as is shown by cost-benefit analysis carried out in so-called "social terms"[4]). By making the maximization of growth the ultimate objective, an absolute value, one reduces social science to economism. However, the discovery in recent years, in connection with criticism of the Soviet experience, that the maximum rate of growth ought not to be sought *regardless of cost* has suddenly rendered labor-intensive techniques attractive, thanks to a medley of hippie ideology, return to the myth of the golden age and the noble savage, and criticism of the reality of the capitalist world. It is on these mistaken foundations that some people have interpreted some aspects of Chinese policy, isolated from their general context and the line of development in which they have occurred.

A socialist plan is certainly not defined in economistic terms, but it includes the economic element and does not reject this: if it did, it would be ineffective. Complete socialism will necessarily be based on a modern high-productivity economy. There is no conflict between modernity and socialism: on the contrary, socialism cannot but be more modern than capitalism. To suppose the contrary is to believe that what is wrong is due to technique and not to the social system within which this technique expresses itself. On the contrary, it is the capitalist mode of production that conflicts with modernization and distorts its potentialities. A great deal has been written about the destructive effects of fragmented, monotonous industrial work *whatever the social system.* Unfortunately, the correctness of these observations has led to a loss of perspective. As time goes by this fragmented type of labor will be seen as characteristic of the capitalist mode of production, which will have fulfilled a historical function—that of accumulation—and so prepared the way for itself to be surpassed. The technical revolution of our time, which I have deliberately emphasized in this work, will replace unskilled detail work, which has been the chief form of labor since the beginning of machinofacture, by automation. It will make possible both an increase in disposable time not devoted to labor, and new, highly skilled forms of labor itself.

How does the present system react to this prospect? It does not see it the dawn of mankind's liberation, but the threat of mass unemployment, the "marginalizing" to an increasing extent of a whole section of mankind (especially in the periphery) in relation to a system that will include only a minority. This is the natural tendency of a calculation of profitability based on profit as the ultimate aim, of the economistic alienation that sees in men only manpower. This is the context to which, in my view, the present wave of neo-Malthusianism on population questions belongs. The racialist nature of this attitude should also be noted: it is forgotten that in 1800 the peoples who today make up the developed world formed an even smaller proportion of the world's total population than in 1970. The problem is misplaced, by treating a real but subordinate question, that of the ratio of demographic growth to economic growth in the accumulation phase, which is a transition phase, as though it were a primary absolute. It is by ridding society of the limits that the capitalist mode of production imposes on it that mankind can emerge from economic alienation, simultaneously freeing the productive forces. There is no conflict between the growth and development of consciously socialist forces and the creation of a world-wide socialist civilization. Whenever there seems to be such a conflict it is because the problem has been wrongly presented, whether this be done in economistic terms or by negation of economics—which is merely the other side of the same coin.

This vitally important way of seeing the line of future development must not be confused with the problem of the stages and strategy of *transition.* Where *this* sphere is concerned I want to emphasize here the theses I have defended in my book. For, if there is a problem, it is indeed a problem of *transition* and not one of the ultimate prospect. It is insofar as the political changes that make the socialist cohesion of the nation as a whole. If it is really a matter of transition to socialism, the end (socialism) cannot be sacrificed to the means (accumulation). The success of a system of transition is therefore not to be measured merely by the rate of growth realized but by its capacity to take upon itself *simultaneously* accumulation *and* progress in the forms of organization and consciousness appropriate to the socialist plan. If this aim is abandoned, then the transition is no longer a transition: it becomes instead the establishment of a capitalist economy, even if this be of a type different from the historical precedents.

This requirement does not rule out the establishment of modern industries, contrary to what is sometimes too hastily asserted. It rules out *confining* oneself to the establishment of these industries, doing this in the same way as capitalism would have done it, that is, subjecting the other sectors of society to this task, reducing them to the passive role of suppliers of cheap labor power, which is what economism or respect for the "laws of the market" dictates. The policy now being carried out in China is an attempt to solve this problem in a practical way.

In a case of a socialist policy of transition, establishment of modern industries does not have the same consequences as in the formations of peripheral capitalism. Here, what has to be challenged is not the choice of modern industries but (1) the exclusively extraverted character of the sectors in which this choice is made and (2) the subjection of the other sectors to the requirements of accumulation in this setting, which is that of the world system. Unless a general policy challenges the types of relations characteristic of capitalism, in which the rest of society is subordinated to the autocentric modern sector that is to be established, the "poles of development" become "poles of development of underdevelopment." This is the thesis that I have emphasized in this book.

My analysis has made some progress since it first appeared, where a few aspects of this problem are concerned. Latin American writing on the subject of marginality, which is the consequence of this establishment of modern sectors in conditions of peripheral capitalism, has begun to attract notice. The rapid rise in unemployment in the Third World is due to the interaction between this choosing of modern techniques and the low level of wages. My theory of the blocking of growth, like the critique of the policy of import-substitution which has been developed in Latin America, obviously has a bearing on this problem. Yet the solution of this difficulty does not consist in renouncing modernization or raising some idyllic plea in favor of agriculture or the inefficient craft techniques of the past. The answer is to organize in a different way the articulation between the modern sector and the less modernized sectors. This important aspect of the problem, on which I have not dwelt sufficiently (it is only outlined), brings up, moreover, the problematic of the prospects of peripheral capitalism, to which I shall return.

China's Cultural Revolution has put its finger on these problems—in the first place on the political aspects of this new articulation that has to be worked out (but also on other aspects that had escaped my attention) and in particular on the absolute necessity of an independent approach to scientific and technological research in the countries of the periphery such as may enable them to break out of the false dilemma: modern techniques copied from the West of today, or old techniques corresponding to conditions in the West a century ago, which are not those of the periphery today. This theme, on which the Chinese alone are giving proof of practical imagination, deserves to be emphasized.

I did not pay enough attention to this theme, for I tended to see technology as a factor external to the problem, an independent variable. Within this narrow context it is clear that the (obligatory) choice of modern industries amounts merely to copying the technology of the West of today, following the example set in their time by Japan and Russia. However, we are beginning to see that technological research follows a direction that accords with the requirements of the system, and, therefore, that technique is not an external factor. Here, too, it is analysis of the problems of underdevelopment that has constituted the starting point for a critique of general economic theory. The domination exercised by the center over the periphery through its technological monopoly, which has been brought out, especially in works on Latin America, by study of the problems of "transfer of technology," has enabled us to see that the economistic assumption of the independence of technology served the function of evading this problem. What is necessary is to direct research toward the invention of *modern* techniques that are better adapted to the problems. It is not, therefore, a question, where the underdeveloped countries are concerned, of "cutting the pear in half," by choosing "intermediate techniques" that are already known, situated halfway between the out-of-date technology of the Europe of 1840 and the ultramodern technology of the United States of 1970, but of defining the economic characteristics of a third, *modern* technique.[5]

3. I therefore still think that it is necessary to start, in any scientific analysis of these problems, not from the exegesis of sacred texts but from reality, and from the way in which reality finds reflection in the theory and ideology of society. It is, accordingly, on the basis of this attitude that I take up discussion of the two fundamental questions set out above.

Analyzing in this way, I began with a critique of the theory of international exchange, pointing out that "a critique of the theory of international exchange, which is the necessary starting-point for formulating the problem, inevitably leads us to go beyond its terms of reference."[6] I am not unaware that, if unequal exchange exists, this is because the social formations of the center and those of the periphery are different. I show with some precision that this is so. But the problems are revealed much more clearly if we start from an analysis of the relations of domination—of inequality—that obtain between these two types of formation integrated in one and the same world system.

The thesis of unequal exchange has provoked widespread indignation against its author, Arghiri Emmanuel.[7] This is not at all a matter for surprise. Emmanuel has been subjected to three types of criticism. The first, made by Bettelheim, has remained within the framework of Emmanuel's argument. But Bettelheim fails to draw the logical conclusion from the extension (which he accepts) of Marx's models of the transformation of values into prices of production to the sphere of international relations, and of his own (incorrect) assumption that the rate of surplus value is higher at the center—for this conclusion would be that it is the developed countries that are the victims of unequal exchange! A second series of critics have claimed that wages are higher at the center because the productivity of labor is higher there, which would "justify" this inequality. Do I need to repeat here, following

Emmanuel, that these commentators are accepting marginalist tautology as their basis, forgetting that, for Marx, the value of labor is independent of its productivity? Outwardly more subtle is the attitude of the third set of critics, who try to deny that the expression "unequal exchange" makes sense, by refusing to allow Emmanuel the right to make use of Marx's models of the transformation of value. These models, according to them, are meaningless outside the context of the capitalist mode of production, and cannot be extended to relations between different formations.[8] This declaration, they suppose, must render their criticism immune to attack. But at what price? At the price of denying that a *single* world capitalist system exists—that is, in fact, of denying the existence of imperialism itself! True, the transformation models cannot be extended so as to apply to *every* situation. For example, there can be no question of using them to analyze trade relations between ancient Greece and Persia. Only marginalist economics, with its striving to create a universal system, can allow itself to indulge in fantasies of that sort. But this is not what we are concerned with here, for center and periphery do form parts of one and the same world capitalist system.

Marx constructed the theory of the capitalist mode of production and defined in abstract terms three conditions of this mode of production: generalization of the commodity form of products (generalized market relations); generalization of the commodity form of labor power (the existence of a—single—labor market); generalization of competition between capitals (the existence of a market—again, a single market—for capital, which is expressed in the equalization of the rate of profit). These three conditions did not fall from the heaven of imagination: they express in abstract terms the reality of the capitalist mode of production, which Marx studied and of which mid-nineteenth-century England provided the concrete model. The world capitalist system is another plane of reality, which also needs to be defined in abstract terms if it is to be analyzed theoretically. Now, at this level of legitimate abstraction, the world system is expressed in the existence of a world market for commodities and of international mobility of capital. Since there is a world commodity market, *there is a problem of values on the international scale.* And since this problem exists, one not only can but *must* use the models of transformation of values. The only question that arises is whether they are used correctly (soundness of the underlying assumptions, etc.). On this plane, I refer my readers to the arguments developed in this book, to which I have nothing to add.

It is certainly not unequal exchange that is the *cause* of inequality in wage levels: quite the contrary. Why are wages higher at the center? Because the social formations there are different from those in the periphery, of course. But saying that only amounts to repeating the same proposition in a different form, without advancing one inch. It is clear that in a closed capitalist economy (the autocentric, central capitalist mode of production that Marx studied) there is a relation between the overall level of productivity (the level of development of the productive forces) and that of wages. If wages fall below a certain level, the system's capacity to produce exceeds its capacity to consume, and production must contract (the phenomenon is a little more complicated if the decline in wages induces a retreat to less efficient techniques). I have devoted many pages of my book to showing this relation, criticizing as necessary the marginalist theory of general equilibrium and of the rate of interest. It is in these terms that it is possible to establish the theoretical reason why the rate of surplus value, in the pure model of the capitalist mode of production, cannot rise indefinitely; it is in this way alone that it is possible to establish the scientific validity of the law of the tendency of the rate of profit to fall, since it is *in this way alone* that one can show that the tendency necessarily gets the better of the countertendencies.

This proof, which is of fundamental importance, accounts for the observed fact that the share taken by wages and by profits in the national income is relatively stable. This fact, which Robinson tries to explain in a different way (by bringing in the rate of interest), remains ultimately unexplained by the marginalist theory of general equilibrium.[9] Obviously, this becomes apparent only if one studies "bourgeois economics" seriously and tries to criticize it in a thorough way, for such a criticism makes it possible to perceive problems that remain unperceived if one remains content merely to repeat that the value of labor-power is not independent of the level of development of the productive forces. Criticism of the theory of general equilibrium enables one to grasp the significance of this relation, by forcing one to retrace the path that Marx followed from concrete reality to theoretical abstraction. Mental laziness, expressed in repetitious enunciation of these theoretical abstractions, leads to Marxism being turned into a dogmatic philosophy, whereas in fact it is a *method.*

I have shown however, along with the foregoing, that for the extraverted capitalist economies of the periphery this necessary link is absent. Wages in the periphery can therefore be frozen at very low levels without extraverted development being hindered. This is the centerpiece of my demonstration that if the capitalist mode of production is autocentric it tends to become exclusive, whereas extraversion blocks its development and so prevents it from becoming exclusive. This explains why the world system does not give rise in the periphery to the same formations as at the center. On this plane, the contributions from Latin America made in recent years coincide completely with my thesis.

What, then, is the significance of the pair constituted by the autocentric economy and the extraverted economy? It means that, in an autocentric economy, there is an organic relation between the two terms of the social contradiction—bourgeoisie and proletariat—that they are both *integrated* into a single *reality,* the *nation.* In an extraverted economy, this unity of opposites is not to be grasped within the national context—this unity is broken, and can be rediscovered only on the world scale.

Differentiated analysis of the essential laws whereby the world system and the capitalist mode of production function thus inevitably leads to important results. Is it surprising that these results call into question the whole problematic of the future of capitalism? The implications of these results cannot be reduced to the economic domain alone, deprived of any political meaning, without thereby abandoning the *ultimate* determining role of the structure of production-relations in order to fall into positivist or structuralist eclecticism. This calling into question is disagreeable only for those who seek unchanging certainties.

The first of these results, which belongs to the plane of immediate economic reality, is unequal exchange—which means transfer of value, nothing more and nothing less. To say that this is meaningless because it concerns relations between different formations would imply that Marx's analysis of primitive accumulation is absurd, because this, too, is concerned with relations between different formations. To say that the theory of unequal exchange means that "the workers of the center exploit those of the periphery" is really to go off the rails, for it is only ownership of capital that makes exploitation possible. This sort of nonsense proves nothing, either for or against unequal exchange. It also means accepting a mechanistic relation between standard of life and political attitudes, thus reducing in childish fashion the dialectic of infrastructure and superstructure to immediate economistic determinations. To say that this theory of unequal exchange also means that the bourgeoisie of the periphery shares the interest of the proletariat of the periphery in winning freedom from domination by the center is to forget that this bourgeoisie was formed from the outset in the wake of the bourgeoisie of the center, and once more to reduce social life to a few simplistic economistic propositions. The purpose of my work is not to discuss all these problems, and I will leave it to lovers of futile polemics to pursue this sort of controversy.

Going deeper, unequal exchange means that the problem of the class struggle must necessarily be considered *on the world scale,* and that national problems cannot be seen as epiphenomena juxtaposed with the essential problem of the "pure" class struggle. At bottom, this is why the theory in question causes so much irritation. It shows that the bourgeoisie (of the center, the only bourgeoisie that exists at the level of the world system) exploits the proletarian and proletarianized masses everywhere, at the center and in the periphery alike, but that it exploits those of the periphery more violently and brutally, and that this can happen because the objective mechanism which is the basis for the unity that links the bourgeoisie with its own proletariat (owing to the autocentric character of the national economy from which it arises), a mechanism that limits exploitation at the center, does not function in the extraverted periphery.

My analysis stops at this point because it does not aim to write the concrete history of the periphery during the last two centuries, and still less to provide prophesies for the future. The world system as I have analyzed it shows that it contains, *at the center just as in the periphery,* both the elements of a socialist challenge to this system and the contrasting elements that oppose such a challenge. No "prophecy," even though it be attributed to Marx, Lenin, or Trotsky, can take the place of the real dialectic of history.

The formation of a world system such as we have today has not merely made possible the development of socialist movements in the periphery. *Up to now* it has led to the shifting of the *principal* nucleus of the forces of socialism from the center to the periphery. This is not an expression of any "Third-World-ist theory" but a plain recognition of the fact that transformations toward socialism have *up to now* broken through nowhere except in the periphery of the system. This fact needs to be explained, like any other—and it can be explained. One way of dodging the question is to deny the socialist character of the transformations in question, either by seeing the revolutions of the periphery as "historical accidents" or by reducing them to "peasant revolts" (as the Trotskyists try to do). This way of denying changes in the system on the world scale—ultimately, of denying the existence of a world system—serves the purpose of safeguarding the sacred character accorded to Marx's analysis of the capitalist mode of production, making of this, instead of the point of departure for analysis, the entirety of a finished body of knowledge. It means forgetting that, as integrated into the world system, the periphery is very largely *proletarianized*, a vital phenomenon that I have stressed in this book.

Can one go on considering the developed world in isolation from its periphery? This means forgetting that the third biggest economic power in the world is made up of American corporations operating outside the United States, so that the proletarians who produce surplus value for U.S. capital are to be found outside the United States to no less an extent than within. Noting this fact, Bettelheim recently arrived at a correct formulation of the problem which coincides almost literally with my own. He wrote:

> I think it very important to draw a sharp line of demarcation, as is done in the article, between Mao Tse-tung's ideas and the Third-World-ist tendencies which see in what are called the underdeveloped countries those that have been left behind by development, or backward countries, whereas they are the *product* of imperialist domination, which has *transformed* them and *integrated* them into the world imperialist system, in which they fulfill a well-defined function, that of a reserve of raw materials and cheap labor power. It is this function that renders the *masses* of these countries ripe for revolution, whether they be *proletarian* masses, in the strict sense of the word, or masses that are *proletarianized* and thereby capable of serving as agents of a proletarian policy.[10]

With this formulation Bettelheim abandons the confused attitudes, which I described as "pre-Leninist," that he had adopted in his dispute with Emmanuel, when he denied the existence of unequal exchange.

It is true, of course, that the mechanisms of proletarianization in the periphery have not worked through to completion, precisely because of thy extroverted character of development in the periphery. A fact of this scope has serious consequences. In the periphery the movement loses its pseudo-"purity": it is both anticapitalist and national. The only successes won by socialism so far have occurred precisely where this merging of socialist and national aims has been most complete (in China and Vietnam). The semi-proletarianized situation of very great masses of the population does, of course, give rise to all sorts of spontaneous tendencies and possible deviations: revival of agrarian capitalism, establishment of state capitalism, or "nationalism." This analysis has nothing in common with that of Frantz Fanon and his followers—who deny that the proletarianized masses of the periphery are capable of fighting for socialism (owing to their alleged material advantages), and who interest themselves exclusively in the peasantry—and only a muddled approach to the controversy can result in these two analyses being confused. The only people who can take offense at this are those who would have preferred history to remain "pure," in accordance with a schema laid down for all time by the "sacred revelation" of 1867. The inability to act upon and transform reality which is characteristic of Trotskyism is what underlies this vain protest against reality.

The distinction I draw between masses that are proletarian, semi-proletarianized, proletarianized, and in course of proletarianization, the emphasis which I put on the need for precise analysis of the mechanisms of proletarianization in the periphery, and the awareness I show of the incomplete stage reached by these processes, all answer *in advance* those hair-splitters who, in the last analysis, are satisfied with recalling that the capitalist mode of production is defined at the level of relations of production, not of exchange. This recalling ad nauseam of a platitude is beside the point, since what is under consideration is the world capitalist system, not the capitalist mode of production. Such analyses, which are incapable of accounting for the *fact* that breaches in the system have so far been effected only in the periphery, are therefore utterly sterile.

We need to go further even than this. The "nationalism" of the East is not a product of its "immaturity" but is the echo of the setbacks suffered in the West, the postponement of the socialist solution in the developed countries. If this delay in the West should continue for a long time—a historical possibility—it is not out of the question that socialism (even if only partial) may coexist for a long time yet with nationalism (even if this be "proletarian" in character).

But the line of development that has been indicated so far is certainly not the only one possible. There is no reason not to expect socialist transformations at the center, and no simplistic economistic argument about the integration of the working-class masses in the system seems to be decisive, for this integration, even if it be a (partial) fact, is not an irreversible one (as it would be if it were total). There is no question of denying this fact of (partial) integration, without which the postponement of the socialist solution in the West would be incomprehensible, except by resorting to subjectivist and anecdotal arguments (about the attitude of the leaders of the trade unions and workers' parties, etc.). This fact also explains why socialist challenging of the system has moved away from the traditional proletariat to the marginal elements of society, and the reflection of this shift in ideology, as we see in the writings of Marcuse. Is it necessary to make clear here, so as to avert further misplaced polemical interpretations, that the alternative line of development, that of social transformations in the West, requires that the system be challenged by more than these marginal elements—that great masses be brought into action, not only the traditional proletariat but also the new proletarianized strata, in particular the white-collar workers and technicians whose numerical importance is growing and will grow more with automation?

Between these two possible lines of development, with their infinite combinations, history alone will decide, and any prophecy must remain illusory.

Finally, the criticism to which the idea of unequal exchange has been subjected has revealed the amazing power of "Europocentrism." People would have liked the proletariat of the center to inherit from its bourgeoisie the leading role in history—that it should inherit the positive aspects of capitalist development without having to inherit its negative aspects. Unfortunately, development is uneven, and this implies transference of the leading role in history from one civilization to another. Greek civilization did not survive the end of slavery. Capitalism will not give way to socialism unless European civilization gives way to a truly worldwide civilization. The vision of the "advanced" proletariat of the West bringing socialism as a "gift" to the "backward" masses of the periphery is not "intolerable"—it is merely refuted by history.

Unequal exchange also draws our attention to the very important fact that the dominant role in the world capitalist system is shifting to *politics.* I make only a brief allusion to this; but it is of vital importance when we tackle the main aspect of the problem, namely, the dynamics and prospects of the peripheral formations.

4. I agree fundamentally with the whole current of thinking which analyzes the origins of underdevelopment as a consequence of the development of capitalism on the world scale, and thereby rejects all the rubbish produced by identifying the concept of underdevelopment with that of "traditionality." For me, development and underdevelopment are the two opposite poles of a dialectical unity. This type of analysis is now that followed by the entire Latin American school (or schools), to which contemporary theory owes its essential conclusions. The differences within this current seem to me to be only minor, and to reflect the commonplace fact that different groups stress different aspects of a problem, depending on the national reality they are concerned with (and these realities are extremely varied)—rarely are they the result of fundamental theoretical divergences.

It is in this way that I, being an Egyptian, have emphasized the role of ground-rent—taken by a class of landowners who are the "beneficiaries" of their country's integration into the international capitalist system—in the genesis of the agrarian crisis in the countries of the periphery, and of the freezing at a very low level of wages and the rewarding of the labor of the small peasants in those countries. Many Latin American writers have pointed out that it is the external character of the market that is responsible for keeping wages down. I agree with them on this point and have in several places in my work shown the close connection between all these phenomena. The critique of the results of the policy of import-substitution which has been also carried out most systematically by Latin Americans, in particular by Raul Prebisch, Celso Furtado, and Maria Conceição Tavarès, likewise coincides with my own."[11]

The problem of the future continues to be the subject of discussions that are not merely possible but also necessary. It is not a taste for futurology that causes me to say this, nor is it my intention to take on the role of the prophets I have criticized. If we have to study what is developing, we must do so with the modesty that is necessary in order to revise our analyses at every stage in the light of the evolution of reality itself.

In recent years, stress has been placed upon the increasing role played by big multinational corporations in the shaping of the world system, and my own analysis is inadequate and out-of-date where this subject is concerned.[12] Nevertheless, I wonder whether the role of these enterprises is not being exaggerated when they are seen as the beginning of a *world capitalist production process*. If one were to anticipate reality, where would the development of this world process lead? I have questioned in this book Marx's analysis of the prospect before the colonies in his day, without the slightest fear of committing "heretical sacrilege," horror of which I leave to the dogmatists. In my turn, however, I must admit that my own view is based on present tendencies, and may also lose its validity as the future unfolds. If a socialist solution is not provided for the increasing contradiction revealed by present tendencies toward the polarization of developed and underdeveloped countries, the world system will itself provide its own solution by evolving in unforeseen directions.

From this angle, is it out of place to ask some questions regarding the semi-industrialized countries of Latin America, notably Brazil and Mexico? In these countries, with the *effect of size* as a factor (which needs to be studied much more systematically, and is practically left out of account in my work), is the possibility of autocentric capitalist development to be altogether ruled out? This prospect must not be reduced to the old problem of national capitalism. Like Canada, could not Mexico (or Brazil?) gradually become a fully developed province of the United States, in the sense that the phenomena of *marginality* that are now apparent would diminish to the point of disappearance? This autocentric development would be undertaken not by national capital but by the capital of the United States, with which the former would of course be associated in a junior capacity (as in Canada). If this should happen, it is clear that the contradiction would shift from the economic sphere to that of culture and politics. Here again we come upon the problem of the shifting of dominance in the system from economics to politics, a matter to which I have already referred.

There is no question of attempting to deal with this problem here, which would require considerable additional work. But it must make us reflect; for I have defined in this book three *symptoms* of underdevelopment (what I have called its "structural characteristics"): unevenness of productivity between sectors, disarticulation, and domination.

It is already clear that disarticulation does not present itself in the same way in Brazil as in tropical Africa. In the case of the semi-industrialized countries of Latin America (Brazil, Mexico, Argentina), there is already an integrated industrial group. This group even tends to become *autocentric,* though in a special way, for it is based not on a large internal market, embracing the whole population, as in the developed countries, but only on a partial internal market, composed of the "rich" and "integrated" fraction of the population. In this way the integrated autocentric industry of these countries leaves out of account a *marginal* population which it does not integrate, and which makes up the bulk of the rural population together with its extension, the inhabitants of the shantytowns. This phenomenon is due to the fact that agriculture, opened up at an earlier stage of the country's integration into the world system, continues to be extraverted and, for this reason, suffers from a very low and stagnant reward for its labor. Disarticulation, which does not appear at the level of industry, is expressed at the national level between agriculture and industry. As we see clearly in the case of Brazil, this phenomenon is expressed in a special structure of external trade, with exports appearing as those of a classical underdeveloped country (predominance of primary products, especially agricultural produce) and imports as those of a developed country (predominance of power, semi-finished goods, equipment goods, and foodstuffs, and not of manufactured consumer goods). This observation leads us to consider more deeply the problem of the relations between agriculture and industry in development. It also leads us to ask whether the "classical" form of disarticulation, which I have described in my book (mainly with Asia and Africa in mind) formed merely a first stage of underdevelopment, or whether the semi-industrialized countries presented from the start specific features that have made this type of solution possible.

Proceeding further, we must ask whether, if disarticulation were to be progressively eliminated through integration of the sectors that are still marginal, underdevelopment would disappear. These are only suppositions, but it is still to be feared that domination will persist, expressing itself particularly in the field of technological initiative. It remains true that, even given this assumption, underdevelopment would look very different from the way it does at present. The fact that Latin American writers stress *dependence* rather than *disarticulation* reflects these preoccupations.

I would suggest, however, that there is nothing to show that the present tendency is for a progressive reduction of the marginal sectors, and their integration. In Mexico, for instance, the marginal population still makes up half of the total, and economic growth is already slowing down—at a level lower than $300 per capita! It seems to me that the prodigious modernization process that this country underwent between 1910 and 1960, and which has nourished this illusion of the progressive absorption of the marginal sectors, was possible owing to the agrarian revolution of 1910 and to the nationalism of the period of Cardenas' presidency (1939-1940). The latter was the first appearance of a current that later developed extensively in other parts of the Third World (India, Egypt, etc.). Until proof appears to the contrary, this type of bourgeois (or petty-bourgeois) nationalism cannot succeed in advancing any further, because it cannot break with the world system. Is it not significant that the pursuit of economic growth in Mexico is based more and more on the export of manpower to the United States (already more than seven million seasonal workers, out of a total population of fifty million), and on tourism—witnessing to other tendencies for the future, characteristic of new forms of dependence and underdevelopment?

The interest offered by analyzing future prospects ought not, therefore, to make us forget present reality. Up to now, the dominant tendency in the world system is for the gulf between center and periphery to get wider, not narrower. In this sense, *imperialism* continues to be the only real problem. The prospect set out in the Pearson Report testifies eloquently to this.[13] And any attempt to hide this basic reality deprives analysis of its scientific character, in order to descend into apologetic ideology, of one sort or another, however subtle. The ultramodern tendencies to a new kind of *unequal* international specialization, however embryonic, seem to me to be a more important field for future research, which is why I have laid much stress on these tendencies. Under the present system, in any case, as in this new system which is beginning to appear, the question of unequal exchange remains, since what is involved is an unequal international division of labor (and so of exchanges). The position occupied by this question is not essential, since exchange continues to be the phenomenon whereby inequality shows itself on the plane of immediate appearances. The essence of the problem lies, as I have emphasized in this book, in the dialectically contradictory pair: *autocentric/extraverted (or developed/underdeveloped).*

It is usual when one confines oneself to the plane of appearances, instead of regarding this as merely the starting-point for analysis, to incur the risk of slipping into positivistic empiricism. In this connection can be mentioned the discussions on the equalization of the rate of profit on the world scale, which is only a tendency, coming up against a countertendency (inequality between monopolies, interference by the national policies of states, and so on). There is also the discussion about the dynamic of the labor market. The fact that the rate of surplus value is higher in the periphery, for reasons I have examined in this book, means that there is transfer of value to the advantage of the center. Along with this, however, a *world labor market,* as yet only embryonic, is coming into existence. Migrations from one continent to another are the beginning of this development. The "brain-drain" after the Second World War was the first sign of this tendency, at that stage affecting only the higher grades of skilled personnel. As always, labor is put at the disposal of capital where the latter wants it, and not vice versa. If, however, these migrations were to become an essential feature of this prospect, then cultural and national differences could be exploited by capital, as can be plainly seen from current experience of the unequal status of immigrant workers in the developed world. In extreme cases, this mass transfer of labor power entails the danger of creating a sort of internal colonial system, as contrasted with the external colonialism that now exists. The model that was once presented by Latin America, and which is today that of the United States and South Africa, where blacks constitute an internal colony, reminds us that this possibility of racism and generalized apartheid needs to be taken seriously. Here, too, politics becomes dominant, and unequal exchange, becoming internal to "developed" society, disappears as a form of *international* exchange.

5. This second edition includes only minor corrections to the original. The style, sometimes too heavy, has not been altered, and reflects the fact that the book was based on a course of lectures: the lengthy expositions have their justification in pedagogical method and in the author's desire to be understood by the mass of social science students, even those not specifically economists. It has seemed to me, for example, more explicit to speak of the comparative evolution of net barter terms of trade and productivities rather than to tackle this problem directly in economistic jargon by analyzing the evolution of the double factoral terms of trade. It did not seem necessary to bring up-to-date my references, often quite old, since many of the ideas set forth here had already been expressed by me as many as fifteen years ago. This is not laziness or affected preference for the old, but is merely due to the fact that more recent texts dealing with the subjects dealt with seem not to contribute anything new. It may be thought that it is useless to criticize the "stages of growth" that were in fashion ten years ago, since Rostow is no longer taken seriously. But it still remains true that he was adviser to a President of the United States, and that the economic policy of many governments continues to be based on the assumptions of the pseudo-theory of stages. The cultural poverty of the technocrats is content with this sort of "social science." Besides, the intellectuals and professors who now smile when mentioning Rostow took him seriously not so long ago, and in most cases have not yet dared to go beyond negative criticism, to work out the theory of the development of underdevelopment. The great period of contemporary university economics seems to me to have been centered on Keynes and the Keynesianism of the 1940s and 1950s. Subsequently, the triumphant technocratic-econometric-positivistic current has merely translated Keynesian and post-Keynesian ideas into the field of practical application. This current, despite the apparent updatings that changing fashion dictates—in this sphere as in that of consumer goods—has now exhausted its potentialities. A genuine bringing up-to-date of this economic theory must start from criticism of the ideas that provided its foundation.

This is why a fundamental criticism of the bases of the marginalist-subjectivist economic theory seemed, and still seems, essential. Piero Sraffa's critique of marginalism has sounded the knell of the subjective theory of value.[14] Sraffa shows again, after Ricardo and Marx, that the macro-economy is fundamental, that the social relations of strength that determine the class sharing of income between the proletariat and the bourgeoisie determine all the conditions of general economic equilibrium, and that calculation of profitability possesses no rationality outside this social relationship of strength. It therefore seems to me that it is necessary, whenever one deals with the theory of underdevelopment, to go to the sources of the ideology of universal harmonies, by carrying out a critique of the subjectivist theory of value. Experience of university teaching has in any case convinced me of the need for this. The crucial role of the rate of surplus value, and consequently the limited and subordinate role of the rate of interest, is of vital significance in the sphere of the economics of development and underdevelopment. This theoretical emphasis has caused me to refer several times to the decisive importance of the contradiction between capacity to produce and capacity to consume: transfers of multiplier mechanisms from the periphery to the center would not be understood without this analysis. However, I stopped at that level. A different book, with a different aim—to give a fundamental critique of the subjective theory—would, needless to say, have had to deal with other problems, in particular those of the transformation of values into prices.[15]

This fundamental criticism having been made, I had to come to grips in this spirit with problems which, though secondary in the theoretical sense, are not less important in practice. The illusions regarding "monetary independence," the ambiguities regarding changes in the conjuncture and the prospect in this connection, especially in the sphere of international relations, positivist empiricism in the outlook on theories and manipulations of the exchange—all need to be examined afresh on the basis of the critique of the theory of development and underdevelopment and of the subjective theory of value that underlies it. This is why I have continually come back to this critique, even at the cost of some repetition. Naturally, a work that criticizes a theory—here, the theory of the economics of development and underdevelopment—demands to be completed by a positive work, which the reader will not find here: a theory of the social formations of capitalism, which is barely sketched out, and even a more general theory of the precapitalist formations and the "facts of civilization."[16]

One final word needs to be said. There can be no doubt that the first edition did not do justice to the debt that I owe, along with all concerned with nonapologetic study of underdevelopment, to the Latin American writers on the subject.[17] Raul Prebisch took the lead in this field, and I have shown in this book that the theory of unequal exchange was founded by him, even if the conjunctural context in which he set it, in his first version, has lost its significance. It is also to the United Nations Economic Commission for Latin America, of which he was the moving spirit, that I owe the essence of the critical theory to which I adhere, for it was this Commission that led the way in the reflections from which all the present currents in Latin American thinking on these matters have developed—criticism of the policy of import-substitution and also theory of dependence.

The amazing theoretical backwardness in Asia, and above all in Africa, where confusion between growth and development still reigns, testifies by contrast to the importance of the contribution from Latin America. When we seek to discover the reasons for this backwardness we are led at once to consider the role of the universities. Since the 1920s the universities of Latin America have been open to the middle classes on a very large scale—sometimes larger than in the developed countries. The old patrician culture, legalistic and positivist, has been subjected to the onslaughts of social science. While in the United States an expansion like this has taken place without serious consequences, thanks to the country's economic dynamism, the European countries which are only now reaching this stage are having difficulty in overcoming the crisis (as is shown by the example of France). In Latin America, where the system was always incapable of digesting this transformation, which peripheral capitalism did not need, a prolonged incubation has helped to create a genuine intelligentsia and resulted in a theoretical harvest of exceptional quality. In Asia and Africa the system of direct colonial rule has prevented this *propulsive contradiction* from arising. It is in this context that the present policy of *systematic destruction* of the universities in the Third World must be seen, especially in the French-speaking countries of Africa, which serves the aim of reducing education to the formation of executive technicians and stifling the formation of real intellectuals capable of reflecting on underdevelopment.

The critique of underdevelopment is thus called upon to play an important part in the bringing up-to-date not only of economics but of social science. The "first decade of development" (the 1960s), in which emphasis was laid on economic growth, with all its illusions of "profitability" and "econometry," ended in obvious defeat—so obvious that the United Nations Organization itself has recognized, at the outset of the "second decade," that "growth is not development." The critique of economism is now subject to the risks of becoming fashionable, that is, of getting diluted in pseudo-synthetical—but really muddled—soothing-syrup. *Structuralism,* by declining to look for the propulsive contradiction within systems, facilitates this process.[18] The fact is that criticism of the theory of underdevelopment leads to criticism of the system, and there is no room for diplomacy in social research.[19]

July 1971

Notes to Volume 2

Notes to Chapter 2, Part 3

177. See the essential work on these structures and this history: Frank, *Capitalism and Underdevelopment in Latin America,* and its very full bibliography of Latin American writings on these problems. See also Gutelman, *L'agriculture socialiste à Cuba,* chapter 1.

178. See Riad, *L'Egypte nassérienne,* and Issawi, ed., *Economic History of the Middle East, 1800-1914.*

179. Rodney, "African Slavery and Other Forms of Social Oppression," points out that the building up of "stocks" of slaves among the inhabitants of the coastal areas led to the formation of new types of slave-owning organization among these peoples. See also Coquery-Vidrovitch, "De la traite négrière à l'exploitation des palmistes du Dahomey," and Dike, *Trade and Politics in the Niger Delta.*

180. Native traders involved in the *economie de traite.* See Dike, op. cit.; Ranger, ed., *Aspects of Central African History;* Oliver and Matew, eds., *History of East Africa.* See also the communication to the IAI Colloquy at Freetown, December 1969.

181. Lacroix, *Industrialisation au Congo.*

182. Amin, "Le développement du capitalisme en Afrique noire."

183. See my book, *Le développement du capitalisme en Côte d'Ivoire.*

184. In six years, from 1960 to 1966, production of foodstuffs for the market multiplied by four in the Lower Congo. For the first time on a big scale the process of capitalist development has been based not on export crops but on food crops, stimulated by the demand of the town of Kinshasa.

185. To use Albert Meister's expressions.

186. See the case of the Ivory Coast, in Amin, *Le développement du capitalisme en Côte d'Ivoire.* See also that of the Gold Coast, which between 1890 and 1914 experienced a "miracle" of the same sort, in Szereszewski, *Structural Changes in the Economy of Ghana.*

187. Examples of such superficial conclusions are not hard to find. It is enough to glance almost at random at the reports produced by the organizations in question. The "green revolution" carried out in some Asian countries (India, Pakistan, Thailand) reflects, as far as certain areas are concerned, the equally rapid progress of "kulakization" among the peasantry.

188. Egypt provides a typical example. See Riad, *L'Egypte nassérienne.*

189. A stimulant that figures in a large-scale traditional trade.

190. Saint-Louis and Gorée were among the earliest European establishments on the African coast.

191. See on this subject the remarkable work by Verhaegen on *Les rébellions au Congo.*

192. Formerly Italian Eritrea experienced a development of capitalism from which the rest of the Ethiopian Empire was immune.

193. Arrighi has correctly emphasized this point. See his communication to the Congress on African Studies (1969).

194. Dobb (*Studies in the Development of Capitalism,* pp. 19-20) also draws attention to the transitional period which in Europe separated the feudal period from that of the Industrial Revolution, and which was marked by an extraordinary development of the simple commodity mode of production.

195. Dobb, op. cit., pp. 3 et seq., rightly emphasizes that capitalism is not synonymous with laissez-faire—that, whenever labor power is lacking, capitalism calls on the state to intervene in order to make labor power available and reduce it to submission.

196. Unpublished study by Samir Amin on the changes in social structure in the Sudan under Mahdi; the author's own observations regarding the Murids. See also Donal O'Brien's research on the Murids (to be published).

197. Studied by Raulin, *La dynamique des techniques agraires.* See also Raulin's communication to the Montreal Congress, October 1969.

198. Delbard, "Les dynamismes sociaux au Sénégal."

199. Amin, *Le monde des affaires sénégalais;* "La bourgeoisie d'affaires sénégalais"; "La politique coloniale francaise."

200. See Amin and Coquery-Vidrovitch, *Du Congo français à l'UDEAC.*

201. Communication to the Congress of African Studies, Montreal, October 1969.

202. When what are involved are important industries, and not mere extensions of commercial activity, as is often the case with light industries producing goods to replace imports—industries that are, moreover, often controlled by the colonial commercial firms themselves.

203. This is the case in Morocco (communication by Abdel Aziz Belal to the Congress of African Studies, Montreal, October 1969) and in Congo-Kinshasa (with the nationalization of the mining companies in Katanga).

204. The expression is from Belal's communication. See also Amin, "Sous-développement et marché international."

205. Aron, *La lutte des classes;* Burnham, *The Managerial Revolution;* Galbraith, *The New Industrial State* and *The Affluent Society.*

206. Hence the decline of parliamentarism in the West. This analysis has been carried out by Edgard Faure, for example, as regards France.

207. A point to which Arrighi has directed our attention (communication to the Montreal Congress, October 1969).

208. See the striking evidence for this in Lacroix, *Industrialisation au Congo.*

209. See the important work on the political and social implications of these changes in Arrighi and Saul, "Nationalism and Revolution in Sub-Saharan Africa"; Arrighi, "The International Corporation"; Arrighi and Saul, "Socialism and Economic Development in Tropical Africa"; also Arrighi's writings on Rhodesia (op. cit.).

210. See Bézy, "La situation économique et sociale du Congo-Kinshasa"; IRES, *Indépendance, inflation, développement;* Ryelandt, *L'inflation congolaise, 1960-1968* (to be published by Mouton), which provides a striking demonstration of this process. It should be mentioned that Ryelandt shows how the intervention of the International Monetary Fund—for the creation of Zaire—has made this retrogression possible: IRES, *Lettre mensuelle,* no. 1, 1967 (on the Union Minière du Katanga).

211. See Amin and Coquery-Vidrovitch, *Du Congo français à l'UDEAC;* Amin, *Trois expériences africaines;* and, bringing these matters up to date, my articles "Ghana," "Guinée," and "Mali" in *Encyclopaedia Universalis,* 1969-70.

Notes to Chapter 3

1. Viner, *Studies in the Theory of International Trade;* Friedman, *Studies in the Quantity Theory of Money;* Von Mises, *Theory of Money and Credit;* Robertson, *Money;* Rist, *Qu'est-ce que la monnaie?;* Nogaro, *La monnaie et les systèmes monétaires;* Marx, *Critique of Political Economy* and *Capital* 1; Schumpeter, *Théorie de l'évolution économique;* Lindhal, *Etudes sur la théorie de la monnaie et du capital;* Myrdal, *L'équilibre monétaire;* Harrod, *Economic Essays;* Keynes, *A Treatise on Money* and *The General Theory;* Hicks, *Value and Capital.* For a general account of monetary theories, see Marchal and Lecaillon, *Les flux monétaires,* and Liau, *La détermination des taux d'intérêt,* which also contain very full bibliographies.

2. Keynes, *The General Theory,* pp. 178-85.

3. Wicksell, *Interest and Prices;* Myrdal, *L'équilibre monétaire;* Keynes, *A Treatise on Money;* Cassel, "The Rate of Interest, the Bank Rate and the Stabilisation of Prices."

4. Robertson, *Money,* pp. 84-107.

5. Don Patinkin, "Price Flexibility and Full Employment"; Courtin, "L'intérêt."

6. Keynes, "The Theory of the Rate of Interest," in *Readings in the Theory of Income Distribution,* p. 418: "Interest . . . is simply the premium obtainable on current cash over deferred cash . . ."

7. Hicks, "Mr. Keynes and the Classics."

8. Keynes, *The General Theory,* pp. 135-64.

9. Robertson, "Mr. Keynes and the Rate of Interest."

10. Denis, *La monnaie.*

11. This is where Gruson finds himself, in *Esquisse d'une théorie générale,* by ultimately identifying saving with amount of money; he is correctly criticized on this point by Courtin (op. cit.).

12. Warburton, "Contemporary Business Fluctuation Theory," p. 284.

13. Harrod, *Towards a Dynamic Economics,* p. 119.

14. Rist, *Histoire des doctrines relatives au crédit et à la monnaie,* pp. 215-18, 404-21.

15. Von Mises, *Theory of Money and Credit.*

16. Hicks, "Simplifying the Theory of Money"; Cannan, "The Theoretical Apparatus of Supply and Demand"; Ellis, "Some Fundamentals in the Theory of Velocity."

17. Modigliana, "Liquidity Preference"; Nogaro, *La méthode de l'économie politique,* pp. 196-245.

18. Friedman, *Studies in the Quantity Theory of Money.*

19. Marjolin, *Prix, monnaie et production,* p. 129; Wicksell, *Interest and Prices,* p. 33; Paish, "Causes of a Change in Gold Supply"; Robertson, *Money,* pp. 82-84.

20. Denis, *La monnaie.*

21. Hicks, *Value and Capital;* Lange, *Price Flexibility and Equilibrium.*

22. Marx, *Capital* 2, ch. 21 ("Accumulation and Reproduction on an Extended Scale").

23. Schumpeter, *Théorie de l'évolution économique.*

24. Perronière, *Les opérations du banque,* pp. 150-70.

25. United Africa Co., Ltd., "The West African Currency Board." Dates of establishment of the other currency boards: East Africa, 1919; Cyprus, 1928; Mauritius, Seychelles, West Indies, 1930; Rhodesia, Malaya, 1938; Central Africa, 1950.

26. See the statistics in Newlyn and Rowan, *Money and Banking in British Colonial Africa,* pp. 51 (West Africa), 64, and 71 (other African colonies); and Greaves, *Colonial Monetary Conditions,* pp. 16, 17, 18 (Malaya and British West Indies).

27. Statistics in Newlyn and Rowan, op. cit., p. 50; the assets represented a percentage of the liabilities varying between 97.2 and 109.4, between 1923 and 1950.

28. Newlyn and Rowan, op. cit., p. 27.

29. Thus, between 1919 and 1942 East Africa gradually built up its reserves, which in 1925 stood at only 43.6 percent of circulation (27.9 in 1930) and eventually, in 1943, attained the figure of 86 percent (Newlyn and Rowan, op. cit., p. 59).

30. "Monetary Systems of the Colonies"; Clausen, "The British Colonial Currency System"; Malkani, "Post-war Currency System in India"; Mikesell, "Financial Problems of the Middle East"; Muhlenfeld, "The Netherlands West Indies"; Shannon, "Evolution of the Colonial Sterling Exchange Standard" and "The Modern Colonial Sterling Exchange Standard"; Vinelli, "The Currency and Exchange System of Honduras."

31. Wallich, *Monetary Problems of an Export Economy,* especially pp. 38, 76, 330.

32. Bloch Lainé, *La zone franc.*

33. Ibid., p. 70.

34. Moursi, *Iqtisadiat al nouqoud,* pp. 184-85.

35. See Brown, *Economic Problems of a Tropical Dependency;* Exter, *The Establishment of a Central Bank in Ceylon;* Frankel, "The

Situation in South Africa"; Shency, "The Currency, Banking and Exchange System of Thailand"; Wallich, "Underdeveloped Countries and the International Monetary Mechanism"; Wallich, *Monetary Problems of an Export Economy,* pp. 40-45; and Chabert, *Structure économique et théorie monétaire,* from which I have taken all the statistics that follow.

36. Newlyn and Rowan, op. cit., pp. 169-76.

37. This distinction is rarely made. The following writers have emphasized its importance: Greaves, "The Sterling Balances of Colonial Territories"; Wightman, "The Sterling Area"; Newlyn, *Money in an African Context.*

38. Figures from the *Annuaires statistiques égyptiens* and the *Annuaire de la SDN* (for Britain). See *Thesis,* p. 407.

39. Chabert, op. cit., pp. 136-39. See also, for the American economy (1800-1945), Warburton, "The Secular Trend in Monetary Velocity" and Hansen, *Monetary Theory and Fiscal Policy.*

40. Bloch Lainé, op. cit., pp. 35, 261, 276, 382; Niveau, "L'organisation de la zone sterling." The figures are taken from Bloch Lainé's book (pp. 488-89) and from *Economie appliquée,* January-March 1953 (p. 189).

41. Fitch and Oppenheimer, *Ghana: End of an Illusion.*

42. Nogaro, *La monnaie et les systèmes monétaires,* p. 153.

43. Spiegel, *Brazil,* pp. 42 et seq.

44. "Ceylon's Central Banking Experiment"; Macrae, "Experiment in Central Banking"; Mikesell, "Sterling Area Currencies of the Middle East"; Newlyn and Rowan, op. cit., ch. 13; Plumptre, *Central Banking in the British Dominions;* Raj, *The Monetary System of Egypt;* Rosenberg, "Banking in a Dependent Economy"; Sayers, ed., *Banking in the British Commonwealth;* Sen, *Central Banking in Undeveloped Money Markets;* Triffin, "Monetary Development in Latin America."

45. Here, too, it is necessary to avoid identifying the relations between the expatriate commercial banks and the central bank in the periphery with the relations maintained by these expatriate banks with the central banks at the center. The spreading network of American banks in Europe (the "only truly European banks," as Kindleberger strikingly puts it in *European Economic Integration* in *Weltwirtschaftliches Archiv,* 1963) raises problems of a different order.

46. Wallich, *Monetary Problems of an Export Economy,* pp. 52–58.

47. Ibid., pp. 256-59.

48. See the special issue of *Revue économique* on "Distribution et

contrôle du crédit" (1951); also Bettelheim, *Problèmes théoriques et pratiques de la planification.*

49. This is the case, for example, in the African countries of the franc area. The history of the (peripheral) bourgeoisie of Senegal, who played an important historical role in the first phase of colonization until they were swept away by this very process, provides an instance (see Amin, *Le monde des affaires sénégalais,* pp. 11-29 and 172-79). Policies of discrimination in the allocation of credit obviously had a lot do with the course taken by this historical development.

50. See the example, in Senegal, of the meat salesmen as compared with the general merchants and *traitants,* which is examined in Amin, op. cit., pp. 97 et seq.

51. There are plenty of well-known facts in this sphere. See, in my work mentioned above, the case of Senegal, pp. 97 et seq. I have given many examples (*Thesis,* ch. 8, pp. 429 et seq.): former French West Africa, Algeria, British colonies in Africa, Cuba, Egypt, South Asia, etc. For a description of the banking system, with in some cases statistics of its functioning, see: Baster, *The Imperial Bank;* Muranjan, *Modern Banking in India;* Mireaux, *L'organisation du crédit dans les territoires d'Outre-Mer;* Newlyn, "The Colonial Banks," in *Banking in the British Commonwealth;* Forté, *Les Banques en Egypte;* UNO, "On the Establishment of Certain Small Loan Banks by Government"; Rowan, "The Native Banking Boom in Nigeria"; "Banking in Nigeria"; "Banking Adaptation in the Gold Coast"; Sayers, ed., *Banking in the British Commonwealth;* Tamagna, *Banking and Finance in China;* Bloch Lainé, *La zone franc,* pp. 234, 241, 242 (for the French Union); Newlyn and Rowan, *Money and Banking in British Colonial Africa,* pp. 79-88 (for the British colonies); Wallich, op. cit., p. 173 (Cuba); Issawi, op. cit., p. 217 (Egypt); UNO, *De la mobilisation des capitaux nationaux en Asie du Sud-Est;* Booker, "Debt in Africa."

52. Chalmers, *History of Currency in the British Colonies;* Crouchley, *Foreign Capital in Egyptian Companies;* Colon Torrès, "Agricultural Credit in the Caribbean"; Dantzala, "Agricultural Credit in India"; FAO, *Agricultural Credit for Small Farmers;* Wallich, op. cit., p. 175.

53. Amin, *Le monde des affaires sénégalais,* pp. 91 et seq.

54. See *Thesis,* pp. 435 et seq., giving examples from the British colonies in Africa and from Egypt, Latin America, and Southeast Asia. Statistical sources taken from Newlyn and Rowan, op. cit., pp. 84, 87, 92 (British Africa); Wallich, op. cit., p. 187 (Cuba); Issawi, op. cit.,

p. 220 (Egypt); League of Nations, *Mémorandum sur les banques commerciales,* p. 57; Jayawardena, "Liquidity in an Underdeveloped Economy"; Newlyn and Rowan, op. cit., p. 79; Moursi, op. cit., p. 258; Amin, *L'utilisation des revenus susceptibles d'épargne.*

55. This is the case of Egypt, for example, for which I have endeavored to measure the (very substantial) volume of hoarding of the income of the large landowners (see Amin, ibid.)

56. Greaves, op. cit., p. 58; Newlyn and Rowan, op. cit., pp. 80, 90, 92.

57. I give some examples in *Thesis,* pp. 445-46, the sources being: UNO, *Mission to Haiti;* Wallich, op. cit., pp. 191-92 (Cuba); Spiegel, op. cit., p. 151 (Brazil); Hazlewood, "Sterling Balances and the Colonial Currency System"; Mars, "The Monetary and Banking System and Loan Market of Nigeria" in *Mining, Commerce and Finance in Nigeria;* Amin, op. cit.

58. Bloch Lainé, op. cit., p. 216; Issawi, op. cit., pp. 222-26.

59. See, e.g., in *Thesis,* the Asian examples quoted from UNO, *De la mobilisation des capitaux nationaux en Asie du Sud-Est et en Extrème-Orient.*

60. Wallich, op. cit., p. 56; Newlyn and Rowan, op. cit., pp. 102-13; Issawi, op. cit., p. 217.

61. Newlyn and Rowan, op. cit., pp. 148, 124; Issawi, op. cit., pp. 216, 221; James, "L'organisation du crédit en Egypte"; UNO, *De la mobilisation des capitaux nationaux;* UNO, *The Economic Development of the Middle East,* p. 41.

62. Described as "rampant" inflation. See, e.g., Biacabe, *Analyses contemporaines de l'inflation* and Bienaymé, *Croissance et monnaie en plein emploi.* Both works contain full bibliographies.

63. Bloch Lainé, op. cit., p. 39.

64. See *Thesis,* p. 453.

65. Nasr, *Essai sur la notion d'inflation;* UNO, *The Economic Development of the Middle East,* p. 20.

66. Durand, *Essai sur la conjoncture de l'Afrique noire,* pp. 53-70.

67. Wallich, op. cit., pp. 87-88, 139-45.

68. Flamant, *Théorie de l'inflation.*

69. Singh, "Monetary Standard in India"; Triffin, "Monetary Development in Latin America."

70. UNO, *The Economic Development of the Middle East,* p. 17; Iversen, *Monetary Policy in Iraq;* International Monetary Fund (IMF), Annual Reports (recent years).

71. Aftalion, *Monnaie, prix et change;* Bresciani-Turoni, *The Eco-*

nomics of Inflation; "Les problèmes monétaires contemporains," *Revue économique,* 1950; Aujac, "L'inflation"; Mikhailevsky, "Le système inflationniste de financement des guerres"; Breguel, "La croissance du fardeau fiscal et l'inflation"; bibliographies in Biacabe and Bienaymé (see note 62).

72. Kondratieff, "The Long Waves in Economic Life"; Nogaro, *La monnaie et les systèmes monétaires;* Akerman, "Discontinuities of Employment Cycles"; "Structural Limits in Economic Development"; Marjolin, *Monnaie, prix et production;* Lescure, *Hausse et baisse des prix de longue durée;* Chamberlin, *The Theory of Monopolistic Competition;* Niebyl, "What Rights Should the Holder of Money Have?" The relation that exists between the monopolistic structure and the steady increase in prices has been the subject of two studies: Abdallah, *Monnaie et structure économique,* and Wilff, "Liaison entre prix et monnaie." A concrete example of how the system works to bring about a price increase is given by Barret, *L'évolution du capitalisme japonais,* vol. 3, pp. 117 et seq. Finally, among studies of the flexibility of prices under a monopoly regime, let me refer to: Backman, *Price Flexibility and Inflexibility;* Burns, "The Organization of Industry and the Theory of Prices"; Dunlop, "Price Flexibility and the Degree of Monopoly"; Galbraith, "Monopoly Power and Price Rigidities"; Hall and Hitch, "Price Theory and Business Behaviour"; Humphrey, "The Nature and Meaning of Rigid Prices"; Robinson, "Imperfect Competition and Falling Supply Price"; Robinson, *The Economics of Imperfect Competition;* Saxton, *The Economics of Price Determination;* Wallace, "Monopoly Prices and Depression," in *Explorations . . . in Honour of Taussig;* Wodd, "Dr. Tucker's Reasons for Price Rigidity."

73. See, e.g., Baran and Sweezy, *Monopoly Capital.*

74. K. Niebyl, quoted in Denis, *La monnaie.*

75. Bernstein and Patel, "Inflation in Relation to Economic Development"; Bronfenbrenner, "The High Cost of Economic Development"; Horsefield, "Inflation in Latin America"; Mendershausen, "Overseas Economic Development in World War II"; UNO, *Courants inflationnistes et déflationnistes actuels* 2, no. 5, 1947; *Les courants inflationnistes et déflationnistes en 1946–48* 2, no. A1; *Report of the U.N. Mission to Chile, 1949–50* 2, no. B6, 1951; Pazos, "Economic Development and Financial Stability"; Prest, *War Economics of Primary Producing Countries;* Rao, "Deficit Financing Capital Formation and Price Behaviour"; League of Nations, *L'inflation, son évolution;* Speigel, op. cit., p. 45; Scheffer, "La banca nei paesi sottosviluppati."

76. See, in my book, *Le monde des affaires sénégalais,* the example of transport (pp. 118 et seq.).

77. See the important studies on this subject in *Income and Wealth,* by Kuznets and others.

78. Emmanuel, *Unequal Exchange.* See also my examination of this problem, in chapter 1.

79. See chapter 2.

80. Lectures given at the Institute of Economic Development and Planning, Dakar, by Eli Löbel in 1966 (duplicated). I here follow this systematic exposition very closely.

81. Spiegel, op. cit., pp. 43, 49, 65; *Thesis*, p. 460.

82. See also the example of the Iranian rial, worth $ .084 in 1928 and $ .018 in 1954, and that of the Mexican peso: the dollar was worth 0.964 pesos in 1823, 0.954 in 1870, 2.062 in 1900, and 5.181 in 1939.

83. I have examined this experience in detail in my *Thesis,* pp. 459 et seq. Sources: Chabert, op. cit., pp. 152, 220, 221.

84. Many examples are available. See, e.g., UNO, *The Economic Development of the Middle East, 1945–54.* This type of inflation has recurred in African countries (Mali, Guinea, Ghana, Egypt, etc.).

85. Grove, "The Role of the Banking System in the Chilean Inflation"; Schloss, "Banking Without a Central Bank." I have studied the case of Egypt in "L'évolution des structures de financement du développement économique en Egypte de 1952 à 1967," in *Studies in the Economic History of the Middle East.*

86. There have been many such experiences, e.g., in Egypt. See UNO, *The Economic Development of the Middle East, 1945–54.*

87. Ryelandt, *L'inflation en pays sous-développés.*

88. Schmitt, *Monetary Policy and Social Conflict in Indonesia;* Amin, *Trois expériences africaines de développement.* Inflation in Latin America has been studied by the Latin American structuralist school. See Félix, "Structural Imbalances, Social Conflict and Inflation"; Furtado, *The Economic Growth of Brazil;* Sears, "Inflation and Growth in Underdeveloped Economies"; Lambert, *Les inflations sud-américaines;* A. Pinto, A. Ferrer, O. Sunkel, etc.

89. The case studied by Calso Furtado in relation to Brazil. See also Amin, "L'évolution des structures de financement," for the sharing of responsibility for the inflation in Egypt.

90. See also Nicolai, *Comportement économique et structures sociales.*

91. Barret, *L'évolution du capitalisme japonais,* vol. 1, pp. 17–23, and vol. 3, pp. 18–60; Allen, *A Short Economic History of Modern Japan.*

92. Okyar, "La théorie keynésienne et les pays sous-développés"; see also Mendershaussen, op. cit.

93. Dobretsberger, "Théorie des territoires économiques," and Perroux, "Les espaces économiques."

94. Anstey, *The Economic Development of India,* p. 412; Jathar and Beri, *Elements of Indian Economics,* p. 129; Haupt, *L'histoire monétaire de notre temps,* pp. 254, 261. See also, in the last-mentioned work, the effects of the devaluation of silver in Java (pp. 236–237).

95. See, e.g., the studies of Fouad Sultan (*La monnaie égyptienne,* 1914) and A. Awad (*L'évolution de la monnaie en Egypte et l'avenir de la livre égyptienne,* 1942). Also: Blowers and Macleod, "Currency Unification in Libya"; Malhotra, *History and Problems of India's Currency;* Mikesell, "Monetary Problems of Saudi Arabia"; Young, "Saudi Arabian Currency and Finance."

96. Löbel, "Liquidités internationales et éléments d'une politique monétaire de l'Afrique."

97. Triffin, *Gold and the Dollar Crisis,* p. 40. (Professor Triffin's "36 percent" appears to be a misprint.—Trans.)

98. See, for recent studies and a bibliography, *A Demand for Money: An International Comparison,* prepared by J. O. Adekunle, Research and Statistics Department, International Monetary Fund, 1965; *Essai d'interprétation de la demande de monnaie,* Paris, Ministry of Finance and Economic Affairs, 1965.

99. The long-term public external debt of the African countries was estimated at the end of 1965 at $5.0 billions units of account (see IBRD Annual Report 1965–66). As this figure did not include the U.A.R., which was included in the Middle East, at least $1.0 billion must be added, given that the external debt of the U.A.R. at the end of 1962 was already $968 million (see Dragoslav Abramović and associates, *Economic Growth and External Debt,* IBRD, 1964).

Notes to Chapter 4

1. Here, in the order in which I discuss them, are the principal writings analyzed: Lutfalla, "Communication to the Washington Meeting"; Lescure, *Les crises générales et périodiques de surproduction;*

Aftalion, *Les crises périodiques de surproduction;* Kaldor, "A Model of the Trade Cycle"; Kalecki, *Studies in Economic Dynamics;* Angell, *Investment and the Business Cycle;* Harrod, *Towards a Dynamic Economics;* Marx, *Capital,* vol. 3, chapter 21 ("Accumulation and Reproduction on an Extended Scale") and chapter 20, sect. 11 ("Replacement of the Fixed Capital"); Dobb, *Political Economy and Capitalism;* Sartre, *Esquisse d'une théorie marxiste des crises périodiques;* Duret, *Le marxisme et les crises;* Sweezy, *The Theory of Capitalist Development;* Hicks, *The Trade Cycle.* See also the articles devoted to these writers in *Les fluctuations économiques* (*La théorie économique du temps présent,* Paris, 1950) and Guitton, *Les fluctuations économiques.*

2. For the theory of maturity see chapter 1. Also, Baran and Sweezy, *Monopoly Capital.*

3. See chapter 3.

4. See Gruson, *Origines et espoirs de la planification française.*

5. Barrère, *Théorie économique et impulsion keynésienne,* p. 86.

6. Haberler, *Prospérité et dépression.*

7. Belshaw, "Stabilization in a Dependent Economy"; Byé, *La transmission internationale des fluctuations économiques;* Clark and Crawford, *The National Income of Australia,* p. 93; UNO, *Mesures pour assurer la stabilité économique internationale;* League of Nations, *Economic Stabilization in the Post-War World;* Prou, *La théorie du multiplicateur d'investissement;* Thomas, "India in the World Depression."

8. Bauer and Paish, "The Reduction of Fluctuations"; Belshaw, "Stabilization in a Dependent Economy"; Black and Tsou, "International Commodity Arrangements"; Brown, "Should Commodity Prices Be Stabilized?"; Davis, "Intergovernmental Commodity Agreements"; FAO, *The Economics of the International Wheat Agreement;* Johnson, "International Commodity Agreements"; Morgan, "International Commodity Problems"; UNO, *Instabilité des marchés d'exportation des pays insuffisamment développés;* Porter, "Buffer Stocks and Economic Stability"; Rieffer, "An International Buffer Stock Agency"; Rowe, *Markets and Men;* Schumann, "Full Employment in South Africa"; League of Nations, *Economic Stabilization in the Post-War World;* Tyszynski, "Economics of the Wheat Agreement"; Whittlesey, "The Stevenson Plan"; Yates and Lamartine, *Commodity Control.*

9. Corea, "Overall Budgetary Policy in an Export Economy"; UNO (Prebisch), *The Economic Development of Latin America,* chapter 7.

10. See *Thesis,* pp. 514–37.

11. The statistics used have been taken from the following works: League of Nations, *Industrialisation et commerce extérieur,* pp. 187–88; UNO, *Commerce des produits de base et développement économique,* p. 11; League of Nations, *L'expérience monétaire internationale,* p. 103. See also: Visine, *La transmission des fluctuations économiques*—the writer reproduces the *Tableaux du commerce international de 1890 à 1938* of Bunle and Rist; League of Nations, *Aperçu du commerce mondial.* For Britain, between 1920 and 1932 the trade balance improved (from a deficit of £391 million to one of £215 million), for France between these dates it worsened (from a deficit of 1 billion francs to one of 10 billion francs) as it did also for the United States, between 1929 and 1933 (from a surplus of $819 million to one of $214 million). For Egypt, however, it improved (from a deficit of £E .3 million in 1929 to zero in 1932), and worsened for India, where the surplus declined from 1.01 billion rupees in 1928–29 to 370 million in 1933–34 (Anstey, op. cit., p. 330). There are thus no precise rules regarding the behavior of the trade balance; imports and exports underwent fluctuations of the same order of magnitude. What is certain is that the price of the exports of the underdeveloped countries fell more than that of the exports of the developed ones. See, for example: Iversen, op. cit., pp. 413, 379. On the evolution of the terms of trade during the cycle, see: League of Nations, *L'expérience monétaire internationale,* p. 234 (the price of exports from Argentina fell by 40 percent, but that of imports by only 3 percent between 1928 and 1932); UNO, *The Economic Development of the Middle East, 1945–54,* pp. 13–15 (improvement in the terms of trade during the Korean War boom); Royal Institute of International Affairs, *The Problem of International Investment,* p. 288 (decline in the gold prices of exports of various commodities, 1929–34). It is the decline in the *prices* of the exports of the underdeveloped countries that is responsible, to a much greater extent than that of their *volume,* for the decline in the import capacity of the underdeveloped countries. See UNO, *Méthodes et problèmes de l'industrialisation des pays sous-développés,* pp. 130–32 (volume of exports and imports of Argentina, Brazil, and Mexico, 1925–29 to 1930–34); Durand, *Essai sur la conjoncture de l'Afrique noire;* Triantis, "Cyclical Changes in the Balance of Merchandise Trade"; Chang, op. cit., chapters devoted to the external balance of Chile and Australia.

12. The statistics relating to Britain, France, and the United States have been constructed on the basis of figures given in the *Annuaire statistique de France* (for the value of exports and imports) and by Iversen (op. cit., pp. 365, 355, 421). The Egyptian figures are taken

from Barrawi, as regards exports, and, for imports, have been worked out with the help of the figures in the *Annuaire statistique de France* and Iversen. My argument can also be checked from the *Tableaux* of Bunle and Rist, for the period 1897–1914, which show the evolution of the indices of the value and volume of exports and imports by continents. It is to be observed that the behavior of the trade balance is not very clear: in 1900 the balances of Britain and China tend toward deficit when the crisis begins, whereas those of Germany, the United States, France, Argentina, and India tend toward surplus. Again, in 1907, those of Britain and India tend toward deficit, those of China, Argentina, the United States, and France toward surplus (Visine, op. cit., p. 127). My argument can also be checked against the example of Algeria. The volume of imports (obtained by dividing the value of imports by the index of French wholesale prices, given in the *Annuaire statistique de France*) increased by 7 percent at the time of the crisis of 1900, and by 21 percent during that of 1907. Similarly, Indonesia's imports increased steadily between 1876 and 1914, as did those of India. This contrasts with the period 1918–38 (Boeke, op. cit., p. 199, for Indonesia; for India, Anstey, op. cit., p. 330, and Jathar and Beri, op. cit., p. 129). See also Tinbergen, *Business Cycles in the United Kingdom;* Tsuru, "Economic Fluctuations in Japan"; Barret, op. cit., vol. 3; Simkin, *The Instability of a Dependent Economy.*

13. The statistics are calculated from the figures given in the *Annuaires statistiques de France* and the *Statistical Abstracts of the United Kingdom.* See also: Legoyt, *La France et l'étranger,* vol. 1, p. 156 (for trade between Britain and the colonies in 1857–58); Matthews, *A Study in Trade Cycle History;* Gayer, Rostow, and Schwarz, *The Growth and Fluctuations of the British Economy.*

14. Sources: Chang, op. cit. (for Britain, Canada, Chile, and Australia); UNO, *Les mouvements internationaux de capitaux entre les deux guerres,* pp. 26 et seq. and pp. 46 et seq. (for Holland, Switzerland, Sweden, China, India, the Dutch East Indies, Argentina, Denmark, Germany, Japan); Wallich, op. cit., pp. 330 et seq. (Cuba), Royal Institute for International Affairs, op. cit., pp. 174 (United States), 200 (France), and 282 (new foreign investments); League of Nations, *L'expérience monétaire internationale,* p. 45 (monetary reserves of creditors and debtors), and pp. 62–67 (sterling balances, etc.).

15. Sources: for France and Britain, Iversen, op. cit., pp. 71, 350, 361; Cairncross, *Home and Foreign Investment,* p. 180; for Argentina, Australia, Canada, and the United States, Iversen, op. cit., pp. 427, 402, 382, 441 (based on Williams, Wood, Viner, and Graham). As regards

Australia between 1883 and 1913, the behavior of the trade balance (annual average for each period of prosperity and depression) does not follow very precise rules. But the close link between the inflow of foreign capital and the conjuncture (except for the prosperity period 1905–1907 the inflow of capital is greater during periods of heightened conjuncture) determines a perfect alternation in the external balance: surplus in a boom, deficit in a depression. For Canada between 1900 and 1913 the upward trend of the inflow of foreign capital conceals the cyclical phenomenon. Nevertheless, the balance (reduced to the trade balance and that of transactions in capital and interest) worsens in 1904, and then again in 1908 and 1909, and improves during the other periods (when the conjuncture is better). It is the same for the United States between 1866 and 1878: the inflow of foreign capital, which was very strong between 1869 and 1873, decreased severely with the crisis of 1873 and the depression that followed, between 1874 and 1876.

16. Sources: League of Nations, *Industrialisation et commerce extérieur,* pp. 158 et seq.; C. Clark, op. cit., p. 70 (industrial unemployment). For calculation of the fluctuations in profits: France and Germany–figures in "L'application du concept de revenu national," *L'actualité économique et financière à l'étranger,* June 1946; Great Britain–C. Clark, op. cit., pp. 497, 412, 397; United States–ibid., p. 48 (figures from Kuznets); Egypt–Issawi, op. cit., p. 80; India–Anstey, op. cit., pp. 420, 637; C. Clark, op. cit., p. 397; Kuznets, *National Income and Its Composition,* vol. 1, p. 269.

17. See chapter 3.

18. Blanchard, "La crise en Egypte" and "La deuxième phase de la crise en Egypte"; Ellsworth, *Chile, An Economy in Transition;* Gayer, Homan, and James, *The Sugar Economy of Puerto Rico;* Ghaleb, *Les capitaux étrangers en Egypte* (see his study of the crisis of 1907).

19. See chapter 2.

20. See chapter 2.

21. See *supra.*

22. See chapter 1.

23. See Luas, "Problèmes actuels du marchè capitaliste."

Notes to Chapter 5

1. Meade, *The Balance of Payments.*
2. See chapter 3.
3. Aftalion, *Monnaie, prix et change,* p. 256.
4. Ibid., pp. 253–55.
5. Byé, *Les structures nationales et l'investissement international.*
6. Chang, *Cyclical Movements of the Balance of Payments.*
7. Viner, *International Trade and Economic Development,* pp. 24–27.
8. Chang, op. cit., and "International Comparisons of Demand for Imports"; "A Statistical Note on World Demand for Imports"; "The British Demand for Imports in the Inter-war Period"; "A Further Note on the British Balance"; Tinbergen, "Some Measurements of Elasticities of Substitution"; "The Problem of Dollar Scarcity"; Machlup, "Elasticity Pessimism in International Trade"; Malinvaud, "Les élasticites prix."
9. Ohlin, *International and Inter-regional Trade;* and, earlier, Longfield, Torrens, and Joplin, quoted by Viner, *Studies in the Theory of International Trade,* p. 297.
10. Mosak, *General Equilibrium Theory in International Trade;* Schiff, "Direct Investment, the Terms of Trade, and the Balance of Payments." Several attempts have been made at a statistical verification of the theory. See, *inter alia:* Bresciani-Turroni, *Theory of International Payments;* Chang, "The British Balance, 1924–1938"; Duncan, "South African Capital Imports"; MacDougal, "Britain's Foreign Trade Problem"; Pandit, *India's Balance of Indebtedness;* Phelps, *The International Economic Position of Argentina.* Iversen (*Aspects of the Theory of International Capital Movements,* Part II-B: Facts) concentrated on criticizing the "classical" explanation. Studying the example of Canada, Viner (*Canada's Balance of International Indebtedness*) thought he had observed an elastic response by the banking system to the influx of gold determining the internal increase in prices and the improvement in the terms of trade that enables the balance to be restored. Iversen explains the course taken by the process by reference to the theory of income. The example of Australia, studied by Wood (*Borrowing and Business in Australia*) and Wilson ("Australian Capital Imports, 1871–1930," and *Capital Imports and the Terms of Trade*) is frankly negative: the terms of trade did not behave in accordance with the classical theory. The history of the United States between 1880 and 1914 (Taussig, *International Trade,* pp. 284 et seq.) is no better. Nor are the experiences of

the big creditor countries: France (White, *The French International Accounts*), where there is no correlation between the situation of the balance and the movement of gold, or between the latter and the movement of credit, or between the movement of credit and the terms of trade; Great Britain (Taussig, op. cit., pp. 236 et seq., and "Great Britain's Foreign Terms of Trade After 1900"); the United States after 1920 (Taussig, op. cit., pp. 318 et seq.).

11. Goschen, *Foreign Exchanges.*

12. A conclusion I have rejected (see chapter 3).

13. This is not the place to discuss why I reject the quantity theory: see chapter 3.

14. See the articles mentioned *supra.* Also: Robinson, "The Foreign Exchange," in *Essays in the Theory of Employment;* Nogaro, *La valeur logique des théories économiques,* chapter 6.

15. Aftalion, *Monnaie, prix et change,* pp. 152–53.

16. See my *Thesis,* chapter 1.

17. Marco Fanno, *Transferimenti anormali dei capitali;* Kindleberger, *International Short-Term Capital Movements.* To these three criticisms —price elasticity, influence of the price of imports on that of home-produced goods, effect of short-term capital movements—must be added the fundamental criticism to which the quantity theory is liable. It is because the quantity of money in circulation depends on what is required, and not on the will of the central bank, that there has never been any correlation between the movement of the international assets of the central bank (gold and foreign currency) and that of national assets, as is shown by Nurkse's statistics, constructed on the basis of 26 countries between 1922 and 1938 (League of Nations, *L'équilibre monétaire international,* pp. 77 et seq.): out of 382 observations, only 121 conform to the classical theory.

18. Boudeville, "Commerce extérieur, revenu national et dévaluation"; Day, "Devaluation and the Balance of Payments"; Hirschman, "Devaluation and Trade Balance"; Polak and Chang, "Effects of Exchange Depreciation"; Zakaria, *Change, commerce extérieur et équilibre économique interne.* Here, too, Iversen has shown how the income effect is superimposed on the exchange effect. The experience of Argentina between 1880 and 1900 has been studied by Williams (*Argentine International Trade Under Inconvertibility*). If we eliminate the upward trend of the gold premium due to internal inflation, we find a good correlation between the price of gold (which functions as the rate of exchange) and the state of the external balance. We also observe that not only does the price of exports (no figure is available for that of

imports) fluctuate with the rate of exchange, but also wages are linked with it. This suggests that all prices, including those of home-produced goods (with which wages are linked), are fixed in accordance with the level of the exchange, which plays a decisive part. For the United States, 1860–1879, see Graham, "International Trade Under Depreciated Paper." Here, too, the state of the balance explains the fluctuations of the price of gold around a downward trend (deflation). In contrast to Argentina, however, the evolution of internal prices (wholesale prices, wages, domestic prices) is regular, independent of the evolution of the rate of exchange. Only the price of imports depends on the rate of exchange: the latter affects internal prices only slightly. These prices depend mainly on the level of the internal equilibrium.

19. Federici, "On the Validity of the Principle of Foreign-trade Multiplier."

20. See chapter 3.

21. Metzler, "The Transfer Problem Reconsidered"; Machlup, *International Trade and the National Income Multiplier;* Gendarme, "Le multiplicateur du commerce extériuer"; Barnerias, *La théorie de l'équilibre international;* Enke and Salera, *International Economics,* chapter 12; Haberler, *Prospérité et dépression;* Clark and Crawford, *The National Income of Australia;* "Determination of the Multiplier"; Harrod, *International Economics;* Byé, *La transmission internationale des fluctuations.*

22. Kindleberger, "International Monetary Stabilization," in *Postwar Economic Problems;* "Foreign Trade Multiplier and Balance Equilibrium"; Duesenberry, "Income Saving, and Consumer Behaviour," in *Essays in Honour of Hansen.*

23. See chapter 2.

24. See Sweezy, *The Theory of Capitalist Development,* and Baran and Sweezy, *Monopoly Capital.*

25. Wallich, *Monetary Problems of an Export Economy,* pp. 210–11, 198.

26. Aftalion, *L'or et sa distribution mondiale.*

27. See my chapter 3; also, Denis, *La monnaie,* from which I have taken my critique of the quantity theory.

28. Nurkse, "International Monetary Equilibrium," in *Essays in International Finance.*

29. Robinson, "The Foreign Exchange," in *Essays in the Theory of Employment.*

30. This is not the place to develop these fundamental ideas, on which see chapter 1. On this subject see, *inter alia,* Frank, *Capitalism*

and Underdevelopment in Latin America. Current non-Marxist writing avoids this subject except in some of its most secondary aspects. As examples, see, *inter alia:* Akerman, "Le problème de l'équilibre international"; Balogh, "Static Models and Current Problems in International Economics"; "The International Equilibrium and U.S. Private Investments"; "South Africa's Hot Money Problem"; Bruton, "Growth Models and Underdeveloped Countries"; Buchanan, *International Investment and Domestic Welfare;* Domar, "Foreign Investment and Underdeveloped Countries"; Institut International de Finances Publiques, *Aspects financiers, fiscaux et budgétaires du développement des pays sous-développés;* Marquez, "Balance of Payments Problems in Latin America"; Saccheti, "Bilancia dei pagamenti dei paesi in sviluppo"; Salant, "Capital Export Under the Point Four Program"; Singer, "The Distribution of Gains Between Investing and Borrowing Countries."

31. See Amin, "Le développement du capitalisme en Afrique noire."

32. See chapter 2.

33. See chapter 2.

34. As an example, see the case of the African countries of the franc area, which are analyzed, so far as former French Equatorial Africa and Cameroon between 1960 and 1968 are concerned, in Amin, "Pour un aménagement du système monétaire des pays africains."

35. See chapter 1. The crucial work on this question is Emmanuel, *Unequal Exchange.*

36. See on this subject the numerous publications of the International Bank for Reconstruction and Development (World Bank), especially the *Cours d'analyse de projets* of its Institute.

37. In UNO, *The Economic Development of Latin America and Its Problems,* chapter 4.

38. Kindleberger, *The Dollar Shortage; International Economics,* 1953; "L'asymètrie dans la balance des paiements"; Harrod, *The Dollar.*

39. See chapter 4.

40. The phenomenon is more complex. See on this question the discussion of the dynamic of the surplus in our time, in Baran and Sweezy, op. cit.

41. See chapter 3.

42. See chapter 3.

43. Sources: League of Nations, *Documents sélectionnés sur la distribution de l'or,* and Haupt, *L'histoire monétaire de notre temps,* pp. 249–53, 243 et seq. (for silver).

44. League of Nations, *Documents sélectionnés.*

45. *Annuaire du commerce extérieur de l'Egypte,* and my own calculations in *L'utilisation des revenus susceptibles d'épargne.*

46. League of Nations, *Rapport provisoire de la délégation de l'or,* Annexe 7, p. 59.

47. League of Nations, *Rapport provisoire de la délégation de l'or* (India); Cairncross, *Home and Foreign Investments* (Britain); Iversen, op. cit., p. 350 (France).

48. League of Nations, *L'expérience monétaire internationale,* pp. 10 et seq.; *Aperçu de la situation monétaire 1937–1938,* vol. 1, p. 14.

49. See on this subject, League of Nations, *Memorandum sur les banques commerciales,* p. 119; *L'expérience monétaire internationale,* pp. 57–62, and Annexe IV, pp. 270–71; UNO, *The Economic Development of Latin America,* p. 31; Spiegel, *Brazil;* Bower, *The Balance of Payments of Nigeria;* Bresciani-Turroni, "Egypt's Balance of Trade"; Central African Statistical Office, *The Balance of Payments of Southern Rhodesia;* Conan, "Balance of Payments of the Colonies"; "India's Balance of Payments Problem"; Franklin, "South Africa's Balance of Payments"; Sweezy, "Mexican Balance of Payments"; Brown, *The International Gold Standard Reinterpreted;* Einzig, *International Gold Movements;* Lambert, *Les inflations sud-américaines.* Details of the facts outlined above will be found in my *Thesis,* chapter 10.

50. De Vries, "The Magnitudes of Exchange Devaluations." Between 1948 and 1967 the European currencies lost 5.2 percent of their value in relation to the dollar; those of the Middle Eastern countries lost 38.4 percent, the rest of Asia (excluding Japan) 46.1 percent, the rest of Africa 47.6 percent, and Latin America 62.2 percent.

51. See, for example, Löbel's study of developments in Africa, 1958–65, "Liquidités internationales et éléments d'une politique monétaire de l'Afrique." Exceptions to this rule are very few, apart from the oil-producing countries, which are exceptional in the other continents too.

52. Theoretically, at least; in practice the persistence of a deficit would cause the metropolitan country to take the initiative in revising the foreign-exchange-standard system. See on this, for the African countries of the franc area, Amin, art. cit. in *Le Mois en Afrique,* May 1969.

53. League of Nations, *L'expérience monétaire internationale,* p. 151.

54. The facts that follow have been taken from ibid., pp. 15, 152, 162.

55. League of Nations, *Rapport sur le contrôle des changes; Enquête sur les accords de clearing;* UNO, *Mesures prises par les gouvernements; Tendances et politiques des balances des paiements, 1950–51;* League of Nations, *L'expérience monétaire internationale,* pp. 185–212.

Notes to Afterword

1. Baran and Sweezy, *Monopoly Capital.*

2. Mandel, "La valeur-travail et le capitalisme monopolistique."

3. An excellent analysis of the disastrous results for nations of taking a "near" horizon in their calculation of profitability will be found in Tanzer, *The Political Economy of International Oil,* especially pp. 32 et seq.

4. This critique of cost-benefit analysis was begun by Sachs in *Environmental Quality, Management and Development Planning.*

5. For an illustration of what might be the economic characteristics of such a technology, see Muller-Plantenberg, "Technologie et dépendance."

6. Discussed in Volume 1.

7. Emmanuel, *Unequal Exchange.* This controversy was echoed in *Le Monde,* 11 November 1969, articles by A. Emmanuel and C. Bettelheim; *Politique Aujourd'hui,* 1969–70, articles by A. Emmanuel, H. Denis, A. Granou, G. Dhoquois, and C. Bettelheim; and *L'homme et la société,* nos. 12, 15, 18, and 19, 1969–71, articles by A. Emmanuel and C. Palloix.

8. This quite unacceptable criticism is offered by Chatelain in "Où mène la thèse de l'échange inégal?" The line taken by Florian ("Emmanuel chez les Philistins") is much more carefully argued. By acknowledging that international transfer of surplus value does take place (p. 103), Florian accepts the existence of unequal exchange, as he explicitly admits (Bailly and Florian, "Contradictions dans les économies semi-industrialisées," p. 39). His polemic really relates to themes connected with the political conclusions too hastily drawn by both supporters and opponents, which have no bearing on the thesis itself.

9. This inadequacy of Robinson's critique of marginalism, as compared with my own, is clearly reflected by Bailly and Florian, op. cit.

10. Bettelheim, "A propos du 'Marxisme de Mao,' " p. 243.

11. Celso Furtado, *Development and Stagnation in Latin America;* Conceicão Tavarès, "Substitucion de importaciones en el Brasil."

12. The literature of this subject is very extensive. I will mention here only: Arrighi, "International Corporations, Labor Aristocracies, and Economic Development in Tropical Africa"; de Cecco, "The Influence of Multinational Corporations"; Hymer, "Excerpt on Mercantilism III"; "The Multinational Corporation and Its Allies"; "The Efficiency of Multinational Corporations"; Hymer and Resnick, "International Trade and Uneven Development"; Kidron, *Western Capitalism Since the War;* Michalet, *L'entreprise plurinationale;* Miller and Carter, "The Modern Dual Economy"; Rowthorn, "Capitalism Since the War"; Sunkel, "Intégration capitaliste transnationale et désintégration nationale"; Sutcliffe, "Outlook for Capitalism in the Seventies"; Tanzer, op. cit.

13. *Partners in Development.* See my criticism of this report in Ward, d'Anjou, and Runnels, eds., *The Widening Gap: Development in the 1970s.*

14. Sraffa, *Production of Commodities by Means of Commodities.*

15. This problem, first raised by Bortkiewicz in 1907, provided the basis of a long controversy in which Moszkowska, Hilferding, Boudin, and others took part. The discussion was resumed by Sweezy in *The Theory of Capitalist Development* (chapter 7) and more recently by Emmanuel, in *L'homme et la société,* no. 18, 1970; see also *Unequal Exchange.* Some have seen a defeat for the labor theory of value in this connection and have consequently attempted a synthesis between it and the subjective theory. Sraffa's work proves, in my opinion, that this view of the matter is wrong, and fully reestablishes the significance of the labor theory of value. It is, of course, not possible to discuss these ideas seriously here.

16. See on this the excellent introduction to the problem in the book by Pelletier and Goblot, *Matérialisme historique et histoire des civilisations;* and, as regards the Arab world, the article by el Kodsy, "Nationalism and Class Struggle in the Arab World."

17. The bibliography could be very lengthy. At the very least I must mention: Casanova, *La démocratie au Mexique;* Cardoso, *Politique et développement dans les sociétés dépendantes* and *Soviologie du développement en Amérique Latine;* Ricardo Cibboti; Enzo Faletto; Cardoso and Faletto, *Dependencia y desarrollo en America latina;* Ferrer, *La economia argentina;* André Gunder Frank; Celso Furtado, *Les Etats-Unis et le sous-développement de l'Amérique latine;* Germani, *Politica y sociedad en una epoca de transicion;* Hinkelammert et al., *Dialectica del desarrollo desigual;* Ianni, *Estado e capitalismo;* Marcos

Kaplan; Jose Martos Mar; Marini, *Subdesarrollo y revolucion;* Luciano Martins; Vilelaluz, *A luta pela industrializacão do Brasil;* Hector Silva and Jose Michelena; Dominguez, Noceto, et al., *El proceso economico del Uruguay;* Ortiz, *Historia economica de la Argentina;* Anibal Pinto; Anibal Quijano; Dos Santos, *Dependencia y cambio social* and *Socialismo o fascismo, dilema latino-americano;* Stavenhagen, *Les classes sociales dans les sociétés africaines;* Osvaldo Sunkel; Maria Conceicão Tavarès; Di Tella, *Una teoria sobre el primer impacto de la industializacion;* Claudio Veliz; Francisco Welfort; Cardoso and Welfort, *Sociologia de la dependencia*; Marshall Wolfe; and many others whose works are still, unfortunately, unknown to me.

18. Here I must mention, if no one else, at least Gunnar Myrdal, (*Asian Drama*); Arthur Lewis (*The Development Process*); Hans Singer ("Distribution of Gains from Trade and Investment"); and the UNRISD team in Geneva working on "a unified approach to development problems." Myrdal's approach, the most systematic, remains structuralist, and, because he does not recognize that production relations are *ultimately* determining, his critique of *economism* lands him in psychologism. While Arthur Lewis's effort fails to go beyond eclectic juxtaposition of the "economic," "social," etc., planes, Hans Singer's courageous self-criticism endeavors really to integrate domination and imperialism in economic analysis.

19. As Gunnar Myrdal has declared.

Bibliography

References in the text to the works of Marx and Lenin are not included in this Bibliography as they are easily accessible to the reader in numerous editions.—Ed.

Abdallah, I. *Monnaie et structure économique.* Cairo, 1952.

Abramović, D., et al. *Economic Growth and External Debt.* 1964.

Ady, P. "Colonial Industrialisation and British Employment." *Review of Economic Studies*, Winter 1943.

Aftalion, A. *Les crises périodiques de surproduction.* Paris, 1913.

——. *Monnaie, prix et change.* Paris, 1935.

——. *L'or et sa distribution mondiale.* Paris, 1932.

Akerman, J. "Discontinuities of Employment Cycles." *Nordisk Tidskrift for Teknisk Økonomie* (1-4), 1948.

——. "Le problème de l'équilibre international dans les économies en voie de développement." *Bulletin Int. Sc. Soc.*, Spring 1951.

——. "Structural Limits in Economic Development." *De Economist*, 1949.

al Said, M. H. *L'Egypte contemporaine.* 1962.

Albertini, J-M. *Les mécanismes du sous-développement.* Paris, 1966.

Allais, M. *Economie et intérêt.* Paris, 1947.

Allen, J. C. *A Short Economic History of Modern Japan.* London, 1963.

Amin, S. *L'Afrique de l'Ouest bloquée: l'économie politique de la colonisation, 1880-1970.* Paris, 1971.

——. "La bourgeoisie d'affaires sénégalaise." *L'homme et la société*, 2d quarter 1969.

——. "Le commerce interafricain." *Le Mois en Afrique,* December 1967.

——. "Le développement du capitalisme en Afrique noire." In *En partant du "Capital,"* edited by Victor Fay. Paris, 1968.

——. *Le développement du capitalisme en Côte d'Ivoire.* Paris, 1967.

——. *L'économie du Maghreb.* 2 vols. Paris, 1966.

——. "Les effets structurels de l'intégration internationale des économies précapitalistes, une étude théorique du mécanisme qui a engendré les économies dites sous-développés." Thesis. Paris, 1957.

——. "L'évolution des structures de financement du développement économique en Egypte de 1952 à 1967." In *Studies in the Economic History of the Middle East.* London, 1970.

——. "L'intégration internationale des sociétés précapitalistes." Duplicated. Paris, 1957.

——. *Le monde des affaires sénégalais.* Paris, 1969.

——. "La politique coloniale française à l'égard de la bourgeoisie commerçante sénégalaise, 1820-1960." Colloque de l'AIA, 1969.

——. "Pour un aménagement du système monétaire des pays africains de la zone franc." *Le Mois en Afrique,* May 1969.

——. "Sous-développement et marché mondial." *Politique aujourd'hui,* September 1969.

——. *Trois expériences africaines de développement: le Mali, la Guinée et le Ghana.* Paris, 1965.

——. *L'utilisation des revenus susceptibles d'épargne en Egypte de 1939 à 1953.* Statistical thesis. Paris, 1955.

Amin, S., and Coquery-Vidrovitch, C. *Du Congo français à l'UDEAC—histoire économique de l'Afrique équatoriale, 1880-1969.* Paris and Dakar, 1969.

Angell, J. W. *Investments and Business Cycles.* 1941. Reprint ed. 1973.

——. *Theory of International Prices.* 1926. Reprint ed. 1972.

Anstey, V. *The Economic Development of India.* London and New York, 1929. Rev. ed. 1936.

Aron, R. *La lutte des classes.* Paris, 1967.

Arrighi, G. Communication to the Congress on African Studies, Montreal, October 1969.

——. "International Corporations, Labor Aristocracies, and Economic Development in Tropical Africa." In *Essays on the Political Economy of Africa,* G. Arrighi and J. S. Saul. New York, 1973.

——. "Labor Supplies in Historical Perspective: A Study of the Proletarianization of the African Peasantry in Rhodesia." In *Essays on the*

Political Economy of Africa, G. Arrighi and J. S. Saul. New York, 1973.

——. "The Political Economy of Rhodesia." In *Essays on the Political Economy of Africa,* G. Arrighi and J. S. Saul. New York, 1973.

Arrighi, G., and Saul, J. S. *Essays on the Political Economy of Africa.* New York, 1973.

——. "Nationalism and Revolution in Sub-Saharan Africa." In Arrighi and Saul, op. cit.

——. "Socialism and Economic Development in Tropical Africa." In Arrighi and Saul, op. cit.

Aubrey, H. G. "Deliberate Industrialisation." *Social Research,* June 1949.

Aujac. "L'inflation: conséquence monétaire du comportement des groupes sociaux." *Economie appliquée,* 1950.

Avineri, S., ed. *Karl Marx on Colonialism and Modernization.* New York, 1969.

Awad, A. *L'évolution de la monnaie en Egypte et l'avenir de la libre égyptienne.* 1942.

Backman, J. *Price Flexibility and Inflexibility.* New York, 1940.

Bailly, J., and Florian, P. "L'exacerbation des contradictions dans les économies semi-industrialisés." *Critique de l'économie politique* 3 (1971).

Bain, J. S. "Measurement of the Degree of Monopoly. A Note." *Economica,* 1943.

Bairoch, P. "Evolution 1960-67 et perspectives à court terme de l'économie du Tiers Monde." Colloquium of the Vienna Institute for Development and Co-operation, June 1968.

——. *Révolution industrielle et sous-développement.* 1963.

Balogh, T. "The International Equilibrium and U.S. Private Investments." *O.U.I.S. Bull. Ag.,* 1951.

——. "Note on Deliberate Industrialisation for Higher Incomes." *Economic Journal,* June 1947.

——. "Some Theoretical Problems of Post-war Foreign Investment Policy." *Oxford Economic Papers,* March 1945.

——. "South Africa's Hot Money Problem." *The Banker,* June 1948.

——. "Static Models and Current Problems in International Economics." *Oxford Economic Papers,* June 1939.

Bank of England. *U.K. Overseas Investments, 1938-1948.* London, 1950.

Baran, P. A. *The Political Economy of Growth.* New York and London, 1957.

Baran, P. A. and Hobsbawm, E. "The Stages of Economic Growth." *Kyklos* 2 (1961).

Baran, P. A. and Sweezy, P. M. *Monopoly Capital: An Essay on the American Economic and Social Order.* New York and London, 1966.

——. "Notes on the Theory of Imperialism. Problems of Economic Dynamics and Planning." In *Essays in Honor of Michael Kalecki.* Oxford, 1963.

Barnerias, J. S. *L'équilibre économique international; nouveaux aspects de la théorie.* Paris, 1952.

Barrère, A. *Théorie économique et impulsion keynésienne.* Paris, 1952.

Barret, F. *L'évolution du capitalisme japonais.* Paris, 1945.

Bastable, C. F. *The Theory of International Trade with Some of Its Applications to Economic Policy.* London, 1887.

Baster, A. S. J. *The Imperial Banks.* London, 1929.

Bauer, P. T., and Paish. "The Reduction of Fluctuations in the Incomes of Primary Producers." *Economic Journal,* December 1952.

Bauer, P. T., and Yamey, B. S. "Economic Progress and Occupational Distribution." *Economic Journal,* December 1951.

Belshaw, M. "Economic Development in Asia." *Economia Internazionale,* November 1952.

——. "Observations on Industrialisation for Higher Incomes." *Economic Journal,* September 1947.

——. "Stabilisation in a Dependent Economy." *Economic Review,* April 1939.

Bénard, J. *La conception marxiste du capital.* Paris, 1951.

Berg, E. "Structure des salaires dans les pays peu développés." Colloquium, Egelund, Denmark, 23-27 October 1967.

Bernstein, E. M., and Patel, I. G. "Inflation in Relation to Economic Development." IMF Staff Papers, November 1952.

Bertin, G. Y. *L'investissement international.* Paris, 1967.

Bettelheim, C. *L'économie allemande sous le nazisme.* Paris, 1945.

——. *Nouveaux aspects de la théorie de l'emploi.* Paris, 1952.

——. "A propos du 'Marxisme de Mao': lettre à Rossana Rossanda" (March 1971). In *Il Manifesto* (Rome).

——. "Revenu national, épargne, investissement chez Marx et Keynes." *Revue d'économie politique* 2, 1948.

——. *Studies in the Theory of Planning.* Bombay and New York, 1961.

Bézy, F. "La situation économique et sociale du Congo-Kinshasa." *Cultures et développement* 1:3 (1969).

Biacabe, P. *Analyses contemporaines de l'inflation.* Paris, 1962.

Bienaymé, A. *Croissance et monnaie en plein emploi.* Paris, 1964.

Black, J., and Tsou, S. "International Commodity Arrangements." *Quarterly Journal of Economics,* August 1944.

Blanchard. "La deuxième phase de la crise en Egypte." *Egypte contemporaine,* 1931.

——. "La crise en Egypte." *Egypte contemporaine,* 1931.

Bloch Lainé. *La zone franc.* Paris, 1956.

Blowers, G. A., and Macleod, A. N. "Currency Unification in Libya." In *IMF Staff Papers,* November 1952.

Boeke, J. H. *Economics and Economic Policy of Dual Societies.* Haarlem, 1953.

Bonné, A. *State and Economics in the Middle East.* 1955. Reprint ed. Greenwich, Conn., 1973.

Booker, H. S. "Debt in Africa." *African Affairs,* April 1949.

Boserup, E. *The Conditions of Agricultural Growth.* Chicago, 1965.

Boudeville. "Commerce extérieur, revenu national et dévaluation." *Revue économique,* October 1950.

Bower, P. A. *The Balance of Payment of Nigeria in 1936.* Oxford, 1949.

Breguel. "La croissance du fardeau fiscal et l'inflation dans les pays capitalistes." *Questions d'économie,* 1953.

Bresciani-Turroni, C. *The Economics of Inflation.* London, 1937. Reprint ed. New York, 1968.

——. "Egypt's Balance of Trade." *Journal of Political Economy,* June 1934.

——. *Inductive Verification of the Theory of International Payments.* Cairo, 1933.

——. "Les problèmes monétaires contemporaines." *Revue économique,* 1950.

Bronfenbrenner, M. "The High Cost of Economic Development." *Land Economy,* May 1953.

Brown, A. J. *Applied Economics.* New York, 1948.

——. *Economic Problems of a Tropical Dependency.* London, 1948.

——. *Industrialisation and Trade.* London, 1943.

——. *The International Gold Standard Reinterpreted.* New York, 1940.

——. "Should Commodity Prices Be Stabilized?" *District Bank Review,* December 1953.

Brus, W. *Problèmes généraux du fonctionnement de l'économie socialiste.* Paris, 1968.

Bruton, H. J. "Growth Models and Underdeveloped Countries." *Journal of Political Economy,* August 1955.

——. "Productivity, the Trade Balance and the Terms of Trade." *Economia internazionale,* August 1955.

Buchanan, D. H. "The Historical Approach to Rent and Price Theory." *Economica,* 1929.

Buchanan, N. S. "Deliberate Industrialisation for Higher Income." *Economic Journal,* December 1956.

——. *International Investment and Domestic Welfare.* New York, 1945.

Bukharin, N. *Imperialism and World Economy.* 1915. Reprint ed. New York, 1973.

Bunle and Rist. *Tableaux du commerce international de 1890 à 1938.* Sirey, 1950.

Burnham, J. *The Managerial Revolution.* New York, 1941.

Burns, A. R. "The Organisation of Industry and the Theory of Prices." *Journal of Political Economy,* February-December 1937.

Byé, M. "La grande unité interterritoriale dans l'industrie extractive et ses plans." In *Cahiers de l'ISEA,* Series F.

——. "Les principes de la spécialisation internationale." Duplicated. Lectures, cours de doctorat, Paris, 1953-54.

——. *Les relations économiques internationales.* Paris, 1969.

——. "Les relations entre l'investissement international et la structure nationale." Lectures, cours de doctorat, Paris, 1950-51.

——. *La spécialisation internationale.* Cours de doctorat, 1953-54.

——. "Stabilité internationale et économies nationales: remarques sur l'exposé du Professeur Lundberg." Rome Congress, September 1956.

——. *La transmission internationale des fluctuations économiques.* Course of lectures, cours du doctorat, Paris, 1952-53.

Cairncross, A. K. *Home and Foreign Investment, 1870-1913.* Cambridge, 1953.

Calcaterra. "La possibiltà di divergenza fra i livelli nazionali dei prezzi." *Revista internazionale di scienze sociali,* September-October 1950.

Cannan, E. "The Application of the Theoretical Apparatus of Supply and Demand to Units of Currency." *Economic Journal,* 1921.

Cardoso, F. H. *Politique et développement dans les sociétés dépendantes.* Paris, 1971.

——. *Sociologie du développement en Amérique latine.* Paris, 1969.

Cardoso, F. H., and Faletto, E. *Dependencia y desarrollo en America latina.* Santiago, 1967.

Cardoso, F. H., and Welfort, F. *Sociologia de la dependencia.* Santiago, 1971.

Carter, P. R. "The Modern Dual Economy, A Cost-Benefit Analysis of Lamco Cy." Duplicated. Conference on Planning, Monrovia, 1971.

Cassel, G. "The Rate of Interest, the Bank Rate and the Stabilisation of Prices." *Quarterly Journal of Economics,* 1928.

Central African Statistical Office. *The Balance of Payments of Southern Rhodesia, 1946-1952.* Salisbury, Rhodesia, 1953.

"Ceylon's Central Banking Experiment." *The Banker,* July 1950.

Chabert, A. *Structure économique et théorique monétaire.* Paris, 1956.

Chalmers, R. *A History of Currency in the British Colonies.* London, 1893.

Chamberlin, E. H. *The Theory of Monopolistic Competition.* 1932.

Chang, T. *Agriculture and Industrialisation.* Cambridge, 1949.

——. "The British Balance, 1924-1938." *Economic Journal,* December 1947.

——. "The British Demand for Imports in the Inter-war Period." *Review of Economics and Statistics,* June 1946.

——. *Cyclical Movements in the Balance of Payments.* Cambridge, 1951.

——. "A Further Note on the British Balance." *Economica,* August 1946.

——. "International Comparisons of Demand for Imports." *Review of Economic Studies* 34, 45, 46.

——. "A Statistical Note on World Demand for Imports." *Review of Economics and Statistics,* May 1948.

Chatelain, E. "Où mène la thèse de l'échange inégal?" *Critiques de l'économie politique* 3, 1971.

Chenery, H. R. "The Application of Investment Criteria." *Quarterly Journal of Economics,* February 1953.

——. *Cartels, Combines and Trusts.* 1944.

Clark, C. *The Conditions of Economic Progress.* London, 1940.

——. "Determination of the Multiplier from National Income Statistics." *Economic Journal,* 1938.

——. "The National Income of Great Britain in 1932." *Economic Journal,* June 1933.

Clark, C., and Crawford, J. C. *The National Income of Australia.* London, 1938.

Clausen, G. L. M. "The British Colonial Currency System." *Economic Journal,* April 1944.

Colon Torrès, R. "Agricultural Credit in the Caribbean." *Caribbean Economic Review,* December 1952.

Conan, A. R. "Balance of Payments of the Colonies." *The Banker,* April 1949.

———. "India's Balance of Payments Problem." *The Banker,* December 1949.

Condliffe, J. B. *The Commerce of Nations.* London, 1951.

Coquery-Vidrovitch, C. "De la traite négrière à l'exploitation des palmistes du Dahomey: XIXe siècle." Communication to the AIA seminar, Freetown, 1969.

———. "Recherches sur une mode de production africaine." *La Pensée,* April 1969.

Corea. "Overall Budgetary Policy in an Export Economy." *Ceylon Economist,* 1950.

Courtin. "L'intérêt." Course of lectures, Paris, 1949-50.

———. *Théorie de l'intérêt.* Cours du doctorat, Paris, 1949-50.

Cox, O. C. *Capitalism as a System.* New York, 1964.

Crouchley, A. E. *The Investment of Foreign Capital in Egyptian Companies and Public Debt.* London, 1936.

d'Alauro, O. "Commercio internazionale e concorrenza monopolistica." *Economia internazionale,* November 1949.

Dantwala, M. L. "Agricultural Credit in India—the Missing Link." *Pacific Affairs,* December 1952.

Das, N. *Industrial Enterprise in India.* 1938. Reprint ed. New York, 1962.

Datta, B. *The Economics of Industrialisation.* 3d rev. ed. Calcutta, 1960.

Davis, S. "Experience Under Intergovernmental Commodity Agreements, 1902-45." *Journal of Political Economy,* June 1946.

Day, A. C. L. "Devaluation and the Balance of Payments." *Economica,* November 1950.

de Cecco, M. "The Influence of Multinational Corporations on the Economic Policies of Underdeveloped Countries." Duplicated. Paper presented at the Tilburg Conference, 1970.

Delbard. "Les dynamismes sociaux au Sénégal." Mimeographed. Dakar, 1965.

Denis, H. *La monnaie.* Paris, 1951.

———. "Le rôle des débouchés préalables dans la croissance économique de l'Europe occidentale et des Etats-Unis." *Cahiers de l'ISEA,* Series P, no. 5, 1961.

——. "Le sens et la portée des coûts comparés." *Revue d'économie politique*, 1940.

de Vries, M. G. "The Magnitudes of Exchange Devaluations." *Finance and Development* 2, 1968.

Dike, K. O. *Trade and Politics in the Niger Delta, 1830-1885*. Oxford, 1956.

"Distribution et contrôle du crédit." *Revue économique*, 1951.

Di Tella, T. *Una teoria sobre el primer impacto de la industrializacion*. Buenos Aires, 1964.

Divatia, M. V., and Trivedi, H. M. *Industrial Capital in India (1938-39)*. Bombay, 1947.

Dobb, M. "Note sur le degré d'intensité capitalistique des investissements dans les pays sous-développés." *Economie appliquée*, 1954.

——. *Political Economy and Capitalism*. 1945. Reprint ed. Greenwich, Conn., 1972.

——. *Studies in the Development of Capitalism*. Rev. ed. New York, 1964.

Dobretsberger, J. "Théorie des territoires économiques." *Economie appliquée*, 1950.

Domar, E. "The Effect of Foreign Investment and Underdeveloped Countries." *Journal of Political Economy*, February 1953.

——. "The Effects of Foreign Investments on the Balance of Payments." *American Economic Review*, December 1940.

Dos Santos, T. *Dependencia y cambio social*. Santiago, 1970.

——. *Socialismo o fascismo, dilema latino-americano*. Santiago, 1969.

Ducros, B. "Les investissements américains à l'étranger et l'équilibre international." *Revue économique*, March 1954.

Dusenberry, J. S. *Income, Saving, and the Theory of Consumer Behavior*. Cambridge, Mass., 1949.

Duncan, A. J. "South African Capital Imports, 1893-98." *Canadian Journal of Economics and Political Science*, February 1948.

Dunlop, J. T. "Price Flexibility and the 'Degree of Monopoly.'" *Quarterly Journal of Economics*, August 1939.

Dupriez, L. H. *Les mouvements économiques généraux*. Louvain, 1947.

Durand, D. *La politique pétrolière internationale*. Paris, 1962.

Durand, H. *Essai sur la conjoncture de l'Afrique Noire*. Paris, 1957.

Duret, J. *Le marxisme et les crises*. Paris, 1933.

Dutt, R. P. *India Today*. London, 1940.

——. *Modern India*. London, 1927.

Edgeworth, F. Y. *Papers Relating to Political Economy.* 1925. Reprint ed. New York, 1970.

——. Review. *Economic Journal,* 1897.

Einzig, P. *International Gold Movements.* London, 1931.

el Kodsy, A. "Nationalism and Class Struggles in the Arab World." *Monthly Review* 22, 1970.

Ellis, H. "Some Fundamentals in the Theory of Velocity." *Quarterly Journal of Economics,* 1938.

Ellsworth, P. T. *Chile, An Economy in Transition.* New York, 1945.

——. *The International Economy.* New York, 1956.

Emmanuel, A. "La question de l'échange inégal." *L'homme et la société* 18, 1970.

——. *Unequal Exchange: A Study of the Imperialism of Trade.* Brian Pearce, trans. New York and London, 1972.

Engler, R. *The Politics of Oil.* New York, 1961.

Enke, S., and Salera, V. *International Economics.* 2d ed. New York, 1953.

Ewing, A. *Industry in Africa.* London, 1968.

Exter. *Report on the Establishment of a Central Bank in Ceylon.* Ceylon Government, 1948.

FAO (Food and Agriculture Organization). *Agricultural Credit for Small Farmers.*

——. *A Reconsideration of the Economics of the International Wheat Agreement.* Rome, 1952.

Falkowski, M. *Problèmes de la croissance du Tiers Monde vus par les économistes des pays socialistes.* Payot, 1968.

Fang, H. *Industrial Capital in China.* Tientsin, 1936.

Fanno, M. *Trasferimenti anormali dei capitali.* Turin, 1935.

Fay, V., ed. *En partant du "Capital."* Paris, 1968.

Federici. "On the Validity of the Principle of Foreign-Trade Multiplier." *Economia internazionale,* August 1950.

Feis, H. *Europe the World's Banker, 1870-1914.* New Haven, Conn., 1930.

Félix, D. "Structural Imbalances, Social Conflict and Inflation." *Economic Development and Cultural Change,* January 1960.

Fellner, W. "The Capital-Output Ratio in Dynamic Economics." In *Money, Trade and Economic Growth: Essays in Honor of John Henry Williams.* New York, 1951.

——. *Competition Among the Few.* New York, 1949.

Fellner, W., and Haley, B. F., eds. *Readings in the Theory of Income Distribution.* Homewood, Ill., 1951.

Ferns, H. S. "Investment and Trade Between Britain and Argentina in the 19th Century." *Economic History Review*, 1950.

Ferrer, A. *La economia argentina, las etapas de su desarrollo y problemas actuales.* Mexico City, 1965.

Fetter, T. A. *A Masquerade of Monopoly.* 1931. Reprint ed. 1966.

Fitch, B., and Oppenheimer, M. *Ghana: End of an Illusion.* New York, 1966.

Flamant, M. *Théorie de l'inflation et politiques anti-inflationnistes: essai d'application des concepts keynésiens.* Paris, 1952.

Florian, P. "Emmanuel chez les philistins." *Critiques de l'économie politiques* 3, 1971.

Forté, A. *Les banques en Egypte.* Paris, 1938.

Frank, A. G. *Capitalism and Underdevelopment in Latin America.* New York, 1967.

——. "The Development of Underdevelopment." In *Latin America: Underdevelopment or Revolution.* New York, 1969.

——. "Sociology of Development and Underdevelopment of Sociology." In op. cit.

——. "Walt Whitman Rostow: Ode to Underdevelopment." *Tricontinental* 7, 1968.

Frankel, S. H. "The Industrialisation of Agricultural Countries and the Possibility of a New International Division of Labour." *Economic Journal,* June-September 1943.

——. "The Situation in South Africa, 1929-32." *Economic Journal,* March 1933.

Franklin, N. N. "South Africa's Balance of Payments and the Sterling Area, 1939-1950." *Economic Journal,* June 1951.

Friedman, M. *Studies in the Quantity Theory of Money.* Chicago, 1956.

Furtado, C. *Development and Stagnation in Latin America: A Structural Approach.* New Haven, Conn., 1965.

——. *The Economic Growth of Brazil: A Survey from Colonial to Modern Times.* Berkeley, Calif., 1963.

——. *Obstacles to Development in Latin America.* New York, 1970.

GATT (General Agreement on Tariffs and Trade). *Rapports annuels sur le commerce mondial.*

Galbraith, J. K. *The Affluent Society.* 1948. 2d rev. ed. 1969.

——. "Monopoly Power and Price Rigidities." *Quarterly Journal of Economics,* May 1936.

——. *The New Industrial State.* New York, 1971.

Gayer, A. D.; Homan, P. T.; and James, E. K. *The Sugar Economy of Puerto Rico.* New York, 1938.

Gayer, A. D.; Rostow, W. W.; and Schwartz, A. J. *The Growth and Fluctuations of the British Economy, 1790-1850.* Oxford, 1953.

Gendarme. "Le multiplicateur du commerce extérieur." *Revue économique,* October 1950.

Germani, G. *Politica y sociedad en una epoca de transicioni de la sociedad tradicional a la sociedad de masas.* Buenos Aires, 1965.

Ghaleb, G. O. *Les capitaux étrangers en Egypte.* Thesis. Paris.

Gonzalez Casanova, P. *Democracy: Mexico.* New York, 1970.

Goschen, G. J. *The Theory of the Foreign Exchanges.* London, 1864. Reprinted 1932.

Graham, F. D. "International Trade Under Depreciated Paper: the United States, 1862-1879." *Quarterly Journal of Economics,* 1922.

——. "Some Aspects of Protection Further Considered." *Quarterly Journal of Economics,* February 1923.

——. "The Theory of International Values Re-examined." *Quarterly Journal of Economics,* November 1923.

Greaves, I. *Colonial Monetary Conditions.* New York, 1953.

——. "The Sterling Balances of Colonial Territories." *Economic Journal,* September 1950.

Gritly. "The Structure of Modern Industry in Egypt." *Egypte contemporain,* 1947.

Grove, D. L. "The Role of the Banking System in the Chilean Inflation." *IMF Staff Papers,* September 1951.

Gruson, C. *Esquisse d'une théorie générale de l'équilibre économique.* Paris, 1949.

——. *Origines et espoirs de la planification française.* Paris, 1968.

Guitton, H. *Les fluctuations économiques.* Paris, 1951.

Gutelman, M. *L'agriculture socialiste à Cuba.* Paris, 1967.

Haberler, G. *Prosperity and Depression.* Cambridge, Mass., 1964.

——. *The Theory of International Trade.* London, 1936.

Hall, R. L., and Hitch, C. J. "Price Theory and Business Behaviour." *Oxford Economic Papers,* May 1939.

Hansen, A. *Monetary Theory and Fiscal Policy.* New York, 1949.

Harrod, R. F. *The Dollar.* London, 1953. Paperback ed. New York, 1963.

——. *Economics Essays.* London, 1952. Rev. ed. New York, 1973.

——. *Towards a Dynamic Economics.* New York, 1948.

Haupt, O. *L'histoire monétaire de notre temps.* Paris, 1886.

Hazlewood, A. "Sterling Balances and the Colonial Currency System." *Economic Journal,* December 1952.

Heaton, H. *Economic History of Europe.* 1948.

Heckscher, E. "The Effect of Foreign Trade on the Distribution of Income." *Ekonomisk Tidskrift* 21, 1919.

Hicks, J. R. *Contribution to the Theory of the Trade Cycle.* Oxford, 1950.

——. "The Foundations of Welfare Economics." *Economic Journal,* December 1939.

——. "Mr. Keynes and the Classics." *Econometrica,* 1937.

——. "A Suggestion for Simplifying the Theory of Money." *Economica,* 1935.

——. *The Theory of Wages.* New York, 1948.

——. *Value and Capital.* Oxford, 1946.

Higgins, B. "The Dualistic Theory of Under-Developed Areas." *Economic Development and Cultural Change,* January 1956.

Hinkelammert, F., et al. "Dialectica del desarrollo desigual." *CEREN* 6, 1970.

Hinschaw, R. "Foreign Investment and American Employment." *American Economic Review,* May 1950.

Hirschman, A. O. "Devaluation and the Trade Balance." *Review of Economics and Statistics,* November 1945.

——. "Industrial Nations and Industrialisation of Under-developed Countries." *Economia internazionale,* August 1951.

——. *National Power and the Structure of Foreign Trade.* 1945. Reprint ed. Berkeley, Calif., 1969.

——. *The Strategy of Economic Development.* New Haven, Conn., 1958.

Hobson, C. K. *The Export of Capital.* 1914. Reprint ed. New York, 1963.

Hobson, J. A. *Imperialism.* London, 1902.

Horsefield, J. K. "Inflation in Latin America." *IMF Staff Papers,* September 1950.

Hubbard, G. E. *Eastern Industrialization and Its Effect on the West.* 1938. Reprint ed. Greenwich, Conn., 1973.

Hume, D. A. "Political Discourses." In *Essays Moral, Political and Literary.* 1875; New York, 1963.

Humphrey, D. D. "The Nature and Meaning of Rigid Prices, 1890-1933." *Journal of Political Economy,* February-December 1937.

Hymer, S. "The Efficiency of Multinational Corporations." Duplicated.

——. "Excerpt on Mercantilism III, The Age of Multinational Corporations." Duplicated. Paper presented at Tilburg Conference, 1970.

——. "The Multinational Corporation and Its Allies." *New Statements* 1, 1971.

IMF (International Monetary Fund). *Annuaires des balances des paiements extérieurs.*

——. Research and Statistics Department. *A Demand for Money: an International Comparison.* J. O. Adekunle, ed. 1965.

——. *Directions of Trade* and *A Supplement to International Financial Statistics (1962-1966).*

Ianni, O. *Estado e capitalismo, estructura social et industrializacão do Brasil.* Rio de Janeiro, 1965.

Imbert, J. *Histoire économique des origines à 1789.* Paris, 1965.

Imlah, A. H. "The Terms of Trade of the United Kingdom." *Journal of Economic History,* November 1950.

INSEE (Institut National de la Statistique et des Etudes Economiques). *L'Egypte, mémento économique.*

Institut International de Finances Publiques. *Aspects financiers, fiscaux et budgétaires du développement des pays sous-développés.* London, 1951.

IRES–Université Lovanium de Kinshasa. *Indépendance, inflation, développement: l'économie congolaise de 1960 à 1965.* Kinshasa, 1968.

——. *Lettre mensuelle* 1, 1967.

Issawi, C. *Egypt in Revolution: An Economic Analysis.* New York, 1963.

——. "Egypt Since 1800: A Study in Lopsided Development." *Journal of Economic History,* March 1961.

——, ed. *The Economic History of the Middle East, 1800-1914.* Chicago, 1966.

Iversen, C. *Aspects of the Theory of International Capital Movements.* London, 1936.

Jalée, P. *Imperialism in 1970.* New York, 1972.

——. *The Third World in World Economy.* New York, 1969.

Jathar, G. B., and Beri, S. G. *Elements of Indian Economics.* Cambridge, 1949.

Jayawardena. "The Problem of Liquidity in an Underdeveloped Economy." *Ceylon Economist,* 2d quarter 1952.

Jenks, L. H. *The Migration of British Capital to 1875.* New York, 1927.

Jewkes, J. "The Growth of World Industry." *Oxford Economic Papers,* February 1951.

Johnson, H. G. "The De-stabilising Effect of International Commodity Agreements on the Prices of Primary Products." *Economic Journal*, September 1950.

——. "Equilibrium Growth in an International Economy." *Canadian Journal of Economic and Political Science*, November 1953.

Kahn, R. "Investment Criteria in Development Programs." *Quarterly Journal of Economics*, February 1951.

Kaldor, N. "Capital Intensity and the Trade Cycle." *Economica*, February 1939.

——. "A Model of the Trade Cycle." *Economic Journal*, 1940.

——. "Welfare Propositions in Economics." *Economic Journal*, September 1939.

Kalecki, M. "Degree of Monopoly. A Comment." *Economic Journal*, 1942.

——. "The Distribution of National Income." In *Theory of Economic Dynamics.* New York, 1968.

——. *Theory of Economic Dynamics.* New York, 1968.

Keynes, J. M. "The Theory of the Rate of Interest." In *Readings in the Theory of Income Distribution*, edited by W. Fellner and B. F. Haley.

——. *A Treatise on Money.* Vol. 5 and 6 of *The Collected Writings of John Maynard Keynes.* New York, 1972.

Kidron, M. *Western Capitalism Since the War.* London, 1970.

Kindleberger, C. "L'assymétrie dans la balance des paiements." *Revue économique*, March 1954.

——. *The Dollar Shortage.* London, 1950.

——. *European Economic Integration and the Development of a Single Financial Centre for Long-Term Capital.* In *Weltwirtschaftliches Archiv*, 1963.

——. "Foreign Trade Multiplier and Balance Equilibrium." *American Economic Review*, March 1949.

——. *International Economics.* New York, 1953.

——. "International Monetary Stabilization." In *Postwar Economic Problems*, edited by S. Harris. New York, 1943.

——. *International Short-Term Capital Movements.* New York, 1937.

——. "Planning for Foreign Investment." *American Economic Review*, March 1943.

——. *The Terms of Trade.* London, 1956.

Klein, L. R. "Theories of Effective Demand and Employment." *Journal of Political Economy*, 1947.

Knight, F. H. "Profit." *Encyclopedia of the Social Sciences* 12, 1934. Reprinted in *Readings in the Theory of Income Distribution,* edited by W. Fellner and B. Haley.

Knight, F. K. "Capital, Time and the Rate of Interest." In *Encyclopedia Brittanica.* 1946.

Kondratieff, N. D. "The Long Waves in Economic Life." *Review of Economic Statistics,* November 1935.

Kuznets, S. S. "Les différences internationales dans la formation du capital." *Economie appliquée,* 1953.

——. *Income and Wealth of the United States.* Cambridge, 1952.

——. *National Income and Its Composition.* Vol. 1. New York, 1941.

——. *National Income of the United States.* 1946.

——. *The National Product Since 1869.* New York, 1946.

Labasse, J. *Les capitaux et la région.* Paris, 1955.

Lacoste, Y. *Géographie du sous-développement.* Paris, 1965.

——. *Ibn Khaldoun.* Paris, 1965.

Lacour-Gayet, J., ed. *Histoire du commerce.* 6 vols. Paris, 1950.

Lacroix, J.-L. *Industrialisation au Congo.* Paris, 1966.

Laidler, H. W. *Concentration of Control in American Industry.* New York, 1931.

Lamartine Yates, P. *Commodity Control.* London, 1943.

Lambert, D. *Les inflations sud-américaines.* Paris, 1959.

Lange, O. *Price Flexibility and Equilibrium.* Bloomington, Ind., 1944.

——. "The Theory of the Multiplier." *Economic Review,* 1943.

Lary, H. B. *Imports of Manufactures from Less Developed Countries.* New York, 1968.

Layton, C. *L'Europe et les investissements américains.* Paris, 1968.

——. *Transatlantic Investments.* Paris, 1966.

League of Nations. *Aperçu du commerce mondial.* 1931.

——. *Aperçu de la situation monétaire 1937-1938.* Vol. 1.

——. *La crise agricole.* 1931.

——. *Documents sélectionnés sur la distribution de l'or.*

——. *Economic Stabilization in the Post-War World.* Geneva, 1945.

——. *Enquête sur les accords de clearing.*

——. *L'équilibre monétaire international.*

——. *L'expérience monétaire internationale.* Geneva, 1944.

——. *Industrialisation et commerce extérieur.* Geneva, 1945.

——. *L'inflation, son évolution.*

——. *Mémorandum sur les banques commerciales, 1913-29.*

——. *Premier rapport provisoire de la délégation de l'or à la commission financière de la S.D.N.*

——. *Rapport sur le contrôle des changes.*

——. *Le réseau du commerce mondial.*

Legoyt, A. *La France et l'étranger, études de statistique comparée.* Paris, 1870.

Leontieff, W. "The Use of Indifference Curves in the Analysis of Foreign Trade." *Quarterly Journal of Economics,* 1933.

Lerner, A. P. "The Concept of Monopoly and the Measurement of Monopoly Power." *Review of Economic Studies,* October 1933–June 1934.

——. "The Diagrammatical Representation of Cost Conditions in International Trade." *Economica,* August 1932.

Lescure, J. *Les crises générales et périodiques de surproduction.* Paris, 1932.

——. *Hausses et baisses des prix de longue durée.* Paris, 1933.

Lewis, C. *America's Stake in International Investment.* Washington, D.C., 1938.

Lewis, W. A. *Development Planning.* New York, 1966.

——. "Economic Development with Unlimited Supplies of Labour." *Manchester School,* May 1954. Reprinted in *Economics of Underdevelopment,* edited by A. N. Agarwala and S. P. Singh. New York, 1963.

——. *The Theory of Economic Growth.* London, 1955. Paperback ed. New York, 1970.

Liau, P. *La détermination des taux d'intérêt.* Paris, 1962.

Liebenstein, H. *Economic Backwardness and Economic Growth.* New York, 1957.

Lindhal, E. *Etudes sur la théorie de la monnaie et du capital.* Paris, 1949.

Löbel, E. Lectures (untitled). Duplicated. Institute of Economic Development and Planning, Dakar, 1966.

——. "Liquidités internationales et éléments d'une politique monétaire de l'Afrique." *Le mois en Afrique,* May 1969.

Luas, E. "Economie, tiers-science." *Front,* October 1969.

——. "Problèmes actuels du marché capitaliste." *Front,* September, October, November, 1969.

Lutfalla, G. "Report of the Washington Meeting, 6-18 September 1947." *Econometrica,* January 1948.

Luxemburg, R. *The Accumulation of Capital.* New York, 1968.

Lynch, D. *The Concentration of Economic Power.* New York, 1946.

MacDougal. "Britain's Foreign Trade Problem." *Economic Journal,* March 1947.

Machlup, F. "Elasticity Pessimism in International Trade." *Economia internazionale,* February 1950.

——. *International Trade and the National Income Multiplier.* New York, 1943.

Macrae, N. A. D. "Experiment in Central Banking: A Study of San Domingo's New Bank." *The Banker,* October 1948.

Magdoff, H. *The Age of Imperialism.* New York, 1968.

Malhotra, D. K. *History and Problems of India's Currency, 1835-1949.* Simla, 1949.

Malinvaud. "Les élasticités prix." *Journal de la Société de Statistique de Paris,* May-June 1950.

Malkani. "Post-war Currency System in India." *Indian Journal of Economics,* 1946.

Mandel, E. "La théorie de la valeur-travail et le capitalisme monopolistique." *Critiques de l'économie politique,* no. 1, 1970.

Mandelbaum, K. *Industrialization of Backward Areas.* New York, 1945.

Manoilesco, M. *Théorie du protectionnisme et du commerce international.* Paris, 1939.

Marchal, A. *Systèmes et structures.* Paris, n.d.

Marchal, J. *Le mécanisme des prix.* Paris, 1951.

Marchal, J., and Lecaillon, J. *Les flux monétaires.* Paris, 1966.

Marjolin, R. *Prix, monnaie et production.* Paris, 1941.

Marquez, J. "Notes on Balance of Payments Problems in Relation to Economic Development of Latin America." *Inter-American Economic Affairs,* September 1947.

Mars. "The Monetary and Banking System and Loan Market of Nigeria." In *Mining, Commerce and Finance in Nigeria.* London, 1948.

Marsh. *World Trade and Investments.* New York, 1951.

Marshall, A. *The Pure Theory of Foreign Trade.* 1897.

Mason, E. S. *Foreign Aid and Foreign Policy.* New York, 1964.

Massé. "Pratique et philosophie de l'investissement." *Economie appliquée,* no. 4, 1952.

Matthews. *Trade Cycle.* New York, 1959.

Mauro, F. *L'expansion européenne 1600-1870.* Paris, 1964.

Mauro Marini, R. *Subdesarrollo y revolucion.* Mexico City, 1969.

Meade, J. E. *The Balance of Payments.* New York, 1951.

Mears, L. A. "Private Foreign Investment and Economic Development: Venezuela, Saudi Arabia and Puerto Rico." *Inter-American Economic Affairs,* Summer 1953.

Mendershausen. "The Pattern of Overseas Economic Development in

World War II and Its Significance." *Economia internazionale*, August 1951.

Metzler, L. A. "Graham's Theory of International Values." *Journal of Political Economy*, February 1950.

——. "The Transfer Problem Reconsidered." *Journal of Political Economy*, 1942.

Michalet, C. A. *L'entreprise plurinationale.* Dunod, 1969.

Mikesell, R. F. "Financial Problems of the Middle East." *Journal of Political Economy*, June 1945.

——. "Monetary Problems of Saudi Arabia." *Middle East Journal*, April 1947.

——. "Sterling Area Currencies of the Middle East." *Middle East Journal*, April 1948.

Mikhailevski. "Le système inflationniste de financement des guerres." *Questions d'économie*, 1952.

Mill, J. S. *Principles of Political Economy.* London, 1848.

Ministry of Finance and Economic Affairs. *Essai d'interprétation de la demande de monnaie.* Paris, 1965.

Mireaux, E. *L'organisation du crédit dans les térritoires d'outre-mer.* Paris, 1954.

Modigliani, F. "Liquidity Preference and the Theory of Interest and Money." *Econometrica*, 1944.

"Monetary Systems of the Colonies." *The Banker*, July 1948 and February 1949.

Moret, M. "Contribution à l'étude des termes de l'échange." *Economie contemporaine*, February 1950.

Morgan, T. "The Approach to International Commodity Problems." *Three Banks Review*, March 1959.

——. "A Measure of Monopoly in Selling." *Quarterly Journal of Economics*, 1946.

Mosak, J. L. *General Equilibrium Theory in International Trade.* New York, 1944.

Mosk, S. A. "Latin America and the World Economy, 1850-1914." *Inter-American Economic Affairs*, Winter 1948.

Mossé, E. *Marx et le problème de la croissance.* Paris, 1957.

Moursi, F. *Iqtisadiat al houqoud.* Cairo, 1952.

Mstislasky. "Some Questions Regarding Investment Efficiency." *Sowjetwissenschaft*, no. 4, 1949.

Muhlenfeld, A. "The Netherlands West Indies: A Financial and Economic Survey." *The Banker*, December 1943.

Muller-Plantenberg, U. "Technologie et dépendance." *Critiques de l'économie politique,* no. 3, 1971.

Mumford, L. *Technics and Civilization.* New York, 1934.

Muranjan, S. *Modern Banking in India.* Bombay, 1952.

Myrdal, G. *Asian Drama: An Inquiry into the Poverty of Nations.* New York, 1968.

——. *Industrialisation and Population.* London, 1933.

——. *Monetary Equilibrium.* New York, 1939.

Nadler, M. "American Foreign Investments." *Banca Nazionale del Lavoro Quarterly Review,* January-March 1950.

Nasr, Z. *Essai sur la notion d'inflation.* Paris, 1949.

Neisser, H. "The Nature of Import Propensities and the Multiplier." *Economia internazionale,* August 1949.

Neisser, H., and Modigliani, F. *National Income and International Trade: A Quantitative Analysis.* Urbana, Ill., 1953.

Newlyn, W. T. "The Colonial Banks." In *Banking in the British Commonwealth,* edited by R. S. Sayers. Oxford, 1952.

——. *Money in an African Context.* New York, 1967.

Newlyn, W. T., and Rowan, D. C. *Money and Banking in British Colonial Africa.* Oxford, 1954.

Nicolai, A. *Comportement économique et structures sociales.* Paris, 1960.

Niebyl, K. "What Rights Should the Holder of Money Have." *American Economic Review,* May 1947.

Niveau, M. "L'organisation de la zone sterling et le rôle international de la livre." *Economie appliquée,* January-March 1953.

Noceto, J. D., et al. *El proceso economico del Uruguay.* Montevideo, 1969.

Nogaro, B. *La monnaie et les systèmes monétaires.* Paris, 1945.

——. *La méthode de l'économie politique.* Paris, 1939.

——. *La valeur logique des théories économiques.* Paris, 1947.

Nurkse, R. "International Monetary Equilibrium." In *Essays in International Finance,* 1945.

——. *Patterns of Trade and Development.* Oxford, 1962.

——. *Problems of Capital-Formation in Underdeveloped Countries.* New York, 1967.

OECD (Organization of Economic Cooperation and Development). *Examen 1968, aide du développement, efforts et politiques poursuivis par les membres du comité d'aide au développement.*

——. *Rapports annuels sur les flux internationaux de capitaux.*

Ohlin, B. *Interregional and International Trade.* Rev. ed. Cambridge, Mass., 1967.

Okyar, O. "La théorie keynésienne et les pays sous-développés." *Economie appliquée,* 1951.

Oliver, R., and Matew, G., eds. *History of East Africa.* Oxford, 1963.

Ortiz, R. M. *Historia economica de la Argentina.* Buenos Aires, 1955.

Owen, G. *Industry in the U.S.A.* New York, 1966.

Paish, F. W. "Causes of a Change in Gold Supply." *Economica,* November 1938.

Palloix, C. *Problèmes de la croissance en économie ouverte.* Paris, 1969.

Pandit, Y. S. *India's Balance of Indebtedness, 1898-1913.* London, 1937.

Patinkin, D. "Price Flexibility and Full Employment." *American Economic Review,* September 1948.

Pazos, F. "Economic Development and Financial Stability." In *IMF Staff Papers,* October 1953.

Pearson Report. *Partners in Development.* New York, 1969.

Pelletier, A., and Goblot, J. J. *Matérialisme historique et histoire des civilisations.* Paris, 1969.

Peltzer, E. "Industrialization of Young Countries and the Change in the International Division of Labor." *Social Research,* September 1940.

Pentland, H. C. "The Role of Capital in Canadian Economic Development Before 1875." *Canadian Journal of Economics,* November 1950.

Perronnière. *Les opérations de banque.* Paris, 1954.

Perroux, F. "L'A.I.O.C. et les effets de domination." *Economie appliquée,* 1952.

——. "Les espaces économiques." *Economie appliquée,* 1950.

——. "Esquisse d'une théorie de l'économie dominante." *Economie appliquée,* 1952.

Peyret, H. *La stratégie des trusts.* Paris, 1966.

Phelps. *The International Economic Position of Argentina.* Philadelphia, 1938.

Pigou, A. C. *The Economics of Welfare.* 1920. Reprint ed. London, 1952.

——. *Wealth and Welfare.* 1912.

Pinto, A. "Structure économique, productivité et salaires en Amérique latine." Colloquium, Egelund, Denmark, 23-27 October 1967.

Plumptre, A. F. W. *Central Banking in the British Dominions.* Toronto, 1940.

Polak, J. J. "Balance-of-Payments Problems of Countries Reconstructing with the Help of Foreign Loans." *Quarterly Journal of Economics,* February 1943.

——. *An International Economic System.* London, 1954.

Polak, J. J., and Chang, T. "Effects of Exchange Depreciation." *IMF Staff Papers,* February 1950.

Porter, R. S. "Buffer Stocks and Economic Stability." *Oxford Economic Papers,* January 1950.

Poulantzas, N. *Pouvoir politique et classes sociales.* Paris, 1958.

Pradel. "L'optimum d'investissement." *Revue d'économie politique,* no. 3, 1953.

Preobrazhensky, E. A. *The New Economics.* 1926. English ed. New York, 1965.

Prest, A. R. *War Economics of Primary Producing Countries.* Cambridge, 1948.

Prokopovicz, S. N. *L'industrialisation des pays agricoles et la structure de l'économie mondiale après la guerre.* Neuchâtel, 1946.

Prou. *Origines et formes récentes de la théorie du multiplicateur d'investissement.* Thesis. Paris, 1948.

Raj. *The Monetary System of Egypt.* London, 1935.

Ranger, T. O., ed. *Aspects of Central African History.* Evanston, Ill., 1968.

Rao. "Deficit Financing, Capital Formation and Price Behaviour in an Underdeveloped Economy." *Indian Economic Review,* February 1953.

——. "Full Employment and Economic Development." *Indian Economic Review,* August 1952.

——. "Investment Income and the Multiplier in Underdeveloped Economies." *Indian Economic Review,* February 1952.

Raulin, H. *La dynamique des techniques agraires en Afrique tropicale du nord.* Paris, 1967.

——. *Techniques et bases socio-économiques des sociétés rurales nigériennes.* Paris, 1966.

Reynolds, L. G., and Gregory, P. *Wages, Productivity and Industrialization in Puerto Rico.* New York, 1965.

Riad, H. *L'Egypte nassérienne.* Paris, 1964.

Richta, R. *La civilisation au carrefour.* Paris, 1969.

Rieffer, W. W. "A Proposal for an International Buffer Stock Agency." *Journal of Political Economy,* December 1946.

Rippy, J. F. "The British Investment 'Boom' of the 1880s in Latin American Mines." *Inter-American Economic Affairs,* March 1948.

Rist, C. *Histoire des doctrines relatives au crédit et à la monnaie depuis John Law jusqu'à nos jours.* Paris, 1938.

——. "Quelques définitions de l'épargne." *Revue d'économie politique,* 1921.

——. *Qu'est-ce que la monnaie?* Paris, 1920.

Robbins. *Essay on the Nature and Significance of Economic Science.* 1932.

Robertson, D. H. *Money.* Cambridge, England, 1947.

——. "Mr. Keynes and the Rate of Interest." In *Essays in Monetary Theory.* 1940.

Robinson, J. "The Classification of Inventions." *Review of Economic Studies,* 1937-1938.

——. *The Economics of Imperfect Competition.* London, 1933.

——. *An Essay on Marxian Economics.* 2d ed. New York, 1966.

——. *Essays in the Theory of Employment.* London, 1937.

——. "The Foreign Exchange." In *Essays in the Theory of Employment,* op. cit.

——. "The Generalisation of the General Theory." In *The Rate of Interest and Other Essays.* London, 1952.

——. "Imperfect Competition and Falling Supply Price." *Economic Journal,* 1932.

——. "Notes on the Economics of Technical Progress." In *The Rate of Interest and Other Essays,* op. cit.

Rodney, W. "African Slavery and Other Forms of Social Oppression on the Upper Guinea Coast in the Context of the Atlantic Slave Trade." *Journal of African History,* no. 3, 1966.

Rosenberg, W. "Banking in a 'Dependent' Economy: New Zealand and Eire Compared." *The Banker,* October 1947.

Rostas, L. "Industrial Production, Productivity and Distribution in Britain, Germany and the United States, 1935-37." *Economic Journal,* April 1943.

Rostow, W. W. *The Stages of Economic Growth.* 2d ed. New York, 1971.

Rothschild, K. W. "The Degree of Monopoly." *Economica,* 1942.

Rottenberg, S. "Note on 'Economic Progress and Occupational Distribution.' " *Review of Economics and Statistics,* May 1953.

Rowan, D. "Banking Adaptation in the Gold Coast: A Critique of the Recent Report by Sir Cecil Trevor, C.I.E." *South African Journal of Economics,* December 1952.

——. "Banking in Nigeria: A Study in Colonial Financial Evolution."

Banca Nazionale del Lavoro Quarterly Review, July-September 1952.

——. "The Native Banking Boom in Nigeria." *The Banker*, October 1951.

Rowe, J. W. F. *Markets and Men.* Cambridge, England, 1936.

Rowthorn, R. "Capitalism Since the War." Duplicated. Tilburg Conference, 1970.

Royal Institute of International Affairs. *The Problem of International Investment.* Oxford, 1937.

Rudloff, M. *Economie politique du Tiers Monde.* Paris, 1968.

Ryelandt, B. *L'inflation congolaise, 1960-1968.* Forthcoming.

——. *L'inflation en pays sous-développés. Origines, mécanismes de propagation et effets réels des pressions inflatoires et des opérations de stabilisation au Congo, 1960-1969.* Thesis. Kinshasa, 1969.

Saccheti. "Bilancia dei pagamenti dei paesi in sviluppo." *L'industria*, no. 4, 1950.

Sachs, I. "Environmental Quality, Management and Development Planning." Duplicated. A contribution at the United Nations Conference on the Environment, Geneva, 1971.

Salant, W. S. "The Domestic Effects of Capital Export Under the Point Four Program." *American Economic Review*, May 1950.

Salter, A. *Foreign Investment.* Princeton, N.J., 1951.

Sammarco, A. *Précis d'histoire de l'Egypte.* Vol. 4. Cairo, 1935.

Samuelson, P. A. *Economics.* 8th ed. New York, 1970.

——. "The Gains from International Trade." *Canadian Journal of Economics and Political Science*, May 1939.

——. "The Price of Factors." *Economic Journal*, June 1948-June 1949.

Sartre, L. *Esquisse d'une théorie marxiste des crises périodiques.* Paris, 1937.

Saxton, C. C. *The Economics of Price Determination.* London and New York, 1942.

Sayers, R. S., ed. *Banking in the British Commonwealth.* Oxford, 1952.

Scheffer. "La banca nei paesi sottosviluppati." *Bancaria*, 1955.

Schiff, E. "Direct Investment, Terms of Trade, and Balance of Payments." *Quarterly Journal of Economics*, February 1942.

Schlesinger, E. R. *Multiple Exchange Rates and Economic Development.* Princeton, N.J., 1952.

Schloss, H., and Millner, H. "Banking Without a Central Bank: A Review of Experience in Palestine." *The Banker*, April 1948.

Schmitt, H. O. *Monetary Policy and Social Conflict in Indonesia.* Berkeley, Calif., 1969.

Schumann, C. G. W. "Aspects of the Problem of Full Employment in South Africa." *South African Journal of Economics,* June 1948.

Schumpeter, J. A. *The Theory of Economic Development.* 1934.

Schurmann, F. *Ideology and Organization in Communist China.* 2d ed. Berkeley, Calif., 1968.

Scitovszky, T. de. "A Reconsideration of the Theory of Tariffs." *Review of Economic Studies,* Summer 1942.

Seers, D. "A Theory of Inflation and Growth in Underdeveloped Economies." *Oxford Economic Papers,* 1962.

Sen, A. K. *Choice of Techniques.* 3d ed. New York, 1968.

Sen, S. *Central Banking in Underdeveloped Money Markets.* Calcutta, 1952.

Shannon, H. A. "Evolution of the Colonial Sterling Exchange Standard." *IMF Staff Papers,* April 1951.

——. "The Modern Colonial Sterling Exchange Standard." *IMF Staff Papers,* April 1952.

Shenoy, B. R. "The Currency, Banking and Exchange System of Thailand." *IMF Staff Papers,* September 1950.

Simkin, C. G. F. *The Instability of a Dependent Economy: Economic Fluctuations in New Zealand, 1840-1914.* London, 1951.

Singer, H. W. "The Distribution of Gains Between Investing and Borrowing Countries." *American Economic Review,* May 1950.

——. *Distribution of Gains from Trade and Investments, Revisited.* Duplicated. Brighton, England, 1971.

Singh. "Monetary Standard in India." *Indian Economic Journal,* July 1953.

Smith, A. D. "Aperçu général des tendances des salaires dans les pays en voie de développement." Colloquium, Egelund, Denmark, 23-27 October 1967.

Spiegel, H. W. *The Brazilian Economy: Chronic Inflation and Sporadic Industrialization and Inflation.* Philadelphia, 1949.

Sraffa, P. *Production of Commodities by Means of Commodities.* New York, 1960.

Staley, E. *World Economic Development: Effects on Advanced Industrial Countries.* Montreal, 1944.

Stamp, L. D. *Our Undeveloped World.* London, 1953.

Stavenhagen, R. *Les classes sociales dans les sociétés africaines.* Paris, 1969.

——. "Seven Erroneous Theses About Latin America." In *Agrarian Problems and Peasant Movements in Latin America,* edited by R. Stavenhagen and O. Feinstein. New York, 1973.

Steindl, J. *Maturity and Stagnation in American Capitalism.* Oxford, 1952.

Stopler, W. F. "A Note on the Multiplier." *Economia internazionale,* August 1950.

Stopler, W. F., and Samuelson, P. A. "Protection and Real Wages." *Review of Economic Studies,* November 1941.

Sunkel, O. "Intégration capitaliste transnationale et désintégration nationale en Amérique latine." *Politique étrangère,* no. 6, 1970.

Sutcliffe, R. B. "Outlook for Capitalism in the Seventies: the Peripheral Capitalist Countries." Duplicated. Tilburg Conference, 1970.

Sweeny, T. D. "The Mexican Balance of Payments, 1947-1950." *IMF Staff Papers,* April 1953.

Sweezy, P. "On the Definition of Monopoly." *Quarterly Journal of Economics,* 1937.

——. *The Theory of Capitalist Development.* New York, 1942.

Sweezy, P. M., et al. *The Transition from Feudalism to Capitalism.* A Symposium. New York, 1954.

Szereszewski, R. *Structural Changes in the Economy of Ghana, 1891-1911.* London, 1965.

Tamagna, F. M. *Banking and Finance in China.* New York, 1942.

Tanzer, M. *The Political Economy of International Oil and the Underdeveloped Countries.* Boston, 1970.

Taussig, F. W. "The Change in Great Britain's Foreign Terms of Trade After 1900." *Economic Journal,* 1925.

——. *International Trade.* New York, 1927.

Tavarès, M. C. "Auge y declinacion del processo de substitucion de importaciones en el Brasil." *Bol. Ec. de America Latina,* 1964.

Terray, E. *Marxism and "Primitive" Societies.* New York, 1972.

Thomas, P. J. "India in the World Depression." *Economic Journal,* September 1935.

Thorner, D. *Investment in Empire.* Philadelphia, 1950.

Tinbergen, J. *Business Cycles in the United Kingdom, 1870-1914.* Amsterdam, 1951.

——. *International Economic Integration.* New York, 1963.

——. "Some Measurements of Elasticities of Substitution." *Review of Economics and Statistics,* August 1946.

——. "Some Remarks on the Problem of Dollar Scarcity." A speech at the meeting of the Econometric Society, Washington, D.C., 1947.

Triantis, S. G. "Cyclical Changes in the Balance of Merchandise Trade of Countries Exporting Chiefly Primary Products." *American Economic Review*, March 1952.

——. "Economic Progress, Occupational Redistribution and the Terms of Trade." *Economic Journal*, September 1953.

Triffin, R. *Gold and the Dollar Crisis.* Rev. ed. New Haven, Conn., 1961.

——. "Monetary Development in Latin America." *Federal Reserve Bulletin*, June 1945.

Tsuru, S. "Economic Fluctuations in Japan, 1868-93." *Review of Economics and Statistics,* November 1941.

——. "On Reproduction Schemes." Appendix to *The Theory of Capitalist Development*, by Sweezy. New York and London, 1942.

Tucker, R. "The Degree of Monopoly." *Quarterly Journal of Economics,* 1940.

Tyszynski, H. "Economics of the Wheat Agreement." *Economica,* February 1949.

U.N.O. *Annuaire du commerce international.*

——. *Commodity Trade and Economic Development.*

——. *Demographic Yearbook.*

——. *Le développement de l'économie de marché en Afrique tropicale.* New York, 1954.

——. *The Economic Development of Latin America and Its Problems.*

——. *Economic Development of the Middle East, 1945 to 1954.*

——. *Economic Survey of Latin America, 1948.*

——. *Etude sur le commerce Asie-Europe.*

——. *Foreign Capital in Latin America.*

——. *Formulation and Economic Appraisal of Development Projects* 1951: 11: B4.

——. *Growth and Stagnation in the European Economy.* 1954.

——. *Inflationary and Deflationary Tendencies 1946-1948.*

——. *Instability in Export Markets of Under-developed Countries.* September 1952, II: A 1.

——. *International Flow of Private Capital.*

——. *International Flow of Private Capital 1946-52.* II, 5.

——. *Measures for the Economic Development of Underdeveloped Countries.* New York, 1951.

——. *Measures for Economic Stability.* 1951. 51 II A 2.

——. *Mesures prises par les gouvernements en matière de chômage, d'inflation et de balance de paiements, 1951-52.*

——. *Méthodes et problèmes de l'industrialisation des pays sous-développés.*

——. *Mission to Haiti.*

——. *Mobilization of Domestic Capital in Certain Countries of Asia and the Far East.* 1951. II, F 3.

——. *Les mouvements internationaux de capitaux entre les deux guerres.*

——. *National Income and Expenditure.*

——. "On the Establishment of Certain Small Loan Banks by Government, with Special Reference to the Experience in Indonesia." *Economic Bulletin, E.C.A.F.E., UNO,* 2nd quarter, 1951.

——. *Prix relatifs des importations et des exportations des pays insuffisament développés.*

——. *Progrès de la réforme agraire.*

——. *The Public Debt.* 1948. XVI 1.

——. *Public Finance Surveys, Foreign Capital in Latin America.*

——. *Report of the U.N. Mission to Chile, 1949-50* 2, no. B 6, 1951.

——. *Le revenu national et sa distribution dans les pays insuffisament développés.*

——. *Scope and Structure of Money Economies in Tropical Africa.* 55 II C 3, 4.

——. *Statistics of National Income and Expenditure* series H. no. 7.

——. *Survey of Current Inflationary and Deflationary Tendencies.*

——. *Tendances et politiques des balance des paiements, 1950-51.*

United Africa Co., Ltd. "The West African Currency Board." *Statistical and Economic Review,* September 1951.

Venkatasubbiah, H. *The Foreign Trade of India, 1900-1940.* New Delhi, 1946.

Vilelaluz, N. *A luta pela industrialização do Brasil, 1808-1930.* São Paulo, 1961.

Vinelli, P. "The Currency and Exchange System of Honduras." *IMF Staff Papers,* April 1951.

Viner, J. *Canada's Balance of International Indebtedness, 1900-1913.*

——. *International Trade and Economic Development.* Oxford, 1953.

——. *Studies in the Theory of International Trade.* London, 1937.

Visine, F. *La transmission des fluctuations économiques par le commerce extérieur.* Thesis. Paris, 1953.

von Burg, W. *La politique des cours différentiels de change selon les pays.* Geneva, 1953.

Von Mises, L. *Theory of Money and Credit.* 1934. Reprint ed. New York, 1971.

Wallace, D. H. "Monopoly Prices and Depression." In *Explorations in Economics: Notes and Essays Contributed in Honor of F. Taussig.* New York, 1936.

Wallich, H. C. *The Monetary Problems of an Export Economy.* Cambridge, England, 1950.

——. "Underdeveloped Countries and the International Monetary Mechanism." In *Money, Trade and Economic Growth,* edited by H. G. Johnson. New York, 1951.

Warburton, C. "The Misplaced Emphasis in Contemporary Business Fluctuation Theory." In *Readings in Monetary Theory,* edited by F. A. Lutz and L. N. Mints. New York, 1951.

——. "The Secular Trend in Monetary Velocity." *Quarterly Journal of Economics,* February 1949.

Ward, B; d'Anjou, L; and Runnels, J. D., eds. *The Widening Gap: Development in the 1970s.* New York, 1971.

White, H. D. *French International Accounts, 1880-1913.* Cambridge, England, 1933.

Whitman, R. H. "A Note on the Concept of Degree of Monopoly." *Economic Journal,* 1941.

Whittlesey, C. R. "The Stevenson Plan: Some Conclusions and Observations." *Journal of Political Economy,* February-December 1931.

Wicksell, K. *Interest and Prices.* London, 1936.

Wightman, D. "The Sterling Area—Part 1: Origins and Development." *Banca Nazionale del Lavoro Quarterly Review,* April-June 1951.

Wilff. "Liaison entre prix et monnaie." *Revue d'économie politique,* 1934.

Williams, E. *Capitalism and Slavery.* 1944.

Williams, J. H. *Argentine International Trade Under Inconvertible Paper Money, 1880-1900.* Cambridge, England, 1920.

Wilson, R. "Australian Capital Imports, 1871-1930." *Economic Record,* May 1931.

——. *Capital Imports and the Terms of Trade.* Melbourne, 1931.

Wood, G. L. *Borrowing and Business in Australia.* London, 1930.

Wood, R. C. "Tucker's Reasons for Price Rigidity." *American Economic Review,* December 1938.

Woodruff, W. *Impact of Western Man.* New York, 1967.

Wu, C. Y. *An Outline of International Price Theories.* London, 1937.

Wu, Y. L. "International Capital Investments and the Development of Poor Countries." *Economic Journal,* March 1946.

Wythe, G. *Industry in Latin America.* New York, 1949.

Yakemtchouk, R. *Assistance économique et pénétration industrielle des pays de l'Est en Afrique.* Kinshasa, n.d.

Young. "Saudi Arabian Currency and Finance." *Middle East Journal,* April 1947.

Zakaria, I. *Change, commerce extérieur et équilibre économique international d'après la doctrine et les expériences françaises, 1919-1950.* Thesis. Paris, 1953.